SAP PRESS Books: Always on hand

Print or e-book, Kindle or iPad, workplace or airplane: Choose where and how to read your SAP PRESS books! You can now get all our titles as e-books, too:

- ▶ By download and online access
- ▶ For all popular devices
- ▶ And, of course, DRM-free

Convinced? Then go to **www.sap-press.com** and get your e-book today.

SAP® CRM: Technical Principles and Programming

 **PRESS**

SAP PRESS is a joint initiative of SAP and Galileo Press. The know-how offered by SAP specialists combined with the expertise of the Galileo Press publishing house offers the reader expert books in the field. SAP PRESS features first-hand information and expert advice, and provides useful skills for professional decision-making.

SAP PRESS offers a variety of books on technical and business-related topics for the SAP user. For further information, please visit our website: *www.sap-press.com*.

Stephen Johannes

SAP® CRM: Technical Principles and Programming

Galileo Press

Bonn • Boston

Galileo Press is named after the Italian physicist, mathematician, and philosopher Galileo Galilei (1564—1642). He is known as one of the founders of modern science and an advocate of our contemporary, heliocentric worldview. His words *Eppur si muove* (And yet it moves) have become legendary. The Galileo Press logo depicts Jupiter orbited by the four Galilean moons, which were discovered by Galileo in 1610.

Editor Laura Korslund
Acquisitions Editor Kelly Grace Harris
Copyeditor Julie McNamee
Cover Design Graham Geary
Photo Credit iStockphoto.com/14798541/CharlotteLake
Layout Design Vera Brauner
Production Graham Geary
Typesetting SatzPro, Krefeld (Germany)
Printed and bound in the United States of America, on paper from sustainable sources

ISBN 978-1-59229-439-8

© 2013 by Galileo Press Inc., Boston (MA)
1st edition 2013

Library of Congress Cataloging-in-Publication Data
Johannes, Stephen.
SAP CRM: technical principles and programming / Stephen Johannes. -- 1st edition.
pages cm
ISBN-13: 978-1-59229-439-8
ISBN-10: 1-59229-439-1
ISBN-13: 978-1-59229-629-3
ISBN-13: 978-1-59229-630-9
1. SAP CRM. 2. Customer relations--Management--Computer programs.
3. Management information systems. I. Title.
HF5415.5.J63 2013
658.8'12028553--dc23
2013011904

Contents at a Glance

Dear Reader,

If you've been working in IT for a while, you don't need me to tell you that one size doesn't fit all. Luckily, this means great job security, even if you have to deal with a few headaches along the way. Up until now, though, there hasn't been a technical resource available that provided guidance on how to tailor the SAP CRM backend. While SAP CRM has come a long way since it was first developed and provides much more options for customization than ever before, there are still many intricacies of the data model that are confusing, and plenty of enhancement options available that might leave you scratching your head.

This book has been written with these SAP CRM-specific matters in mind. Aided by years of experience and a sense of humor (which he claims is a must when working with SAP CRM), Stephen Johannes has compiled years of personal experience and countless hours of community research into a developer's reference of the most essential and useful information to use when working with the SAP CRM system. I'm confident that the advice and direction he provides will help establish a more consistent approach to developing SAP CRM.

We at SAP PRESS are always eager to hear your opinion. What do you think about *SAP CRM: Technical Principles and Programming*? As your comments and suggestions are our most useful tools to help us make our books the best they can be, we encourage you to visit our website at *www.sap-press.com* and share your feedback.

Thank you for purchasing a book from SAP PRESS!

Laura Korslund
Editor, SAP PRESS

Galileo Press
Boston, MA

laura.korslund@galileo-press.com
www.sap-press.com

Contents

6   The Post Processing Framework: Output and Actions   245

7   Common Enhancement Requests in Sales and Service   293

Acknowledgments

About a year or so ago I started out with a crazy idea that I could write a book and train for a half marathon at the same time. Over the past year, I found out that writing a book and running a half marathon require similar types of dedication, motivation, and preparation in order to achieve the goal. I realized that this book has been a long journey after many years and support from several people.

Even though the writing of this book did not take place until last year, my journey to gain the qualifications to write this book began many years ago.

My journey with SAP started with my father Cyril suggesting that I look at working with SAP as a career. I thank my dad for directing me to look at something that I would never have considered. I also thank my parents for supporting me throughout my schooling, and in later years helping myself and my wife with the kids for those nights that were a needed break during the writing process.

I would also like to thank Mark Pirkl, who introduced me to the world of SAP E-Commerce, which eventually led me to SAP CRM.

I would like to acknowledge those people who I worked with on my first SAP CRM project including Jung Yeo, Bill Wynne, Stephen Shellenberger, and Don Yopp.

This book would not be possible if I had not started contributing to the SAP Developer Network (SDN), which is now the SAP Community Network. My early inspiration on that network was Gregor Wolf. When SAP introduced the CRM forum on SDN in early 2005, Gregor was one of the most active and early contributors in that space. His example led me to share and write one of my first blogs on the XIF adapter, which was quite popular and is the basis for Chapter 5 of this book. Through my participation on SDN, I started to look at ways to improve CRM developer knowledge as a community project. I would like to thank

Marilyn Pratt for encouraging me to become a moderator on SDN. I would also like to thank Anne Fish for helping me to connect with SAP CRM product management on a regular basis. Also, a thank you to Mark Finnern for supporting me in the SAP Mentor Program during my time in the program.

Through my participation in the community I would like to thank all those in the SAP CRM community on SCN that participate on a regular basis. I'd like to think about this book as a way of giving back to a common request, for which we can we find more knowledge about SAP CRM for developers. I would like to thank Harshit Kumar, Nicolas Busson, Carsten Kasper, and many others who challenge me to do better and keep me honest.

In St. Louis, there a few people in the local ASUG community that I would like to thank. First of all, Mike Narducci, who is the ASUG chapter chair, for helping with SAP Inside Track Events in St. Louis. During the first SAP Inside Track Event, I presented a presentation that was one of the early pre-cursors to the content of this book. Jamie Oswald for being a "game-changer" and partner in crime for SAP Mentor activities in St. Louis. Eric Vallo, who is another SAP Mentor from Saint Louis and an SAP PRESS author, gave me the advice that you will never have enough time, which turned out to be absolutely true.

Because much of my knowledge is based on my support of a productive SAP CRM system, I would like to acknowledge some of my past co-workers who helped me along the way: Keith Linneman, Steve Lee, Desmonde Thomas, Luke Browning, Tom Mann, Scott Gill, Prabhat Kumar, Rhonda Lange, Doug Meyer, Vince Gibbs, Nilesh Shinde, and Ben Ambaye.

My current co-workers at my current employer including those who put up with discussions about the book: Carrie Rudberg, Barb Hassler, Joe Moore, and Tim Sarvis.

For Tandra Williams, who currently supports SAP CRM with me at my current employer, it has been a great three years working together so far. It has been great working with someone who is passionate and understands SAP CRM from business perspective as much as you do.

Additionally, this book would not be possible without one very generous individual: Paparao Undavali. Paparao provided me with complimentary access to an SAP CRM system so that I could complete the remainder of this book after there were some technical issues with the system that I was using. I am completely grateful for Paparao's assistance.

I would also like to thank my editor Laura Korslund for putting up with a writer who decided to buy a Mac that doesn't quite act like the regular template used to publish the book. In addition, a thank you to Kelly Grace Harris for allowing me to run with the idea of a different book than the need she was trying to fill.

Finally, after a list that makes most academy awards winners look short, I want to thank my family and my wife Karon in particular for putting up with me for the last year. Without her support I would not have been able to finish this book, as she has provided countless encouragement as I encountered writer's block and other forms of frustration during this process.

If I have managed to miss anyone here, please note that you are not forgotten, and that my editor said that people were not buying the book due to a cool acknowledgment section, but rather great technical content.

Stephen Johannes
March 2013

Introduction

SAP Customer Relationship Management (which we'll refer to throughout the book as SAP CRM) is a software solution delivered by SAP to aid businesses in their management of relationships between the company, their current customers, and their potential customers. A successful SAP CRM implementation provides tools that allow the business to manage relationships and the experience with the customer. This book will give you the technical foundation you need to be more effective on an SAP CRM project as a developer. By reading this book, you should gain the knowledge needed to implement enhancements that will allow you to meet many different business requirements and increase the success of your SAP CRM implementation.

The information gathered is based on multiple SAP CRM projects and years of experience supporting SAP CRM productively. We'll reveal information that was learned only by working on SAP CRM projects, or by searching and reading hundreds of articles on the Internet.

Who This Book Is For

This book is aimed at developers and consultants who are currently working with SAP CRM or who are new to SAP CRM. We recommend that you have a general working knowledge of ABAP, ABAP Objects, and general programing. You should be able to read and write ABAP code without difficulty in order to understand the examples in this book. Some basic experience in SAP configuration may be helpful in setting up parts of the system required for the examples; however, we do cover the basic configuration required.

What This Book Covers

This book provides an introduction to customer relationship management in general and to SAP CRM specifically. We introduce the business processes supported by SAP CRM and cover the basic overall technical architecture.

Key concepts   Throughout the book, we examine key concepts such as the data model of SAP CRM. This knowledge will serve as the foundation in how to enhance SAP CRM to meet key business requirements. As we go through the book, we cover various tools provided by SAP CRM in the system that can be used to meet various requirements. In addition to examining the tools available, we provide several examples of business requirements and how to solve those business requirements using the available tools. As every project needs a fallback plan, we also explore options that should be considered only as a last resort, but kept on hand if necessary.

The book starts with an overview of the SAP CRM system. It then dives into the SAP CRM data model and explores how to enhance that data model. The next three chapters focus on three major technical areas of the business transaction: business transaction event framework (BTE framework), XIF adapter, and Post Processing Framework (PPF). These technical areas cover custom logic, data loads and extracts, and finally output for the business transaction. We then look at common enhancement requests in the Sales, Service, and Marketing modules of SAP CRM found in most SAP CRM projects. We then move to cover enhancements for analytics and reporting. We end the book by examining methods of last resort, when there are no other options left to meet your requirements.

Chapter   The chapters are organized as follows:
breakdown

- ▶ **Chapter 1**

  This chapter provides an introduction to SAP CRM. We explain what SAP CRM is and why we have a separate SAP CRM system, instead of SAP CRM being a component in SAP ERP. We also take a look at the basic technical landscape of SAP CRM.

- ▶ **Chapter 2**

  This chapter discusses the SAP CRM data model for business partners, products, business transactions, and marketing attributes. If you only read one chapter in full in this book, we recommend you read this chapter. The information in this chapter will be foundational for all other chapters.

▶ **Chapter 3**

This chapter explains how to enhance the data model of SAP CRM. We'll look at four different tools: EEWB, AET, marketing attributes, and product attributes for data model enhancements. Enhancing the data model is the number one requirement for most SAP CRM projects.

▶ **Chapter 4**

This chapter discusses the business transaction event framework (BTE framework). The BTE framework is a function module-based framework that allows for custom logic to be added within your SAP CRM system for business transactions. We look at the customizing of this framework and provide an example of how to build on the BTE function module.

▶ **Chapter 5**

This chapter discusses data extraction and loading using the XIF adapter. We examine how to load data and extract into SAP CRM using the XIF adapter via two main methods: LSMW and custom code. If you need to load legacy data into SAP CRM or extract data from SAP CRM, we encourage you to review this chaper.

▶ **Chapter 6**

This chapter discusses the Post Processing Framework (PPF), which is the SAP CRM version of output control for business transactions. In addition, it can be used for custom business logic. We cover the customizing of this logic and how to create custom logic within this framework.

▶ **Chapter 7**

This chapter discusses common enhancements in sales and service. We show you how to make fields be required and values be default in the business transaction. Through configuration and coding, we examine how date rules can be used for complex time calculations in a business transaction. Finally, we look at how to extend partner and organizational model determination.

▶ **Chapter 8**

This chapter discusses common enhancements in marketing. Our focus will be on two BAdIs. The first BAdI deals with External List Management (ELM) used in the import of list data into SAP CRM. The second BAdI deals with exporting data to the open channel when executing a marketing campaign in SAP CRM.

▶ **Chapter 9**

This chapter discusses common enhancements in analytics and reporting. We show you how to extend data sources for SAP NetWeaver Business Warehouse (SAP NetWeaver BW). A brief look at enhancing interactive reporting is also provided. Finally, we illustrate how the Transaction Launcher can be used to display custom reports.

▶ **Chapter 10**

This chapter discusses other techniques that can be used when all else fails. We look at implicit enhancements, core modifications, and community resources.

Technical specifications All coding samples and screenshots were prepared using the initial SAP CRM 7.0 and SAP CRM 7.0 EHP1 available at the time of the writing of this book (January 2013). Unless noted, coding examples aren't specific to either release. Based on past experience, examples may work on SAP CRM 7.0 with the exception of examples concerning the Application Enhancement Tool. Using a sandbox system to practice or follow the examples is strongly encouraged.

Example Scenario: Developing a Social Call Report

Throughout the book we'll discuss the concept of a social call report as a business example for the enhancements. The business requirements are scattered through each chapter and organized by the technical nature of each enhancement, so we'd like to elaborate on how all of these enhancements fit within a typical SAP CRM implementation and explain which areas of the book cover those requirements. Here, we're assuming that you're an SAP CRM functional consultant who needs to verify the development effort of your project.

Business Background and Need

The example company has recently entered the world of social media through a corporate account on Facebook and Twitter. Up until this point, the company's only interactions with their customers was through phone, email, and the corporate website. However, the company started to notice that customers were talking about them on these social channels. The company already had a great SAP CRM system implemented that was providing a good view of their customer interactions; however, they were missing the social interactions and honest feedback and suggestions about the direction of the company.

Their sales representatives were already logging their interactions with customers in SAP CRM using an activity business transaction called a call report. The company decided that they'd like to have their sales force interact with customers on social media directly and record those interactions manually in the SAP CRM system until they could upgrade/purchase a social media integration package. While not the optimal solution, the modifications would allow the company to start listening, responding, and capturing these conversations to prevent them from losing some of their customer base.

Fit Gap Analysis

The development team determined that the standard SAP CRM system did not contain any specific tools out of the book for recording social media interactions. In reviewing the system, we noticed several gaps, which included business partner master data, transaction data and processing, loading data into the system, and reporting.

The first major gap we noticed was that we didn't see any specific fields on the business partner where we could specify the Facebook or Twitter account of a business partner. The information contained in Chapter 2 will allowed us to confirm our findings. We will need to add these fields to the business partner in order to be able to understand who the company's customers are on Twitter. To resolve this, we'll use the Application Enhancement Tool to add two new fields for Facebook ID and Twitter account ID for business partners. You can use the information in Section 3.2 of this book to understand how the AET can be used to add those fields to the business partner in your system.

Add fields

The second major gap we noticed is that the standard activity transaction did not contain all the fields we need to capture. Also, when creating the transaction, we noticed that it did not perform the necessary checks and validations to properly record a social media interaction. Accordingly, we'll need to create a new business transaction type called a *social call report* that will store all of our social media interactions in the SAP CRM system. The call report will need to be able to record notes and the applicable hashtag of the social media interaction to provide the company with a rich view of the conversation. The standard SAP CRM business activity does not contain a field to record a hashtag, so we will need to add the field using the AET tool as explained in Section 3.2.

Required fields For all interactions, we would like to require that the hashtag is filled out. Now we understand that not all tweets or Facebook interactions will use a hashtag, so we will have our sales representative put a one or two word description of the primary subject of the interaction if there is no hashtag provided in the tweet. It's important that this field is always maintained by the company's sales representative in order to have accurate analytics on the type of conversations that are occurring. We can use the information in Section 7.1 to achieve this requirement. However, we may want to default a subject, as initial feedback from the company's sales representatives indicates that trying to pick a single appropriate word is next to impossible. Section 7.2 provides an example of how you can default this value within the business transaction. Chapter 4 also gives other options you can use for inserting custom business logic rules into the social call report business transaction.

Automatic field population When we create the transaction, we want the dates of when it occurred to be populated automatically to the current date, so the sales representatives have less work to do. The information in Section 7.3 will allow you to achieve this requirement. We also want the correct contact person to be suggested when the transaction is created. If the system could figure out or suggest other people that we know that might have similar tweets or influence the interaction, we want it to provide a list of suggestions so that we can record that into the social call report. The information in Section 7.4 will help you to meet that requirement.

Even though the company communicates electronically, the sales representatives would still like a formatted output of the social call report, similar to how they have a print output of their standard call report. The company also wants to send email notifications to their marketing group, as these social call reports are being created so they can make sure that their sales force is properly aligned with the branding message. The Post Processing Framework can be used to achieve this requirement; refer to Chapter 6.

Formatted report output

Now that the social media interactions can be stored in the SAP CRM system, we would like to have some historical data available upon launch. It will be hard for the team to have a complete view of the customer without some historical information that shows what happened in the last two years. We've hired some great web programmers to download and create a few flat files that contain interactions relevant to the company from Facebook and Twitter. The sales representatives have even agreed to clean and review the data so that it will end up in a structured tab delimited file. To meet this requirement, we could examine either using the XIF adapter (Chapter 5) or look at extending External List management (Section 8.1). Either option could work; it's just a matter of determining whether the data should be loaded on a recurring basis, or this will be a one-time conversion. If this is a one-time conversion, our development team suggests XIF, while if this is a recurring process they think the marketing group should own this and they are willing to extend ELM so that going forward, the marketing group can be self sufficient.

Historical data

Senior management has requested that they track and analyze how many social interactions the company is receiving, and if any correlation to sales volume can be determined. The company currently has an SAP NetWeaver BW system in place that contains the sales volume data. We would like to send over information about the social media interactions to the SAP NetWeaver BW system to create combine reports on the number of social media interactions for the customer versus the ordering volume. (In Section 9.1, you'll learn how to extend SAP CRM to provide this information to the SAP NetWeaver BW system.) The company also wants to do some simple reporting on a weekly basis of all social media interactions at a detailed level received based on the hashtag

Reporting and analysis

entered. They believe that with those metrics, they'll have a better understanding of their customer base. In Section 9.3, you'll learn how you can launch some simple custom reports that you could develop to meet this requirement.

The company wants to accomplish all these requirements using the existing SAP CRM support staff within six to eight weeks. They're hoping to handle this all in-house, as they don't have the budget to pay for external consulting resources. Chapter 10 provides some resources to acccss when you've run out of solutions to solve the business requirements.

Summary

Although this scenario is purely fictional, the discussion of the requirements and how to meet those requirements is close what you will find on actual SAP CRM project when talking with your technical team. We hope that by matching the tools we've presented with this business scenario, your team can better use this book to solve your SAP CRM implementation requirements. In addition, we've chosen the social media example as it is simple to explain, but has several required technical components and is hopefully more relevant to your business than a flight reservation system. If for some reason you do actually end up productively implementing this social media scenario in your SAP CRM system, please let us know via Twitter *@sapcrmtpp*.

Information technology professionals face unique challenges in providing a solution that allows the business to focus on the customer instead of internal operations. SAP CRM provides a software solution to lessen those challenges through a deep integration with SAP ERP and the capability to capture a 360 degree view of the customer.

1   Understanding the Basic Architecture of SAP CRM

Working with customer relationship management (CRM) solutions offers a unique challenge. CRM developers need to be more than great technical programmers when working with business software solutions such as those delivered by SAP. A key challenge of working as developers on these SAP products is that you need to understand the associated business process as well as how the processes and software work in tandem.

For SAP CRM specifically, you must first understand what CRM is to be able to help adapt the software solution to meet the needs of your business users. In this chapter, we'll explain what CRM is in general, describe how SAP CRM is used to support a CRM methodology, and provide a brief overview of the major business processes supported by SAP CRM. We'll dive into an overview of the technical design of SAP CRM that will provide a foundation for our discussions later in this book on how to enhance and modify the SAP CRM system.

1.1   Defining Customer Relationship Management

In general, customer relationship management (CRM) is a methodology that is used by a business to establish, manage, and grow relationships with the customers that buy or purchase the goods or services the company

SAP CRM:
a software solution

offers. At the heart of CRM is the knowledge gained by tracking the interactions with customers. SAP Customer Relationship Management (SAP CRM) is a software solution delivered by SAP to help businesses manage and work with their different customers and vendors.

In CRM, there are three primary types of data captured about a customer:

Customer data

- Profile attributes that explain who they are
- Relationship attributes that explain where they fit in
- Transactional data that explains how they interact

Customer lifecycle

When implemented, a CRM system collects this data into a single view of the customer that is also known as the 360 degree or complete view of a customer, as shown in Figure 1.1. This view consists of the three major aspects of the customer lifecycle, which starts out in marketing or creating interest for a customer, moves to sales where you are pitching and selling the actual good or service, and ends with service, which may involve the service offered or service after the sale.

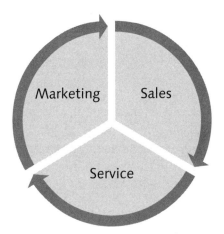

Figure 1.1 The 360 Degree View of a Customer

Social CRM

CRM has evolved over the last several years to focus on "social CRM" and customer experience management. Social CRM is the company's response to the fact that the customer is in control of the conversation as defined by Paul Greenberg in *CRM at the Speed of Light* (4th edition, McGraw-Hill Osborne Media, 2009).

Customer experience management is the methodology of considering the experience of the customer as the most critical focus in conducting business. The primary difference between social CRM and customer experience management is the scope of focus within an organization. Social CRM is traditionally focused more on the social interaction methods with a customer involving social media. Customer experience management goes beyond just the standard communication channels and looks at the operations of an enterprise, including noncustomer-facing functions that could impact the customer experience such as internal procurement, staffing procedures, and so on. An excellent resource on how customer experience management relates to CRM is *The Customer Experience Edge: Technology and Techniques for Delivering an Enduring, Profitable and Positive Experience to Your Customers* by Volker Hildebrand, Vinay Iyer, and Reza Soudagar (McGraw-Hill, 2011).

Customer experience management

> **Note**
>
> These books have been mentioned because they provide the business motivation on why to implement a CRM software system. As SAP CRM developers, we strongly suggest spending some time reviewing those books after you've finished this text.

SAP CRM supports tracking customer attributes, relationships, and interactions with a company. CRM interactions can be any type of event that happens with the customer, including but not limited to a sales order, complaint, phone call, in-person meeting, email, tweet, Facebook update, return, and so on. Due to the vast nature of possible customer interactions that could be recorded in SAP CRM, a decision is typically made by business sponsors for CRM implementation in a company on what type of interactions will be recorded in the SAP CRM system.

The primary reason to implement SAP CRM is to better support your CRM or customer experience business processes that focus on the customer. A successful SAP CRM implementation will provide tools that allow the business to manage relationships and the experience with the customer. This requires that the business take the lead in driving the SAP CRM implementation and adoption instead of allowing that to be the job of the developers and IT. As a developer, your role is to be a trusted technical adviser that can help achieve the goals of the business.

SAP CRM: customer-support tool

From a business perspective, SAP CRM supports functions related to sales, service, marketing, and e-commerce. For each area, there are specific functions that relate to that aspect of CRM. However, because a CRM system is designed to provide a single, comprehensive view of the customer, many features will be shared across major areas.

In the next sections, we provide a high-level overview of the key modules of the SAP CRM system.

> **Note**
>
> For a more in-depth review of these features, we recommend the book *Discover SAP CRM* by Srini Katta (2nd Edition SAP PRESS, 2013), which is an excellent reference on the business features of SAP CRM.

1.1.1 Sales

Sales Force Automation

A core function of any CRM software tool and one of the most widely implemented features of any CRM software solution is called *Sales Force Automation (SFA)*. The goal of SFA is to provide functionality that will enable a company's sales force to better understand and interact with their customers. Three primary areas of SFA include Account and Contact Management, Activity Management, and Opportunity and Pipeline Management, as you'll see in the following subsections. In addition, SAP CRM provides traditional sales order and sales contract management functionality.

Account and Contact Management

The core function of Account and Contact Management is to track the attributes and relationships of all customers, prospects, vendors, and employees that interact with a company. To track this, the SAP CRM system provides the concept of the business partner, along with business partner relationships.

Business partner

A *business partner* is defined as any person, organization, or group that interacts with a business and/or employees of a business. As you'll learn in Chapter 2, the business partner is central to the SAP CRM system. Figure 1.2 shows an example of a business partner in SAP CRM. The primary information of a business partner that is common to all types of business partners is a name, address, and communication details. In communication details we might record the phone number, email address, or website of a business partner.

> **Note**
>
> In Chapter 2, we'll cover in detail how SAP defines the business partner in SAP CRM, along with the data model.

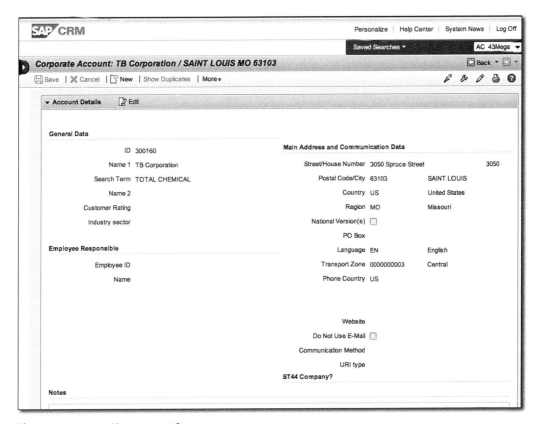

Figure 1.2 Account Management Screen

Activity Management

The tracking of nonfinancial interactions with a customer and/or prospect is the heart of Activity Management. *Activities* are any type of significant

Activities

interaction with a business partner that takes place. Common examples include a phone call, email, customer visit, and so on. The goal of Activity Management is to track these interactions and provide a means to allow everyone within an organization to understand nonfinancial interactions with a customer or prospect.

Lead Management

Tracking business interests

Lead Management is the tracking of potential interests in buying a good or service from a company. The key difference between Lead Management and Opportunity Management is that a lead has not yet been qualified when received as potential future sales and instead could just represent a simple interest in a company.

The process of converting potential interest to an actual interest is called qualification. *Qualification* determines whether the potential buyer ("prospect") has a strong interest in the good or service, the timeframe to purchase (now versus future), and the purchasing power to buy the good or service.

Opportunity and Pipeline Management

Tracking potential and current sales

Opportunity Management is the process of managing and tracking potential sales to existing customers or prospects. In Opportunity Management, you track the progress of a potential sale as it moves from "pitch" to "close." Some of the goals of Opportunity Management include the following:

▶ Determine how much sales you could have in the future

▶ Learn when and possibly why you lose business

▶ Track the effectiveness of sales forces in converting pitches to signed deals

The tracking of opportunities across the various phases in a sales cycle is known as Pipeline Management. The pipeline data captured in SAP CRM is normally transferred to a business analytics tool for detailed analysis.

Order Management

As an alternative to the order-entry functionality found in SAP ERP, SAP CRM allows for the management of sales orders. The sales orders created in SAP CRM are normally transferred back to an SAP ERP or other ERP system. The primary reason for using Order Management in SAP CRM is that you can combine traditional ordering processes with enhanced cross-selling functionality that uses the marketing features of SAP CRM.

Sales Order Management

In the newer versions, you can use SAP CRM as a frontend to place orders in SAP ERP. The advantage is that there is less setup work than the traditional configuration, and you still benefit from the enhanced marketing features of SAP CRM.

Contract Management

You can also track and manage sales contracts in SAP CRM. By having sales contracts in SAP CRM, you can manage the complete sales process from lead to order within SAP CRM.

1.1.2   Service

After a customer has purchased a product from a company, there is an expectation of providing service to the customer if something is wrong with the purchase or of providing support after the sale. In some cases, the support itself may be the product you're selling. SAP CRM provides tools to support Complaint and Return Management, Warranty Management, and IT Service Management (ITSM).

Complaint and Return Management

One of the most common but least desired customer interactions involves complaints from a customer about a good or service. Complaint Management allows a company to track and monitor customer complaints received in order to identify issues involving sales, product quality, or customer service.

Complaints and returns

Warranty Management

Warranties

Warranties are contracts from a company that provide a means of remediation if a good or service is found to be defective within a given period of time. SAP CRM enables the management of warranties for products sold to a customer and the claims filed against those warranties.

IT Service Management

ITSM provides an IT Infrastructure Library (ITIL)-complaint solution for management of IT support processes within SAP CRM. Some of the processes supported include Incident Management, Change Request Management, and IT Asset Management.

1.1.3 Marketing

Manage marketing activities in SAP CRM

Marketing is an important aspect of the customer lifecycle and SAP CRM. Each prospect starts out as a potential customer or prospect that first needs to be made aware of the product or service and then eventually is identified as someone interested in buying that product or service. After a prospect becomes a customer, you still need to keep the customer engaged with your company. SAP CRM provides tools that help manage your marketing activities. Those tools include Campaign Management, Loyalty Management, Segmentation Management, List Management, and Trade Promotion Management (TPM).

Campaign Management

Manage marketing campaigns

The management of marketing campaigns is a key feature supported by SAP CRM. A marketing campaign is a defined set of tactics and techniques used to influence or make potential buyers aware of a set of goods or services. Each marketing campaign normally targets a predefined audience or market that best fits the potential purchasers of a product or service. The Campaign Management module of SAP CRM allows you to define, manage the execution of, and track the results of those campaigns. In SAP CRM, you can set up a marketing calendar that allows you to arrange the timing of when campaigns will occur. For each campaign, you can define the method of communication that will be used along with who you're targeting. You can also group several related campaigns together as subcampaigns of a much larger overall marketing campaign. The system then provides methods to execute certain types of campaigns, such as email campaigns, and track the responses received. You can also manually import the results of any campaign activity into SAP CRM even if the campaign was not executed from SAP CRM. A positive interest in buying the good or service advertised from a campaign is considered a lead.

Loyalty Management

Loyalty Management allows for the management of customer loyalty programs. A customer loyalty programs is a marketing technique used to retain and reward customers. A common example is a frequent buyer program that provides discounts or free merchandise after a qualifying amount of purchases has been made.

Customer loyalty

Segmentation Management and List Management

One of the most powerful features of SAP CRM is the capability to group similar customers together via common attributes. The Segment Builder in SAP CRM allows you to group together customers by common attributes in a dynamic fashion. The marketing attributes in SAP CRM are defined via an end-user tool that extends the database model of SAP CRM without the need to manually create new tables to store the attributes. The tools are designed so that a marketing professional can set up the attributes without needing intervention from their IT professional.

Grouping customers by common attributes

List Management allows companies to import and manage lists of prospects that may be bought from various vendors. SAP CRM provides a tool called External List Management (ELM) that allows for the import of owned and rented lists of prospects into SAP CRM for use in marketing campaigns or other business processes.

List Management

Trade Promotion Management

Trade Promotion Management (TPM) primarily focuses on managing trade promotions used in the selling of a product by a company's distributors or by selling directly to a customer. The two primary areas tracked

Tracking customer rebates and trade spend funds

by TPM are customer rebates and trade spend funds. Rebates are based on volume bought/sold and are typically given as credits on an invoice when a customer has bought (or a distributor has sold) a certain amount of a particular product. Trade spend funds are credits that accumulate like a rebate but are instead used for advertising the product for a particular distributor. The trade promotions are set up in SAP CRM and will typically result in SAP CRM sending back information to SAP ERP on rebate conditions to be set up based on the trade promotion.

1.1.4 E-Commerce

SAP CRM Web Channel Experience Management

E-commerce for SAP CRM is also known as SAP CRM Web Channel Experience Management (which we'll also refer to as the Web Channel). The primary function of this module allows a customer to place orders, view product catalogs, and check on order statuses via the Internet using a web browser. The Web Channel can be used for either business-to-business (B2B) transactions, which require a user ID and password to access the information and is for established customers, or for business-to-consumer (B2C), which allows for anyone with Internet access to place an order. This module was one of the key drivers for having SAP CRM set up as a separate technical system from SAP ERP.

1.1.5 Interaction Center

The Interaction Center supports tracking and management of customer interactions via a traditional phone call center in SAP CRM and other channels such as online chat and email. The Interaction Center does not include the telephony software itself, but it provides a standard interface that can be set up to integrate with most major telephony systems. *Maximizing Your SAP CRM Interaction Center* by John Burton (SAP PRESS, 2009) provides an excellent deep dive on this topic, including a discussion on the Computer Telephony Integration (CTI) tool used to connect SAP CRM with a telephony system.

1.2   Reasons for a Separate SAP CRM System

One of the first technical questions that many ABAP developers ask when getting started with SAP CRM is why SAP has a separate system. There are many reasons SAP CRM has been created as its own system; in this section, we'll take a look at five factors that influenced the design.

1.2.1   Performance

Even though the SAP R/3 Basis System, or now known as the SAP NetWeaver Application Server ABAP (AS ABAP), could scale to handle load, it didn't always meet the demands posed by e-commerce applications. An e-commerce application needs to be up 24/7 and exposed to the Internet. SAP tried to expose this functionality via the Internet Transaction Server (ITS) but failed. The biggest issues were that the built-in pricing engine of SAP ERP and product catalog did not respond fast enough for web-based transactions. The existing engines were considered too far away from the web server, which increased the network latency. In addition, the design of the SAP ERP database wasn't considered optimized for web-based ordering, especially for e-commerce sites with a large product catalog stored in the backend SAP ERP system.

To solve this problem, the design placed the e-commerce applications on a separate system that could use additional hardware for the database and application layers. In addition, by switching to a separate system, the catalog and pricing engines in the SAP R/3 system could be redesigned toward web applications. In this design, one of SAP's first in-memory computing applications—SAP Text and Retrieval Engine (TREX)—was created with the primary function of serving product catalog information.

TREX

Another aspect of performance was reducing the overall size of the database on the SAP ERP system. The SAP R/3 system was already a huge monolith when the development SAP CRM started. Breaking SAP CRM into a separate database reduced the overall size of the SAP ERP system.

1.2.2 Development Cycles

One of the biggest drawbacks of the SAP R/3 solution and the current SAP ERP solution is the fact that because everything is integrated, upgrade cycles are quite time consuming. The need for new functionality in established back-office processes is more about covering the "gaps" rather than supporting a new evolving methodology. SAP CRM as a process was not as established as many traditional back-office processes in the late 90s and needed constant refinement. Compared to traditional ERP systems such as SAP R/3, the original versions of SAP CRM were an early attempt at covering key parts of CRM but still were missing key parts to support the entire methodology.

This issue of maturity led to the need to have versions of the software released more rapidly. The versions could be compatible with an older R/3 or SAP ERP system but allow for rapid innovation. Until SAP CRM 7.0, SAP CRM was on a separate release cycle from other solutions. SAP has now unified the release cycle of new versions with other solutions with the advent of SAP Business Suite Innovations 2010. Although this reduces much of the system complexity, this now has caused the SAP CRM system to be extended with new innovations at a much slower pace than before.

Let's also look at development cycles from the customer operations perspective. In many companies, the project lifecycles are quite different between SAP ERP and SAP CRM. SAP CRM projects tend to be shorter and more frequent. By having a separate system, it allows the IT department supporting the system to add more functionality to the SAP CRM system at a much more rapid pace without disrupting the work in the core SAP ERP system, which tends to be more stable.

1.2.3 Mobility

One of the earliest processes targeted to be supported by SAP CRM was mobile sales and mobile service. The idea was that a sales representative or field service worker could work with an offline copy of the knowledge stored in an SAP CRM system and then replicate the changes they made and receive new updates for their accounts when back in the office or via dial-up modem. This concept of mobility existed long before smartphones, tablets, and other mobile devices that redefined how we interact with computers. Instead the focus was on "mobile laptops," which are bulky compared to current devices such as an Apple MacBook Air.

To solve the mobility issue, there needed to be a central database that could handle the replication and realignment of data that was sent to mobile devices. Even though the SAP R/3 system could have been modified for this task, the result would still have performance and development cycle issues. The SAP CRM central database also allowed keeping the staging area for replication separate from the operational data.

SAP CRM as a central database to communicate with remote devices

This long-standing requirement and need for mobility for SAP CRM has created a design that can send data to other systems for mobile access, even though the target mobile technology has changed.

1.2.4 Non-SAP Systems

One of the many goals of SAP CRM was to provide a way for customers who might have multiple ERP or different backend systems to get one view of their customers. The problem that both business and IT often face is that a single customer ends up as many different entities across several disconnected systems and there is no easy way to get one view. If SAP CRM were implemented as just another module of SAP ERP, then SAP ERP would need to be extended to handle the data of multiple ERP systems.

The problem with this is that the customer master, vendor master, material master, and many other transactional tables are only designed or sometimes configured to handle one business model. To overcome this issue, the data models for the customer master, vendor master, material master, sales orders, and others had to be redesigned to support more than one business model at the same time. In addition, the SAP R/3 system traditionally did not support the import or export of all data. A new system design was needed that would by default support the import or export of all major data objects.

Integrate third-party systems and tools

Even though the use of SAP CRM against an ERP backend that is not SAP ERP isn't as common, there are still benefits for those customers running the traditional scenario of a single SAP CRM system connected to a single SAP ERP system. One of those benefits is that all objects in SAP CRM have well-defined application programming interfaces (API) for importing and exporting data. This feature typically reduces the time required for building programs in SAP CRM to import or export data into the system.

1.2.5 Target User Base

Operational selling vs. financial model

Ideally, a CRM process should involve all employees of a company and not just those in sales, service, and marketing. However, in most cases, the employees in sales, service, and marketing are the key users of a system designed to a support CRM. As result, the system was designed with those users in mind, instead of being designed like an ERP system with a finance-centric view of the world. One classic example is the SAP CRM organizational model. In SAP CRM, you can set up an organizational model that reflects how your sales force operates, instead of how the books are organized. If you look at the traditional ERP system, the organizational model for sales documents is primarily focused on how revenue will be booked in accounting, rather than how you sell. Although making sure that you can keep track of the books is important, SAP CRM allows you to map your operational selling model to the financial model required for proper accounting.

Usually, business structures that map to a CRM system change more frequently than other areas. By having a separate system for some of the more rapidly changing processes, you can allow for the system to change without impacting the core ERP system of a company. These changes typically aren't as complex as completely revising an order-to-cash process, but they are needed for the SAP CRM processes to be effective.

1.3 Technical Landscape of SAP CRM

The technical landscape of SAP CRM has evolved over many years. The original landscape involved many standalone engines on separate hardware in order to implement a single module of SAP CRM. Over the years, this design has been simplified to a more manageable setup without sacrificing performance. As a developer, it's always crucial to understand the design and components of a software solution to enhance and/or make modifications to that system. To better understand SAP CRM as a developer, you need to review the components, landscape, and development tools that make up the technical infrastructure of SAP CRM.

1.3.1 System Components

The system components in SAP CRM vary by business scenario and for each release. The SAP CRM Master Guide always has the most up-to-date requirements for each scenario.

Let's examine some of the commonly used components and how they function within the SAP CRM setup. These components include the SAP CRM ABAP Application Server, SAP CRM Java Application Server, and SAP TREX. In addition to the SAP CRM system components, an associated SAP ERP system may serve as the backend data source for SAP CRM. A backend data source provides information such as customizing, master data, and transactional information to the SAP CRM system. Figure 1.3 shows a basic SAP CRM landscape consisting of SAP ERP and SAP CRM. Both systems in this diagram have an ABAP Application Server and a Java Application Server.

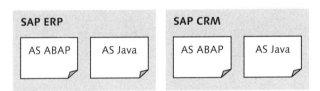

Figure 1.3 Basic SAP CRM Landscape

SAP CRM ABAP Server

The SAP CRM ABAP Server is the heart of the system. It's based on SAP NetWeaver AS ABAP and contains the core business logic and programs for SAP CRM. The ABAP Server component is core to almost every business scenario except the Web Channel for SAP ERP. ABAP is the proprietary programming language developed by SAP for business applications.

One of the first things you'll notice about the SAP CRM ABAP Server is despite it sharing the same common ABAP foundation as an SAP ERP system on a similar SAP NetWeaver release, the design and code contained are completely different. The SAP CRM ABAP system was built from scratch, and with the exception of the business partner in SAP and SAP Classification System, there is little shared business application-level code used by both SAP CRM and SAP ERP.

Object-oriented code

As you review the ABAP code found in the SAP CRM system, you'll notice that most of it is object based and much of it is object oriented. Object-based code is a method of writing structured non object-oriented code that uses object-oriented concepts without full object orientation. An object-based design still uses procedural language elements of SAP ABAP but does not use object-oriented concepts such as classes. The benefits of an object-based design include a strong element of abstraction and a separation of layers. Object-based code tends not to exhibit the "spaghetti-string" attributes of normal procedural-based programming.

Modern ABAP language constructs

In addition to the object-oriented design orientation of SAP CRM, you'll find that most modern ABAP language constructs are used. Historically, the SAP CRM system has been on a newer version of ABAP than the SAP ERP system, and the developers of SAP CRM tend to take advantage of the new features delivered with each release of the ABAP AS. As a developer, you'll need to be familiar with current ABAP concepts to understand the newest features of SAP CRM. If you don't already understand ABAP Objects, we strongly recommend that you become familiar with it before working with SAP CRM as an ABAP developer. Ideally, you have worked with ABAP for at least one year with a focus on SAP ERP Materials Management/Sales and Distribution (MM/SD) components before starting your work with SAP CRM.

SAP CRM Java Server

The SAP CRM Java Server is primarily used by the SAP CRM Interaction Center and Web Channel. The SAP CRM Java Server is based on the SAP NetWeaver AS Java and is a J2EE-complaint application server based on the Java programming language. It is primarily used for e-commerce and interaction scenarios on SAP CRM.

The SAP CRM Java Server is typically kept at the same technical release level of SAP NetWeaver as the SAP CRM ABAP system. Recently, SAP has released an option that allows SAP CRM Java components to be run on an SAP NetWeaver 7.3 system while keeping the SAP CRM ABAP system using the SAP NetWeaver 7.0 technology. The primary benefits of this change are that it allows for a modern Java Virtual Machine (JVM) to be used, provides for easier system administration, and results in better performance than the earlier versions of SAP NetWeaver Java.

SAP CRM ABAP Java Virtual Machine Container

One of the strangest concepts within the SAP world is the SAP NetWeaver ABAP Server JVM Container. This subsystem of the SAP NetWeaver AS is a container that holds a J2EE virtual machine. This is designed so that the pricing engine of SAP CRM—known as the Internet Pricing Configurator (IPC)—doesn't require a separate Java AS. This allows for a reduction of hardware because originally an SAP CRM landscape required the IPC on separate hardware.

SAP TREX

The SAP Text and Retrieval Engine (TREX) was originally designed to support the indexing and searching of product catalog data for the SAP CRM Web Channel. This technology has now been expanded to support the central/simple search for SAP CRM business transactions and master data. It allows for the full text search of information that has been indexed to the TREX server.

Indexing & search

1.3.2 User Interface

Like most ABAP-based systems, the SAP CRM system can be accessed using the SAP GUI as shown in Figure 1.4. Historically, this was the first interface and was supported by SAP for business user access until SAP CRM 2006s. With the release of SAP CRM 2006s, a new UI called the

SAP Web Client

SAP CRM Web Client was introduced as shown in Figure 1.5. This interface is browser based and intended to be used for all business user access to the system. Administrative functions of SAP CRM, including configuration, development, and system administration, are still possible with the SAP GUI.

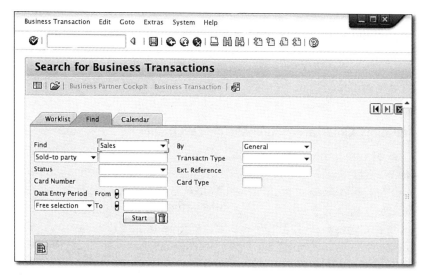

Figure 1.4 SAP GUI for SAP CRM

> **Note**
>
> The SAP CRM Web Client is also known as the *SAP Web Client*, or just the *Web Client*. In this book we will primarily use the term Web Client to refer to this user interface of SAP CRM, as you'll most likely refer to it in this shortened form in your daily job.

People-Centric UI
In addition to the SAP GUI and Web Client, two other user interfaces have been used on an SAP CRM system that you may encounter on an older release of the software. The first is called the People-Centric User Interface (PCUI) and was the first replacement for the SAP GUI. This interface was found on SAP CRM 3.1, 4.0, and 5.0. Although strongly marketed by SAP, it was poorly received by most SAP CRM end users, and SAP never required the use of PCUI instead of the SAP GUI transactions.

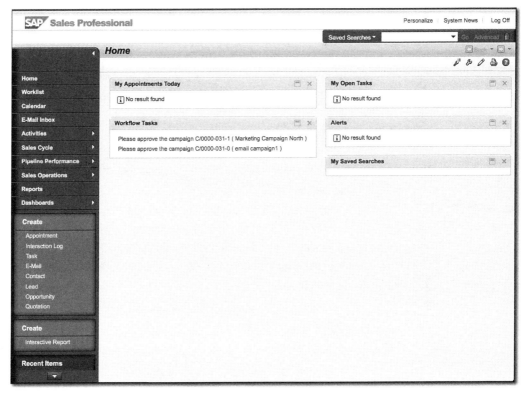

Figure 1.5 SAP Web Client User Interface

The second UI was called the IC Web Client. This UI was primarily intended for the Interaction Center and was found on SAP CRM 4.0 and SAP CRM 5.0 in general use. The technical design foundations of this UI were used in creating the Web Client and offered an alternative interface from the SAP GUI for the interaction center.

IC Web Client

In SAP CRM 7.0 and above, a typical ABAP developer will still be spending most of his time in the ABAP Workbench. However, certain tools, such as the Application Enhancement Tool (AET), are only available via the Web Client UI. In addition, debugging most SAP CRM applications requires the use of external breakpoints even though the code being created is not in the UI layer.

Why Is the User Interface Important for SAP CRM?

Before SAP CRM 2006/s was introduced, the most common complaint about the application was the UI. Even though the PCUI interface was people centric, it was considered unfriendly by the majority of end users at most companies running the solution. After an SAP CRM system was implemented, it wasn't uncommon for the system to be left unused due to the complexity of the UI. Many users commonly ignored the SAP CRM system, even if it was written into their job duties. If the Web Client UI had not been introduced, there may have been no need for this book, as many SAP CRM customers would not have been using the solution.

In this book, we won't focus on the customization or development of the Web Client; rather, our focus will be on the UI-independent business logic layers that have remained relatively stable since SAP CRM 3.0. There are two excellent resources on Web Client development that delve into further detail:

- *SAP Web Client Customizing and Development* by Michael Füschle and Matthias Zierke (SAP PRESS, 2010)
- *SAP Web Client: A Comprehensive Guide for Developers* by Tzanko Stefanov, Armand Serzikeye, and Sanjeet Mall (SAP PRESS, 2011)

1.3.3   Recommended Landscape

The SAP CRM system and associated components normally reside as a separate technical SAP NetWeaver AS instance with a separate database. There is typically one SAP CRM system per each SAP ERP system contained in the SAP landscape. Your SAP CRM landscape should mirror your SAP ERP landscape with one exception. By mirroring, there should be an instance of SAP CRM for each level of SAP ERP system that you have. The primary exception is that a normal SAP CRM system should only have one client, which is paired to the primary client in each SAP ERP system that contains all of the configuration, master data, and transactional data that will be replicated to SAP CRM.

Avoid multiple clients
We can't stress enough that having multiple clients in your SAP CRM system will cause multiple headaches unless you're doing a nontraditional SAP CRM setup; that is, you're working with multiple SAP ERP or legacy

ERP systems that point to your SAP CRM system. However, even for those scenarios, we still recommend only one client per SAP CRM instance. The most important reason is that SAP CRM retrieves its customizing data via the SAP CRM Middleware from the SAP ERP system. Due to the design of SAP CRM, you can only have one connection between SAP CRM and an SAP ERP system. A gold client in SAP CRM that contains no transactional data doesn't make sense because you always need to download data from SAP ERP before you can start the customization of SAP CRM. Even if you connect multiple SAP ERP systems to your SAP CRM system, you'll still need to have the customization from those systems available before you can begin your SAP CRM customization. The one major exception to this rule is if you run SAP CRM as a standalone system with no connections to an ERP system (SAP or other vendor). In this case, the gold client might make some sense, but we still don't recommend it if you ever plan to connect your SAP CRM to another system.

1.3.4   SAP CRM Middleware

The SAP CRM Middleware refers to collection of ABAP code contained in SAP ERP and SAP CRM based on queued remote function call (qRFC) that allows for the transfer of master and transactional data from SAP ERP to SAP CRM and from SAP CRM to SAP ERP. The ABAP code on the SAP ERP side consists of a modifying plug-in, which is considered part of the standard SAP ERP system as of SAP ERP 6.0. Earlier versions of SAP ERP or SAP   R/3 required this code to be installed. The code itself is a series of changes to standard SAP Transactions VA01 (create sales order), XD01 (create customer), MM01 (create material), and so on. These changes transfer data to special user exits known as the OPEN FI user exits, which are only active upon setup of the middleware data transfer between the SAP ERP and SAP CRM systems. The OPEN FI exits make a special qRFC call that encapsulates the data from the transferring system to the target system via a structure called a business document (BDoc). A BDoc is similar in structure to the SAP IDoc structure; however, only the SAP CRM Middleware for data transfer uses it.

qRFC is special type of report functional call technology that uses ordered queues in the execution of remote function calls (RFCs) between two systems. During data transfer from SAP ERP to SAP CRM

qRFC

and from SAP CRM to SAP ERP, the call parameters are written into a queue in a distinct logical unit of work known as a transaction. Each transaction is processed in a first in first out order (FIFO) to preserve the data integrity of the updates. This design allows for asynchronous updates to be sent between the systems, which provide a restart and error-handling mechanism in case of errors. To improve the performance of the data transfer, multiple queues are used and are typically based on the type of data being updated (customers, materials, orders, etc.). Due to the use of queues, both systems are no longer required to be available to transfer updates between systems without data loss.

Even though the word "middleware" is used, be careful not to confuse it with enterprise application integration (EAI) software such as SAP NetWeaver Process Integration (SAP NetWeaver PI), Microsoft BizTalk, TIBCO, or IBM WebSphere. Although it's technically possible not to use the middleware to integrate SAP CRM with SAP ERP, normally we advise against that because the standard middleware scenarios cover the majority if not every integration requirement between SAP CRM and SAP ERP.

Middleware setup   The middleware setup involves configuration on both the SAP ERP and SAP CRM systems. SAP has predefined the mapping of standard customizing, master, organizational, and transactional data between the two systems. For the middleware configuration, you set up RFC destinations between the two systems and what data should be transferred. If you have extended the data model of either system, you can use *middleware exits* to extend the data transfer model on both systems or change the default mapping provided by SAP. The middleware is also the foundation for the external interface adapter (XIF adapter), which allows for transfer of data into and from the SAP CRM system from/to non-SAP ERP systems. We'll cover the XIF adapter in greater detail later in this book.

The only drawback to the approach of the middleware is that it requires a resource with a strong knowledge of SAP ERP and SAP CRM who can act as an SAP renaissance resource. An effective SAP CRM Middleware person can configure both systems, debug and write ABAP, and troubleshoot basic system administration functions. For this book, we won't cover the details of the middleware as an entire volume has been written on this topic and eventually will be written again.

1.3.5   Data Model

In the next chapter, we'll spend a significant amount of time discussing the data model of SAP CRM. As stated earlier, the data model of SAP CRM differs significantly from SAP ERP, even though the two systems were designed to work together. You'll also find that the SAP CRM data is only a subset of the general SAP ERP data model.

The terminology of the SAP CRM data model is different from normal SAP ERP terminology. Customers are known as business partners, materials are known as partners, and sales orders are known as business transactions. This difference in terminology sometimes poses a challenge to experienced ABAP developers who understand SAP ERP Sales and Distribution (SD) but are new to SAP CRM.

1.3.6   Development Tools

SAP CRM provides additional tools for development beyond the standard ABAP Workbench. In this book, we'll cover the Easy Enhancement Workbench (EEWB), Application Enhancement Tool (AET), external interface adapter (XIF adapter), and Post Processing Framework (PPF). These tools allow the developer to spend more time focusing on developing the business logic requirements. Although some of these tools, such as EEWB and AET, were designed to be executed by non-IT personnel, due to the complexity of the tools and the fact that they update the schema of the SAP CRM database tables, we advise that they are supervised by technical resources personnel who understand how these tools change the system.

Business logic development

Easy Enhancement Workbench (EEWB)

The EEWB is the original data model extension tool for SAP CRM. It was made available with SAP CRM 4.0 and was replaced by the AET in SAP CRM 7.0. EEWB is an SAP GUI-based transaction as show in Figure 1.6. The goal of the tool was to automate the creation of extensions to common

EEWB

SAP CRM data objects such as business partners, products, and business transactions. The tool proved quite useful and reduced the amount of effort to customize the system. Common extension requirements to the SAP Business Partner were reduced from a week of development to only 15 minutes. Even though EEWB isn't used for new development on SAP CRM version 7.0 or higher, we'll cover the details in Chapter 3 because it will help to understand existing enhancements in older SAP CRM systems.

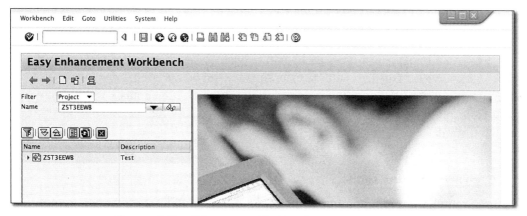

Figure 1.6 Easy Enhancement Workbench

Application Enhancement Tool (AET)

Reusable extensions The AET is the replacement for the EEWB. It isn't based on the SAP GUI like the EEWB but instead is built for the Web Client UI as show in Figure 1.7. The key difference is that AET extensions are reusable instead of just being built for one-time use. The AET also can import and use previous extensions made by the EEWB, allowing for backward compatibility. Chapter 3 explains how to use this development tool.

External Interface (XIF) Adapter

The XIF adapter is a framework that sits on top of the SAP CRM Middleware. It is delivered as a series of remote function modules and IDocs that translate a data structure into a BDoc for inbound processing or outbound extraction. Chapter 5 covers the XIF adapter in further detail.

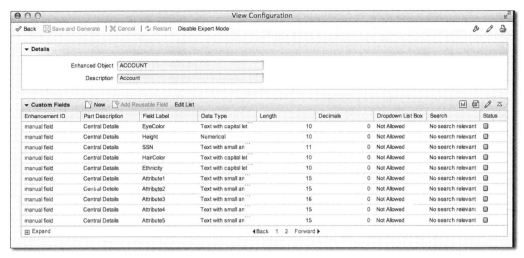

Figure 1.7 Application Enhancement Tool

Post Processing Framework

The Post Processing Framework (PPF) is used to create print outputs from SAP CRM. It can also be used to execute business logic on an immediate or scheduled basis similar to SAP Business Workflow. As a developer, you'll use this tool when you need to generate print output via SAP Smart Forms or update an SAP CRM transaction based on certain logic. More information about this tool is provided in Chapter 6.

1.3.7   Reporting

The SAP CRM system didn't provide out-of-the-box reports with the system. Instead, the approach was to allow connectivity to reporting tools such as SAP NetWeaver Business Warehouse (BW) to handle reporting requirements. With the release of SAP CRM 2006s, a new reporting tool was provided to allow users to create their own reports without a need for a BW system. In addition, SAP has started to deliver enhanced reporting content such as the SAP BusinessObjects Dashboards with version 7.0 EHP1 based on the BusinessObjects set of analytics tools.

1.3.8   Supporting SAP CRM

Technical support for SAP CRM often mirrors the support model for an SAP ERP system. A normal SAP CRM system will have system administrators, database administrators, SAP security administrators, ABAP developers, configuration specialists, and so on. Most of the best practices for supporting SAP ERP will apply—keeping in mind the exceptions pointed out already.

Key Characteristics of a Successful SAP CRM Developer

Understanding SAP CRM as an ABAP developer requires a different focus from the traditional SAP ERP projects. The first skill you'll be forced to use and learn is object-oriented ABAP in order to enhance the existing system.

Next, you'll need to understand the data model of SAP CRM. As the majority of business requirements for SAP will involve extensions to the data model, it's imperative to understand what can be extended and how to make those extensions.

Call timing   Finally, you'll need to develop a good understanding of call timing in the SAP CRM system. *Call timing* refers to when certain code is executed on the SAP CRM system, which can be anything from standard function modules to Business Add-Ins (BAdIs).

One other aspect that has always been a heavy restriction on learning SAP CRM has been the lack of available training courses and books on the technical side of the solution. For most SAP CRM developers, knowledge has been traditionally gained from project experience or from using the SAP Community Network (SCN) forums on SAP CRM. The most common question we get is how did you learn everything you know about SAP CRM? Our normal answer is through many years of project experience. Our goal for you as a reader is to be able to gain a quick jump-start on the design of SAP CRM and how to enhance the system, so that you don't have to spend as much time as we have in discovering the design and technical limits of the system.

Life as an SAP CRM Developer

After spending 10 years working with SAP CRM as an ABAP developer, you realize that your typical day isn't quite the same as someone just working with SAP ERP. You typically have more "projects" during a year than an SAP ERP group and normally these go in three to six month "bursts." If you're also responsible for the middleware, you'll be constantly trying to reconcile issues in data transfer, primarily due to bad data or lack of communication on configuration changes.

In addition, you may have to explain to your Basis, security, management, and business teams why SAP CRM just technically does everything different from SAP ERP. Even though this can be a huge challenge, after reading this book you'll be able to start to deliver the impossible for your end users. When you make your SAP CRM end users happy, you'll feel like their champion.

1.4 Summary

This chapter explained that the SAP CRM software tool supports the customer relationship management (CRM) methodology used by a company. SAP CRM consists of modules that support processes in sales, service, marketing, and e-commerce. These modules have been developed to provide a complete 360 degree view of the relationship of a customer or prospect with a given company.

SAP CRM has been set up as a separate technical system from SAP ERP due to four major factors: performance, development cycles, mobility, and non-SAP systems. Even though some of these factors are no longer primary drivers to keep SAP CRM as a separate system, their influence on the design of the system is still present. These design motivations have also allowed SAP CRM to more rapidly evolve over the past 10 years.

The technical landscape of SAP CRM consists of three components: SAP CRM ABAP Server, SAP CRM Java Server, and TREX. The SAP CRM ABAP Server is the component used in most business scenarios and implementations with the exception of the Web Channel for an SAP ERP scenario.

SAP CRM has a very unique technical design compared to SAP ERP even though the two share a common SAP NetWeaver AS ABAP foundation. This design requires that an SAP CRM ABAP developer have additional skills beyond those required for SAP ERP.

In the following chapters, you'll learn the details of the data model, including how to enhance that data model, import/extract data to and from the system, and perform other enhancements for common business requirements.

The heart of customer relationship management is the customer; therefore, the heart of SAP CRM is the business partner. Understanding the data model for the business partner will help you understand the core of SAP CRM.

2   The SAP CRM Data Model

SAP CRM is centered on a 360 degree view of the customer. To provide that view, you must have a data model that supports all attributes of a customer. Because the data about a customer is the heart of SAP CRM, we'll help you to understand how this model is set up so you can extend it to meet your business requirements.

In this chapter, we'll explore the design principles behind the SAP CRM data model and examine the data model of major business objects in SAP CRM, including the business partner, product master, business transaction, and marketing attributes.

2.1   Data Model Background

SAP R/3 was a great product but was primarily focused on making sure that all functions were integrated and that the financial books could be maintained. This left little consideration to creating a customer-centric view of the enterprise. To solve this issue and fix some of the problems from the original R/3 design, the data model of SAP CRM was created from a blank slate.

In the following sections, we'll go over the specifics of the modern SAP ERP system as it relates to SAP CRM.

2.1.1   SAP ERP Data Model for Sales

R/3   In the SAP R/3 system, the data model was designed with one purpose: the perfect posting of financial transactions. This meant that organizational structure, customers, vendors, materials, and sales orders were all geared toward correct financial postings. In short, the focus was on a successful order-to-cash lifecycle rather than the customer lifecycle. Organizational data such as sales organizations were mapped to correspond to the financial reporting structure of a company rather than to the sales management structure, for example.

2.1.2   Segments and Tables

SAP ERP design   The SAP ERP system features huge tables that contain hundreds of attributes due to previous limitations and designs. Part of the primary drivers behind this design was the fact that database management systems had a physical limit on the number of tables contained in a schema. SAP had implemented several different techniques to get around this issue while only keeping the most important tables as standalone in the database. As the late 1990s ended, these restrictions were no longer an issue. However, due to the growing install base of the R/3 solution, it was no longer feasible to redesign the underlying data model to take advantage of the new technology.

Table redesign   In designing SAP CRM, the underlying table design was approached as series of logical objects that contained a traditional header and segments. The *header* is a table that contains the primary key and descriptive attributes to uniquely identify an object. A *segment* is a group of related attributes for an object.

This model was quite different from traditional SAP ERP tables such as MARA, which contain both unique and descriptive attributes resulting in tables with more than 200 fields. The SAP CRM approach takes large table designs such as MARA and breaks them up into a series of smaller tables.

GUIDs   Another design difference for SAP CRM was the introduction of GUIDs (globally unique identifiers) as the primary key for data objects. GUIDs make it possible to store unique table entries with a single key, even though several fields may comprise the full key of the object.

2.1.3   Major Objects of the SAP CRM Data Model

SAP has several major data objects that are key to the application: *busi-*   Data objects
ness partners, *products*, *business transactions*, and *marketing attributes*.
Every SAP CRM module uses at least one of these four objects to support
the business process represented by that module.

Now that you know about the design of the data model, we'll discuss
each of these major objects in SAP CRM in detail.

2.2   Business Partners

The primary focus of CRM is on managing the relationship with the customer. In SAP CRM, the business partner is used to model the customer
in the software solution. You first need to learn the business definition
of the business partner and then understand how this is technically
translated into a database model, which we'll explain in the following
sections. Finally, we'll discuss some common techniques used to
retrieve business partner information from the database model.

2.2.1   Business Definition

As we've mentioned, the customer is the heart of CRM, and so the business partner is the heart of SAP CRM. It's impossible to execute any scenario in SAP CRM without a business partner. A *business partner* is any
person, company, or organization that is part of a relationship between
a company and its customers. A business partner can be a customer,
vendor, contact person, employee, third party, or other entity that
needs to be tracked or is involved in a customer interaction. In traditional SAP ERP, customers, vendors, and contact persons are stored separately and act as different entities. In SAP CRM, all business partners
are stored centrally and function based on the role provided.

Everything Is a Partner

One of the hardest concepts to understand for new SAP CRM users is that a
business partner isn't just a customer but rather can represent any party
involved in an interaction. One complaint or result from this is that if your

55

master data in your SAP ERP system isn't clean or is set up in a confusing manner, it will be the same in SAP CRM. Keep this in mind when you get requests about eliminating duplicate data from your SAP CRM system.

2.2.2 Technical Definition

SAP Business Partner concept

The SAP CRM business partner is based on the generic SAP Business Partner concept. In creating the SAP CRM business partner, new extensions to the SAP Business Partner were created that are only found in SAP CRM. This data is normally referred to as SAP CRM-specific data. The SAP Business Partner is used in other applications such as Financial Supply Chain Management (FSCM) within the SAP ERP system. You'll also find the SAP Business Partner used in SAP Supplier Relationship Management (SAP SRM) due to the fact that SAP CRM and SAP SRM originally shared a common technical foundation.

Three technical divisions of the data model

The SAP CRM overall data model features three technical divisions:

- General data is primarily part of the Business Partner data model and was traditionally modeled via the Business Data Toolset (BDT).
- Address data is based on the generic address management services provided by SAP.
- Relationship data allows connecting and/or relating business partners in the system together.

The four tables illustrated in Table 2.1 (and discussed in the following subsections) are the primary tables of the business partner in SAP CRM that connect the business partner to each technical division of data.

Table Name	Description
BUT000	General data
BUT020	Address data
BUT050	Relationships
BUT100	Business partner roles

Table 2.1 Primary Business Partner Data Tables

General Data

Because the business partner was designed to be an application service not unique to SAP CRM, the design is different in several aspects from other data objects. The SAP CRM business partner is the only major data object in SAP CRM not using a GUID as a primary key.

The business partner consists of several key tables, each starting with "BUT".

Key tables

Table BUT000

Table BUT000 is considered the primary or header table for the business partner. The primary key is the PARTNER, which is a 10-digit alphanumeric field modeled by the data element BU_PARTNER. The table also has a secondary index based on the field PARTNER_GUID, which is used to link the standard business partner data to SAP CRM extension data and business transactions. The PARTNER_GUID field is found toward the end of the table as shown in Figure 2.1.

Transp. Table	BUT000	Active
Short Description	BP: General data I	

Attributes | Delivery and Maintenance | Fields | Entry help/check | Currency/Quantity Fields

Srch Help | Predefined Type

Field	Key	Ini...	Data element	Data T...	Length	Deci...	Short Description
.INCLUDE	☐	☐	BUS000_INT	STRU	0	0	BP: General Data I (Data Fields – Internal)
.INCLUDE	☐	☐	BUS000AINT	STRU	0	0	CBP: Internal general data (not dependent on partner cat.)
MC_NAME1	☐	☐	BU_MCNAME1	CHAR	35	0	Search Help Field 1 (Name 1/Last Name)
MC_NAME2	☐	☐	BU_MCNAME2	CHAR	35	0	Search Help Field 2 (Name 2/First Name)
CRUSR	☐	☐	BU_CRUSR	CHAR	12	0	User who created the object
CRDAT	☐	☐	BU_CRDAT	DATS	8	0	Date on Which Object Was Created
CRTIM	☐	☐	BU_CRTIM	TIMS	6	0	Time at which the object was created
CHUSR	☐	☐	BU_CHUSR	CHAR	12	0	Last user to change object
CHDAT	☐	☐	BU_CHDAT	DATS	8	0	Date on which the object was last changed
CHTIM	☐	☐	BU_CHTIM	TIMS	6	0	Time at which object was last changed
PARTNER_GUID	☐	☐	BU_PARTNER_GUID	RAW	16	0	Business Partner GUID
ADDRCOMM	☐	☐	BU_ADDRCOMM	CHAR	10	0	Address Number
TD_SWITCH	☐	☐	BU_TD_SWITCH	CHAR	1	0	Planned Change Documents for Partner Were Converted
VALID_FROM	☐	☐	BU_BP_VALID_FROM	DEC	15	0	Validity Start BUT000 BP Data
VALID_TO	☐	☐	BU_BP_VALID_TO	DEC	15	0	Validity End BUT000 BP Data

Figure 2.1 Partner GUID on Table BUT000

Other important fields include TYPE, BPKIND, and BU_GROUP, as shown in Figure 2.2.

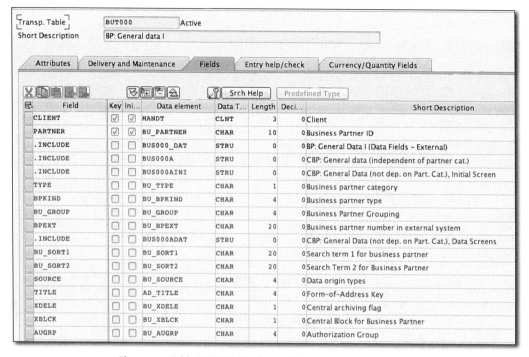

Figure 2.2 Table BUT000 Header Fields

TYPE field   The TYPE field is one of the most misunderstood fields for the business partner. The sole purpose of this field is to determine the form of address for the business partner (i.e., whether the business partner is a person, organization, or group). You have the following options:

▸ A person is typically a contact person or employee in SAP CRM.

▸ An organization normally represents a company or other legal entity in SAP CRM.

▸ The group isn't normally used in most typical SAP installations.

BPKIND field   BPKIND was designed for field control in the BDT. This field isn't normally used in newer installations, except as a way to classify SAP CRM partners. BU_GROUP is an important field because it's the technical equivalent of the account group found in SAP ERP. This field controls the number range that will be created for a business partner.

Another interesting aspect of Table BUT000 is the storage of the business partner name. The name storage consists of many different fields and varies based on the type of partner (person, organization, or group). These fields are shown in Table 2.2.

Field Name	Field Description
NAME_LAST	Last name of person
NAME_FIRST	First name of person
NAME_ORG1	Name 1 of organization
NAME_ORG2	Name 2 of organization
NAME_ORG3	Name 3 of organization
NAME_ORG4	Name 4 of organization
NAME_GRP1	Name 1 of a group
NAME_GRP2	Name 2 of a group

Table 2.2 Multiple Name Fields in Table BUT000

It's important to note that NAME_ORG1 is equivalent to NAME_LAST, and NAME_ORG2 is equivalent to NAME_FIRST. In several applications where you search for business partners by name, these fields are typically combined for both search input and output.

The final feature of the table that we'll mention is the CI include for customer attributes. This include—called `CI_EEW_BUT000`—is delivered by SAP for enhancing the business partner with new attributes that are of a 1:1 relationship to the business partner. In Chapter 3, we'll explain how to extend the SAP CRM business partner.

CI include

Table BUT100

Table BUT100 describes the role of a business partner in SAP CRM. This originally controlled the tab order for the SAP GUI Transaction BP, and now it's used primarily for classification of business partners. This differs

Business partner role

from the partner function assignment of the business partner in the sales area data.

SAP CRM-specific data for a business partner consists of the segments detailed in Table 2.3, which are centered on the sales area data of the customer.

Data Segment	Table Name
Business hours	CRMM_BUT_FRG0060
Partner function	CRMM_BUT_FRG0081
Sales employee	CRMM_BUT_SEMPL00
Sales classification	CRMM_BUT_FRG0041
Status	CRMM_BUT_FRG0100
Sales Area Data (Sales, Billing, Shipping)	
Sales rule	CRMM_BUT_LNK0011
Sales data	CRMM_BUT_SET0010
Shipping rule	CRMM_BUT_LNK0021
Shipping data	CRMM_BUT_SET0020
Bill rule	CRMM_BUT_LNK0031
Billing data	CRMM_BUT_SET0030
Organization rule	CRMM_BUT_LNK0141

Table 2.3 Data Segment Tables of the Business Partner

Sales area data   The sales area data in SAP CRM corresponds to the sales area data normally found in SAP ERP. This data is normally used to control the creation of sales orders and assign the business partner to particular sales areas. There are two tables per sales area-related table. The tables that start with CRMM_BUT_LNK link a set of attribute data to a business partner. The tables that start with CRMM_BUT_SET contain a unique set of attributes for a given period of time. Each set has a set of Business Application Programming Interfaces (BAPIs) that follows the naming pattern BAPI_BUPA_FRG<number>_*, where <number> is the four-digit number of the attribute set.

The full data model for the SAP CRM business partner can be viewed via Transaction SD11 and looking at the data model PRM_BP.

Business Partner BAPIs

Normally when reading business partner data, you can use the delivered BAPIs. A BAPI is a remote-enabled function module delivered by SAP. These BAPIs normally start with `BAPI_BUPA`; some of the more commonly used BAPIs are listed here:

▶ `BAPI_BUPA_SEARCH`

▶ `BAPI_BUPA_CENTRAL_GETDETAIL`

▶ `BAPI_BUPA_CREATE_FROM_DATA`

Common BAPIs

As a general rule, ABAP programs in SAP CRM should not be created to directly read data from the tables unless performing a search. Instead, we recommend using the business partner BAPIs and API function modules to retrieve any data required. The primary benefit of this method is that you'll take advantage of the buffering logic built by SAP and the most optimized path to read this data.

We'll now look at three coding examples for business partner search, retrieving the details of a business partner, and creating a new business by using the business partner BAPIs.

Listing 2.1 shows a common coding example to search for business partner data.

Business partner data search

```
data: telephone type AD_TELNRCL,
      email type AD_SMTPADR,
      url type AD_URI2,
      addressdata type BAPIBUS1006_ADDR_SEARCH,
      centraldata type BAPIBUS1006_CENTRAL_SEARCH,
      businesspartnerrole type BU_ROLE,
      country_for_telephone type AD_COMCTRY,
      fax_data type BAPIBUS1006_FAX_DATA,
      others = BAPIBUS1006_OTHER_DATA ,
      searchresult type table of BAPIBUS1006_BP_ADDR,
      return type table of BAPIRET2.

  CALL FUNCTION 'BAPI_BUPA_SEARCH'
    EXPORTING
      TELEPHONE                   = telephone
```

```
        EMAIL                           = email
        URL                             = url
        ADDRESSDATA                     = addressdata
        CENTRALDATA                     = centraldata
        BUSINESSPARTNERROLE             = businesspartnerrole
        COUNTRY_FOR_TELEPHONE           = countryfortelephone
        FAX_DATA                        = fax_data
        OTHERS                          = others
      TABLES
        searchresult                    = searchresult
        return                          = return.
```

Listing 2.1 BAPI_BUPA_SEARCH

Find business partner details

Listing 2.2 shows a typical coding example to retrieve the central details for a business partner. Note we're using the function module BUPA_CENTRAL_GET_DETAIL instead of the BAPI because the BAPI won't return whether the business partner is a person, organization, or group. You only need to pass the partner number to retrieve the primary details of the business partner. Also keep in mind that the business partner number should be zero filled, so you may need to call CONVERSION_EXIT_ALPHA_INPUT to properly format the partner number.

```
DATA: lv_partner type bu_partner,
      ls_data type BAPIBUS1006_CENTRAL,
      ls_data_person type BAPIBUS1006_CENTRAL_PERSON,
      ls_data_organ type BAPIBUS1006_CENTRAL_ORGAN,
      ls_data_group type BAPIBUS1006_CENTRAL_GROUP,
      ls_data_info type BAPIBUS1006_CENTRAL_INFO,
      lv_category type BU_TYPE,
      lv_fullname_converted type AD_NAMCONV,
      ls_central_customer_ext type BUPA_CENTR_CUST_EXT,
      return TYPE table of BAPIRET2
* Retrieve the central data for a business partner(non-
address)
* Also includes any extension data we created
CALL FUNCTION 'BUPA_CENTRAL_GET_DETAIL'
  EXPORTING
    IV_PARTNER                   = iv_partner
  IMPORTING
    ES_DATA                      = ls_data
    ES_DATA_PERSON               = ls_data_person
    ES_DATA_ORGAN                = ls_data_organ
```

```
  ES_DATA_GROUP                   = ls_data_group
  ES_DATA_INFO                    = ls_data_info
  EV_CATEGORY                     = lv_category
  EV_FULLNAME_CONVERTED           = lv_fullname_converted
  ES_CENTRAL_CUSTOMER_EXT         = ls_central_customer_ext
TABLES
  ET_RETURN                       = lt_return.


CASE LV_CATEGORY.
  WHEN '1'.
* Retrieve information from ls_data_person
  WHEN '2'.
* Retrieve information from ls_data_organ
  WHEN '3'.
* Retrieve information from ls_data_group
  WHEN OTHERS.
* Do Nothing
ENDCASE.
```

Listing 2.2 BUPA_CENTRAL_GET_DETAIL

Listing 2.3 shows a common coding example to create a new business partner from scratch. A business partner in SAP CRM only requires that two fields are maintained to be created. The first field is the country of the business partner. The second field will be LAST_NAME for a person, NAME_ORG1 for an organization, or NAME_GRP1 for a group. All other fields are considered optional unless you've configured or extended the system to make a field required.

Create new business partner

```
DATA:  lt_error          TYPE bapiret2_t,
       ls_error          TYPE bapiret2,
       lt_telephone      TYPE STANDARD TABLE OF bapiadtel,
       lt_fax            TYPE STANDARD TABLE OF bapiadfax,
       lt_uri            TYPE STANDARD TABLE OF bapiaduri,
       ls_mktlist_adr    TYPE crmt_mktlist_adr,
       ls_mktlist_org    TYPE crmt_mktlist_org,
       ls_bp_org         TYPE bapibus1006_central_organ,
       ls_telephone_org  TYPE bapiadtel,
       ls_fax_org        TYPE bapiadfax,
       ls_uri_org        TYPE bapiaduri,
       ls_central        TYPE bapibus1006_central,
       ls_bp_add         TYPE bapibus1006_address.
```

```
data:  lv_no_duplicate_check
              TYPE BAPIBUS1006_HEAD-CONTROLDUPLICATEMESSAGE.
data: lv_bp                    TYPE bu_partner,
      lv_address_num           TYPE AD_ADDRNUM,
      lv_address_guid          TYPE BU_ADDRESS_GUID,
      lv_partner_guid          TYPE BU_PARTNER_GUID.

CALL FUNCTION 'BUPA_CREATE_FROM_DATA'
   EXPORTING
      iv_category                  = '2'
      is_data                      = ls_central
      is_data_organ                = ls_bp_org
      is_address                   = ls_bp_add
      iv_duplicate_message_type = lv_no_duplicate_check
   IMPORTING
      ev_partner                   = lv_bp
      ev_partner_guid              = lv_partner_guid
      ev_addrnumber                = lv_address_num
      ev_addrguid                  = lv_address_guid
   TABLES
      it_adtel                     = lt_telephone
      it_adfax                     = lt_fax
      it_aduri                     = lt_uri
      et_return                    = lt_error.
```

Listing 2.3 BUPA_CREATE_FROM_DATA

Address Data

Address data for a business partner includes the mailing address and communication data. The mailing address contains all of the necessary fields to support a postal or physical address. The communication data consists of contact information storage such as telephone numbers (including mobile), fax numbers, email address, and URI for web addresses or other Internet resources.

The address data for an SAP CRM business partner is maintained using the Business Address Service (BAS) or Central Address Management (CAM) of the SAP NetWeaver ABAP AS. The business partner data model maintains a link to the address management system via Table BUT020.

Normally, you don't read the address data directly from the database tables. Instead, you can use several function modules to handle this:

Call function modules

▶ BUPA_ADDRESSES_GET
Gets the list of addresses for a business partner

▶ BUPA_ADDRESS_GET_DETAIL
Gets the details for a particular address

For contact persons and the relationship address information, the function modules are different:

▶ BUPR_CONTP_ADDRESSES_GET
Retrieves the addresses for a conact person relationship

▶ BUPR_CONTP_ADDR_GET_DETAIL
Retrieves the details of a contract persoon relationship address

Listing 2.4 shows a typical example for retrieving the address data for a given business partner.

```
DATA: lv_partner TYPE bu_partner,
      lv_standard_addrnumber TYPE AD_ADDRNUM,
      lv_standard_addrguid TYPE BU_ADDRESS_GUID,
      lt_return TYPE TABLE OF BAPIRET2,
      ls_address TYPE BAPIBUS1006_ADDRESS,
      lt_adtel TYPE TABLE OF BAPIADTEL,
      lt_adfax TYPE TABLE OF BAPIADFAX,
      lt_adsmtp TYPE TABLE OF BAPIADSMTP,
      lt_aduri TYPE TABLE OF BAPIADURI.

CALL FUNCTION 'BUPA_ADDRESSES_GET'
  EXPORTING
    IV_PARTNER                  = lv_partner
  IMPORTING
    EV_STANDARD_ADDRNUMBER      = lv_standard_addrnumber
    EV_STANDARD_ADDRGUID        = lv_standard_addrguid
  TABLES
    ET_RETURN                   = lt_return.

REFRESH: lt_return.

CALL FUNCTION 'BUPA_ADDRESS_GET_DETAIL'
  EXPORTING
    IV_PARTNER              = lv_partner
```

65

```
    IV_ADDRNUMBER                = lv_standard_addrnumber
    IV_ADDRGUID                  = lv_standard_addrguid
  IMPORTING
    ES_ADDRESS                    = ls_address
  TABLES
    ET_ADTEL                     = lt_adtel
    ET_ADFAX                     = lt_adfax
    ET_ADSMTP                    = lt_adsmtp
    ET_ADURI                     = lt_aduri
    ET_RETURN                    = lt_return.
```

Listing 2.4 Retrieve Address Data for a Business Partner

Relationship Data

Business partner interaction
Relationship data describes how two business partners in SAP CRM interact. Typical examples of relationships include contact person and employee responsible for a business partner such as a sales representative.

Table BUT050

Table BUT050 stores the relationships between business partners. This is the second-most important table in the SAP CRM business partner data model next to Table BUT000. The primary key consists of RELNR, PARTNER1, PARTNER2, and DATE_TO. PARTNER1 is the parent partner in a relationship that is expressed by PARTNER1 HAS RELATED PARTNER2. If you look at a contact person relationship, PARTNER1 is the company, and PARTNER2 is the contact person. The table contains a validity date, which means relationships can be time dependent. However, extra configuration work is required to activate this feature for end users of the system.

An important field not included in the primary key of this table is REL-TYP, which defines the type of relationship. The most common relationships you'll see in your SAP CRM system are BUR001 (HAS CONTACT PERSON) and BUR010 (HAS THE EMPLOYEE RESPONSIBLE). SAP provides two secondary indexes for this table that allow lookup on PARTNER1 and PARTNER2 based on the relationship type.

Table BUT051

Table BUT051 contains specific information for a contact person relationship. In SAP CRM, a contact contains personal and work address information. Table BUT051 contains the work address, which is equivalent to the relationship address for the contact person.

Listing 2.5 shows how to retrieve all of the contact persons for a given business partner. This is a common requirement for reporting within an SAP CRM system.

Retrieve contacts for business partner

```
DATA: lv_partner TYPE bu_partner,
      lt_partner type table of bu partner,
      lt_addresses type table of BAPIBUS1006002_ADDRESSES_I,
      lt_return type table of bapiret2.
field-symbols: <fs_partner> type bu_partner.
* LV_PARTNER is the main partner that you wish to find contact
* persons for
SELECT partner2 FROM but050 INTO TABLE lt_partner
          WHERE partner1 = lv_partner
          AND date_to le sy-datum
          AND reltyp = 'BUR001'.

LOOP AT lt_partner ASSIGNING <fs_partner>.
  refresh: lt_addresses, lt_return.
  CALL FUNCTION 'BUPR_CONTP_ADDRESSES_GET'
    EXPORTING
      IV_PARTNER              = lv_partner
      IV_CONTACTPERSON        = <fs_partner>
    TABLES
      ET_ADDRESSES            = lt_addresses
      ET_RETURN               = lt_return .
ENDLOOP.
```

Listing 2.5 Contact Person Retrieval for a Business Partner

Attachments

Attachments for business partners are typically files such as pictures, Microsoft documents, or other types of files. They are stored in the SAP CRM Document Management system, and the best way to access them is using the CL_CRM_DOCUMENTS API. We don't recommend even trying to retrieve related documents outside of this API. The layers of abstraction

CL_CRM_DOCUMENTS API

for this piece of SAP CRM normally befuddle the most senior developers working with the solution.

Listing 2.6 is an example to retrieve a list of documents for a business partner and then retrieve each individual document. This example calls the method `CL_CRM_DOCUMENTS_API=>GET_WITH_FILE` to download them to the end-user's PC directly via the SAP GUI. You can also call the method `GET_WITH_TABLE` to store the document into an internal table instead.

```
DATA: ls_business_object TYPE SIBFLPORB,
      lt_phioloios TYPE SKWF_LPIOS,
      lt_ios_properties_result TYPE CRM_KW_PROPST,
      ls_ios_properties_result type crm_kw_props.
DATA: ls_loio TYPE SKWF_IO,
      ls_phio TYPE SKWF_IO,
      lt_bad_ios TYPE SKWF_IOERRS,
      ls_properties TYPE SDOKPROPTL,
      lv_filename TYPE SDOK_FILNM,
      lv_directory TYPE SDOK_CHTRD.
FIELD-SYMBOLS: <fs_phioloios> TYPE SKWF_LPIO.
* The instance ID is the GUID of the partner
* The type ID is business object BUS1006, which is SAP Busine
ss Partner
lv_directory = 'C:'.
ls_business_object-instid = iv_guid.
ls_business_object-typeid = 'BUS1006'.
ls_business_object-catid = 'BO'.
CALL METHOD CL_CRM_DOCUMENTS=>GET_INFO
  EXPORTING
    BUSINESS_OBJECT = ls_business_object
  IMPORTING
    PHIOLOIOS = lt_phioloios
    IOS_PROPERTIES_RESULT   = lt_ios_properties_result.

LOOP AT lt_phioloios ASSIGNING <fs_phioloios>.
  CLEAR: ls_loio, ls_phio, ls_ios_properties_result,
         lv_filename, ls_properties.
  ls_loio-OBJTYPE = <fs_phioloios>-OBJTYPELO.
  ls_loio-class = <fs_phioloios>-CLASSLO.
  ls_loio-objid = <fs_phioloios>-OBJIDLO.
  ls_phio-OBJTYPE = <fs_phioloios>-OBJTYPEPH.
```

```
 ls_phio-class = <fs_phioloios>-CLASSPH.
 ls_phio-objid = <fs_phioloios>-OBJIDPH.
READ TABLE lt_ios_properties_result INTO ls_ios_properties_
result
      WITH KEY objtype = ls_loio-objtype
               class = ls_loio-class
               objid = ls_loio-objid.
READ TABLE ls_ios_properties_result-properties INTO ls_
properties
      WITH KEY name = 'KW_RELATIVE_URL'.
lv_filename = ls_properties-value.
CALL METHOD CL_CRM_DOCUMENTS=>GET_WITH_FILE
   EXPORTING
    LOIO = ls_loio
    PHIO = ls_phio
    FILE_NAME = lv_filename
    DIRECTORY = lv_directory
   IMPORTING
    BAD_IOS = lt_bad_ios
   EXCEPTIONS
    NOT_TRANSFERRED = 1
    others          = 2.
ENDLOOP.
```

Listing 2.6 Retrieve Document Attachments for a Business Partner

Now that we've reviewed the data model of the business partner, let's examine how the goods and services that are sold to the business partners are modeled within your SAP CRM system.

2.3 Products

An important part of the relationship between a company and its customers are the goods and services sold. In SAP CRM, products are used to model and track those goods and services sold. To better understand the product in SAP CRM, we'll review the business definition and the underlying technical design of the product master in the following sections. Finally, we review some of the common APIs available in SAP CRM to access or update the product master data.

Track goods and services

2.3.1 Business Definition

A *product* is a good or service that a company may purchase or sell. In SAP ERP terms, a product is a material. Additional types of products include services and financial products. Pest Control Visit is an example of a service material. Car Leasing is an example of a financial product. Each type of product has unique attributes specific to that product type.

2.3.2 Technical Definition

Material product

For this book, we'll examine the data model for products that are of the type material. A material product consists of three major data areas: general, category, and fragment:

- General data contains the header information of the product along with the relationship to the fragment data.
- Category data allows you to group products into related sets.
- Fragment data are the specific attributes of the product that are dependent on the type of product and the categories associated with that product.

We'll explain each of these types of data in the following subsections.

General Data

The data model for a product consists of a primary header table, a segment relationship table, and segment tables that contain attributes. In Table 2.4 we list the two primary tables of the product master. By technical definition, a product in SAP CRM doesn't have any attributes until it's assigned a product category. For normal SAP CRM scenarios connected to SAP ERP, these attributes are defined when a category from the hierarchy R3PRODSTYP is assigned to a material such as MAT_FERT.

Table Name	Description
COMM_PRODUCT	Primary header table
COMM_PR_FRG_REL	Segment relationship table

Table 2.4 General Header Tables of the Product Master

If you examine Table COMM_PRODUCT shown in Figure 2.3, you see   **Product ID**
the primary key for a product is the PRODUCT_GUID field and not the
PRODUCT_ID field. In standard SAP CRM design, the key to a table is a
GUID.

Transp. Table	COMM_PRODUCT	Active
Short Description	Product	

| Attributes | Delivery and Maintenance | Fields | Entry help/check | Currency/Quantity Fields |

Srch Help   Predefined Type

Field	Key	Ini...	Data element	Data T...	Length	Deci...	Short Description
.INCLUDE	☑	☑	COMT_PRODUCT_KEY	STRU	0	0	Product Key Fields
CLIENT	☑	☑	MANDT	CLNT	3	0	Client
PRODUCT_GUID	☑	☑	COMT_PRODUCT_GU...	RAW	16	0	Internal Unique ID of Product
.INCLUDE	☐	☑	COMT_PRODUCT_DA...	STRU	0	0	Product Header Data
PRODUCT_ID	☐	☐	COMT_PRODUCT_ID	CHAR	40	0	Product ID
PRODUCT_TYPE	☐	☐	COMT_PRODUCT_TY...	CHAR	2	0	Product Type
CONFIG	☐	☐	COMT_PRODUCT_CO...	CHAR	1	0	Determines Whether a Product Is Configurable
XNOSEARCH	☐	☑	COMT_PRODUCT_XN...	CHAR	1	0	Product Is Not Relevant for Search Help
OBJECT_FAMILY	☐	☑	COMT_PRODUCT_OB...	CHAR	4	0	Object Family
BATCH_DEDICATED	☐	☑	COMT_BATCH_DEDI...	CHAR	1	0	Specifies Whether Batches Are Maintained for Product
COMPETITOR_PROD	☐	☑	COMT_PR_COMP	CHAR	1	0	Indicates Product Is a Competitor Product
.INCLUDE	☐	☐	COMT_PRODUCT_ADM	STRU	0	0	Product Administration Data
VALID_FROM	☐	☐	COMT_VALID_FROM	DEC	15	0	Valid From (Time Stamp)
VALID_TO	☐	☐	COMT_VALID_TO	DEC	15	0	Valid To (Time Stamp)
UPNAME	☐	☐	COMT_UPNAME	CHAR	12	0	Name of the User Who Last Changed the Set
HISTEX	☐	☐	COMT_HISTEX	CHAR	1	0	History Exists
LOGSYS	☐	☐	COMT_LOGSYS	CHAR	10	0	Original System

Figure 2.3 Table COMM_PRODUCT

There is an additional reason for the product master key not being the
PRODUCT_ID field: to support multiple SAP ERP backend systems, the
product ID must be allowed to be repeated. This means that material
1000 could exist in two different backend systems, and you would need
to have both materials in the system to download any related sales
orders for customers that exist in both systems. As a result of this
design, PRODUCT_ID isn't considered a unique identifier in SAP CRM.
Instead, by reviewing the delivered indexes on that table, you'll see that
the combination of PRODUCT_ID, PRODUCT_TYPE, OBJECT_FAMILY,
and LOGSYS fields is what makes PRODUCT_ID unique.

Table COMM_PR_FRG_REL has a primary key that consists of the
PRODUCT_GUID and the GUID of the associated fragment (FRAG-

MENT_TYPE). The actual GUID of the data associated with the product in the fragment table is an attribute of the table called FRAGMENT_GUID.

Category Data

Hierarchies The product master of SAP CRM can be extended through the associate of new product attributes associated via categories. The categories are defined in SAP CRM in Table COMM_CATEGORY. These categories are associated together in a grouping called a *hierarchy*. Unlike SAP ERP, there can be multiple hierarchies of products that represent different logical groupings of the materials. Three basic hierarchies are downloaded from SAP ERP to SAP CRM for materials as shown in Table 2.5.

Hierarchy Name	Description
R3MATCLASS	Material group
R3PRODHIER	Product hierarchy
R3PRODSTYP	Product subtype

Table 2.5 Product: Basic Material Hierarchies for SAP CRM Products

Hierarchy R3PRODSTYP To properly create a product of type material in SAP CRM, you must have at least one category from the hierarchy R3PRODSTYP assigned to the product. A typical category assignment would use category MAT_FERT to maintain this assignment. The assignment of the category to the product is found in Table COMM_PRCAT.

The categories in R3PRODSTYP typically contain the assignment of the associated fragment data that can be maintained for a product associated with that category. The definition of what fragments are associated with a category is found in Table COMM_CATFRGR.

Fragment Data

Fragment data (also known as attribute sets) contains all of the non-general data of the product master. The fragments for a product are dependent on both the product type and categories assigned to the product. Table 2.6 shows the common attribute sets used by a material.

Set Name	Database Table	Description
COMM_PR_MAT	COMM_PRMAT	Division and item category group
COMM_PR_SHTEXT	COMM_PRSHTEXT	Short description
COMM_PR_UNIT	COMM_PR_UNIT	Base unit of measure
COMM_PR_LGTEXT1	COMM_PR_LGTEXT1	Long text
COMM_PR_GTIN	COMM_PR_GTIN	Global trade identification number
CRMM_PR_TAX	CRMM_PR_TAX	Tax information

Table 2.6 Attribute Sets for the Product Master

Attribute sets are defined in Table COMC_SETTYPE. The entries in this table are delivered by SAP and should not be changed manually. In Chapter 3, Section 3.5, we'll show you how to create new attribute sets using the tools delivered by SAP. For each attribute set, there is a definition of the database table where the data will be stored, names of read and update function modules for the attribute set, and a definition of what type of product can be used for this attribute set (see Figure 2.4).

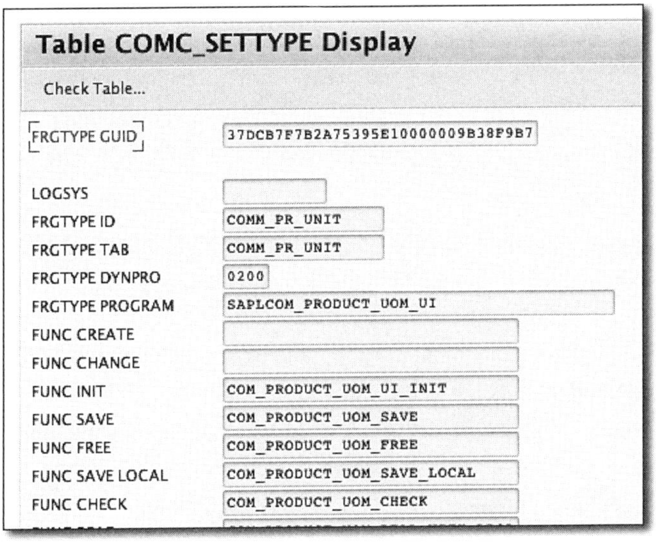

Attribute sets

Figure 2.4 Definition of COMM_PR_UNIT Attribute Set in COMC_SETTYPE

Product Master APIs

The product master follows the consistent design of the SAP CRM system that all data can be created, read, updated, and deleted via an API. For the product master, there are two primary function modules that will meet most common requirements. For creating or updating an existing product, you can use the function module COM_PRODUCT_MAT_ MAINT_MULT_API. If you only need to retrieve the product data, you can use the function module COM_PRODUCT_GETDETAIL_API.

Example

Because it can be difficult to create a new material using a function module, we'll look at an example of how to call COM_PRODUCT_MAT_MAINT_ MULT_API to create a new material. This example requires several pieces of data to create the material. The minimum data required are a GUID, unique product ID, product type, logical system, product short description, base unit of measure, and associated product subtype category.

Helper function modules

The coding example in Listing 2.7 calls two helper function modules that are used quite often in SAP CRM. The first function module OWN_ LOGICAL_SYSTEM_GET provides a way to determine the logical system of the current client without the need for hardcoding. This is important because as you move among development, test, and productions systems, this value is changed. The second function module, GUID_CREATE, will create a GUID for the product that you want to create. It's sometimes necessary to provide a GUID to an API in SAP CRM because the API will use the provided GUID to link the passed-in data together in a logical fashion.

For products of type material, another useful helper function module is COM_PRODUCT_BASE_CATEGORY_READ, which finds all of the product categories available for a product type. The product categories are downloaded each time into an SAP CRM client, so the GUIDs for the categories will vary. This prevents you from having to know the GUID for a category and instead allows you to specify the name of the corresponding product subtype.

```
data: lt_product type COMT_PRODUCT_MAT_MAINTAIN_APIT,
      ls_product type COMT_PRODUCT_MAT_MAINTAIN_API,
      et_product type COMT_PRODUCT_MAT_MAINTAIN_APIT,
```

```
        ls_unit              type comt_pr_unit_maintain,
        lt_bapireturn type BAPIRET2_TAB,
        lv_logsys type LOGSYS,
        lv_product_guid type COMT_PRODUCT_GUID.

data: lt_base_category type COMT_CATEGORY_TAB,
        ls_base_category type COMT_CATEGORY,
        ls_short_texts type COMT_PR_SHTEXT_MAINTAIN,
        ls_categories type COMT_PROD_CAT_REL_MAINTAIN.

call function 'OWN_LOGICAL_SYSTEM_GET'
    importing
       own_logical_system            = lv_logsys
    exceptions
       own_logical_system_not_defined = 1
       others                        = 2.

* Generate a GUID in order link-related tables
CALL FUNCTION 'GUID_CREATE'
 IMPORTING
   EV_GUID_16       = lv_product_guid.

ls_product-header-com_product-product_guid = lv_product_guid.
ls_product-header-com_product-product_id = 'TESTMATNUM'.
* Product Type is Material
ls_product-header-com_product-product_type = '01'.
ls_product-header-com_product-logsys = lv_logsys.
ls_product-header-update_type = 'I'.

ls_short_texts-data-product_guid = lv_product_guid.
ls_short_texts-data-short_text = 'Test Material Description'.
ls_short_texts-data-langu = sy-langu.
ls_short_texts-data-logsys = lv_logsys.
ls_short_texts-data_x-short_text = 'X'.
ls_short_texts-update_type = 'I'.

append ls_short_texts  to ls_product-header-short_texts.

* Assign the category MAT_FERT to the product
call function 'COM_PRODUCT_BASE_CATEGORY_READ'
    exporting
       iv_product_type       = '01'
       iv_read_text          = ' '
```

```
      importing
        et_category               = lt_base_category
*       ET_VALUE                  =
      exceptions
        nothing_found             = 1
        others                    = 2.


read table lt_base_category into ls_base_category
                  with key category_id = 'MAT_FERT'.

ls_categories-data-product_guid = lv_product_guid.
ls_categories-data-hierarchy_guid = ls_base_category-
hierarchy_guid.
ls_categories-data-category_guid = ls_base_category-category_
guid.
ls_categories-data-category_id = ls_base_category-category_
id.
ls_categories-data-logsys = lv_logsys.
ls_categories-update_type = 'I'.

append ls_categories to ls_product-header-categories.

* prepare base unit of measurement
ls_unit-data-product_guid = lv_product_guid.
ls_unit-data-unit = 'KG'.
ls_unit-data-numerator = 1.
ls_unit-data-denominator = 1.
ls_unit-data-logsys = lv_logsys.
ls_unit-data-is_base_unit = 'X'.
append ls_unit to ls_product-data-comm_pr_unit.

append ls_product to lt_product.

CALL FUNCTION 'COM_PRODUCT_MAT_MAINT_MULT_API'
  EXPORTING
    IT_PRODUCT                    = lt_product
  IMPORTING
    ET_PRODUCT                    = et_product
    ET_BAPIRETURN                 = lt_bapireturn
  EXCEPTIONS
    INTERNAL_ERROR                = 1
    OTHERS                        = 2.
```

```
call function 'COM_PRODUCT_SAVE_API'
      exceptions
         internal_error = 1
         others         = 2.

* If successful, then commit work
call function 'BAPI_TRANSACTION_COMMIT'
      exporting
          wait = 'X'.

call function 'COM_PRODUCT_FREE_API'.
```

Listing 2.7 Create a New Product via a Function Module

The next major business object we need to discuss is the business transaction.

2.4   One Order: SAP Business Transaction

In the early days of SAP ERP, each different type of document in SD occupied its own set of tables. This method was efficient due to the available database technology, but it lacked the capability to share data information across transactions and required maintenance of many different transaction codes to maintain similar patterns of data.

In creating SAP CRM, SAP tackled one of the biggest issues surrounding the SD component of SAP ERP. Instead of copying the SAP ERP data model for sales orders and other types of transactions in a 1:1 fashion to the SAP CRM system, SAP came up with a new data model called *one order*, which is designed to eliminate some of the drawbacks of the SAP ERP model. The one order data model and framework is the technical foundation for business transactions within SAP CRM.

The big drawbacks of the model in SAP ERP include tables with hundreds of fields, large programs with a central include for user exits MV45AFZZ, and related transactions set up as individual modules instead of one unique framework. The design of one order attempts to solve these problems by creating many tables with smaller sets of data; that is, a modular design of programs along with user exits and the one order

Drawback of SAP ERP model

framework for many different types of transactions. However, this approach comes with a price. Many developers new to SAP CRM will find one order complicated due to the many different tables and APIs associated with the one order data model.

Learning the one order framework does involves some effort; however, after you learn the framework, it's much easier to learn the technical aspects of a new business transaction type in SAP CRM as your company may implement additional business processes using SAP CRM.

To learn the one order data model and framework, you should first ignore any knowledge of how SAP ERP is structured and start with a blank slate. In SAP CRM, a business transaction isn't restricted to a single business process type such as a sales order. Even though you'll see the name "ORDER" in the technical naming of the one order function modules and tables, this refers to "one order" and not a sales order. This means that the data model and APIs that we'll explore are used against all business transaction types in the system.

2.4.1 General Design

Business transaction

The business transaction is a document in SAP CRM that contains the information surrounding a business process involving one or more business partners in the SAP CRM system. These business transactions include but aren't limited to processes in sales, service, and marketing. Common business transaction types include sales orders, service orders, customer complaints, leads, activities, opportunities, quotations, contracts, and tasks.

In the one order data model, the business transaction is modeled through a concept of central administration tables and segment data tables at both the header and item levels. Only the central header administration table is maintained for every transaction type. It's possible to have transactions without item data such as a task or business activity. The data segment tables used will depend on the type of transaction being maintained. The data segment tables can be further classified as a header extension, an item extension, or a set.

Primary Table

In the one order data model, the central administration table at the header level is Table CRMD_ORDERADM_H. This table contains the primary key of the business transaction, which is known as the GUID. This table typically contains fewer than 40 fields and doesn't contain transaction detail information. This is in stark contrast to the sales order header table in SAP ERP's Table VBAK, which contains many more fields and details about the sales order document.

Central administration table

In viewing the data model of one order, we commonly refer to each portion as a *data segment*. We won't cover all data segments in this chapter, but Table 2.7 provides a listing of commonly used segments, and whether the primary key is identical to the key of ORDERADM_H. The complete list of all possible segments can be found in view CRMV_OBJECTS.

Data segments

Segment Name	Table Name	Description
ACTIVITY_H	CRMD_ACTIVITY_H	Activity header data
CUSTOMER_H	CRMD_CUSTOMER_H	Customer extension data
LEAD_H	CRMD_LEAD_H	Lead header data
OPPORT_H	CRMD_OPPORT_H	Opportunity header data
PRICING	CRMD_PRICING	Pricing parameter data
SALES	CRMD_SALES	Sales data
SERVICE_H	CRMD_SERVICE_H	Service header data

Table 2.7 Header Extension Tables

Item Data

Business transactions in SAP CRM can store information at a line-item level. Table CRMD_ORDERADM_I serves as the central administration table and contains a reference to the header table through the header attribute. Like the header portion of the business transaction, the items of the business transaction contain additional data segments. Some of these additional data segments are listed in Table 2.8.

Segment Name	Table Name	Description
CUSTOMER_I	CRMD_CUSTOMER_I	Line item customer extension
OPPORT_I	CRMD_OPPORT_I	Line item opportunity data
PRODUCT_I	CRMD_PRODUCT_I	Line item product data
PRICING_I	CRMD_PRICING_I	Line item pricing data
SERVICE_I	CRMD_SERVICE_I	Line item service data

Table 2.8 Item Extension Tables

Set Tables

The segments of the business transaction are linked to the primary business transaction table through the use of Table CRMD_LINK for those tables whose primary key GUID isn't equal to the GUID of Table CRMD_ORDERADM_H. You can use the definition of each segment to find out the set ID. This is contained in the CRMV_OBJECTS view by looking at the detail of a given entry. The PARTNER segment is a classic example of this setup (see Figure 2.5).

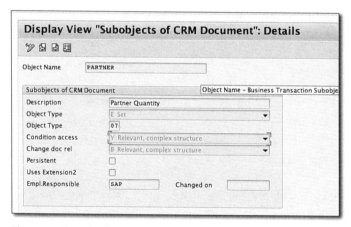

Figure 2.5 Details of Partner Segment Definition

Business Object Types

Mapping Now that you understand the various segments of the data model, you need to understand how the different business process types that will be created as business transactions map the various segments to the process type. To achieve this, the one order model works on the concept of business object types that represent a business process. These business object types are modeled in the standard Business Object Builder along with the one order customizing. The base business object type for all transactions is BUS2001 as shown in Figure 2.6. These codes are important to know because applications such as the Web Client use a technical abbreviation, and the business workflow in SAP CRM uses these object types.

Display View "Business Transaction – Object Type": Overview

Business Transaction – Object Type

Trans.Cat.	Descriptn	Descript.	Appl.
BUS20001	CRM Bus Transactions	CRM Business Transaction	CRM One Order...
BUS2000106	CRM Know. Article	CRM Knowledge Article	CRM One Order...
BUS2000107	Group Contract	Group Contract	CRM One Order...
BUS2000108	Lead	CRM Lead	CRM One Order...
BUS2000110	Activity (don't use)	(Use business activity or task)	CRM One Order...
BUS2000111	Opportunity	CRM Opportunity	CRM One Order...
BUS2000112	Service Contract	Service Contract	CRM One Order...
BUS2000113	Purchase Contract	Purchase Contract EBP	CRM One Order...
BUS2000114	Financing Contract	Financing Contract	CRM One Order...
BUS2000115	Sales	Sales	CRM One Order...
BUS2000116	Service Process	Service Process	CRM One Order...
BUS2000117	Service Confirmation	Service Confirmation	CRM One Order...
BUS2000118	Pur. Schd. Agreement	Purchase Scheduling Agreement EBP	CRM One Order...
BUS2000120	Complaints	CRM Complaints Transaction	CRM One Order...
BUS2000121	Sales Contract	Sales Contract	CRM One Order...
BUS2000125	Task	Task	CRM One Order...
BUS2000126	Business Activity	Business Activity	CRM One Order...
BUS2000210	Prod.Service Letter	Product Service Letter	CRM One Order...
BUS2000215	Rebate Agreement	Rebate Agreement CRM	CRM One Order...
BUS2000220	Project	Project	CRM One Order...
BUS2000223	CRM Service Request	CRM Service Request	CRM One Order...
BUS2000224	CRM Master Request	CRM Master Request	CRM One Order...
BUS2000230	License Sales Contr.	CRM License Sales Contract	CRM One Order...
BUS2000231	License Acqu.Contr.	CRM License Acquisition Contract	CRM One Order...

Position...   Entry 1 of 61

Figure 2.6 Business Object Types for Business Transactions

We won't list object types in this book, but the cross reference table in Table 2.9 lists the business object type, description, and corresponding

Web Client object type along with the process type of the standard delivered SAP business transaction that represents this process. The view CRMV_SUBOB_CAT provides a listing of the possible business object types used by the one order framework for business transactions.

Business Object Type	Process Description	Web Client Header Component	Example Process Type
BUS2000108	Lead	BT108_LEA	LEAD
BUS2000111	Opportunity	BT111_OPPT	OPPT
BUS2000115	Sales order	BT115H_SLSO	TA
BUS2000115	Quotation	BT115H_SLSQ	AG
BUS2000116	Service order	BT116_SRVO	SRVO
BUS2000120	Complaint	BT120H_CPL	CRMC
BUS2000121	Sales contract	BT121H_SLSC	QCTR
BUS2000125	Task	BT125H_TASK	1003
BUS2000126	Activity – appointment	BT126H_APPT	0000
BUS2000126	Activity – interaction log	BT126H_CALL	0001

Table 2.9 Business Object Types

Object Type, Transaction Type, and UI Component Type

The relationship between business object type, process type, and UI component type is not always clear. To better understand how these are related, let's look at how to find this information for a leads business transaction. Leads are modeled as a business transaction in SAP CRM. SAP delivers a standard transaction type called LEAD. If you go into the IMG and look at the customizing definition of the LEAD which is found via CRM • TRANSACTIONS • BASIC SETTINGS • DEFINE TRANSACTION TYPES, you will find that the LEAD transaction type has a leading transaction category of BUS2000108 which is "Lead." The leading transaction category of a business transaction type will control which UI component is used to display that process.

To figure out which UI component is used for the display of the header details of the transaction type, we'll take the last three digits of the leading transaction category which would be "108" in this case. We then know that the lead UI component for the header will start with BT108H_<OBJ>. We can easily search for UI components starting with BT108 to find everything related to leads from a technical perspective.

Now if you want to cheat to figure out the UI component, you can always click F2 when you're on the screen displaying the transaction and you'll see what UI component was used. The method we describe here allows you to figure out the UI component without needing to log into the Web Client.

Assignment of Segments to Business Object Types

After you've defined the business object types, you can then assign what segments should be allowed for the various business object types. The view CRMV_OBJECT_ASSI defines which segments of the business transaction are available for a business transaction object type (see Figure 2.7). If you look at the values for business activity, you can see that not all segments are available, such as OPPORT_H. If we were to look at the entries in the table for CRMV_OBJECT_ASSI, we would find that ACTIVITY_H would not appear, but OPPORT_H would appear in the list of assigned segments.

CRMV_OBJECT_ ASSI

Display View "Assignment: Application Area – Sub-object": Overview

Appl. area	Desc.: Appl. areas	Object	Object descripti
BUS2000126	Business Activity	ACTION	Actions
BUS2000126	Business Activity	ACTIVITY_H	Header data activity
BUS2000126	Business Activity	APPOINTMENT	Dates
BUS2000126	Business Activity	CUSTOMER_H	Customer Header Data
BUS2000126	Business Activity	DOC_FLOW	Document Flow
BUS2000126	Business Activity	EXT_REF	Additional External References
BUS2000126	Business Activity	LAWREF_H	Header extension for Law Referer
BUS2000126	Business Activity	MESSAGES	Message Handler
BUS2000126	Business Activity	ORDERADM_H	Administration Header
BUS2000126	Business Activity	ORDERADM_I	Administration item
BUS2000126	Business Activity	ORGMAN	Organizational Data
BUS2000126	Business Activity	PARTNER	Partner Quantity
BUS2000126	Business Activity	QUALIF	Qualification Requirement Set
BUS2000126	Business Activity	SERVICE_OS	Service reference object subject
BUS2000126	Business Activity	STATUS	Status
BUS2000126	Business Activity	SUBJECT	Service Subject
BUS2000126	Business Activity	SURVEY	Questionnaire
BUS2000126	Business Activity	TEXTS	Texts

Figure 2.7 Business Object Type to Segment Assignment

Process Types

Now that you've defined the segments of the one order data model, business object types, and how those are related, you're missing one last piece of the model: each business transaction corresponds to a process type in the system.

Customizing
The process type defines a unique business process based on one or more business object types but will, however, have one business object type for control purposes. To understand this further, you need to take a look at the Customizing for business transactions within the IMG. The path for defining a new business transaction is CUSTOMER RELATIONSHIP MANAGEMENT • TRANSACTIONS • BASIC SETTINGS • DEFINE TRANSACTION TYPES.

Standard delivered transaction types
Figure 2.8 shows the standard delivered transaction type 0001, which is an interaction log and a business activity. You can see it has a leading transaction category of BUS2000126, which is the business activity object type. However, you'll also notice on the left-hand side of the screen that you can assign other business transaction categories to your process. This is useful if you need to create a business transaction type that behaves mostly like one business object type but needs some additional data only found in another business object type. The view CRMV_PROC_TYPE can be used to get a basic listing of the business transaction types.

New transaction type
To create a new transaction type, we recommend that you copy an existing transaction type to a transaction type that starts with either "Z" or "Y". You should never change the customizing on the SAP-delivered transaction type because upgrades to your SAP CRM system could overwrite the changes made.

> **Note**
>
> For the purposes of this book, we've copied the standard interaction log 0001 transaction type over to ZSCR, which is our social media call report (see Figure 2.9). Throughout this book, we'll make enhancements to this transaction type.

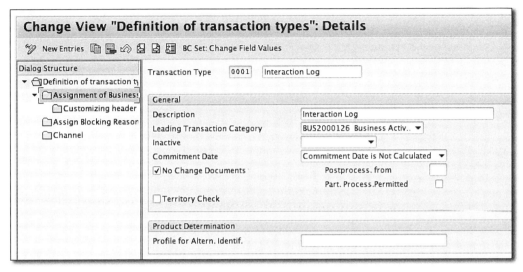

Figure 2.8 Standard Transaction Type Interaction Log

| Transaction Type | ZSCR | Social Call Report |

General

Description	Social Call Report
Leading Transaction Category	BUS2000126 Business Activ.. ▾
Inactive	▾
Commitment Date	Commitment Date is Not Calculated ▾
☑ No Change Documents	Postprocess. from
	Part. Process.Permitted ☐
☐ Territory Check	

Figure 2.9 Social Call Report Transaction

2.4.2   Programming with One Order

As an SAP CRM developer, you'll find that the majority of your enhancement requirements in sales and service will involve you having to manipulate data within the one order framework. Due to the importance and complexity of the one order framework, you'll find separate chapters in this book on business transaction events (BTEs) and common enhancement requests in sales and service. To prepare you to better understand those chapters, let's walk through the API used by the one order framework for common segments and consider a coding example that shows how to update a business transaction within your SAP CRM system.

One Order API

The one order API consists of one order data model

The one order data model is updated through the one order API. This API is used by all code within the SAP CRM system that updates business transaction data. (Remember, you should never update any SAP-delivered table through a direct SQL update; instead, use an SAP-provided BAPI or function module to perform the update.) The API of the one order framework takes care of all of the buffering and other development headaches that you may encounter when trying to keep a huge, complex data model in sync with several database tables.

SAP does provide several publicly released BAPIs for updating business transaction data in your SAP CRM system. We recommend that you use these BAPIs when writing load programs or extracts into your SAP CRM system. However, we don't recommend using the BAPIs when building enhancements within a BAdI or BTE in the one order framework; instead, we recommend you use the one order API layer to handle those updates.

Function modules

The one order API consists of a series of function modules that manage and update the various segments of the business transaction. They typically follow a naming pattern of CRM_<SEGMENTNAME>_<OPERATION>_OW. Common operations include READ, MAINTAIN, and so on.

CUSTOMER_H segment

To understand this further, let's review the CUSTOMER_H segment. If you perform a search for corresponding function modules that follow that pattern, you'll find several in the system. However, based on practice and experience, the two that you'll most commonly use are CRM_CUSTOMER_H_READ_OW and CRM_CUSTOMER_H_MAINTAIN_OW (see Figure 2.10). These function modules will allow you to get the current value of the CUSTOMER_H segment that is in memory and then update/create that segment as needed. For most enhancement logic that you'll need to write, you'll need to use this kind of function module for every segment to fulfill the basic requirement to read and write data.

Repository Info System: Function Modules Find (9 Hits)	
Function group	Function group short text
Function Module Name	Short text for function module
CRM_CUSTOMER_H_OW	Header: Maintenance Modules
CRM_CUSTOMER_H_CHANGE_OW	Ändern der Kopfdaten
CRM_CUSTOMER_H_CHECK_OW	Kopfdaten auf Konsistenz prüfen
CRM_CUSTOMER_H_CREATE_OW	Anlegen eines Kopfes
CRM_CUSTOMER_H_FILL_OW	Filling Header Data
CRM_CUSTOMER_H_INIT_OW	Initialisierung des Objektes
CRM_CUSTOMER_H_MAINTAIN_OW	Pflegen (Anlegen oder Ändern) von Kopfdaten
CRM_CUSTOMER_H_MERGE_OW	Merge Data
CRM_CUSTOMER_H_PUBLISH_OW	Event für andere Objekte auslösen
CRM_CUSTOMER_H_READ_OW	Informationen zum Kopf

Figure 2.10 OW Function Modules for the CUSTOMER_H Segment

Another point in using these function modules is that you shouldn't use these in the UI layer of SAP CRM. Instead, the Business Object Layer (BOL) model for one order contains ways to access this data. We'll look at the BOL model for one order later in this chapter, as it's important to understand how the object segments translate into the BOL model.

CRM_ORDER_READ

In some cases, you may want to retrieve all data contained within the business transaction. To do this, you don't need to read each segment individually, but rather you can call the function module CRM_ORDER_READ. One of the advantages of the CRM_ORDER_READ function module is that there is a corresponding example program called CRM_ORDER_READ that allows you to see what data will be returned in each segment.

To execute this program, run Transaction SE38 and enter "CRM_ORDER_READ" as the program name. A screen as shown in Figure 2.11 appears, asking for either the object ID or header GUID of the transaction. Provide the appropriate information, and click the EXECUTE button.

Once executed, the CRM_ORDER_READ display shows what data segments will be filled in by the READ by highlighting those rows and a record count, as shown in Figure 2.12.

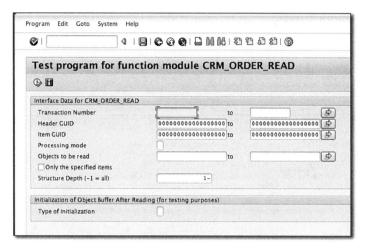

Figure 2.11 Selection Screen for CRM_ORDER_READ

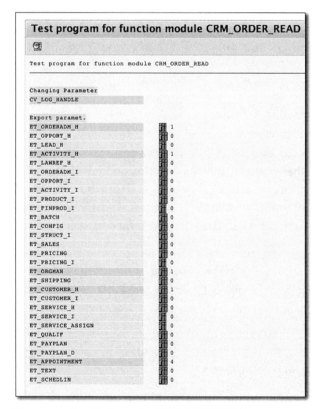

Figure 2.12 Results Screen for CRM_ORDER_READ

Double-click on any row with a record count to see the details of the values presented (see Figure 2.13). This is a useful way of determining whether a segment will contain the data you need, when you're not quite sure where the data is stored within the business transaction one order model inside of SAP CRM.

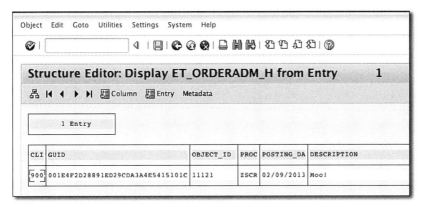

Figure 2.13 Drill Down into ET_ORDERADM_H Results

CRM_ORDER_MAINTAIN

Another commonly used function module for one order is CRM_ORDER_MAINTAIN. When used in combination with CRM_ORDER_SAVE, this function allows for the creation or change of business transaction data within your system. The coding example in Listing 2.8 shows how to use the function module to change an existing transaction. This example changes the description of the transaction and the priority of the transaction. The description is located in the ORDERADM_H segment, and the priority is located in the ACTIVITY_H segment.

Create/change business transaction data

```
*&--------------------------------------------------------------
*& Report    ZCRM_BOOK_MAINTAIN
*&
*&--------------------------------------------------------------
REPORT  ZCRM_BOOK_MAINTAIN.

INCLUDE crm_object_kinds_con.
INCLUDE crm_object_names_con.
INCLUDE crm_mode_con.
```

```
data: lv_trans_guid type crmt_object_guid,
      lv_description type crmt_process_description,
      lv_priority type CRMT_PRIORITY.

data: lt_input_fields       type CRMT_INPUT_FIELD_TAB.
DATA: lt_input_field_names  TYPE crmt_input_field_names_tab.
DATA: ls_input_field_names  TYPE crmt_input_field_names.
DATA: ls_input_fields       TYPE crmt_input_field,
      lt_exception          type CRMT_EXCEPTION_T.

data: lt_objects_to_save    TYPE CRMT_OBJECT_GUID_TAB,
      lt_objects_not_saved  type CRMT_OBJECT_GUID_TAB.

data: lt_orderadm_h         type crmt_orderadm_h_comt,
      lt_activity_h         type crmt_activity_h_comt,
      ls_orderadm_h         TYPE crmt_orderadm_h_com,
      ls_activity_h         TYPE crmt_activity_h_com.


lv_trans_guid = '001E4F2D28891ED29CDA3A4E5415101C'.
lv_description = 'New Description'.
lv_priority = '1'.

*****************************************************************
*    Activity Header
ls_activity_h-mode        = gc_mode-change.
ls_activity_h-priority    = lv_priority.
INSERT ls_activity_h INTO TABLE lt_activity_h.

ls_input_field_names-fieldname   = 'PRIORITY'.
INSERT ls_input_field_names INTO TABLE lt_input_field_names.

CLEAR ls_input_fields.
ls_input_fields-ref_guid     = lv_trans_guid.
ls_input_fields-ref_kind     = gc_object_kind-orderadm_h.
ls_input_fields-objectname   = gc_object_name-activity_h.
ls_input_fields-field_names  = lt_input_field_names.
INSERT ls_input_fields INTO TABLE lt_input_fields.

*****************************************************************
* Order Header
ls_orderadm_h-mode           = gc_mode-change.
ls_orderadm_h-guid           = lv_trans_guid.
```

```
ls_orderadm_h-description  = lv_description.
INSERT ls_orderadm_h INTO TABLE lt_orderadm_h.

*build table with change fields
FREE lt_input_field_names.
IF ls_orderadm_h-description IS NOT INITIAL.
  ls_input_field_names-fieldname = 'DESCRIPTION'.
  INSERT ls_input_field_names INTO TABLE lt_input_field_
names.
ENDIF.

CLEAR ls_input_fields.

ls_input_fields-ref_guid    = lv_trans_guid.
ls_input_fields-ref_kind    = gc_object_kind-orderadm_h.
ls_input_fields-objectname  = gc_object_name-orderadm_h.
ls_input_fields-field_names = lt_input_field_names.
INSERT ls_input_fields INTO TABLE lt_input_fields.
*************************************************************

CALL FUNCTION 'CRM_ORDER_MAINTAIN'
  EXPORTING
    it_activity_h     = lt_activity_h
  IMPORTING
    et_exception      = lt_exception
  CHANGING
    ct_orderadm_h     = lt_orderadm_h
    ct_input_fields   = lt_input_fields
  EXCEPTIONS
    error_occurred    = 1
    document_locked   = 2
    no_change_allowed = 3
    no_authority      = 4
    OTHERS            = 5.

read table lt_exception transporting no fields
    with key guid = lv_trans_guid.
if sy-subrc ne 0.


  insert lv_trans_guid into table lt_objects_to_save.

  IF lt_objects_to_save IS NOT INITIAL.
```

```
*     save object
      refresh: lt_exception.
      CALL FUNCTION 'CRM_ORDER_SAVE'
        EXPORTING
          it_objects_to_save   = lt_objects_to_save
        IMPORTING
          et_objects_not_saved = lt_objects_not_saved
          et_exception         = lt_exception
        EXCEPTIONS
          document_not_saved   = 1
          OTHERS               = 2.

      read table lt_exception transporting no fields
              with key guid = lv_trans_guid.

    if sy-subrc ne 0.
      commit work.
    endif.
  ENDIF.
endif.
```

Listing 2.8 Change Existing Transaction

Searching for Transactional Data

CRMD_ORDER_
INDEX

After reviewing the data model for the business transaction, you may have thought that building the SQL statements to search for data in your programs will be complex. Although this is generally true, there are a few tables and views that can be helpful in your searches. One of the most commonly used tables for searching is Table CRMD_ORDER_INDEX. This table was created by SAP to allow the searching of transactions by business partner in a more efficient fashion. Without this table, the SQL statement to join the order header, segment link, and partner table would be very inefficient to run on a standard database. In the future, database technology such as SAP HANA may also use this table.

In addition to Table CRMD_ORDER_INDEX, another useful view is Table CRMV_INDEX_JEST. This allows you to select transactions by status by combining Table CRMD_ORDER_INDEX with the status Table CRM_JEST.

Web Client BOL Model with One Order

A major hurdle that developers face when starting with SAP CRM is that they understand the Web Client development tools but don't understand how the data updates are passed from the Web Client screens into the SAP CRM database. To help overcome this obstacle, let's take a look at the Business Object Layer (BOL) model for SAP CRM business transactions and how it's related to the SAP CRM one order data model and API.

The BOL is an abstraction layer used by Web Client to separate UI logic from business logic. This layer typical represents the model layer in the Model View Controller (MVC) paradigm used by the Web Client. (To learn more about Web Client programming, review the book *SAP Web Client: A Comprehensive Guide for Developers* by Tzanko Stefanov, Armand Sezikeye, and Sanjeet Mall [SAP PRESS 2011] for further details.)

UI logic

For the business transaction, SAP has set up the BOL model to mirror the one order data model as closely as possible. BOL objects for segments generally start with naming convention of BT<segmentname>. The objects also follow a pattern where the root object of the model will correspond to the ORDERADM_H, and all other segments will be children of this root segment. You can also find out which BOL object corresponds to a segment name by looking in the view CRMV_OBJ_BTIL, as shown in Figure 2.14. It's important to keep this in mind because the objects of the BOL for the business transaction will use the one order API for creating, changing, reading, and deleting the business transaction maintained in the Web Client interface.

External Object Name	Object Name	Description	ObjectType	Structure name	Structure name
BTAUISearchResult	< >		E Search Result Object ▾	CRMS_AUI_SRCH_RESULT	CRMT_OBJECT_GUID
BTAUIView	< >		F View Object ▾	CRMST_INBOX_RESULTLIST	
BTAcAssignSet	AC_ASSIGN	Settlement Account Assi...	C Dependent Object ▾	CRMST_ACASSIGNSET_BTIL	CRMST_ACASSIGNSET_KEY
BTActivityH	ACTIVITY_H	Header data activity	C Dependent Object ▾	CRMST_ACTIVITYH_BTIL	CRMST_ACTIVITYH_KEY
BTActivityI	ACTIVITY_I	Activity Item Data	C Dependent Object ▾	CRMST_ACTIVITYI_BTIL	CRMST_ACTIVITYI_KEY
BTAdminH	ORDERADM_H	Administration Header	B Access Object ▾	CRMST_ADMINH_BTIL	CRMT_OBJECT_GUID
BTAdminI	ORDERADM_I	Administration Item	B Access Object ▾	CRMST_ADMINI_BTIL	CRMT_OBJECT_GUID

Figure 2.14 View CRMV_OBJ_BTIL

Another interesting point of reference in understanding how the one order API function modules are used in the BOL is to examine the package `CRM_BTIL_OBJ`. This package contains most of the classes used to implement most of the segments of the one order data model.

2.5   Marketing Attributes

Customer-specific attributes

One of the most interesting challenges a business faces is how to organize the customer base into similar groups to effectively market and sell to those customers with similar sets of attributes. To solve this problem, you need to a way to identify certain common attributes of your customers. The problem with having a common set of attributes is that no two companies may want to group their customers in the same fashion. Marketing attributes in SAP CRM resolve this problem by providing a framework to create specific attributes for customers that don't necessarily have to be assigned to all customers.

2.5.1   Business Definition

Marketing attributes are common characteristics or attributes of a business partner that can be used to classify or group one or more common customers together within a group.

An attribute normally consists of a predefined set of values that describes a characteristic. An example attribute could be sales volume, which might be defined as high, medium, or low instead of a specific number.

Attribute set

Similar attributes that describe related characteristics of a business partner can be put together as an *attribute set*. An attribute set is a set of related attributes that have been grouped together to ensure easy and complete maintenance of particular characteristics of a business partner. An example of an attribute set could be "Buying Pattern," which would consist of two attributes: sales volume and order frequency. Even though both attributes can be maintained independently when maintained together, they provide a more complete view of that type of information for a business partner.

2.5.2 Technical Definition

In your SAP CRM system, you can access the definition of marketing attributes using the Web Client. Log in to the Web Client under the MARKETINGPRO business role. Once inside the SAP CRM system, go to the MARKETING work center, and choose the ATTRIBUTES option under the SEARCH menu.

Marketing attributes in SAP CRM have been implemented by creating an API on top of the standard SAP classification system that is delivered in both SAP ERP and SAP CRM. The classification system allows you to create characteristics, which are attributes that describe a business object. A business object can be something such as a customer or material when looking at SAP ERP. Those characteristics when grouped together are called a *class*. The assignment of the class to a business object then allows you to maintain those characteristics in relationship to that business object.

The process of creating characteristics and classes has been abstracted in SAP CRM to a specific process for business partner data. In this abstraction, characteristics are modeled as marketing attributes or attributes, and classes are known as attribute sets. These attributes have been designed to be specific to the business partner in SAP CRM, so there is no need to associate these attributes with a specific business object type—unlike how classification works in SAP ERP.

Skip Ahead and Turn Back

We strongly recommend that you consider going through the examples in Chapter 3, Section 3.4, of this book to create your own marketing attributes. You then can review the data model after you've created your own marketing attributes because it's easier to explore in your own system with actual data.

Attributes

As we discussed earlier, attributes are abstractions on top of characteristics in the classification system. Characteristics are defined in Table CABN and can be viewed using Transaction CT04 as shown in Figure 2.15.

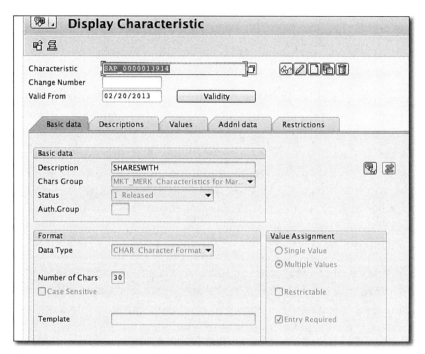

Figure 2.15 Custom Characteristic in Transaction CT04

When you create the characteristics through the standard tools available in the Web Client, the system then creates an automatically generated system name as the technical ID. The technical ID displayed in the Web Client is in the DESCRIPTION field. The CHARS GROUP for these characteristics is "MKT_MERK". The characteristic definition also defines the type of data being stored, whether it can be used once or many times in a class, and whether the entry is mandatory.

Now if you compare this to how the underlying characteristic is shown as a marketing attribute, you see much less technical detail as show in

Figure 2.16. The primary reason for this is that marketing attributes were designed to be created by business users and not IT support staff. The problem with classification as you can immediately determine from this screen comparison is that the UI is unfriendly and too complicated, except for those with strong technical skills.

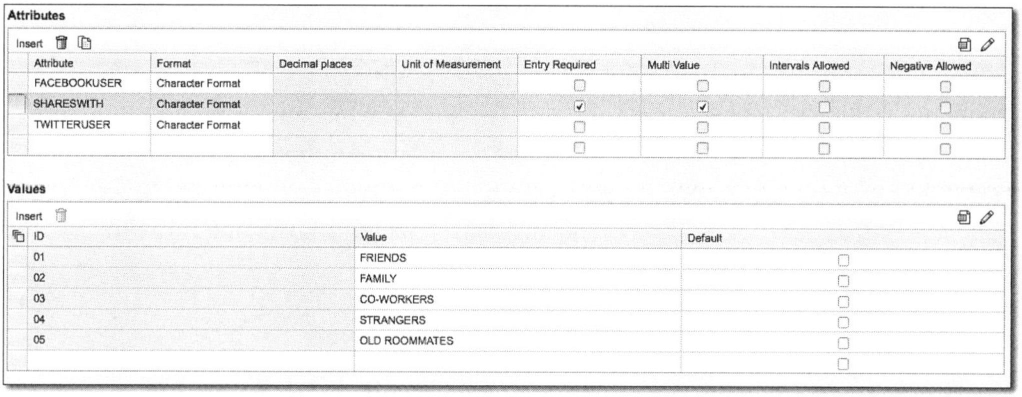

Attributes

Insert 🗑 🗋

Attribute	Format	Decimal places	Unit of Measurement	Entry Required	Multi Value	Intervals Allowed	Negative Allowed
FACEBOOKUSER	Character Format			☐	☐	☐	☐
SHARESWITH	Character Format			☑	☑	☐	☐
TWITTERUSER	Character Format			☐	☐	☐	☐
				☐	☐	☐	☐

Values

Insert 🗑

ID	Value	Default
01	FRIENDS	☐
02	FAMILY	☐
03	CO-WORKERS	☐
04	STRANGERS	☐
05	OLD ROOMMATES	☐
		☐

Figure 2.16 Marketing Attribute in the Web Client

Attribute Set Header

The attribute set header is stored as a class header in Table KLAH. The attribute sets are always created with a CLASS TYPE of "BUP", which is the business partner, and a CLASS GROUP of "MKT_PT", which is the group for profile templates.

You can review the classification system definition of an existing class by running Transaction CL03. In Figure 2.17, you see the class definition of the attribute set "ZCRM_TPP_BOOK", which we'll define in Chapter 3, Section 3.4. Click on the CHAR. tab on this screen to see the attributes assigned as shown in Figure 2.18.

> **Note**
>
> Even though you can view the underlying data of the attributes through the standard delivered classification transaction, you shouldn't change the data in this fashion. Instead, we recommend that you always use the provided tools in the Web Client or in Transaction CRMD_MKT_TOOLS to adjust your attribute set in your SAP CRM system.

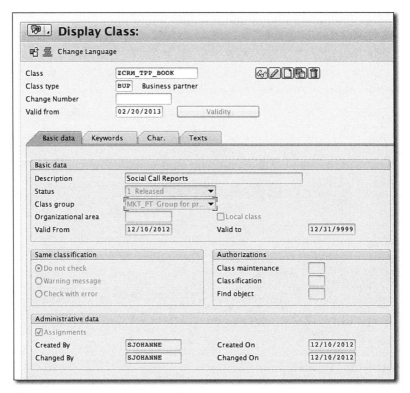

Figure 2.17 Class Header in Transaction CL03

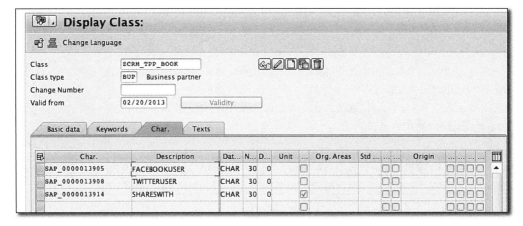

Figure 2.18 Characteristics Assigned to a Class in Transaction CL03

To complete the comparison, bring up the marketing attribute set in the Web Client for a much simpler view of the data as shown in Figure 2.19.

Simple view

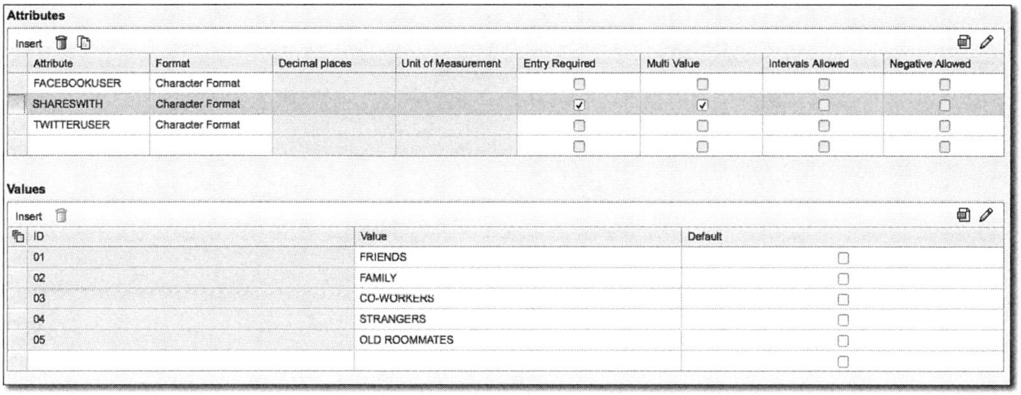

Attributes

Insert 🗑 ⬒

Attribute	Format	Decimal places	Unit of Measurement	Entry Required	Multi Value	Intervals Allowed	Negative Allowed
FACEBOOKUSER	Character Format			☐	☐	☐	☐
SHARESWITH	Character Format			☑	☑	☐	☐
TWITTERUSER	Character Format			☐	☐	☐	☐
				☐	☐	☐	☐

Values

Insert 🗑

ID	Value	Default
01	FRIENDS	☐
02	FAMILY	☐
03	CO-WORKERS	☐
04	STRANGERS	☐
05	OLD ROOMMATES	☐
		☐

Figure 2.19 Attribute Set in the Web Client

In the Web Client, the assignment of marketing attributes to a business partner is done through an assignment block on the account overview screen. This block allows you to pick the attribute set and then maintain attributes for the business partner.

Assignment block

Figure 2.20 shows how the attributes appear to the end user from the Web Client.

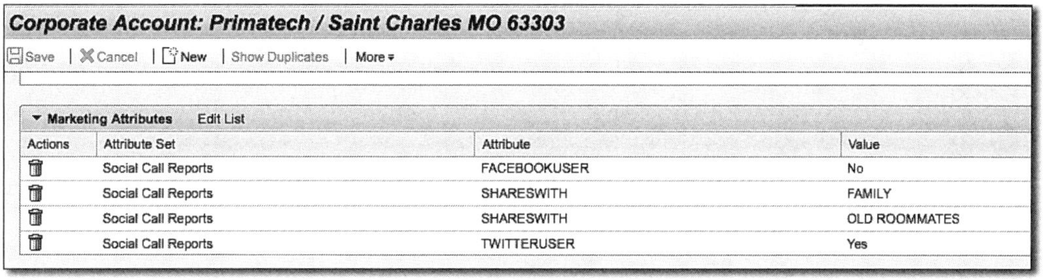

Corporate Account: Primatech / Saint Charles MO 63303

🖫 Save | ✖ Cancel | 🗋 New | Show Duplicates | More ▾

▼ Marketing Attributes   Edit List

Actions	Attribute Set	Attribute	Value
🗑	Social Call Reports	FACEBOOKUSER	No
🗑	Social Call Reports	SHARESWITH	FAMILY
🗑	Social Call Reports	SHARESWITH	OLD ROOMMATES
🗑	Social Call Reports	TWITTERUSER	Yes

Figure 2.20 Marketing Attributes Assigned to a Business Partner

After the data is saved, the system uses the marketing attributes API to store this information in the classification system within several tables. This representation will look different from the screen representation given to the end user.

Tables

The physical representation consists of three primary tables: INOB, KSSK, and AUSP. Each table is used to store a specific part of the business object to class assignment (see Table 2.10).

Table Name	Description
CABN	Characteristic – Contains Attribute Details: Cars
CAWN	Characteristic Values – Contains Attribute Values: Under Cars (Ford, Chevy, Porsche)
KLAH	Class Header Data: Attribute Set ID or Class ID
SWOR	Classification System: Keywords
KSSK	Allocation Table – Object to Class: Attribute Set ID to Object ID
INOB	Link between Internal Number and Object: Object ID to BP ID
AUSP	Characteristic Values: BP GUID for an Attribute ID, Value, and Object ID

Table 2.10 Assignment of Attributes to a Business Partner in the Web Client

INOB

Table INOB serves as a link between the external key of the object, which is the business partner key, and the key for the set of characteristic values maintained. In Figure 2.21, you see that for the assignment to the business partner 422021, there is a single entry. The primary key of the table is the CUOBJ field, which is short for configuration object. In the classification system, the assignment of values to attributes of a specific class is also known as a configuration object. In the OBJEK field, you see the partner ID that has been assigned to the configuration object.

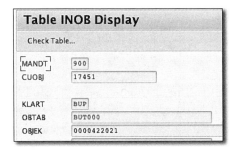

Figure 2.21 Linkage to a Business Partner in Table INOB: Marketing Tables

Table KSSK links the configuration object with the corresponding class. **KSSK**
The OBJEK field is the configuration object key, and the CLINT field is
the technical identifier of the class, which corresponds to the attribute
set as shown in Figure 2.22.

Data Browser: Table KSSK Select Entries   1

Table: KSSK
Displayed Fields: 13 of 13   Fixed Columns: ⌈6⌉   List Width 0250

MANDT	OBJEK	MAFID	KLART	CLINT	AD2HL	ZAEHL	STATU	STDCL	REKRI	AENNR	DATUV	LKENZ
900	000000000000017451	O	BUP	0000003932	0000	0	1				00/00/0000	

Figure 2.22 Entries in Table KSSK

Finally, Table AUSP contains the actual values of the attributes that were **AUSP**
assigned to the business partner as shown in Figure 2.23. One interesting note about this assignment is that SAP has extended Table AUSP to
include the GUID of the business partner. This is to improve the performance of reading the attributes from your SAP CRM system because it
allows the direct lookup of attributes assigned to an account without the
need to read Tables KSSK and INOB.

Data Browser: Table AUSP Select Entries   4

Table: AUSP
Displayed Fields: 14 of 29   Fixed Columns: ⌈7⌉   List Width 0250

MANDT	OBJEK	ATINN	ATZHL	MAFID	KLART	AD2HL	ATWRT
900	000000000000017451	0000013907	001	O	BUP	0000	N
900	000000000000017451	0000013910	001	O	BUP	0000	Y
900	000000000000017451	0000013916	001	O	BUP	0000	02
900	000000000000017451	0000013916	002	O	BUP	0000	05

Figure 2.23 Entries in Table AUSP

You can view the assignment of marketing attribute data from the clas- **Marketing**
sification point of view by using Transaction CL24N as shown in Figure **attribute data**
2.24. We don't recommend that you change the data displayed by this **assignment**
transaction, but we wanted to show it to give you a deeper understanding of how the marketing attributes have been modeled in SAP CRM.

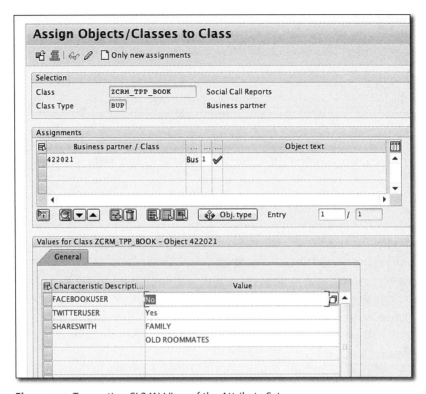

Figure 2.24 Transaction CL24N View of the Attribute Set

2.5.3 API Function Modules

Change metadata

There are many function modules to retrieve and change data for marketing attributes and the business partners they are attached to. Whenever you're making changes to or viewing the metadata of marketing attributes, you should use the API and function modules. It's much more efficient and you have less of an opportunity to corrupt the data in the system. The following function modules are quite useful when writing custom logic that reads or updates marketing attributes for a business partner:

Custom logic

▶ CRM_MKTBP_READ_BP_DATA

With function module CRM_MKTBP_READ_DATA, you can get the value sets for a particular business partner. You must pass the business partner GUID and also the name of the profile set.

▶ CRM_MKTPFTPL_READ

With function module CRM_MKTPFTPL_READ, you can receive metadata of an attribute set. You'll need to pass the attribute set name.

▶ CRM_MKTBP_CHANGE_BP

With function module CRM_MKTBP_CHANGE_BP, you can update attribute set values for a particular business partner.

> **Tips & Tricks**
>
> Search CRM_MKT* in Transaction SE37 for additional function modules.

2.6 Summary

Understanding the SAP CRM data model is key to becoming an effective developer of enhancements in the SAP CRM system. Understanding the key business objects of business partners, business transactions, products, and marketing attributes will allow you to build enhancements for most processes implemented on an SAP CRM system.

In the next chapter, we'll examine techniques to extend the data model that we just reviewed.

Any properly designed data model should have easy-to-use tools that allow you to extend the model to meet your business requirements. SAP CRM benefits from having simple but powerful tools to allow for easy extension of the data model without coding.

3 Data Model Extension Techniques

The standard data model of SAP CRM contains many different attributes that cover the various aspects of the relationships between a company and its customers. However, it's impossible for SAP to deliver a set of attributes that meets all requirements for every single customer of SAP CRM. Instead, SAP provides several different tools to enhance the data model of SAP CRM. These tools include the Easy Enhancement Workbench (EEWB), Application Enhancement Tool (AET), manual techniques, marketing attributes, and product master attributes. In this chapter, we'll examine each tool in further detail so you'll know exactly when to use a particular tool.

3.1 Easy Enhancement Workbench

The Easy Enhancement Workbench (EEWB) was the original tool delivered by SAP to enhance the SAP CRM data model for business transactions and business partner data. Until SAP CRM 7.0, this was the primary method of adding new fields in SAP CRM. The EEWB is delivered in SAP CRM as Transaction EEWB.

> **Note**
>
> It's important to note that SAP no longer recommends using the EEWB for enhancements as of SAP CRM 7.0. The EEWB has been replaced by the Application Enhancement Tool (AET) for enhancements because even though the

> EEWB creates fields automatically for you, it's difficult to use and doesn't work perfectly.

EEWB drawbacks The EEWB is very confusing to use for a new user. As you'll see from the example in this section, it's easy to pick the wrong extension types when using the EEWB. It's also based on the old SAP GUI for SAP CRM, which means it's not available via the Web Client. The EEWB also doesn't generate any code for the Web Client use.

Another major drawback of the EEWB is that it doesn't support currency or quantity fields. This becomes an issue if you want to add a new attribute to your business transaction that needs to be associated with a unit of measure or a monetary value. Finally, the EEWB doesn't support changing the structures that it generates. Instead, after you generate an extension and move it past the development environment, you can't delete fields, and adding new fields can cause the existing extension not to generate properly.

The EEWB is a good tool if you only need to add new fields or create new extensions; however, the EEWB limits the number of extensions you can create. An extension can have one or more fields, but the total number of extensions has a hardcoded limit. This poses problems if you choose to add fields one at a time or want to add many fields at once because an extension can only support a fixed limit of new fields. These limitations and the revamping of the SAP UI is what drove SAP to introduce the AET, which we'll discuss in Section 3.2.

Due to the widespread use of the EEWB by many SAP CRM customers, we'll explore the tool even though it should no longer be used. Our exploration of the EEWB will focus on the enhancements generated by the tool.

3.1.1 Add a New Field

To gain a better understanding of how the tool works, let's examine how to add a new field on an interaction log business transaction type. The interaction log is a business activity transaction. This example adds an additional field to store a related "hashtag" for a social media call report based on the interaction log.

1. First go to Transaction EEWB. Click on the NEW button, and you're prompted to create a project.

2. All EEWB work is organized within projects. The project asks you to define the package to store the enhancements and prefixes. This example uses the ZCRM_TPP_BOOK package and "Z" as the namespace prefix as shown in Figure 3.1.

Projects

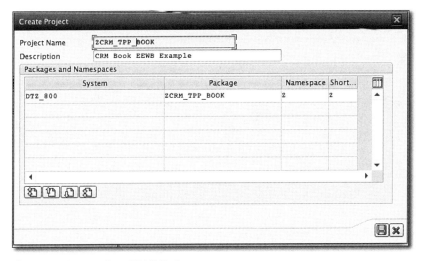

Figure 3.1 Create a New EEWB Project

3. Next, define transport requests for that project that will save all of the associated objects. You'll either use existing transports or create a new transport. You must specify both a WORKBENCH and CUSTOMIZING transport for the project as shown in Figure 3.2.

Define transport requests

4. After this is done, click SAVE, and you'll be moved to the CHANGE PROJECT screen. This screen provides the general details about the project, including the description, creation date, created by, package, and user responsible for the project as shown in Figure 3.3.

Project details

We'll now move on to the next step, which is creating an extension.

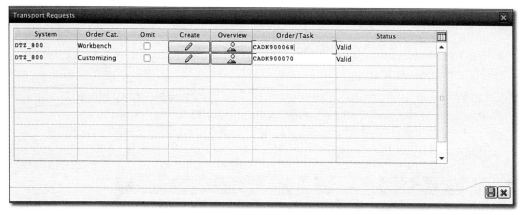

Figure 3.2 Transport Definition for the EEWB Project

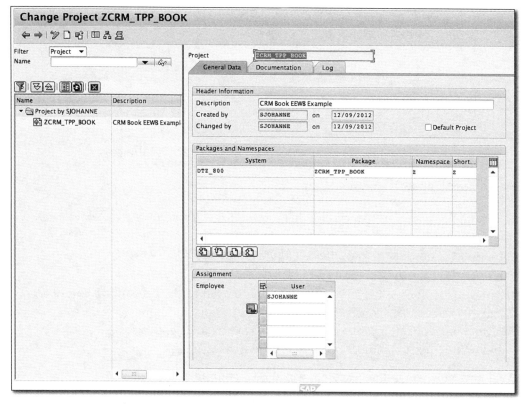

Figure 3.3 Created EEWB Project

3.1.2   Create an Extension

An *extension* is a group of new fields or a new table on an SAP CRM business object. An EEWB project is a folder that can house multiple extensions. The extension is the actual enhancement of the data model by the EEWB.

Create an extension by right-clicking on the project name in the left-hand navigation tree and choosing CREATE EXTENSION as shown in Figure 3.4. If you're on a newer version of SAP CRM that contains the AET, you'll get a warning message strongly encouraging you to use the AET as shown in Figure 3.5.

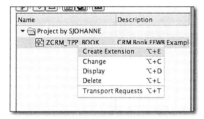

Figure 3.4 Create an EEWB Extension

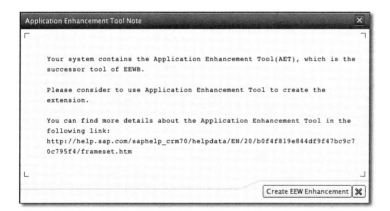

Figure 3.5 Use AET Instead Warning Message

> Warning: recommendation to use AET

Note

We also would recommend that you don't use the EEWB on SAP CRM 7.0 and above, but for this book, we'll continue with the example so you can understand the older method of doing things. This is important because many

SAP CRM systems were upgraded from the older versions and used EEWB extensively for enhancements. If you're working on a fresh install of SAP CRM 7.0 or higher, you can skip this section.

After you ignore the warning given by SAP, a popup asks you for some information about your extension as shown in Figure 3.6. Give the extension a name, description, business object, and extension type:

▶ For the NAME field, enter "ZCRM_TPP_BOOK"

▶ For DESCRIPTION, enter "TPP Book"

▶ For EEW BUS. OBJECT, enter "BUSINESS_TRANSACTION"

▶ For EXTENSION TYPE, enter "CUSTOMER_H"

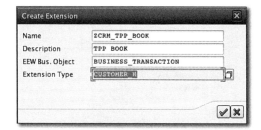

Figure 3.6 Create Extension CUSTOMER_H

Warning!

Once again, you should not be playing with the EEWB in a system that is in a production landscape. This means that unless you're using a sandbox system, please click CANCEL now, and read the rest of this section before trying anything. A sandbox is a standalone system that doesn't have a transport path to a production system. A true sandbox system is one that can be restored from a backup if the changes made cause the system to become inoperable without any impact to the production landscape. It's quite possible to make an SAP CRM system completely unusable for maintaining business transactions via the EEWB. Now that you know the dangers, let's continue.

Incorrect object type

Note

One of the biggest mistakes made with the EEWB is picking the wrong object type. It had been a while since we used the EEWB when writing this book, and we made this exact error when creating our example. The only valid object type that you should use for business transactions is BUSINESS TRANS-ACTION. The other available options won't give you the correct enhancement options. There is an object type for business activity, but once again don't use this if you decide for some reason to use the EEWB even though we recommend that you do not.

The final part of the information you need to specify is the extension type. For this example, choose CUSTOMER_H.

Extension type

We strongly advise putting fields on CUSTOMER_H because then any business transaction type can reuse the fields, which keeps the header of the business transaction less cluttered. Even ORDERADM_H is an option, although we don't recommend putting any custom fields on segments besides CUSTOMER_H unless absolutely needed in the business transaction. A great example is if you put a field on OPPORT_H and then need it in an activity, you can't use it without adding it to ACTIVITY_H. Instead, if the field was put on CUSTOMER_H, it would have been shared between both sections.

After you provide the basic data about the extension type, a wizard dialog pops up that will guide you through several steps as shown in Figure 3.7.

Wizard for new fields in a business transaction

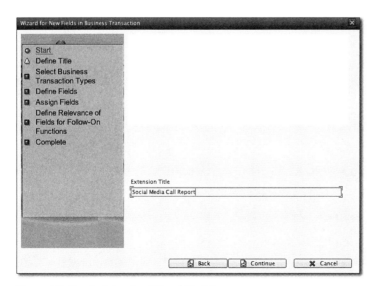

Figure 3.7 Create Extension Wizard Start Screen

Wizards in the SAP GUI part of SAP CRM are guided procedures that walk you through the creation process of data. The wizard first asks you what the title of this data should be. For our purposes, use SOCIAL MEDIA CALL REPORT. This title labels the structure that is created, and when this generates screens in the SAP GUI, it will be the title of the area within the screen. Click CONTINUE.

Business transaction object type The next screen asks you to pick the relevance of your custom field as shown in Figure 3.8. This transaction type isn't the business transaction *process* type but rather the business transaction *object* type. Select the BUSINESS ACTIVITY to drive the display of the field in the old SAP GUI CRMD_ORDER transaction used to maintain business transactions in SAP CRM.

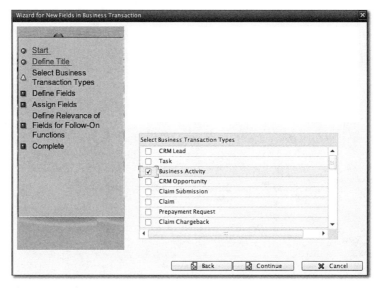

Figure 3.8 Select Business Transaction Type

3.1.3 Specify New Fields to Be Added

Expansion Finally, you've reached point where you can start specifying the new fields to be added.

1. Click on the EXPANSION button below the table entry area to put the table in expert mode as shown in Figure 3.9. If you don't use expert mode, SAP generates hard to remember names for your fields.

Instead, you can specify valid names for the field and the data element. For this example, you'll want your field to start with "ZZ", which is in the customer namespace for appending fields. This is important because the CUSTOMER_H fields are included in other structures that mix non-CUSTOMER_H fields with standard tables such as search.

Use expansion mode to choose specific names

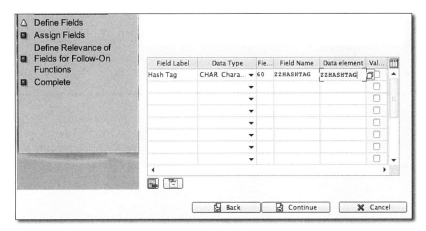

Figure 3.9 Define Fields for Extension

2. In the table shown in Figure 3.9, provide information in the FIELD LABEL, FIELD TYPE, FIELD LENGTH, FIELD NAME, and DATA ELEMENT columns.

   ▹ The DATA ELEMENT should be a name of a data element not yet created

   ▹ Enter "Hash Tag" for the FIELD LABEL

   ▹ Enter "Character" for the FIELD TYPE

   ▹ Enter "60" for the FIELD LENGTH

   ▹ Enter "ZZHASHTAG" for the FIELD NAME

   ▹ Enter "ZZHASHTAG" for the DATA ELEMENT

3. After you've made this entry, click on the CONTINUE button.

   You can now specify where the field should be placed within the business transaction as shown in Figure 3.10.

Specify where the field will appear in the business transaction

4. Click the HEADER flag, and then choose the SUBOBJECT CUSTOMER HEADER DATA using the FIELD HELP popup as shown in Figure 3.11.

This will cause the fields to be created on the Table CRMD_ CUSTOMER_H. Click CONTINUE to move on to the next step.

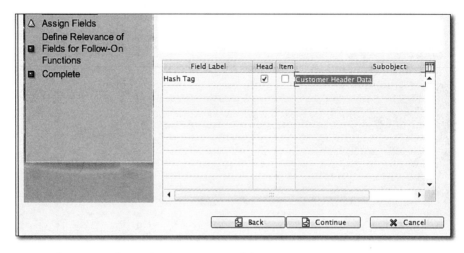

Figure 3.10 Choose the Data Segment of the Transaction

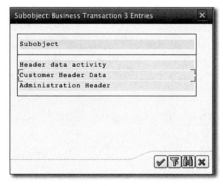

Figure 3.11 Picking the Proper Data Segment

5. The next screen as shown in Figure 3.12 allows you to have the fields extend either the middleware data transfer to SAP ERP, SAP Net-Weaver BW extractors, mobile extractors, or search. For this example don't choose any of these options because you don't need the field sent elsewhere.

6. Click CONTINUE for the final review screen. The final review screen shown in Figure 3.13 displays what you're about to create and starts to generate the extension in the system when you click COMPLETE.

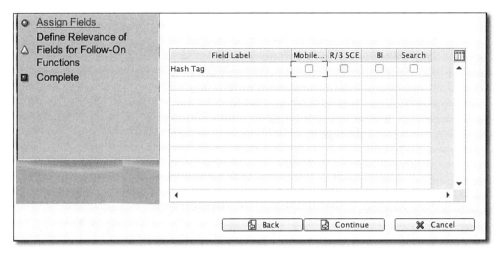

Figure 3.12 Selecting Follow-On Options

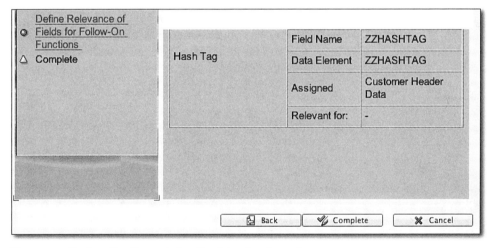

Figure 3.13 Confirmation Screen before the Extension Generates

If you already have structures/fields within the CRMD_CUSTOMER_H system, this step can cause your existing enhancements to no longer work. Cleaning up the generation failures by the EEWB is something that takes way too much effort. If you did make the mistake of clicking COMPLETE in your development system and it's no longer working, then please see Chapter 10 of this book to explore the community resources that are available. You'll definitely need to use the SAP CRM Community on SCN to resolve your issue, unless you want to pay a consultant or SAP to come in and fix this problem.

After you click the COMPLETE button (unless you have really fast servers for your SAP CRM system), this is a great point to take a coffee or soda break. The generation normally takes about 5 to 15 minutes depending on the speed of your system. After it's complete, you'll see a generation log in the project overview as shown in Figure 3.14 that provides some details on what happened.

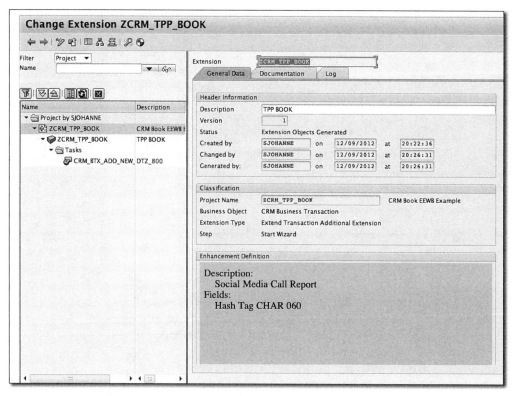

Figure 3.14 Generation Results Screen

It's very important to see a green check next to your extension name on the left-hand navigation bar because this means that your extension generated properly with no errors. This doesn't mean your system will work correctly, but you'll have less chance of a short dump. After you see the green checkmark, double-click on your extension name and get a list of generated objects as shown in Figure 3.15. The object list is a combination of Data Dictionary objects and ABAP programs that are generated. You can also verify that the field was added to Table CRMD_CUSTOMER_H in Transaction SE11 as shown in Figure 3.16. As you can see, the field exists in the CI_EEW_CUSTOMER_H include.

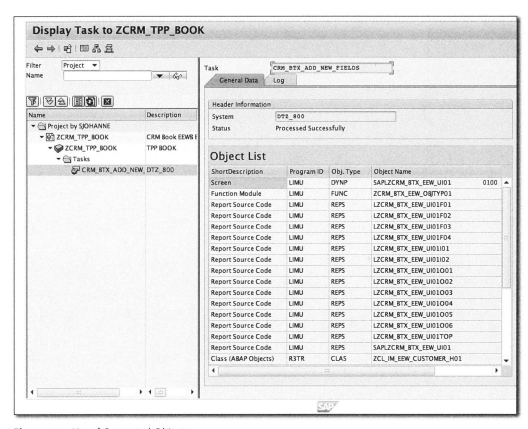

Figure 3.15 List of Generated Objects

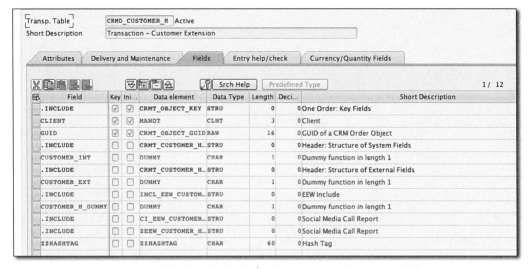

Figure 3.16 Newly Created Field in Table CRMD_CUSTOMER_H

3.2 Application Enhancement Tool

The Application Enhancement Tool (AET) was introduced to replace the EEWB in SAP CRM. The goal was to provide a tool within the Web Client interface that allows for the easy extension of new fields in SAP CRM. The AET achieved that and doesn't have all of the limitations that the EEWB faced. In this section, we'll take a look at how to use the AET to create a new field on the business transaction for a business activity transaction type.

> **Note**
>
> A big difference with using the AET is how you start the process. You're no longer in the SAP GUI, but rather in the actual Web Client UI, where you want the new field to be displayed. One of the key design goals when SAP created the Web Client was for it to be easy to use for both end users and administrators. This is one of the primary reasons why the enhancement work starts from where you want to enhance, instead of having to use an unfriendly SAP GUI transaction.

3.2.1 Launching the AET

To start working with the AET, you need to first access the Web Client
via a supported web browser to get to the primary end-user interface of
SAP CRM. There are two methods to bring up the Web Client. The easiest way if your SAP CRM system is configured properly is to launch
Transaction CRM_UI from the SAP GUI, which opens a new external
web browser that prompts you to log in to the SAP CRM system.

Accessing the Web Client

The other alternative is to use the *crm_logon* link to your system. This
URL link is in the format *http://<fqdn>:<port>/sap/crm_logon*. *<FQDN>*
is the fully qualified domain name of your SAP CRM system, and the
<port> is the port you've configured for HTTP communication on your
SAP CRM system. Your SAP NetWeaver administrator will be able to
provide this information.

The AET is embedded in the configuration tools of the Web Client. The
tools are normally accessed by going into the view that you want to
enhance in the same fashion as an end user and then clicking on a special SHOW CONFIGURABLE AREAS button. You then choose an area to configure to bring up the configuration tool for a particular view.

3.2.2 Adding a New Field

Even though the data model of SAP CRM covers many different business
processes, not all attributes of those processes may be covered by the
software. To remedy this, you can use the AET to extend the data model
of the business transaction and business partner to add additional
attributes as needed. For this chapter we will look how the AET can be
used to extend the business model of the business transaction. We will
review the associated business scenario and technical configuration
steps related to extending the data model.

Extend business model

> **Business Scenario**
>
> We have already added the hashtag related to the social media interaction to
> our social call report. We would now like to add a field to allow us to capture
> the Facebook ID that's related to the social interaction when applicable. In
> this scenario, we'll want to add the field to the DETAILS section of the CREATE
> ACTIVITY screen in the Web Client.

Technical Configuration

First, log in to SAP CRM under a business role that has the link to create activities, and then click on that link to open the CREATE ACTIVITY screen.

1. Click on the SHOW CONFIGURABLE AREAS button in the upper-right corner of the screen.

2. Click on the DETAILS section to bring up the configuration for view.

3. Start the enhancement process using the AET by bringing up the configuration for the view and choosing the CREATE FIELD option as shown in Figure 3.17. The benefit of starting where the field needs to be enhanced is that you no longer have to guess or figure out the correct business object.

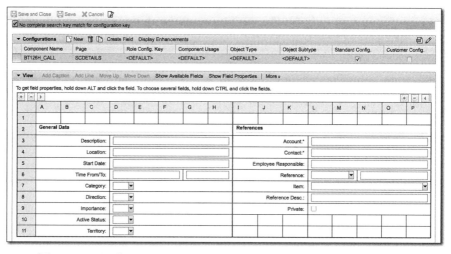

Figure 3.17 Configuration Screen

Choose object type 4. A popup appears as shown in Figure 3.18 due to the fact that there are two object types that can be enhanced for this screen. Choose INTERACTION_LOG.

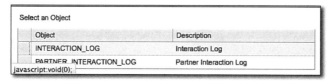

Figure 3.18 Select the Object for Enhancement

The next popup asks you where to place the field. The options here show you whether the field will end up in a context node of the underlying view of the Web Client. For those of you unfamiliar with the Web Client, the context nodes represent the data within a business transaction that will be displayed on the screen.

Field placement

> **Note**
>
> For more information on Web Client development, the book *SAP Web Client: A Comprehensive Guide for Developers* (SAP PRESS, 2011) by Tzanko Stefanov, Armand Sezikeye, and Sanjeet Mall is an excellent reference.

5. Choose CUSTOMER_H, and click the OK button as shown in Figure 3.19.

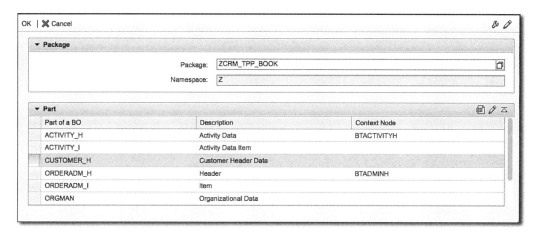

Figure 3.19 Define the Package and Part for the Enhancement

You're now presented with the nonexpert mode screen of the AET as shown in Figure 3.20. The primary difference between the nonexpert mode and expert mode (see Figure 3.21) is the ability to define the technical names for your field and the data element name. You don't want to use the system-generated names because, similar to the EEWB, SAP uses a ZZFLDXXXXXX naming convention for the technical field name. This name is generally not friendly if you need to code against it or have to review the names of the fields in the generated extension.

Nonexpert mode

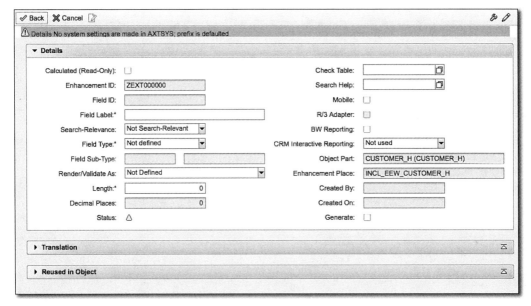

Figure 3.20 Define Field Attributes in Nonexpert Mode

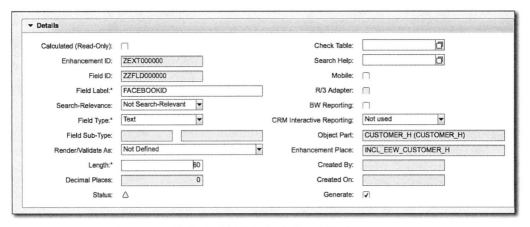

Figure 3.21 Define Field Attributes in Expert Mode

In addition, the data element name is generated as "ZDETLXXXXXX". The generic naming convention is something you normally should avoid when designing a data model for your enterprise. You should always enable expert mode in the AET and provide values for your own field names and data elements. Note that all fields you create should always start with "ZZ" because this is the customer namespace for fields that are part of the append structures to standard delivered SAP tables. All of the additional field extensions created by the AET are considered extensions to standard SAP-delivered tables.

The definition screen for the field you're adding in expert mode features several options as shown in Figure 3.21. Let's go over the different screen options (please note that this is not a complete list of what is available):

Expert mode options

▶ ENHANCEMENT ID
The technical name of the new enhancement you created.

▶ FIELD ID
The name of the field in the data object that you're enhancing, which should always begin with "ZZ".

▶ SEARCH-RELEVANCE
Defines whether the fields should be included as part of the SAP CRM search for that business object.

▶ FIELD TYPE
Defines the type of field that is being added in terms of data type. If the field is CURRENCY or QUANTITY, the reference FIELD ID provides the respective quantity or currency unit for the field.

▶ DATA ELEMENT
The name of the data element that will respect the field attributes in the Data Dictionary.

▶ RENDER VALIDATE/AS
Defines how the field should be displayed in the Web Client UI.

▶ LENGTH
Describes how long the field should be. If the field is numeric, you can specify the number of decimal places in the DECIMAL PLACES field.

▶ CHECK TABLE
Defines whether there is a specific set of possible values for your field. You can also specify a standard SAP search help to be used as possible values for your field.

- ▶ MOBILE
  Indicates that the field should be part of the data transfer interface of the SAP CRM Middleware for mobile data.

- ▶ R/3 ADAPTER
  Indicates that the BDoc for business transactions should be extended to include this field.

- ▶ BW REPORTING
  Indicates that the data source for the SAP NetWeaver BW system for the business object type should be extended to include the field.

- ▶ CRM INTERACTIVE REPORTING
  Indicates that the Interactive Reporting data sources should be extended to include this new field.

- ▶ OBJECT PART
  Defines the object that you're extending.

- ▶ ENHANCEMENT PLACE
  Defines the technical name of the Data Dictionary include in which the new field will be placed.

- ▶ CREATED BY/CREATED ON
  Shows who created the new field and when it was created.

- ▶ STATUS
  Indicates whether the field is fully generated, in draft status, or generated with errors.

- ▶ GENERATE
  Indicates that this field is ready for system generation.

For this example, rename the technical field name to "ZZFACE-BOOKID", as shown in Figure 3.22. However, keep the system-generated data element name. After you've maintained the entries as appropriate, click the BACK button to continue.

The newly created field and any other extensions on CUSTOMER_H, including the field you created via the EEWB are shown in the next screen (see Figure 3.23).

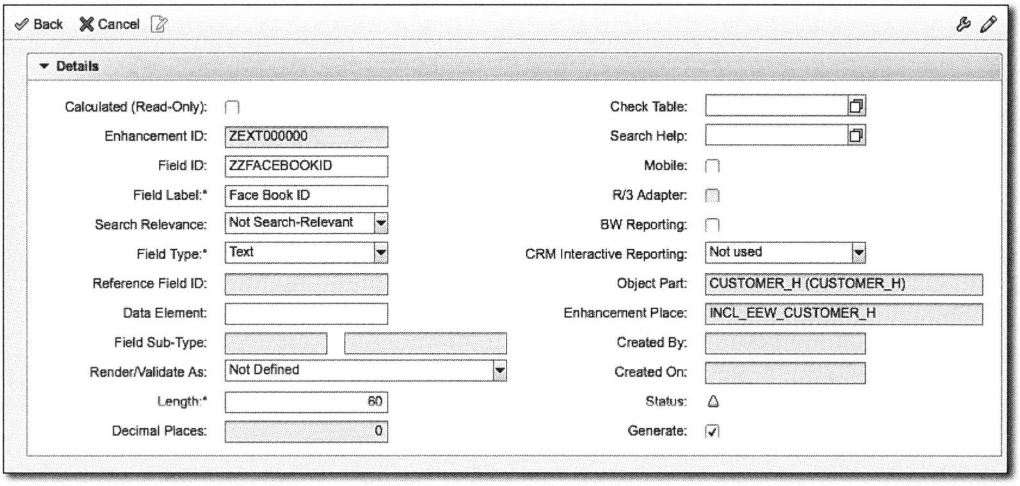

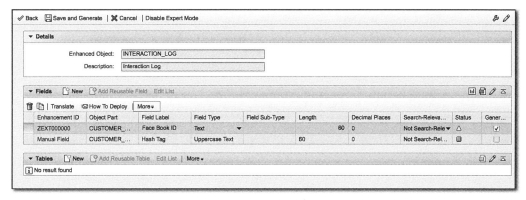

Figure 3.22 Rename Field to New Values

Figure 3.23 Enhancement Overview

For systems that were previously enhanced by the EEWB, the ability for the AET to recognize and not write over previous EEWB enhancements is a major advantage over the EEWB. At this point, if you're ready for the changes to be saved, click on the SAVE AND GENERATE button, and the system adds your field.

Add the Field to the System

Generation Before generation, the system prompts for a transport request that you'll provide as shown in Figure 3.24.

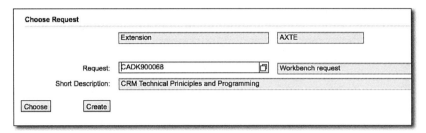

Figure 3.24 Prompt for Transport Request

After the generation is complete, you'll see a green status indicator for your field indicating that it's ready for use now as shown in Figure 3.25.

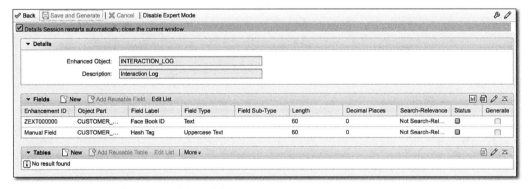

Figure 3.25 Successful Generation

In addition, Table CRMD_CUSTOMER_H has a new append that has been created with your field as shown in Figure 3.26.

In the background, the system registers the generated fields in several tables: AXT_RUN_BO_PART, AXT_RUN_FIELDDEF, and AXT_RUN_FIELDUSE. You can view the metadata structure of the enhancement in Transaction AXTREG and objects generated in Transaction AXTSHOW.

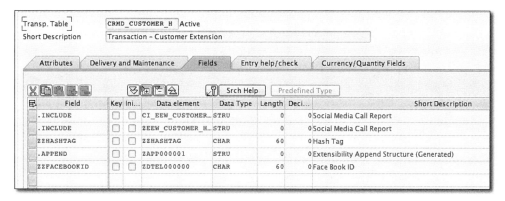

Figure 3.26 New Field in Table CRMD_CUSTOMER_H

3.2.3   Adding a New Table

In many projects we've encountered, there is a need to add additional data to the business transaction that is not related to the line items of a transaction, but is instead related to the header of the transaction in a 1:*N* relationship. In earlier releases of SAP CRM without the AET, this was almost impossible, due to the exhaustive effort required to implement this requirement. Now with the AET we can extend the business transaction with additional tabular data using the wizard, without needing any coding.

Add data to business transaction

Business Scenario

For this example we would like to capture the "likes" and comments of our social interaction. In Facebook, comments and likes can be associated with a posting and will indicate who either liked or made the comment to the original post. Our problem is that the CURRENT PARTIES INVOLVED section only allows us to list who was involved in the interaction, and we can't indicate whether they liked the interaction or had an additional comment.

In order to resolve this problem, we would like to create a new comments and likes section that allows us to indicate who commented or liked the interaction, whether it was a comment or like, and provide a short summary of the comment if one exists. We would like to store this on the social call report without needing to create new unique social call report to see the details of the comments. In order to achieve this, we can use the *create new table* feature of the AET.

Technical Steps

The creation of the new table requires us to set up the system to allow for table enhancements by the AET. All screens of the Web Client are stored in a UI component. The standard delivered SAP CRM system does not have a UI component available for table extensions generated by the AET. This UI component must be generated using the AET Systems Settings transaction. Follow these steps:

1. Launch Transaction AXTSYS, which will allow you to create a UI component to hold your new table enhancements. On the initial screen, specify the package that will be assigned to the UI component as shown in Figure 3.27. For this example we will use the ZCRM_TPP_BOOK package.

UI component 2. Once this has been specified, click the CREATE UI COMPONENT button to start the creation process.

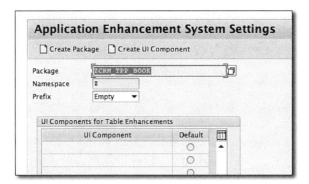

Figure 3.27 Specify Package for UI Component

3. You'll then receive a popup window asking us to name the UI component that will be generated. Enter ZCRM_TPP_BOOK as the name of the UI component and then press the green check button. The system will now generate the UI component.

4. Once the system is finished with generation, press the SAVE button to set the generated UI component as the default location to store table enhancements in your system as shown in Figure 3.28.

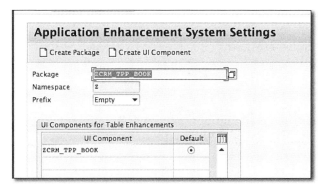

Figure 3.28 Completed UI Component Settings for Table Generation

Now that the system has been set up for the AET to create table extensions, we will start the process of adding a new table to the social call report.

Add new table to report

1. Log in into the Web Client using a business role that contains the CREATE INTERACTION LOG link. For this example we will use the standard business role SALESPRO.

2. After you've logged into the Web Client, choose the link INTERACTION LOG under the CREATE menu on the left-hand navigation bar.

3. You'll then receive a popup asking you to choose a type of interaction log to create. For this example, we've chosen our ZSCR social call report.

4. You'll then be taken to the CREATE INTERACTION LOG overview screen. Click the CONFIGURE PAGE button in the upper right-hand part of the screen.

5. You'll now receive a popup showing the configuration that's available for the current screen. Click the CREATE TABLE button in the Configurations table to start the process of creating a new table.

6. You'll be prompted to choose a package for the new table and review the business object part that the extension should be a part of. Choose

the package to be the ZCRM_TPP_BOOK (or another appropriate package) and then click the OK button.

7. You may be prompted for a transport request to record your changes at this time. After you specify the transport request, you'll receive a new popup, which is the start screen for creating a new table.

8. On this screen shown in Figure 3.29, define the attributes of the table and fields that will be contained in the table.

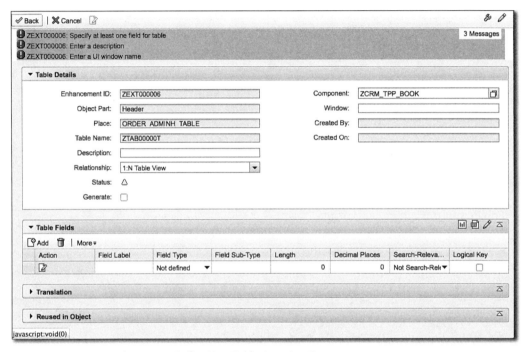

Figure 3.29 Define New Table Overview Screen

9. In the TABLE DETAILS section as shown in Figure 3.30, enter "Comments and Likes" as the description.

Note

Please make sure that when you enter this description, it's displayed in the way you wish the new table to appear to the end user.

10. For the window, enter ZCOMMENTSLIKES. This window name should be a technical name of the window that will contain the table on the Web Client screen.

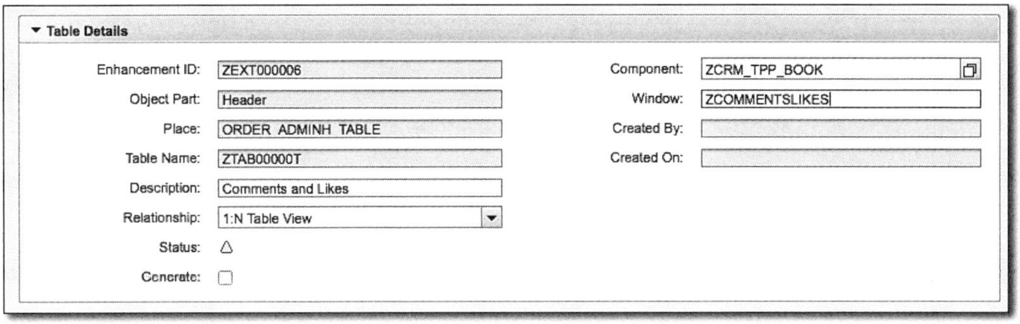

Figure 3.30 Table Details for New Table

Once the header attributes of the table are defined, you can now define the fields of the table.

Define table fields

1. To define a new field, click on the EDIT button on the first row in the table fields table. This will bring you into the FIELD DETAILS screen. The first field to define is to document who either commented or liked the interaction. For this field, make the following settings:

   ▶ The FIELD LABEL should be set as "Commenter"

   ▶ The FIELD TYPE will be set as an application reference. The APPLICATION REFERENCE TYPE allows us to link our field to use an existing business object type within in CRM.

   ▶ For the FIELD SUB-TYPE we will choose CONTACT

   ▶ We will leave the remaining options as is

   ▶ We will also check the LOGICAL KEY checkbox. This will indicate that this field is part of the key relationship between business transaction and the individual record.

2. Our completed screen should appear similar to Figure 3.31. Once everything is verified, click the green checkmark button to return to the overview screen and move on to the next field.

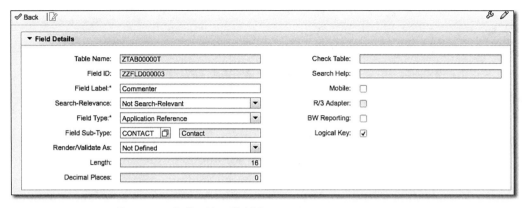

Figure 3.31 Define New Field Commenter

3. To define the next field, click on the EDIT button on the second row in the table fields table. This will bring you into the FIELD DETAILS screen. The second field you want to define is whether this was a comment or like made on the interaction. Set the following fields:

  ▶ Set the FIELD LABEL as "Remark Type"

  ▶ Set the FIELD TYPE as UPPER CASE TEXT

  ▶ For the FIELD LENGTH, enter a value of 2

4. Now, expand the assignment block dropdown list and add two new entries under that list:

  ▶ The first entry will have input code of 01 and description of "Like"

  ▶ The second entry will have an input code of 02 and description of "Comment"

5. Leave the remaining options as is, and your completed screen should look similar to what's shown in Figure 3.32.

6. Once complete, press the green checkmark button to return to the overview screen and move on to the next field.

7. To define the last field, click on the EDIT button on the third row in the table fields table to go to the FIELD DETAILS screen. The last field will provide the details of the comment. Enter the following settings:

  ▶ Set the FIELD LABEL as "Comment Details"

  ▶ Set the FIELD TYPE as "Text"

  ▶ Set the FIELD LENGTH to 60

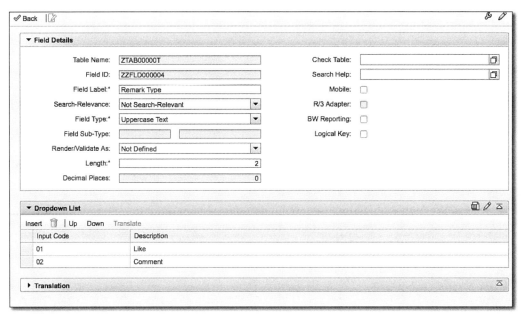

Figure 3.32 Define Field Remark Type

8. Leave the remaining options as is; your completed screen should look similar to what's shown in Figure 3.33.

9. Once complete, press the green checkmark button to return to the overview screen and move on to the next field.

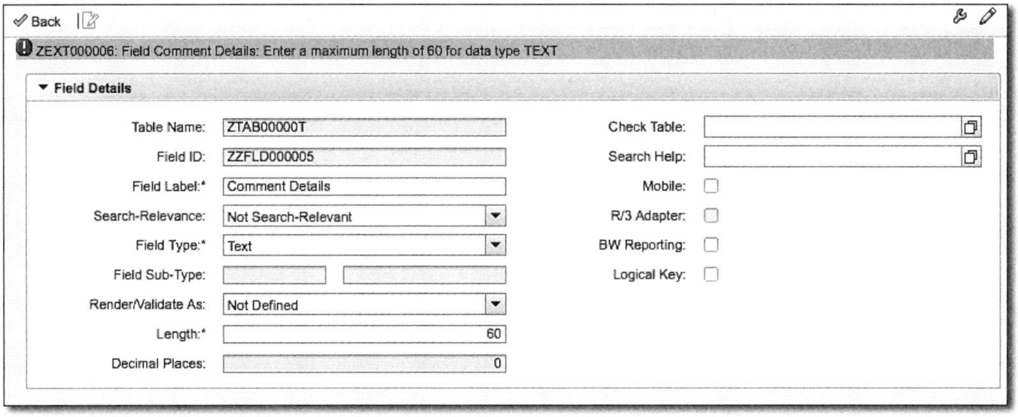

Figure 3.33 Define Field Comments Details

Complete
generation

10. Now that you've defined all the fields for the table, click the green checkmark button to the list on the EXTENSION OVERVIEW screen. The completed table definition will appear similar to what's shown in Figure 3.34.

11. Press the SAVE AND GENERATE button. The system will now create our new table and insert screens for editing the table in the UI component that we defined in Transaction AXTSYS. Once the generation is complete, there should be a green button icon in the STATUS icon for our table extension on the overview screen for the enhancements of the INTERACTION_LOG object.

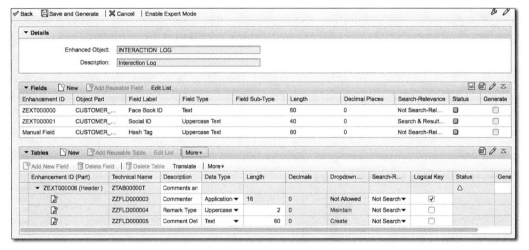

Figure 3.34 Extension Overview Before Save

Display new table
in the report

Even though generation is complete, you still need to display the new table on the screen of our social call report.

1. Click the green checkmark arrow to go back to the CONFIGURATION OVERVIEW screen for the INTERACTION LOG overview page. Recall that we used this screen to start the process of creating the new table. The view for the new table should now appear listed under the table labelled AVAILABLE ASSIGNMENT BLOCKS in the bottom left-hand portion of the VIEW CONFIGURATION screen as shown in Figure 3.35.

2. Select this row and press the right arrow in the middle of the screen to input the displayed assignment blocks section as show in Figure 3.36.

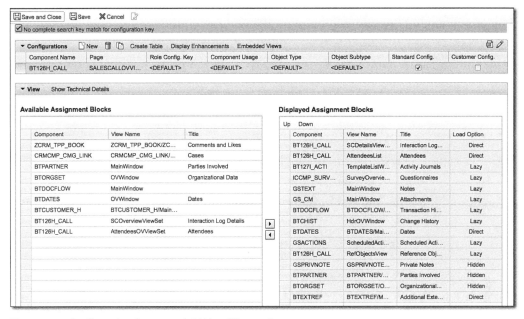

Figure 3.35 Configuration Screen to Add New View to Screen

Displayed Assignment Blocks			
Up Down			
Component	View Name ▲	Title	Load Option
BT126H_CALL	SCDetailsView...	Interaction Log...	Direct
ZCRM_TPP_B...	ZCRM_TPP_B...	Comments and Lik	Direct ▼
BT126H_CALL	AttendeesList	Attendees	Direct
BT127I_ACTI	TemplateListW...	Activity Journals	Lazy
ICCMP_SURV...	SurveyOvervie...	Questionnaires	Lazy
GSTEXT	MainWindow	Notes	Lazy

Figure 3.36 Assignment of New Table to Screen

3. Once this is done, press the SAVE AND CLOSE button to go back to the CREATE OVERVIEW screen of our social call report.

Results
You will now have a new assignment block labeled COMMENTS AND LIKE that appears on the OVERVIEW screen of the social call report, which should look similar to Figure 3.37.

135

Social Call Report: New
Back
Save and Back
Save
Cancel
New
More
(3)
Comments and Likes
Edit List
Insert
Actions
Commenter
Commenter (Link)
Remark Type
Comment Details

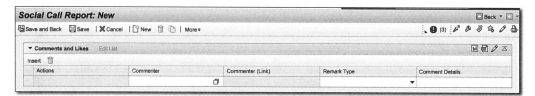

Figure 3.37 Comments and Like Table Default End-User View

We have successfully created a table extension to our existing business transaction data without the need to write any code or use the ABAP Data Dictionary. If we were to look into the Data Dictionary, we would find that our table that was generated there with the name ZTAB00000T and appear similar to what's shown in Figure 3.38.

Tips & Tricks

This generated name will vary by system. If you're in the expert mode of the AET when you created a table, you can generate your own name.

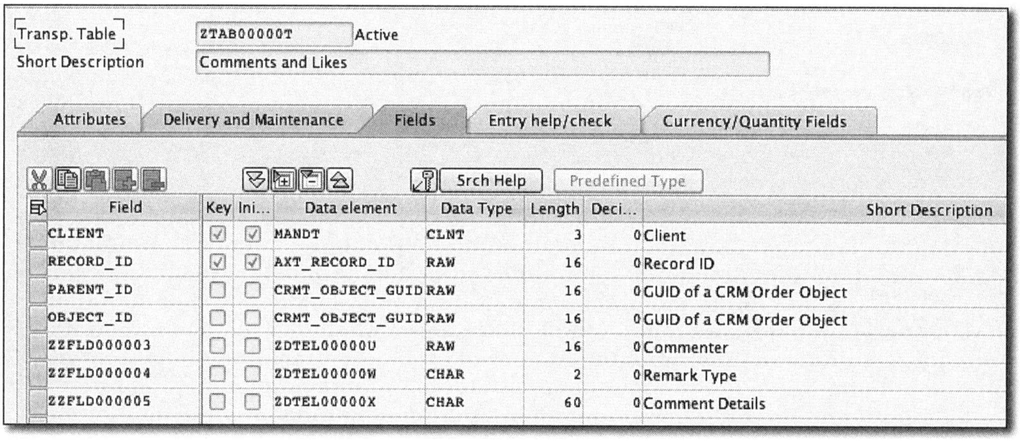

Transp. Table
ZTAB00000T
Active
Short Description
Comments and Likes
Attributes
Delivery and Maintenance
Fields
Entry help/check
Currency/Quantity Fields
Srch Help
Predefined Type
Field
Key
Ini...
Data element
Data Type
Length
Deci...
Short Description
CLIENT
MANDT
CLNT
3
0
Client
RECORD_ID
AXT_RECORD_ID
RAW
16
0
Record ID
PARENT_ID
CRMT_OBJECT_GUID
RAW
16
0
GUID of a CRM Order Object
OBJECT_ID
CRMT_OBJECT_GUID
RAW
16
0
GUID of a CRM Order Object
ZZFLD000003
ZDTEL00000U
RAW
16
0
Commenter
ZZFLD000004
ZDTEL00000W
CHAR
2
0
Remark Type
ZZFLD000005
ZDTEL00000X
CHAR
60
0
Comment Details

Figure 3.38 Generated Table ZTAB00000T

In addition to the generated table, the system will also generate two function groups—ZCRM_ZOBJ000000_EC and ZFUGR00000—which were automatically named that manage the updates of the table into the database.

3.2.4 Conclusion

As we've discussed, the AET offers much more flexibility than the EEWB in generating new fields in SAP CRM and is easier to use. The AET is also better able to recognize existing enhancements without destroying those existing enhancements. Although the AET should be your primary tool of choice for enhancements on SAP CRM 7.0 and above, there are still two areas of enhancement that require different tools. Marketing attributes and product attributes require you to use different tool sets, as we'll describe in the next section.

3.3 Manual Enhancements: Don't Try This at Home

You may be wondering if any of the enhancements to the data model can be performed manually. The answer is that business transactions and business partners can be enhanced manually, while the product master and marketing attributes are next to impossible to create manually.

With the delivery of the AET, there is no reason not to use the AET to extend the business partner and the business transaction data types. However, when the EEWB was the only available tool for enhancements, there were issues in adding more enhancements after one enhancement to a business transaction or business partner was created. To resolve these issues, a common tactic is to insert additional fields in the customer include of the respective tables that is also used by the EEWB to add new field enhancements. The drawback is that not all of the enhancement areas are covered.

Manual enhancements for business transactions and business partners

In general, we no longer recommend that you manually enhance the data model of the SAP CRM system through the ABAP Data Dictionary and ABAP Workbench coding alone. For an example of why this should not be done, consider that a manual enhancement of the SAP CRM business partner could take about one week to build without the use of the AET. If you use the AET, that same enhancement could take at most 15

Transaction AXTREG

minutes to create. If you're interested in seeing the objects built by the AET, however, you can look at Transaction AXTREG, which shows the structure of what is built when part of the system is enhanced.

3.4 Marketing Attributes

Group organization

One of the most interesting challenges a business faces is how to organize the customer base into similar groups to effectively market and sell to those customers with similar sets of attributes. To solve this problem, you need to find a way to identify certain common attributes of your customers. The problem with having a common set of attributes is that no two companies may want to group their customers in the same fashion. *Marketing attributes* in SAP CRM resolve this problem by providing a framework to create specific attributes for customers that don't necessarily have to be assigned to all customers. In this section, we'll look at how to create new marketing attributes.

3.4.1 Creating New Marketing Attribute Sets

Common marketing attributes

Marketing attributes originally were maintained through SAP GUI transactions in SAP CRM. With the introduction of the Web Client, you can maintain those via the Web Client interface.

1. To get started, open up the search screen for marketing attribute sets in the MARKETINGPRO business role in SAP CRM.

Create the attribute set

2. In this search screen, click on the NEW button as shown in Figure 3.39 to create a new attribute set. All marketing attributes are grouped together in SAP CRM in logical sets. The marketing attributes as discussed earlier sit on top of the classification system, which is why you don't maintain attributes individually.

3. Provide an ID and description for your attribute set as shown in Figure 3.40. Indicate whether this attribute set should be automatically assigned to new business partners and the type of business partner that the attributes are valid for. In this case, choose PERSONS, ORGANIZATIONS, or MARKETING PROSPECT.

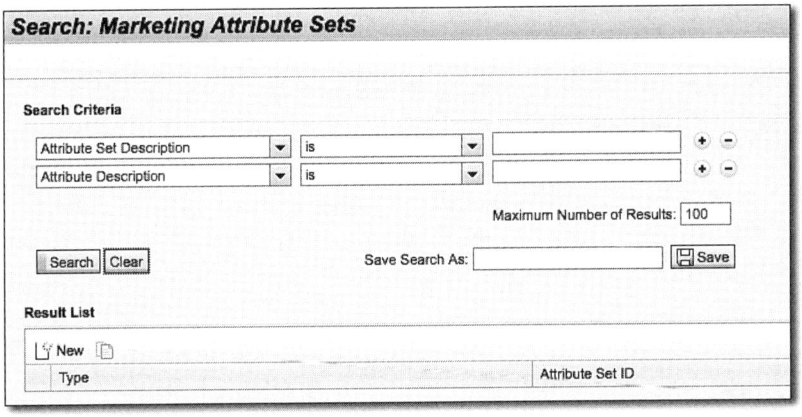

Figure 3.39 Search for Marketing Attribute Sets

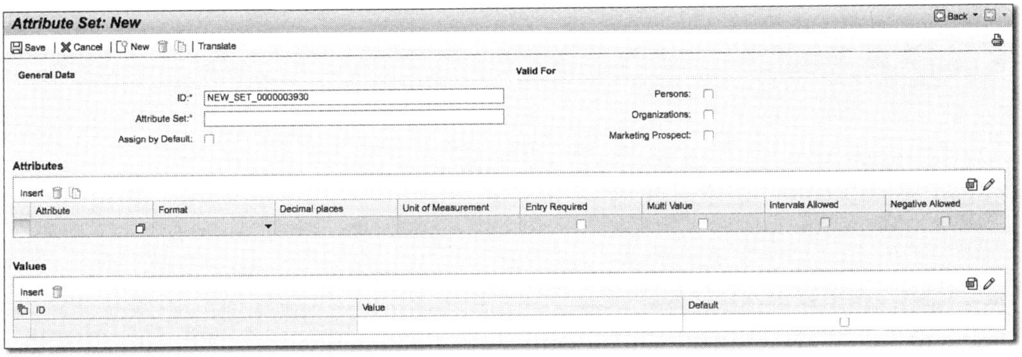

Figure 3.40 Create a New Marketing Attribute Set

3.4.2 Create a New Attribute or Choose an Existing Attribute

After you've made your choices, you can start creating new attributes or pick an existing attribute to add to your set. For this example, you'll create a new attribute by following these steps:

1. Click on the INSERT button on the toolbar in the table labeled ATTRIBUTES on the screen. This will create a blank line for you to enter your information.

New attribute steps

2. In the ATTRIBUTE column, enter "FACEBOOKUSER".

3. Under the FORMAT column, choose CHARACTER FORMAT from the dropdown list of values for that column.

4. For the remaining columns—DECIMAL PLACES, UNIT OF MEASURE-MENT, ENTRY REQUIRED, MULTI VALUE, INTERVALS ALLOWED, and NEGATIVE ALLOWED—don't make any entries.

5. Specify possible values for your attribute and pick a default value. The possible values can be defined by clicking on the INSERT button in the table labeled VALUES. This creates a new line. For your first value, enter "Y" as the value under the ID column, and enter "Yes" as the value under VALUE. Don't select the DEFAULT checkbox for this entry.

6. Click the INSERT button, and another blank line appears. For this row, enter "N" as the value under the ID column, and enter "No" as the value under VALUE. For this row, check the DEFAULT checkbox.

7. Save your work by clicking the SAVE button as shown in Figure 3.41.

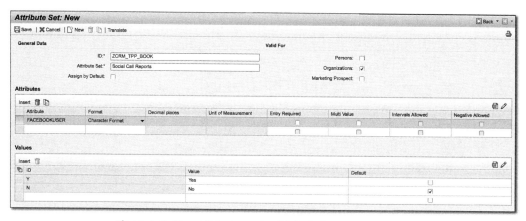

Figure 3.41 New Attribute on the Attribute Set

8. To add more than one attribute to your set, click on the INSERT button on the ATTRIBUTES table. A new blank row is created.

9. For this entry, enter "TWITTERUSER" as the ATTRIBUTE ID, and choose CHARACTER FORMAT from the dropdown list in the FORMAT column. Don't maintain the remaining columns.

10. Add the possible values in the same fashion that you added them for the FACEBOOKUSER attribute. After your second attribute is added, the set should look similar to the entries show in Figure 3.42.

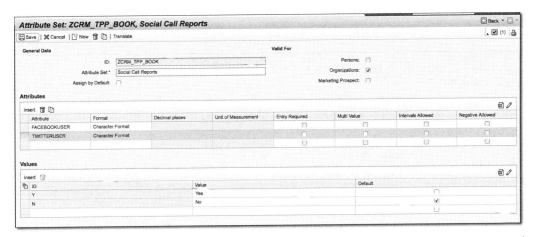

Figure 3.42 Additional New Attribute on the Attribute Set

The attribute set is now available to use in your business partner.

Assign an attribute to a business partner

1. Pull up a business partner of type organization, scroll down to the MARKETING ATTRIBUTES assignment block, and click EDIT to choose an attribute set to assign to your business partner.

2. In this case, choose the social media call report, and immediately the two attributes associated with your attribute set appear as shown in Figure 3.43.

3. Either accept the default values or click SAVE.

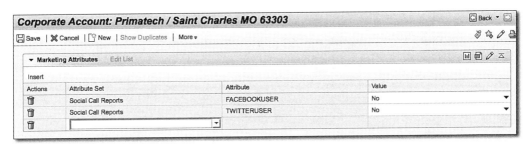

Figure 3.43 Assignment of Attributes to the Account

A great benefit of attribute sets is that you can add additional attributes to a set even if they are already assigned to a business partner. To add an additional attribute, edit the existing set by following these steps:

Edit an existing attribute set

1. Search for your existing set by going to the SEARCH screen for marketing attributes in the Web Client.

2. On the SEARCH screen, use the attribute set ID "ZCRM_TPP_BOOK" as your search criteria.

3. Click on the name of the attribute set in your search results. This will bring up the attribute set definition in edit mode. You now can add a new attribute to this set.

4. Click on the INSERT button on the toolbar under the ATTRIBUTES section to create a new line for you to enter your new attribute. Enter "SHARESWITH" in the ATTRIBUTE column. Choose CHARACTER FORMAT under the FORMAT column for your row.

5. For the last setting on this entry, click the ENTRY REQUIRED and MULTI VALUE checkboxes. Your entry now should look as shown in Figure 3.44.

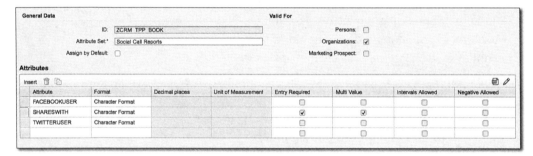

Figure 3.44 Multiple Value Attributes

6. Now that you've defined the attribute, you need to define the list of possible values. For this example, you'll do this manually. You'll follow the same procedure of adding values that was used for the other attributes, but you'll use the values listed in Table 3.1 for your entries.

ID	Value
01	FRIENDS
02	FAMILY
03	CO-WORKERS

Table 3.1 Possible Values for the SHARESWITH Attribute

ID	Value
04	STRANGERS
05	OLD ROOMMATES

Table 3.1 Possible Values for the SHARESWITH Attribute (Cont.)

7. After you've entered all of the values, they should appear as shown in Figure 3.45. Save your attribute set.

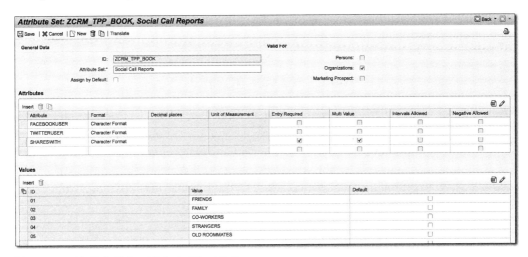

Figure 3.45 Multiple Value Attribute Direct Entry

8. Now go back into the MARKETING ATTRIBUTES assignment block on the business partner overview screen to see that multiple entries are possible for a single attribute as shown in Figure 3.46. The benefit of this is that you can assign multiple values without having to create additional attributes or use a table type structure to handle the multiple associations to a single a business partner.

Actions	Attribute Set	Attribute	Value
🗑	Social Call Reports	FACEBOOKUSER	No
🗑	Social Call Reports	SHARESWITH	FAMILY
🗑	Social Call Reports	SHARESWITH	OLD ROOMMATES
🗑	Social Call Reports	TWITTERUSER	Yes

Figure 3.46 Multiple Value Maintenance on an Account

Web Client: search
for attribute via
business partner One last great benefit of marketing attributes is that they are automatically included in the business partner search. If you bring up the search in the Web Client and choose SEARCH BY MARKETING ATTRIBUTE, you can search on any of the new attributes chosen.

Marketing attributes are a powerful yet easy way to track additional data on your business partners and provide a foundation for segmentation. The tools are aimed at business users; however, we strongly recommend that the creation of attributes should be part of an overall data model maintenance process for your enterprise instead of being kept in your marketing department.

3.5   Product Master Attribute Sets

In many situations, you might need additional attributes added to the product master in SAP CRM. A common example is the need for specific product attributes that can be used for product catalogs, or additional fields that might impact pricing. SAP has provided a different method for adding additional fields to the product master through the use of attributes and attribute sets for products. If you recall in the previous chapter, a product technically has no attributes until assigned to a category that has attribute sets associated with that category. SAP provides standard attribute sets, which are then associated to a product when the corresponding category is assigned. This general concept also works for customer-defined attributes.

Customer-defined
attributes
In SAP CRM, the customer-defined attributes are maintained via Transaction COMM_ATTRSET. This extension technique predates the EEWB and was available as early as release 2.0C, unlike the EEWB, which wasn't available until release 4.0. In the first screen of the transaction, you can maintain two options: attributes and set types. Attributes correspond to individual fields that describe a particular characteristic of a product. A set type is a logical grouping of attributes.

3.5.1   Create a New Attribute for a Product

Let's walk through the steps needed to create a new attribute for your product:

1. Open Transaction COMM_ATTR_SET as shown in Figure 3.47.

2. On the initial screen, select ATTRIBUTE, enter the name of the attribute, and click the CREATE button.

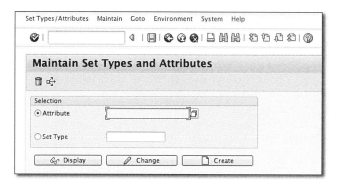

Figure 3.47 Maintain Set Types and Attributes

For this example, you'll create a new attribute called "ZZSTORAGE" as shown in Figure 3.48. This attribute allows you to specify how much storage your smartphone product contains inside of your SAP CRM system.

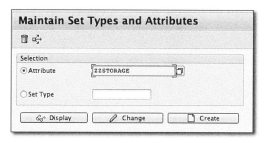

Figure 3.48 Create New Attribute ZZSTORAGE

3. After you click CREATE, a screen appears that prompts you to enter the details of the new attribute as shown in Figure 3.49. Enter a description, attribute type, and length.

4. You can then either allow the field to be free text or specify a list of possible values as shown in Figure 3.50. For this example, specify a list of possible values. You can pull this information either by specifying a value table or by directly entering a list on this transaction.

5. After you're finished, save your work.

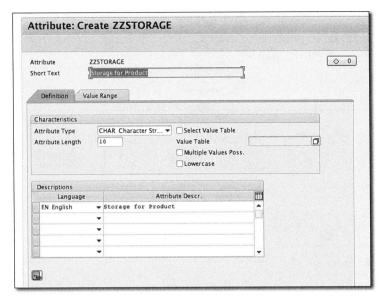

Figure 3.49 Details for Creating New Attribute ZZSTORAGE

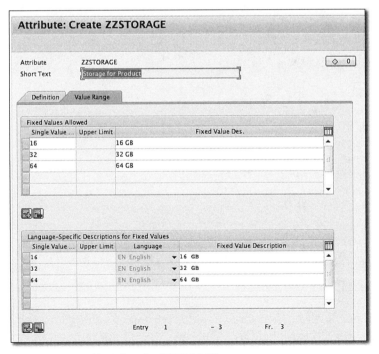

Figure 3.50 Possible Values for ZZSTORAGE

3.5.2   Create a New Set Type

Next, you need to create a new set type. As you recall from Chapter 2,   Set type
the data model for the master consists of a series of attribute sets delivered by SAP, and you can add additional attribute sets through this technique.

1. Go once again to the initial screen of Transaction COMM_ATTR_SET.

2. Choose SET TYPE, enter the name of your new set type, and click CRE-
   ATE as shown in Figure 3.51. For this example, call the attribute set
   "ZSMARTPHONE".

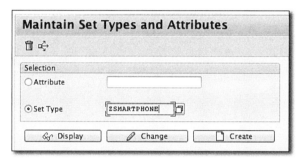

Figure 3.51 Create the New Set Type ZSMARTPHONE

3. A screen appears asking you to define the details of your set type as
   shown in Figure 3.52. Enter a description and the product type. Specify whether the attributes are at a particular org level or at a general
   product level.

4. Specify the list of attributes that should exist in your set type. In this
   step, you'll use the attribute that you previously created to be
   included in your set type as shown in Figure 3.53.

5. Click SAVE, and now your set type is ready to use.

As we discussed in Chapter 2, the attribute set now needs to be assigned
to a product category, and that category needs to be assigned to a product before the attribute can be maintained on the product.

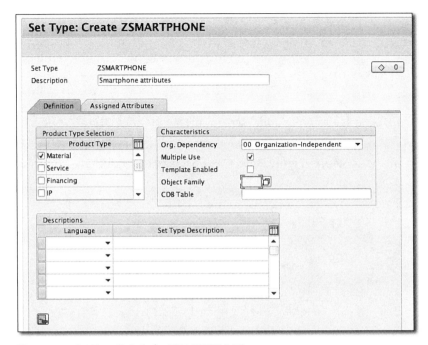

Figure 3.52 Set Type Details for ZSMARTPHONE

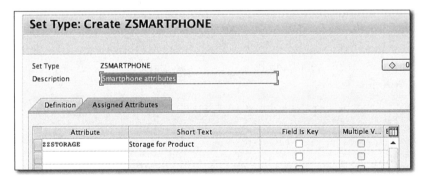

Figure 3.53 Assigned Attributes for the ZSMARTPHONE Set

Generate the
Web Client
configuration
To see your set type on the Web Client screens, you must run two transactions that will generate the Web Client configuration.

1. First, use Transaction CRMM_UIU_PROD_GEN to insert the new attribute set into the overview page of the transaction. When you first run the transaction, you'll see a screen as shown in Figure 3.54. On

this screen, specify the name of the new attribute set you created. Provide the enhancement set for the Web Client that you're using, and pick the type of the product overview page on which this should appear. Your choices include the product overview, competitor product overview, or product object overview.

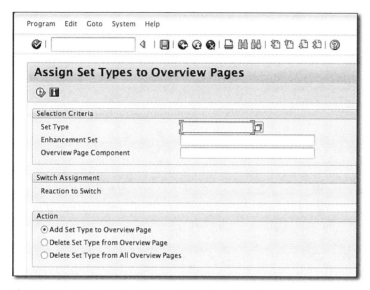

Figure 3.54 Generate the Set Type in the Overview Page

2. After you choose the values, click the EXECUTE button. This generates the entries in the *repository.xml* file of the component for your view of the attribute set. The generated entry is a component usage, which has a name that corresponds to the set type. The used component is the PRDGENSET, and the interface view is PRDGENSET/SLSetOVE.

3. The system then adds the view based on the component usage To list Views of views for the view area of the overview page. However, you still need to configure the UI for this new set type.

4. Use Transaction CRMM_UIU_PROD_CONFIG, which generates a view configuration for the new component usage of the generated component. This allows the fields in the set type to be displayed on the screen. You'll need to provide the name of the setup as input to this transaction as shown in Figure 3.55.

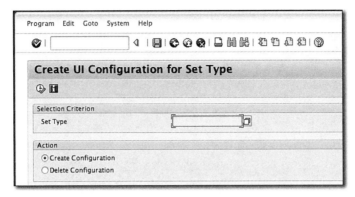

Figure 3.55 Generate UI Configuration for the Set Type

3.5.3 Assign the Set Type to a Product Category

After all of the technical configuration is finished, you must finally assign your set type to a product category. The normal approach is to create a new custom hierarchy and then a new category within that category. You then assign all products that need the new attributes to use that category.

Create a new product hierarchy — To begin, you'll create the new product hierarchy by going to the CREATE PRODUCT HIERARCHY link in the Web Client. This link can be found in the standard business role SERVICEPRO under the ACCOUNTS AND PRODUCTS work center. Follow these steps:

1. Choose the link PRODUCT HIERARCHY in the CREATE section of the work center. You'll then see the create hierarchy screen.

2. Enter a hierarchy ID; for our example, use "ZCRM_BOOK" and enter a description of "CRM Book Example".

3. Click the SAVE button. The resulting entry for the hierarchy details should be similar to Figure 3.56.

Figure 3.56 ZCRM_BOOK Product Hierarchy Details

Now that you've defined the header information of the hierarchy, you need to build the categories or structure of the hierarchy by following these steps:

Build structure

1. Go to the CATEGORIES assignment block of the hierarchy overview screen, and click on the EDIT HIERARCHY button. A blank line appears in the table grid in that block.

2. Enter "CRMBOOKDEMO" under the HIERARCHY STRUCTURE column, and enter "CRMBOOKDEMO" as the CATEGORY. For the PRODUCT TYPE column, choose MATERIAL, and leave the OBJECT FAMILY TYPE blank.

3. Click SAVE. Your entry under the CATEGORIES section should look similar to Figure 3.57.

Figure 3.57 Category CRMBOOKDEMO in the ZCRM_BOOK Hierarchy

4. Select the CRMBOOKDEMO entry under the CATEGORIES table to bring up the assigned set types for your category. This is the section where the product attribute set that you created is assigned to your product category.

5. Click the EDIT LIST button, and a blank row appears. Enter "ZSMART-PHONE" under the SET TYPE ID column, and click Enter. The system validates your entry and brings back the description of your set type.

6. After this validation is done, click SAVE to save your work. The screen should now look similar to Figure 3.58, which shows that the ZSMARTPHONE attribute set is assigned to the category CRMBOOK-DEMO of the product hierarchy ZCRM_BOOK.

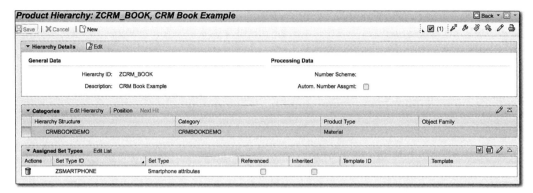

Figure 3.58 Set Type ZSMARTSHONE Assignment to the CRMBOOKDEMO Category

Assign a category to a product

Now that the hierarchy has been created and a category assigned, you can assign this category to a product to allow the new attribute in your product attribute set ZSMARTPHONE to be maintained for an existing product. Follow these steps:

1. Go back to the Web Client, and search for an existing product.

2. After you bring up the details of an existing product, go the CATEGO-RIES assignment block of the product overview page, and click on the EDIT LIST button. This will bring up a list with an empty row as shown in Figure 3.59.

Figure 3.59 Maintain Categories for a Product

3. Because you know the name of your category, enter "CRMBOOK-DEMO" in the CATEGORY ID column, and then click SAVE. The CATE-GORIES assignment block should now show the list of categories as seen in Figure 3.60.

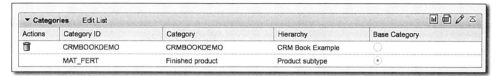

Figure 3.60 CRMBOOKDEMO Category Assigned to a Product

4. Due to the dynamic nature of product attribute assignment in SAP CRM, your product overview screen will now automatically include an assignment block for the ZSMARTPHONE attribute as shown in Figure 3.61.

Figure 3.61 ZSMARTPHONE Attribute Maintenance Screen

5. Pick a possible value for STORAGE FOR PRODUCT by clicking on the SEARCH HELP button. A popup window appears that shows the values you defined earlier in this chapter. Choose the 64 GB option if desired to be maintained on your product as shown in Figure 3.62.

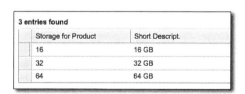

Figure 3.62 Popup Choices for Product Storage for the ZZSTORAGE Attribute

153

3.6   Summary

SAP provides very powerful but easy-to-use tools to extend the data model of SAP CRM. The earlier version of the tool called the EEWB was replaced with the newer version known as the AET. The AET can be used to extend business transaction and business partner data.

If you need to extend the product master or create marketing attributes, you must use specific tools for those extensions. We no longer recommend creating extensions manually in the newer versions of SAP CRM because the delivered tools reduce tasks that used to take a week into a 15-minute exercise. These data model extension tools allow you to meet almost all business requirements and allow for an efficient implementation of the SAP CRM system.

In the next chapter, we'll take a look at how the business transaction event framework (BTE framework) can be used to extend the logic in the business transaction.

The processing of a business transaction can be modeled as a series of events. The business transaction event framework allows you to manage the processing of those events.

4 Business Transaction Event Framework

The business transaction event framework (BTE framework) is a powerful mechanism used by SAP to further separate the BusinessObject-specific logic from the rest of the general business transaction logic in the SAP CRM system. This framework is embedded into the processing logic of every business transaction that will be created in your SAP CRM system. It allows for the dynamic execution of business logic based on the type of business transaction, segment of data in the business transaction, and activity performed. This framework allows SAP to separate specific business process logic from the general business transaction logic. The logic is executed through a series of function module calls, which are defined through customizing tables maintained in Transaction CRMV_ EVENT. This framework is useful when the standard delivered BADIs for the business transaction are not executed at the proper time required for a business requirement.

Dynamic execution of business logic

The standard SAP CRM system contains several event function modules that are considered part of the standard logic of the SAP CRM system. These event function modules can be executed at various times throughout the lifecycle of the business transaction.

The BTE framework is quite flexible and allows you to meet most, if not all, of the most complex business logic requirements in SAP CRM.

In this chapter, we'll examine the concept in further detail, look at standard delivered events within the system, examine how to trace the call of these events, and discuss how to build your own event handler function module. After learning how the BTE framework functions, you'll be able to extend the BTE framework to handle the most complex of business requirements.

4.1 Introduction to the Business Transaction Event Framework

One order framework

As you learned in Chapter 2, business transactions in SAP CRM are based on a one order framework. In designing the SAP CRM system, there is a unique problem of how to provide users with different application logic for a single data model that incorporates many disparate business processes within the one order framework. To solve this issue and prevent the need to duplicate code in several places, SAP introduced the concept of the *business transaction event framework* (*BTE framework*) inside of the one order framework. The BTE framework allows for the processing of logic based on logical events within the lifecycle of the business transaction. Data segments of the business transaction are known as *objects* within the framework. Objects can be used to further restrict the selection of logic to be processed.

A primary benefit of creating this framework is that you no longer have to code all of the logic for all business object types in the general framework of the business transaction. This means you can further separate SAP BusinessObject-specific application logic from the remainder of the business transaction processing logic. Additionally, this provides a side effect of a highly flexible user-exit style framework that allows you to insert your specific business logic into the SAP CRM system when the delivered BAdIs for the business won't meet your requirements.

The BTE framework acts like a plumbing system that manipulates and moves data within the business transaction for all business scenarios that require the maintenance of a business transaction. Like a plumbing system, in which your understanding of how joints, valves, and fixtures are attached can be transferred to different settings such as kitchens and bathrooms, you can do the same with your understanding of business transactions. A change of partner within one type of transaction will retain logic similar to the change of partner within a different type of business transaction. You need to understand that one order isn't simply just a data model, but rather a unified business logic framework. By learning how the BTE framework is set up and used in SAP CRM, you understand how to run the "engine" in the business transactions.

4.2 The Three Main Components of the Business Transaction Event Framework

The BTE framework consists of three main components: customizing data, framework code, and event handler function modules.

▶ *Customizing data* defines the logic of execution and what will be executed at certain points in processing.

▶ *Framework code* refers to the function modules that are part of the standard one order function module calls that publish and process the BTE logic.

▶ *Event handler function modules* contain the specific business logic for a given business object type.

We'll discuss each main component in more detail in the following sections.

4.2.1 Customizing Data

The heart of the BTE framework is a series of customizing tables that define what events will be raised, what logic can be invoked, and when that logic can be invoked. The Customizing for the BTE framework can be accessed through Transaction CRMV_EVENT, as shown in Figure 4.1. For most SAP customers, the customizing data in Transaction CRMV_EVENT will serve as a reference, as SAP has provided a customer-specific customizing area that is accessed through a separate menu path in the IMG.

Transaction
CRMV_EVENT

In the startup of Transaction CRMV_EVENT, you can see that many different options are available. The ASSIGNMENT block of the screen deals with the assignment of event handlers for a given event. The DEFINITIONS block contains options to view the various aspects of the framework. In the CHECKS block, there is an option to run checks to see what event handlers will be triggered—either a transaction type or combination of a transaction type and item category. Most options are used to maintain the data that defines the framework customizing.

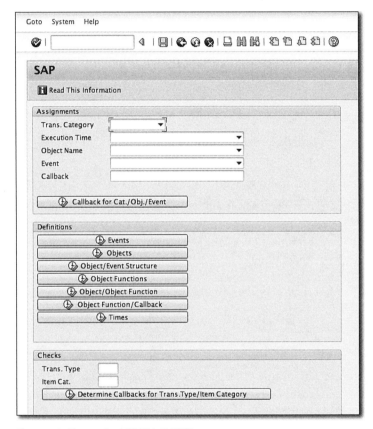

Figure 4.1 Transaction CRMV_EVENT

Transaction lifecycle definition

As you may recall from Chapter 2, a business transaction within SAP CRM consists of a series of logical segments. The creation, change, and deletion of the data within segments of the business transaction may not always occur in the same physical sequence. The reason for this is that an SAP CRM user doesn't always update all of the data on a business transaction in the same logical sequence due to differences between business object types or business processes. Because you can't predict when certain updates may occur during the creation, update, and/or deletion of a business transaction, you need a mechanism that allows you to execute certain logic when the transaction reaches a certain point or "event" within processing. This sequence is also known as the "lifecycle" of the business transaction, which describes the activities performed throughout the existence of a business transaction from creation to deletion.

To better understand the lifecycle of a business transaction, let's look at an example of how to create an activity and how even something as simple as an activity can be updated in a different sequence.

Example: activity creation

As you may remember, an *activity* in SAP CRM is the recording of a significant interaction between a company and its customers and/or prospects. When you first create an activity in SAP CRM, the system automatically creates the ORDERADM_H segment in memory. This segment contains information about the transaction type, including the GUID of the transaction and the transaction object ID. This creation occurs when the user clicks NEW in the Web Client.

Normally, the next step for your user includes entering text in the required fields, which are typically a description and the related activity partner. The description actually resides in segment ORDERADM_H, which means that you'll be making a "change" to ORDERADM_H. In addition, when the activity partner was added, this "created" the PARTNER segment of the business transaction.

After the end user has entered the header data of the business transaction, he can continue adding data and editing the business transaction. In one scenario, the user may decide to first add in additional notes to the business transaction. This action creates the TEXT segment of the business transaction. The user then decides to add some additional attendees to the activity, such as a meeting. This creates additional PARTNER entries for the attendee partner function. However, it's just as possible that the user will decide to first add the attendees to the activity and then update the notes.

As you can see, there are no guarantees of the order in which the user will update the data in a business transaction except that the user always creates the header of the business transaction first. This then poses a problem if you need business logic based on when data is updated within a business transaction. To solve this issue, the BTE framework allows you to logically track how the business transaction is being updated without worrying about the physical timing sequence of the business transaction.

The BTE lifecycle has been split up into three areas that are defined by the customizing tables as structured in the CRMV_EVENT main screen, shown previously in Figure 4.1. The first area focuses on the timing, the second area focuses on the data being acted upon, and the last area focuses on what should be executed. The EVENTS and TIMES sections are used to define the timing of the lifecycle. EVENTS define what actions could occur during the lifecycle, and TIMES are the possible execution times for business logic during the lifecycle. The OBJECTS, OBJECT FUNCTIONS, and OBJECT/OBJECT FUNCTION sections describe the parts of the business transaction. Finally, the OBJECT FUNCTION/CALLBACK and CALLBACK FOR CAT./OBJ./EVENT describe what logic can be executed in the form of a function module.

The customizing tables for the framework are grouped into the following sections: EVENTS, OBJECTS, OBJECT/EVENT STRUCTURE, OBJECT FUNCTIONS, OBJECT FUNCTION/CALLBACK, TIMES, and CALLBACK FOR CAT./OBJ./EVENT. The primary section is the CALLBACK FOR CAT./OBJ./EVENT. This is a customizing table that contains a listing of function modules, also known as event handlers, that will be executed at a particular point in the lifecycle of processing a business transaction in SAP CRM.

Events

Events are predefined points in time in the business transaction that describes a particular activity. This activity could be classified as initialize, check, change, delete, save, or general. Some examples of events include INIT, BEFORE_CHANGE, AFTER_CHANGE, AFTER_DELETE, SAVE, and CONFIRM, as shown in Figure 4.2.

Each object defined may cause these events to be triggered. The INIT event normally occurs when the OBJECT is first created within the business transaction. This first creation doesn't mean creation on the database but rather the first logical creation during the business transaction lifecycle. The BEFORE_CHANGE and AFTER_CHANGE events typically correspond to point in times that occur when an object is changed. The events for the business transaction are defined in Table CRMC_EVENTS and maintained in the CRMV_EVENTS view. Each event is defined by a technical name and the category of the event.

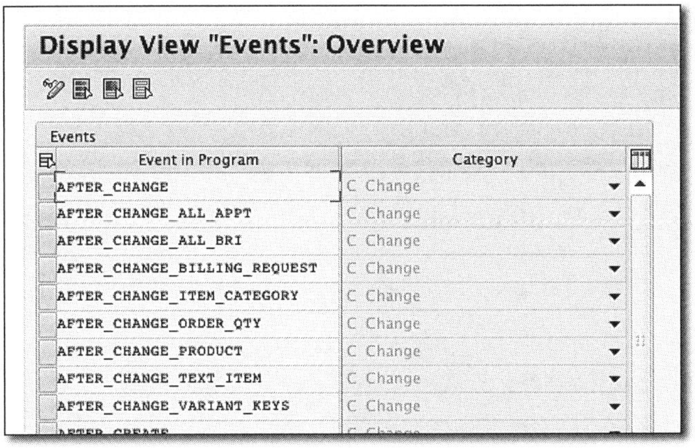

Figure 4.2 Event Definition Table for Business Transaction Event Framework

If you look once again at your SAP CRM activity, you can see how the events work. Not all events are used or published for all segments of the business transaction because there may not be a logical need for those events. When you create an activity, the system automatically creates the ORDERADM_H segment in memory and then initializes all of the other segments.

How events work

As you enter data into those segments, they are then created during the maintenance. This might be something as simple as entering the priority on the activity document. Depending on whether this data was entered in the segment, this segment will change the type of events that may be entered. If the segment has not been entered before then, you could trigger an AFTER_CREATE event. However, if you changed the data, then you may receive the AFTER_CHANGE event.

The events correspond to the logical action that is being performed on the segment. Thus, if you enter the priority on the activity for the first time, you'll trigger the AFTER_CREATE event. However, if you change the priority on the activity, you could trigger the AFTER_CHANGE event. The difference between the events and the BAdI calls for the segment is that the BAdI is executed regardless of whether you change or create the data, while the events give you a precise timing of what just happened to the data within a segment of the business transaction.

Objects *Objects* in the BTE framework correspond to the logical data segments of the business transaction. If you look at Figure 4.3, you can see a few examples of the objects defined in the SAP CRM system for the BTE framework. These objects correspond 1:1 to the logical business transaction data model; however, there may be cases where there isn't a complete match between models. These objects are defined in the CRMV_OBJECTS view, which is a logical join on Table CRMC_OBJECTS and Table CRMC_OBJECTS_T. The entries for this view consist of two primary fields: the technical name of the object and the object description.

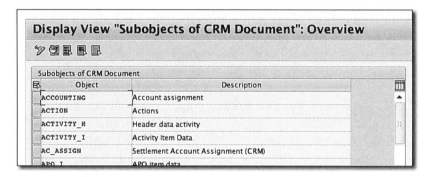

Figure 4.3 Objects of the Business Transaction Event Framework

Object Event/Structure

The object/event structure defines data structures that will be passed to an event function module when called. The assignment is made based on the combination of the object of the business transaction and event. This definition is stored in Table CRMC_EVENT_STRUC and maintained using the CRMV_EVENT_STRUC view, as shown in Figure 4.4. In this view, you specify the technical name of the object, the technical name of the event, and finally the name of the data structure that describes the data that will be passed to the event handler function module. This structure name should be a valid structure name that has been specified in the ABAP Data Dictionary using Transaction SE11.

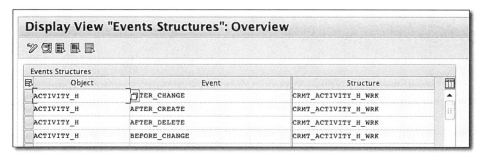

Figure 4.4 Object Event Structure

Object Functions

Object functions provide a logical grouping of event handlers to make it easier to determine what handlers are available for a given transaction type. These are stored in Table CRMC_OBJ_FUNC and maintained through the CRMV_OBJ_FUNC view. In Figure 4.5, you see a listing of object functions that can be found in your SAP CRM system.

Logical grouping of event handlers

Figure 4.5 Object Functions

Assigning an object function to an object, which is accessed through the OBJECT/OBJECT FUNCTION button on the initial screen of Transaction CRMV_EVENT, allows you to permit a more specific separation of event handlers for a given object type. This data is maintained using the CRMV_OBJECT_FUNC view. As shown in Figure 4.6, the ACTIVITY_H object is mapped to three different object functions, which makes it possible to create distinct event handlers mapped to each object function instead of the entire object.

Assign object function to object

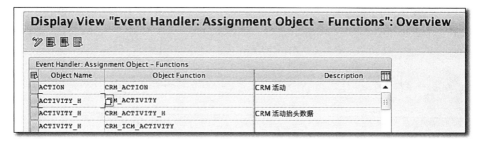

Figure 4.6 Object Function to Object Assignment

Execution Times

To access the Execution Times table, click the Times button in the initial screen of Transaction CRMV_EVENT shown earlier in Figure 4.1. Describe when the actual invocation of an event handler function module will occur. These are stored and maintained through the maintenance view CRMV_EVENT_EXTI. Figure 4.7 shows the execution times in the SAP CRM system that will be used for most business transactions.

Display View "Execution Times": Overview

Zeitp.	Ze...	P...	NoP...	Descript.
1	0	0	☑	Immediately
10	30	40	☐	End of Item Processing
30	30	60	☐	End of Header Processing
40	0	0	☑	End of Deletion
50	50	50	☐	End of Document Processing
70	70	50	☐	End of All Documents
78	0	0	☑	Before Saving
80	0	0	☑	Save Document
82	0	0	☑	Save Header
84	0	0	☑	Save Item
88	0	0	☑	Initialize Document
101	20	50	☐	END ACTIVITY_H

Figure 4.7 Execution Times

Logical times The description of all of the execution times is logically straightforward because the description is a definition of when the execution of the function module will occur. The END OF <OBJECT> time corresponds to the final part of processing a segment of the business object that corresponds to the <OBJECT> name specified in the time. Each segment has its own END OF <OBJECT> time.

As you can tell, these times are "logical" times, especially the END OF <OBJECT> time. As we discussed earlier, the exact physical sequence of the times may vary, so you shouldn't expect that they will be executed in a particular order for END OF <OBJECT>. This means that you shouldn't build or create any logic that assumes that end of a particular segment will be before the end of another segment. You can, however, be assured that certain times such as *initialize document* and *save document* should be executed at the start of document creation and near the save of the business transaction, respectively.

Race Summary versus Race Detail

In dealing with business transactions in SAP CRM, enhancements tend to focus on two key times: during the processing of the business transaction and during the consuming of the business transaction on the system. The amount of timing information for those enhancements is different. A great analogy is the difference between the summary of a race such as a half marathon made by someone watching it, and the detail of the race by the actual participant.

In a half-marathon race that covers a great distance, an observer can't actively track the participants unless they are running next to that participant or the participant has some type of real-time tracking. Instead, the observer waits at the observation point (which may be the finish line) to see the person complete that course. The type of information they receive is a total time for that participant. This information is useful because it's the key information that needs to be consumed and no further details are necessary.

On the other hand, the participant is interested during the course of that race on his actual progress and how far he has gone. The participant will typically pass by mile marker signs and, at key milestone intervals, will see a timer showing how much time has elapsed in the overall race. The runner may also have devices showing his pace and other key information that describes how the race is progressing.

All of this in-race data allows the participant to determine if he needs to make adjustments in how he is running. This race detail is similar to the type of information that the BTE framework is providing so that business logic can be executed at the right moment in time.

If you're only interested in the summary results of a business transaction (what was saved) to the database, then the information provided by the BTE

---

framework isn't necessary. Instead, the creation/change and deletion of a business transaction is much like a race where you need to know where you are along a given path to be able to execute the correct logic and complete the process at the proper finish.

Object Event/Handlers

CRMV_FUNC_ ASSIGN

The object function/event handler is defined through the maintenance view CRMV_FUNC_ASSIGN as shown in Figure 4.8. This table allows you to assign the individual event handler function modules that could occur at any possible event to a particular object function. The table structure consists of the function module name as the key and the corresponding object function. This means that a function module can only be used by one object function.

Display View "Assignment: Event Handler Modules for Object Function":

Assignment: Event Handler Modules for Object Function

Function Module	Object Function
CRM_ACTIVITY_H_COMPLETION_EC	CRM_ACTIVITY_H
CRM_ACTIVITY_H_COPY_EC	CRM_ACTIVITY_H
CRM_ACTIVITY_H_DELETE_CHECK_EC	CRM_ACTIVITY
CRM_ACTIVITY_H_DELETE_EC	CRM_ACTIVITY_H
CRM_ACTIVITY_H_INIT_EC	CRM_ACTIVITY_H
CRM_ACTIVITY_H_SAVE_EC	CRM_ACTIVITY_H
CRM_ACTIVITY_H_STATREASON_EC	CRM_ACTIVITY_H
CRM_ACTIVITY_H_STATUSTRANS_EC	CRM_ACTIVITY_H
CRM_ACTIVITY_H_STATUS_COPY_EC	CRM_ACTIVITY

Figure 4.8 Event Handlers per Object Function

One function module for one object function

In general, you should create new function modules for each object function even if the logic executed is similar. The primary reason for this is that each object function will use a different data structure when passing data to the event handler function module. Because each data segment of the business transaction has a unique update structure, it's a logical choice to only allow an event handler function module to be assigned to a single object. Allowing for multiple assignments goes against the ability to add logic for new segments without having to change code for existing segments when building new functionality in the SAP CRM system.

CRMV_EVC_ALL is the primary maintenance view that defines the actual business logic that will be invoked based on several attributes. The entries maintained through CRMV_EVC_ALL are the core of the BTE framework logic. Figure 4.9 shows a listing of entries in the CRMV_EVENT_CALL view for the ACTIVITY_H object. All of the previous tables that you've explored support the definition of entries in this table. An SAP CRM 7.0 system typically has around 4,000 or more entries in this table.

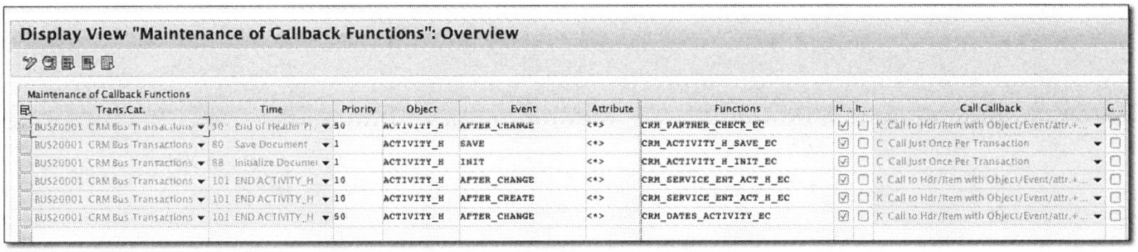

CRMV_EVC_ALL

Figure 4.9 CRMV_EVC_ALL Maintenance View

This view maintains entries in CRMC_EVENT_CALL. The fields in Table 4.1 determine what data is selected for use.

Field	Description
Trans.Cat.	The type of business transaction such as sales order, complaint, activity, service order, and so on.
Time	When to execute the event handler function module.
Priority	The order of execution of the event handler function modules when there is more than one for a given event. The lowest number entry is processed first.
Object	The data segment of the business transaction that is related to the event.
Event	The type of activity performed on an object within the business transaction.
Attribute	A value set by the event that distinguishes between different parts of an object being updated. Normally <*>, however, some objects such as PARTNER will provide a value.

Table 4.1 Description of Fields in CRMC_EVENT_CALL

Field	Description
FUNCTION	The name of an ABAP function module to be executed when the event is triggered.
HEADER	Whether the logic is executed for the header part of the document.
ITEM	Whether the logic is executed for the item part of the document.
CALL CALLBACK	The type of call of the function module along with the type of data being communicated to the function module.
DO NOT PROCESS	If there were errors, don't process this logic.

Table 4.1 Description of Fields in CRMC_EVENT_CALL (Cont.)

The possible entry fields TRANS.CAT., TIME, OBJECT, EVENT, and FUNCTION were defined in the previous customizing tables that you examined. For the CALLBACK field, you have five possible options:

Callback field options
▶ " " (blank): CALL TO HEADER/ITEM WITH OBJECT, EVENT, ATTR., OLD/NEW DATA
Use this value if your execution time is IMMEDIATELY.

▶ A: CALL TO HEADER/ITEM WITH OBJECT, EVENT, ATTR. W/OUT OLD/NEW DATA
Use this value if the event does not provide changed data or is not needed.

▶ B: CALL TO HEADER/ITEM W/OUT OBJECT, EVENT, ATTR., OLD/NEW DATA
Use this value if you do not need all of the data surrounding the event to perform your update. This is normally used by the AFTER_DELETE event.

▶ C: CALL JUST ONCE PER TRANSACTION
Use this value for events that should only be executed once during the lifecycle of the transaction. This is normally used for the AFTER_CREATE event of ORDERADM_H.

▶ K: CALL TO HDR/ITEM WITH OBJECT/EVENT/ATTR + COMPRESSED OLD/NEW
Use this value if you don't need any intermediate changes between data. However, it can't be used for the PARTNER segment.

The CRMV_EVC_ALL maintenance view is intended for use by SAP only. However, in earlier releases of SAP CRM, you were able to insert entries in this table to handle your requirements. In newer versions of SAP CRM, the CRMV_EVENT_CUST maintenance view for Table CRMC_EVENT_CUST allows customers to register their entries as needed. The table structure is identical to the CRMV_EVC_ALL view as illustrated in Figure 4.10.

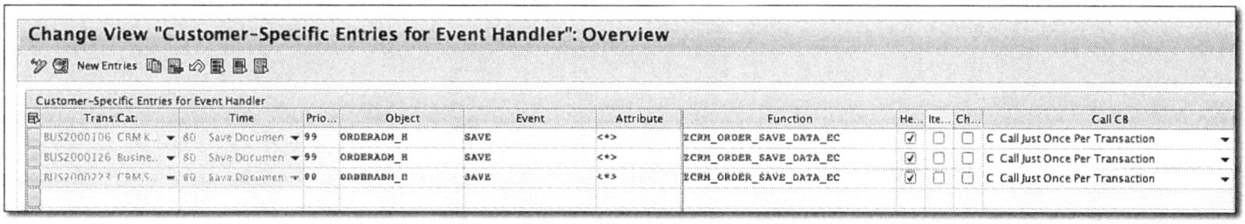

Figure 4.10 CRMV_EVENT_CUST Maintenance View

All entries in this table are included in the logic to determine what event handlers will be called. The only benefit is that SAP won't overwrite entries in this table during an upgrade. The entries in this table are added to the list of possible callback entries after the entries from CRMC_EVENT_CALL have been read.

Customer Customizing Tables

Customizing tables

Most SAP applications based on the SAP NetWeaver AS ABAP contain a concept of *customizing tables*. Customizing tables are essentially database tables that define a list of possible values or business logic rules in a system. SAP normally splits these tables into three major types: SAP customizing tables that are not to be changed by a customer, SAP customizing tables that can be changed by a customer, and customer-created customizing tables.

The term *customer* refers to the customer who licensed the software product from SAP and not your customers. This terminology can lead to confusion as the data segment CUSTOMER_H refers to "customer data fields," which isn't the same as the PARTNER segment. Normally, you assume that the "sold-to" party information about a business transaction in a CUSTOMER segment when in fact it's stored in the PARTNER segment. When looking at technical naming in SAP CRM, "CUSTOMER" always refers to your own customizations and not the customers that you are keeping track of in SAP CRM.

In the case of the customer event customizing tables, there is one missing customer-only table for the BTE framework. This table is the OBJECT FUNCTION/ CALLBACK table. In this case, we need to put the function module developed into this table before we can put it in the customer-specific event handler table. Usually, another table is delivered for this purpose; however, because a customer should never name its function modules within the SAP namespace, a collision during upgrades shouldn't occur.

Determine callbacks

If you look at the last part of the Transaction CRMV_EVENT screen shown earlier in Figure 4.1, there is a button labeled DETERMINE CALL-BACKS FOR TRANS. TYPE/ITEM CATEGORY. This button executes a report that allows you to receive a listing of all of the callbacks that will occur at either the header level for a particular transaction type or at the item level for a particular item category. If you click on the DETERMINE CALL-BACKS FOR TRANS. TYPE/ITEM CATEGORY button, a screen appears that allows you to enter only a transaction type or a valid combination of a transaction type and item category as shown in Figure 4.11.

After you've entered a valid transaction type into the field on the TRANS-ACTION TYPE screen, click the EXECUTE button to see a listing of the planned event handler function modules that will be executed for a given transaction type.

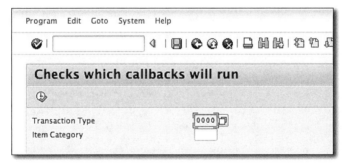

Figure 4.11 Check Report for Event Handlers to be Executed

The list provides several pieces of information regarding what will be executed as shown in Figure 4.12. The list is sorted by the OBJECT NAME and also contains the corresponding OBJECT FUNCTION, along with the EXECUTION TIME, PRIORITY, and CALL FREQUENCY of each event handler call. You'll also see which specific attributes will trigger the call.

Checks which callbacks will run

Function Module CRMV_EVENT

Trans. Category	Execution Time	Priority	Object Name	Event in Program	Attribute	Object Function	Callback Function	...	...	Current Date	User Name	...
BUS20001	88	1	ACTION	INIT	<*>	CRM_ACTION	CRM_ACTION_INIT_EC					C
BUS20001	80	1	ACTION	SAVE	<*>	CRM_ORDER	<DUMMY>					C
BUS20001	30	50	ACTIVITY_H	AFTER_CHANGE	<*>	CRM_PARTNER_CHECK	CRM_PARTNER_CHECK_EC					K
BUS20001	101	50	ACTIVITY_H	AFTER_CHANGE	<*>	CRM_APPOINTMENT	CRM_DATES_ACTIVITY_EC					K
BUS20001	88	1	ACTIVITY_H	INIT	<*>	CRM_ACTIVITY_H	CRM_ACTIVITY_H_INIT_EC					C
BUS20001	80	1	ACTIVITY_H	SAVE	<*>	CRM_ACTIVITY_H	CRM_ACTIVITY_H_SAVE_EC					C
BUS20001	50	50	APPOINTMENT	AFTER_CHANGE	CANCDATE	CRM_APPOINTMENT	CRM_DATES_CONTEND_SET_EC					
BUS20001	1	2	APPOINTMENT	AFTER_CHANGE	XBILLFREQ	CRM_APPOINTMENT	CRM_RECCURING_BILLFREQ_UPD_EC					
BUS20001	50	50	APPOINTMENT	AFTER_CREATE	CANCDATE	CRM_APPOINTMENT	CRM_DATES_CONTEND_SET_EC					
BUS20001	1	2	APPOINTMENT	AFTER_CREATE	XBILLFREQ	CRM_APPOINTMENT	CRM_RECCURING_BILLFREQ_UPD_EC					
BUS20001	88	1	APPOINTMENT	INIT	<*>	INIT	CRM_DATES_INIT_EC					C
BUS20001	80	1	APPOINTMENT	SAVE	<*>	CRM_APPOINTMENT	CRM_DATES_SAVE_EC					C
BUS20001	88	2	CUSTOMER_H	INIT	<*>	CRM_CUSTOMER_H	CRM_CUSTOMER_H_INIT_EC					C
BUS20001	80	1	CUSTOMER_H	SAVE	<*>	CRM_CUSTOMER_H	CRM_CUSTOMER_H_SAVE_EC					C
BUS20001	88	1	DOC_FLOW	INIT	<*>	CRM_DOC_FLOW	CRM_DOC_FLOW_INIT_EC					C
BUS20001	88	5	DOC_FLOW	INIT	<*>	CRM_DOC_FLOW	CRM_PNT_INIT_EC					C
BUS20001	80	99	DOC_FLOW	SAVE	<*>	CRM_DOC_FLOW	CRM_DOC_FLOW_SAVE_EC					C
BUS20001	88	1	EXT_REF	INIT	<*>	CRM_EXT_REF	CRM_EXT_REF_INIT_EC					C
BUS20001	80	1	EXT_REF	SAVE	<*>	CRM_EXT_REF	CRM_EXT_REF_SAVE_EC					C
BUS20001	88	1	LAWREF_H	INIT	<*>	CRM_LAWREF_H	CRM_LAWREF_H_INIT_EC					C
BUS20001	80	1	LAWREF_H	SAVE	<*>	CRM_LAWREF_H	CRM_LAWREF_H_SAVE_EC					C
BUS20001	80	1	MESSAGES	SAVE	<*>	CRM_ORDER	<DUMMY>					C

Figure 4.12 Results for the Check Report on Event Handlers

When we executed this for the 0000 transaction type, we received back an entry for CUSTOMER_H based on the BUS2001 business object, which is a general SAP CRM business transaction. This entry was executed during the initial document time frame, and the priority/sequence was "2". The event was INIT and was executed regardless of any attribute data because the attribute filter value was <*>. The object function was CRM_CUSTOMER_H, and it executed the CRM_CUSTOMER_H_INIT_EC event handle function module.

4.2.2 Framework Code

Now that you've examined the customizing data that defines the BTE framework, you also need to see how this framework is executed. The framework is embedded within the one order framework through a series of function module calls. Two specific function modules trigger most of the logic calls that comprise the BTE framework, which we'll discuss in the following subsections.

CRM_EVENT_PUBLISH_OW

The first function module—CRM_EVENT_PUBLISH_OW—publishes events to the framework. The publishing process passes several pieces of information to the global buffer table. This information includes the object

Publish events to BTE framework

name, header GUID, object kind, event name, attribute of the event, and new and old values of the object.

One example of this call is found in the function module CRM_ACTIVITY_H_PUBLISH_OW. This function module is called when the ACTIVITY_H data is changed. In this function module, the CRM_EVENT_PUBLISH_OW function module is called and passes the object name, header GUID, object kind, event name (AFTER_CREATE or AFTER_CHANGE), the old values of ACTIVITY_H, and the new values of ACTIVITY_H. This information is then provided to the event handler function module calls that execute the actual business logic for the event that was triggered.

A key aspect of this call is that the timing of the event trigger corresponds to the exact spot in the update cycle of the business transaction due to BTE framework code being "embedded" within the standard logic of the one order framework. One question that comes to mind is why not just implement a BAdI instead of publishing the event? The main reason for not implementing a BAdI is that the BAdI would need to be executed immediately instead of being delayed for later.

Import parameters If you examine the CRM_EVENT_PUBLISH_OW function module, you first notice that only four import parameters are required:

- IV_OBJ_NAME: Name of segment within the business transaction.
- IV_GUID_HI: GUID of the parent of the segment being changed.
- IV_KIND_HI: Type of parent object.
- IV_EVENT: Event that occurred.

This means technically you can raise an event without providing any data about that event. This could occur in the AFTER_CHANGE event for the TEXT segment as seen in the function module CRM_TEXT_MAINTAIN_OW. This, however, is generally the exception because if you examine the AFTER_CHANGE event for ACTIVITY_H, you notice that the following import parameters have been populated:

- IV_TABVAL_OLD: The values of the segment before the update or change.
- IV_TABVAL_NEW: The values of the segment after the update or change.

If you look at the events for the PARTNER segment, you find that the IV_ ATTRIL is also used. In this case, it communicates the partner function.

When the function module CRM_EVENT_PUBLISH_OW is called, it takes the data provided to publish the event. The event publishing process consists of two general steps: first to determine the correct buffer table to insert the published event, and second to execute any event handlers that should be processed immediately upon raise of the event. Those event handlers that don't need to be processed immediately will be executed when the framework is notified that time in the lifecycle has occurred.

The logic to determine what event handlers should be selected works in the following way for header-level event handlers:

Event handler selection logic

1. Determine whether the transaction is "new" and if so, then determine the process type.
2. Build a list of all available event handlers for the process type using the function module CRM_EVENT_FILTER_PROC_TYPE_OW.
3. If it's a *change type* event, publish the data to the save event.
4. If it's a *create* event, then publish the data to the create event buffer.
5. Determine whether the event handler needs to be executed now. If so, publish it to the immediate execution table; otherwise, move it to the appropriate planned execution buffer.

After the buffers have been filled, a subroutine called execute_ callbacks_at_once will process all the entries placed in the immediate execution buffer. The logic for this module is very simple as you loop through the immediate execution buffer and call each event handler function module with the data that was stored in the buffer.

CRM_EVENT_SET_EXETIME_OW

At this point, you've handled all immediate calls and published the data for calls to be processed later. The key for processing calls later is that the system must know when a certain time has been reached in the business transaction processing lifecycle. To achieve this, the function

Signal end of segment processing

173

module `CRM_EVENT_SET_EXETIME_OW` is used to signal the end of processing for a segment.

If you continue to examine the change of `ACTIVITY_H` data, you can find that the `END of ACTIVITY_H` processing occurs at the end of the `CRM_ACTIVITY_H_MAINTAIN_OW` function module. This signals that all work on `ACTIVITY_H` as a result of a change or creation has been completed. In calling the `CRM_EVENT_SET_EXETIME_OW` function module, the following import parameters are used:

Import parameters
- `IV_EXETIME`: The current time of execution such as `END of ACTIVITY_H`.
- `IV_GUID_HI`: The parent GUID of the object being processed.
- `IV_KIND_HI`: The type of parent GUID (header or item).

After the `CRM_EVENT_SET_EXETIME_OW` function module receives this data, the function sets the current execution time into the memory buffers of the BTE framework. After that, you go through and look for any callbacks that should be executed now from the planned callback buffer.

By understanding these two key function modules used to execute the BTE framework, you now have a better insight into how the event handler function modules are invoked in the BTE framework.

Later in this chapter, we'll look at the event trace (Section 4.4), which will also help you determine what events are being raised and what event handler function modules are being invoked without needing to read the standard delivered code or use the debugger to determine the call sequence.

4.2.3   Event Handlers

Callbacks   During our examination of the customizing data, you learned that the BTE framework specifies which function modules will be called when a certain event is reached during the lifecycle of a business transaction. These function modules are what SAP CRM terms as *callbacks*. For our purposes, we'll call these event handlers because they process business logic related to events in the BTE framework.

If you examine the event handler function modules that were delivered by SAP as part of the standard SAP CRM system, you can see that they follow a certain interface pattern and naming convention. To designate that they are an event handler function module, all function modules should end with "_EC". For the actual interface or signature of the function module, you'll see a series of import parameters that are received and a single exception. You won't see any export parameters, however, because the function modules don't return any data and can only manipulate data indirectly through the one order API.

Naming conventions

The import parameters consist of the required parameters outlined in Table 4.2.

Import parameters

Parameter Name	Use
IV_OBJECT_NAME	Name of the segment, such as ACTIVITY_H
IV_EVENT_EXETIME	When the event is being executed
IV_EVENT	Which event is being executed

Table 4.2 Required Import Parameters for Event Handlers

Additionally, the parameters in Table 4.3 are optional, as we've discovered by looking at the framework code that values for these parameters aren't always published.

Optional parameters

Parameter Name	Use
IV_ATTRIBUT	An attribute such as the partner function being published
IV_HEADER_GUID	The header GUID of the object
IV_OBJECT_GUID	The GUID of the segment
IV_STRVAL_OLD	The old values of the segment
IV_STRVAL_NEW	The new values of the segment
IV_STRUC_NAME	The name of the structure that describes the data being passed to the function module

Table 4.3 Optional Parameters for Event Handlers

> ### Why Function Modules Instead of Business Rules or Methods?
>
> When SAP CRM was first developed in the late 1990s and early 2000s, the ABAP language was a much different system. In fact, Object-Oriented ABAP was relatively new, and tools, such as the Business Rules Framework plus (BRF+), were not created yet. Even concepts such as the BAdI were not widely used. As we discussed earlier, SAP CRM was one of the first applications to make wide use of BAdIs and ABAP objects. At the time that SAP CRM was built, dynamic calls with ABAP object methods were not as practiced.
>
> Another application that uses function module exits instead of BAdIs in some cases is the SAP CRM Middleware. The OPEN FI exits that exist in the SAP ERP system used by the SAP CRM Middleware are in many aspects similar to the BTE framework. There is a concept of events and a central registration table for function modules that should be executed at a particular event. A key difference, however, is that the function modules are executed immediately and don't provide an option to be executed at a later point in processing.
>
> You can build events that invoke BRF+ rules within your function module. This might be beneficial if you have logic that involves complex rule tables or needs to meet a threshold set by the business users that could change on a frequent basis.

Later in this chapter, we'll examine how to build a custom event handler for your own specific business logic. For now, let's review the standard delivered event handlers provided by SAP in the SAP CRM system.

4.3 Standard Delivered Events

An interesting aspect of the BTE framework is that the original use was for SAP and not necessarily as an exit mechanism for SAP CRM customers to implement their own business logic. Due to that fact, the SAP CRM system contains many event handler function modules that are delivered as part of the standard system and comprise the standard logic of the business transaction in SAP CRM.

In this section, we'll review the standard delivered entries in Transaction CRMV_EVENT, examine standard delivered event handlers, and review how to find event handlers delivered by SAP.

4.3.1 Review Business Transaction Event Framework Customizing

As we discussed earlier when reviewing the customizing of the BTE framework, you can use Transaction CRMV_EVENT to review which event handler function modules have been delivered by SAP. To do this, run Transaction CRMV_EVENT, and then choose the transaction category and/or the object name to restrict your selections. Click the CALL-BACK FOR CAT/OBJ./EVENT button to bring up a listing that shows what is available. For this example, take a look at the ACTIVITY_H segment.

For ACTIVITY_H, the amount of registered events is minimal, as Figure 4.13 shows those function modules that are listed. This, however, isn't always the case; for example, the number of entries registered for the PARTNER totals several hundred.

Display View "Assignment: Event Handler Modules for Object Function":

Function Module	Object Function
CRM_1OIIE_ORDPRP_I_CHNG_EC	CRM_ORDPRP
CRM_1OIIE_ORGMAN_CHNG_EC	CRM_ORGMAN
CRM_1OIIE_PRIDOC_CHNG_EC	CRM_PRIDOC
CRM_1OIIE_RESTART_EC	CRM_ORDERADM_H
CRM_1OIIE_START_ACCEPTING_EC	CRM_ORDERADM_H
CRM_1O_SVY_DELETE_LINK_EC	CRM_SURVEY
CRM_1O_SVY_INIT_EC	CRM_SURVEY
CRM_1O_SVY_SAVE_EC	CRM_SURVEY
CRM_ACTION_DELETE_EC	CRM_ACTION
CRM_ACTION_INIT_EC	CRM_ACTION
CRM_ACTION_REGISTER_EC	CRM_ACTION
CRM_ACTIVITY_DATES_CHANGE_EC	CRM_ACTIVITY_I
CRM_ACTIVITY_H_COMPLETION_EC	CRM_ACTIVITY_H
CRM_ACTIVITY_H_COPY_EC	CRM_ACTIVITY_H
CRM_ACTIVITY_H_DELETE_CHECK_EC	CRM_ACTIVITY
CRM_ACTIVITY_H_DELETE_EC	CRM_ACTIVITY_H
CRM_ACTIVITY_H_INIT_EC	CRM_ACTIVITY_H
CRM_ACTIVITY_H_SAVE_EC	CRM_ACTIVITY_H
CRM_ACTIVITY_H_STATREASON_EC	CRM_ACTIVITY_H

Figure 4.13 Example List of Registered Event Handlers for ACTIVITY_H

4.3.2 Review Logic

The next step to take when looking at these entries is to determine what logic is being performed that could not have been incorporated in the

One order function modules

standard one order function modules. To determine this, examine the function module CRM_ACTIVITY_H_SAVE_EC, which saves the object buffer entries to the physical database. The key part about this call is that timing is fixed. The call only occurs when the transaction is saved and isn't a multiple call during the transaction lifecycle. Although you could technically hardcode the physical save call within the business transaction, in this fashion, you allow for a more precise timing.

> **Note**
>
> As you may remember, CRM_ORDER_SAVE is called when a business transaction is saved.

More flexibility   If you dig further in the code, you'll find that the CRM_ORDER_SAVE_OW function module calls CRM_EVENT_SET_EXETIME_MULTI_OW. The primary benefit of this structure is that code that performs the physical save of the SAP CRM business transaction can be made more generic. This means that if in the future you added a new segment, you wouldn't have to modify the code that handles the save of the business transaction to database to handle each new segment. This allows better separation of the physical and logical update layers within the SAP CRM business transaction.

You gain flexibility because you can generically define logic and allow the events handler function modules to handle the specific logic for a given business segment. The drawback of course is that tracing how parts of the business transaction are physically updated on the database becomes more difficult.

4.3.3   Business Object Categories for Transactions

You've seen how the BTE framework can be used to prevent you from coding logic specific to a particular segment of business transaction; now let's take look at how the BTE framework is used to distinguish different business object categories for transactions. The business object categories allow you to separate which event handler function modules will be called for a similar set of business transaction process types. Without the specification of the business object category in the BTE framework, all event handler function modules would be called for all business processes. For this example you'll pick the lead business object type because they're similar to activities, but you'll add another layer of logic.

A perfect example is the CRM_LEAD_H_STATUSSINCE_EC module. In the customizing in Transaction CRMV_EVENT, this function module is called at the end of document processing and is triggered by a change of status on the lead. The logic of this function module is to track on the LEAD_H segment how long the lead has been in a current status.

> **Business Application**
>
> It's a common business requirement in Lead Management to know how long a lead has been in a current status. However, for other business object categories, this requirement may not be necessary.

The traditional logic would have put a case statement in the code that updates the status, but then it would become cluttered and hard to maintain. Instead, the status update code only needs to trigger the event. This is once again a perfect example of how the standard delivered event handler function modules keep update function modules for the one order framework generic but allow for specific business logic for different cases. The benefit is that you can introduce new business object types for business transactions without having to rewrite the entire business transaction processing code.

Trigger event

> **Note**
>
> Keep in mind that creating a new business object type for a business transaction type is something reserved by SAP but allows SAP to deliver new functionality with less effort. A great example of this is that SAP created new service business transaction types with SAP CRM 7.0 and didn't have to completely rewrite the one order framework.

4.3.4   Code Field Updates

Another problem solved by the BTE framework is where to code the field updates on the business transaction that are copied from data contained on a business partner in the transaction. If you were to code this logic without the BTEs, you would have to hardcode in the `PARTNER` segment function module's logic for every possible partner update that is needed. You then wouldn't be able to create new partner functions without changing the `PARTNER` segment code.

Instead, you can create new event handler function modules that provide for the update. One example of a standard delivered event handler function module is `CRM_SALES_PARTNER_CHANGE_EC`. This function module updates the `SALES` segment on the business transaction when the sold-to or ship-to parties on a business transaction have been changed.

Another example is `CRM_PRICING_PARTNER_CHANGE_EC`, which updates several of the pricing communication fields when the sold-to party on a document changes. A final example is the `CRM_TEXT_COLLECT_CHANGE_EC` function module. As the partner changes, the text determination procedure for the document is validated again.

All of these called function modules for the `PARTNER` segment allow for a more flexible method of defaulting values when a partner is added or changed within the SAP CRM business transaction.

4.3.5   List SAP-Delivered Event Handlers

Our discussion of the standard delivered event handlers would not be complete without a quick review of how to get a list of all event handlers delivered by SAP. In general, there are two methods to find these function modules:

▸ Search for function modules whose name ends in "`EC`" in Transaction SE37.

▸ Launch Transaction CRMV_EVENT, and click the OBJECT FUNCTION/ CALLBACK button (this is the more accurate method of the two). You'll then see a list of all function modules for each given object. A look into the SAP CRM 7.0 system that has been used for writing this book reveals around 2,000 entries in this table.

Keep in mind that not all 2,000 function modules will be used for a given business transaction type, but this shows how much logic has been separated from the standard one order function modules. If this logic was not separated, it wouldn't be hard to imagine the difficulty of building the one order framework to support all business processes on the SAP CRM system.

Complexity versus Flexibility

The biggest complaint from ABAP developers who are new to SAP CRM is that the system is too complex. The problem is that SAP CRM wasn't designed to support one process but almost any "business process" within three major areas. In addition, the design was done before there were modern tools such as the BRF that could have eliminated the need for some of the logic. The BTE framework is such an example where the ability to easily trace through the logical execution of code using the standard ABAP Debugger has been given up for the flexibility to add logic as needed.

4.4 Event Trace

The most common piece of information that people want to know about the BTE framework is when an event handler function module will be called. Even though you can logically guess the call order, this isn't always an accurate or efficient way of determining the sequence of calls.

The other option for tracing calls—via the ABAP Debugger—will only give you a partial picture of which events are being raised.

Note

Remember, events are raised by the one order function modules for each particular segment.

If you were to insert a breakpoint in one of the event handler function modules, you would only then see a call stack that reflects either an immediate call from that function module or a delayed call later. You would have to insert breakpoints in all function modules that could possibly be called to get a complete picture of the events being called if you only had the ABAP Debugger available.

To resolve this problem, SAP has provided the Event Trace tool inside of SAP CRM, to see which events are raised and which event handlers were called. You can access this tool by running Transaction CRMD_EVENT_ TRACE.

4.4.1 Prerequisites

Before you can use the tool, you first need to set up a user or another account for the trace. To do this, run Transaction SU3, and go to the PARAMETERS tab. Add the parameter ID "CRM_EVENT_TRACE", and set the value of the parameter ID to "X" as shown in Figure 4.14. After this is done, you're ready to create a trace file.

Creating or changing a transaction from the Web Client will create this trace file. After you've performed the activities in the business transaction for which you want to examine the triggered events, you're ready to review the trace.

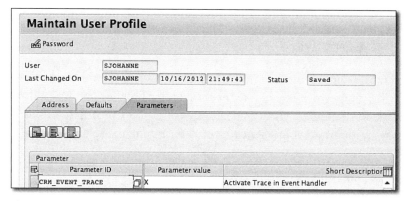

Figure 4.14 User Parameter for CRM_EVENT_TRACE

4.4.2 Review the Trace

Common use We've found the most common usage of the event trace is when we're first trying to see if an event exists for the new logic that we may want to insert in business transaction. In addition, there have been times when we've registered new event handlers by guessing the correct timing and needed to figure out why the event handler wasn't called by the system. After doing the guess and test method several times, we've found it's much easier to take the approach of tracing and then "locating" instead.

In this example, create a new interaction log transaction type 0001. Then go to Transaction CRMD_EVENT_TRACE, and click the EXECUTE button as shown in Figure 4.15.

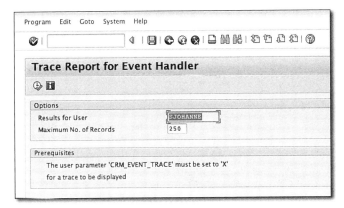

Figure 4.15 Initial Screen for Transaction CRMD_EVENT_TRACE

You'll get a report that lists the current trace for the transaction. The report consists of several columns that provide details of each event step, including the triggering of the event. The first row in Figure 4.16 shows that when the transaction was created, an event was published for ORDERADM_H called AFTER_CREATE. As a result of that event being published, several function modules were called immediately. In addition, new events were triggered along with lifecycle changes for the event. Line 9 shows that the END OF ORDERADM_H processing was reached and also triggered a function module call based on that time.

Report details

Trace Report for Event Handler

Refresh | Callstack | Function Module | CRMV_EVENT

	Line	Rec...	What happened?	Runti...	Exctn Time	Object Name	Event in Program	Attribute	Function Module Name	Legacy Dat	New Data
	1		Event Published			ORDERADM_H	AFTER_CREATE				
	2	1	FM Called		Immediately	ORDERADM_H	AFTER_CREATE		CRM_TSRV_STATUS_LOG_EC	X	X
	3		Callback Return	458	Immediately	ORDERADM_H	AFTER_CREATE		CRM_TSRV_STATUS_LOG_EC		
	4	1	FM Called		Immediately	ORDERADM_H	AFTER_CREATE		CRM_TEXT_COLLECT_CHANGE_EC	X	X
	5		Callback Return	670	Immediately	ORDERADM_H	AFTER_CREATE		CRM_TEXT_COLLECT_CHANGE_EC		
	6		Event Published			STATUS	AFTER_CHANGE	I1002			
	7	1	FM Called		Immediately	STATUS	AFTER_CHANGE	I1002	CRM_ORDERADM_H_STAT_PROFILE_EC	X	X
	8		Callback Return	763	Immediately				CRM_ORDERADM_H_STAT_PROFILE_EC		
	9		Exctn Time Set		END OF ORDERADM_H						
	10	1	FM Called		END OF ORDERADM_H	ORDERADM_H	AFTER_CREATE		CRM_DATES_DETERM_INITIAL_EC		
	11		Event Published			APPOINTMENT	BEFORE_CHANGE	BILL_DATE			
	12		Event Published			APPOINTMENT	SAVE				
	13		Event Published			APPOINTMENT	AFTER_CREATE	BILL_DATE			
	14	2	FM Called		Immediately	APPOINTMENT	AFTER_CREATE	BILL_DATE	CRM_BILLING_DATES_CHANGED_EC		X
	15		Callback Return	510	Immediately	APPOINTMENT	AFTER_CREATE	BILL_DATE	CRM_BILLING_DATES_CHANGED_EC		
	16	2	FM Called		Immediately	APPOINTMENT	AFTER_CREATE	BILL_DATE	CRM_PMM_BTX_QUT_APPOINTMEN_EC		X
	17		Callback Return	517	Immediately	APPOINTMENT	AFTER_CREATE	BILL_DATE	CRM_PMM_BTX_QUT_APPOINTMEN_EC		
	18		Event Published			APPOINTMENT	BEFORE_CHANGE	INVCR_DATE			
	19		Event Published			APPOINTMENT	SAVE				
	20		Event Published			APPOINTMENT	AFTER_CREATE	INVCR_DATE			
	21	2	FM Called		Immediately	APPOINTMENT	AFTER_CREATE	INVCR_DATE	CRM_BILLING_DATES_CHANGED_EC		X
	22		Callback Return	7,153	Immediately	APPOINTMENT	AFTER_CREATE	INVCR_DATE	CRM_BILLING_DATES_CHANGED_EC		
	23	2	FM Called		Immediately	APPOINTMENT	AFTER_CREATE	INVCR_DATE	CRM_PMM_BTX_QUT_APPOINTMEN_EC		X
	24		Callback Return	7,225	Immediately	APPOINTMENT	AFTER_CREATE	INVCR_DATE	CRM_PMM_BTX_QUT_APPOINTMEN_EC		
	25		Event Published			APPOINTMENT	BEFORE_CHANGE	REQ_DLV_DATE			

Figure 4.16 Example Event Trace for Interaction Log Creation

183

One of the most interesting aspects of the trace is that it shows how much processing is executed for the BTE framework. For this simple example of updating the interaction log, it generated almost 400 entries on the SAP CRM 7.0 system.

View enhancements

In addition to the listing, you can select a row and then click on the FUNCTION MODULE button, which will show the source code of the function module that will be called. If you click on the CRMV_EVENT button, it will prefill the selection screen for the row selected in the CRMV_EVENT button so you can look at the customizing entries responsible for that function module call. In the far right columns, there are entries for LEGACY DATA and NEW DATA. Click the underlined cell to see the data structure passed into the function module for old and/or new data.

> **Note**
>
> Keep in mind this doesn't always work correctly and can create short dumps in your system when there is a type mismatch between the call and the data that was passed in. This normally occurs when a structure was enhanced with a new field, or a system code was recently generated.

Overwrite existing entries

Another aspect of using the event trace is that new entries will overwrite existing entries. This means that the trace isn't permanently stored when activated. If you need to perform a lengthy analysis on the results, it's recommended that you export the results to a Microsoft Excel spreadsheet to be retained. We also strongly recommend that you turn off the trace immediately after it's finished because it can be a performance drain on your system and increase the size of your database if being used across multiple users. We don't recommend turning on the trace for multiple users unless absolutely necessary to determine a problem with your system.

The trace itself is integrated into the BTE framework through the parameter ID CRM_EVENT_TRACE. This parameter is read when the function group CRM_EVENT_OW is loaded into memory. This function group contains the function modules that initialize the BTE framework and the processing of the framework. The trace is stored out on the database Table INDX under the cluster (EV) with the key being the user ID of the active user. This is why you shouldn't turn on the trace for multiple users in a system; it can cause major performance issues with your system.

Table INDX

Table INDX in the SAP CRM system allowed developers to get around the limitations of relational database management systems (RDBMSs) in the early 1990s. Originally, most RDBMSs had a limit on the maximum number of tables that could be created in a single schema.

Due to the complex design of enterprise software, SAP found the applications it developed pushing the limit of that system. To get around that limit, SAP created the concept of *cluster tables*. The idea of cluster tables is that you could store several different "tables" in only one physical database table. The drawback is that all of those tables had to share and use the same primary key, and there was no way to index those tables by a secondary key.

Cluster tables

As the technology progressed with RDBMSs, the number of tables restriction was lifted, and the need to store multiple tables in a single physical table was no longer necessary. However, some cluster tables such as Table INDX still remain and tend to be used when a developer doesn't want to create a separate table to store information and only needs direct primary key access to information. We don't recommend using Table INDX for new developments, but because you may encounter the table in different places, it's useful to be familiar with its existence. One other key area in SAP CRM that stores data in Table INDX is the sales organization data customizing for SAP CRM.

4.5 Creating an Event Module

Now that we've examined how the BTE framework functions, let's examine how you can use it to add your own custom business logic to a business transaction. To do this, you'll proceed through these steps in the following sections:

- Decide which event should trigger your logic.

Step overview

- Create a new function group to hold the function module that will contain your function module.

- Create the function module by copying an existing event function module or from scratch with a predefined interface.

- Register the function module to be called in the customer settings for the event handler.

After everything is set up, you'll be able to test to see if your logic is called. Let's get started with the first step.

4.5.1 Determining the Correct Event

Before you start the process of determining the correct event, you should always ask whether there's a BAdI available that meets your business requirements. In Chapter 7, Section 7.4, we've provide some suggestions on finding BAdIs within the one order framework of SAP CRM.

Should I Use the BTE Framework?

Even though the BTE framework can meet almost all of your business requirements, you should use it sparingly. In many cases, most of the standard delivered BAdIs for the segments of the business transactions will meet your requirements. In addition, due to the restricted nature of the BAdIs, it's more difficult to create an infinite update loop within them. The problem though is that the BAdIs tend not to offer the precision needed to have the business transaction updated and/or validated at the correct time. The benefit then of using the BTE framework is that you can use precise timing to ensure that the transaction works. In general, the framework should be used for business requirements where the timing of the logic to be executed can't be met by the available BAdIs.

Precise timing

With precise timing, you end up with the coding being more difficult than your typical BAdI implementation. The first problem is that if you choose the wrong event, nothing will happen. The second problem is that if you accidently call something that calls the event that triggers your function module, you could end up in an infinite loop or trigger a short dump. When first working with the BTE framework, this can be a common mistake.

The difference between working with the BAdI implementation and the event function module is similar to using a chisel versus laser. Both tools will cut the rock in the shape you want, but each tool provides a different margin of error. Most people can easily start working with hand tools; lasers, on the other hand, require more advanced training and special equipment. The BTE framework is like a laser in the toolset for developers who support SAP CRM. It's very useful, but you need to make sure you use it properly and with extreme caution when using it for your own developments.

Chapter 7 provides examples using the business requirement of a field for entry when the BTE framework is appropriate for use.

In the previous section, you learned how to use the CRMD_EVENT trace to see which events are triggered as a business transaction is created and changed. In creating a new event module, you'll normally decide which object needs either an update or validation of data and when it should occur. After you've made these decision, you can then use the event trace to validate that your new event module will get called when expected based on your choices.

For this section of the chapter, we'll use the example of adding a new validation check on the social media call report. The social media call report is a custom transaction type with the technical name ZSCR that is based on the interaction log activity transaction in SAP CRM. For this example, we'll walk through the steps needed to create a new event handler that will execute business logic after values on the CUSTOMER_H section of the transaction have been changed. It's quite common to add new logic and validations when custom fields have been added to the business transaction.

Example

4.5.2 Creating the Function Group

As you may recall from your first ABAP development book or course, a function module belongs to a function group, and you must first create a function group before creating a function module. In most development scenarios, the standard recommendation is to use any function group as appropriate if one exists.

For these event handler function modules, we instead recommend putting them in a separate function group. The two primary reasons for this are maintainability and prevention of global memory conflicts. For maintenance purposes, it's easier to have all of your event handlers related to a particular business transaction type stored in a single function group. Because event handlers are a hook into the core business transaction code of SAP CRM, you can remove dependencies from other code you create. In addition, as the global memory of a function group is shared among all function modules within that group, you can run into issues if global memory isn't shared correctly.

Event handler function modules

For most custom programs, this isn't an issue, but because called event handlers will live for the lifetime of the business transaction process, you'll need to ensure that global memory is used sparingly and is managed properly. Therefore, by isolating the event handler function modules to a separate function group, you reduce the impact of any side effects that could be caused if you instead chose to put your event handler in the same function group with several other nonrelated function modules. You may write the body of the event handler in an object-oriented fashion using ABAP objects; however, the event handlers themselves must remain an ABAP function module.

Create function
group

To create the function group, follow these steps:

1. Go into Transaction SE80. In the REPOSITORY BROWSER view of the explorer, choose FUNCTION GROUP from the dropdown, and enter the name of the function group you want to create.

2. For this example, enter "ZSCR_EC" as shown in Figure 4.17.

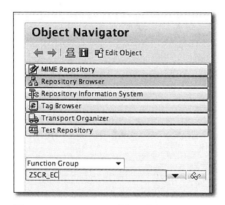

Figure 4.17 ABAP Workbench: Enter Function Group Name

3. Click the DISPLAY button next to the name you just entered; a popup will appear stating that your function group doesn't exist and asking whether you want to create an object (see Figure 4.18).

4. Choose YES, and then you'll be prompted to create a function group.

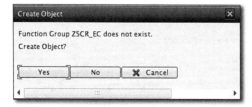

Figure 4.18 Create Object Prompt for Function Module

5. Enter a description for the function group, and click the SAVE button as shown in Figure 4.19. You'll be prompted to assign a package to your object. If you place the object in a transportable package, you'll need to place the function group in a workbench request.

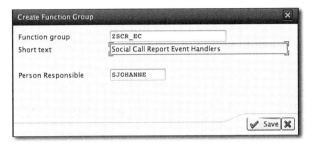

Figure 4.19 Create Function Group Popup Window

After the function group is created, you need to activate the function group by following these steps:

Activate a function group

1. Right-click on the NAME function group in the left-hand navigation pane of the ABAP Workbench. For SAP GUI Java on a Mac, press Cmd + click.

2. After the function group is activated, you can create a function module within the function group. As discussed earlier, we strongly recommend that your event handlers are kept in a separate function group from the rest of your development. The created function group would look similar in structure to the function group shown in Figure 4.20.

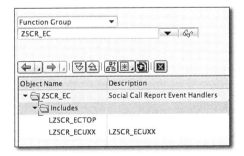

Figure 4.20 Newly Created Function Group ZSCR_EC

4.5.3   Building the Function Module

Validate call A normal event handler function module follows a standard pattern of logic execution. When building your own code logic, the first step is to validate that the call of the function module is receiving the correct data structure for processing. Because it's technically possible to register any event handler against any object and event, this prevents the system from creating a short dump if the table was maintained incorrectly.

Assign field symbol The next step is to assign a field symbol to the old and/or new values when working with the AFTER_CHANGE type event situations. After that's done, you'll review the data passed in, based on your logic and either perform updates or issue error messages as needed. You shouldn't issue a commit work in your function modules, however, because the business transaction program is responsible for managing whether updates should be committed to the database or not.

Another rule is that your function module must not issue or create any dialog popups within the coding. The event handler calls should be treated like a batch call or call without a Dynpro screen. This is especially important because the UI of SAP CRM doesn't use any Dynpro screens, so if you make any calls that involve a Dynpro screen, your end user will receive a short dump indicating that you attempted to call a dialog screen without output.

Create Event Handler

For this example, you'll create a new event handler by following these steps:

1. Copy the function CRM_DATES_ACTIVITY_EC. Figure 4.21 shows the import parameters and exceptions of this standard delivered function module. To start the copy process, bring up the function module in Transaction SE37.

2. Choose the COPY icon as show in Figure 4.22.

> **Transporting BTE Customizing and Code**
>
> The customizing and code for the BTE framework is handled in the same fashion as typical transport requests with the exception of when you should move

it. It's extremely important that you don't move changes to the customizing and function modules used by the BTE framework when end users are active on the system creating business transactions. Although this may sound logical, moving transports into a production system while users are actively working on it can cause data issues or system errors. The last thing you or your end user, want to see is a short-dump error message as a result of a transport you recently made into your production system. The best practices for managing transports for an ABAP system still apply for an SAP CRM system even when the data being entered may not be as time sensitive as data entered in SAP ERP.

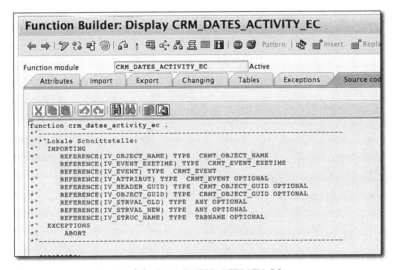

Figure 4.21 Function Module CRM_DATES_ACTIVITY_EC

Function Builder: Initial Screen

Function Module CRM DATES ACTIVITY EC

Display   Change   Create

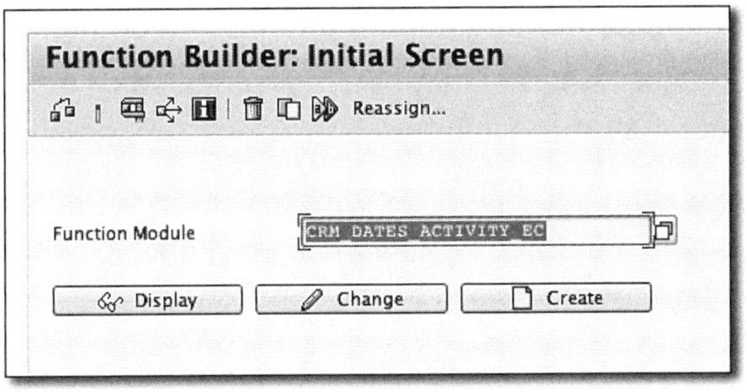

Figure 4.22 Transaction SE37: Function Module Copy

3. A popup window appears asking for the name of the copy and the function group in which to place the copy. Name your function module "Z_SCR_BTE_EC", and choose the FUNCTION GROUP ZSCR_EC, as shown in Figure 4.23. You'll then receive a message that the function module was copied.

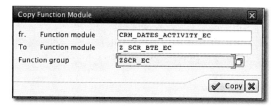

Figure 4.23 Copy Function Module Popup Window

Tips & Tricks

Keep in mind that when you copy a function module in this fashion, you need to be careful of any global variables and common subroutines that are referenced by the original function module. A copy of an individual function module to a new function group doesn't copy over anything contained in the shared part of the original function group of the original function module.

Because it's common for global variables to be used in existing function modules, you should probably delete most if not all of the code in your copy of the existing function module. This will allow your function module to pass the syntax check and generate successfully.

Modify Copied Function Module

Now you can go into Transaction SE80 and start changing your copied function module to meet your needs. Open up the function group that you created earlier: ZSCR_EC. You should see your new function module listed as shown in Figure 4.24.

You can now edit the function module. The primary benefit of doing a copy in this fashion is that you don't have to manually build the interface for the event handler. However, you could have created a new function module from scratch and added the necessary import parameters.

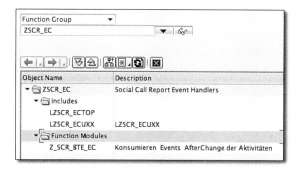

Figure 4.24 Z_SCR_BTE_EC in ZSCR_EC Function Group

If you need to create the function module from scratch, follow these steps:

Create the function module

1. Access Transaction SE80, and bring up your function group ZSCR_EC.
2. Right-click (Cmd + click on a Mac) on the function group, and choose NEW FUNCTION MODULE. A popup window appears asking for the name of the function module and a description.
3. Enter the name, and make sure that it begins with "Y_", "Z_", or your registered namespace prefix.
4. Define several import parameters with the predefined types as listed in Table 4.4.

Parameter Name	Data Type	Optional
IV_OBJECT_NAME	CRMT_OBJECT_NAME	No
IV_EVENT_EXETIME	CRMT_EVENT_EXETIME	No
IV_EVENT	CRMT_EVENT	No
IV_ATTRIBUT	CRMT_EVENT	Yes
IV_HEADER_GUID	CRMT_OBJECT_GUID	Yes
IV_OBJECT_GUID	CRMT_OBJECT_GUID	Yes
IV_STRVAL_OLD	ANY	Yes
IV_STRVAL_NEW	ANY	Yes
IV_STRUC_NAME	TABNAME	Yes

Table 4.4 Import Parameters for a Custom Built Event Handler

4.5.4 Common Code Structure

If you examine the code for your event handler and other event handlers you'll find a common structure.

Validate The first step involves validating that the data structure received matches the expected type for your event handler. This prevents any possible type mismatch errors that happen when calling your event handler. This is normally handled by a check on the IV_STRUC_NAME attribute that is received by your function module.

Access segment data After this check passes, you'll need to provide access to the segment data that's passed into your function module. If you notice that the IV_STRVAL_OLD and IV_STRVAL_NEW parameters are generically typed to access the components of the structures that they represent, you must assign a typed field symbol to work the data. The field symbol will be of the type of data defined for the segment. In this case, you'll type the field symbol with the CRMT_ACTIVITY_H_WRK structure.

Data check Finally, you can start working with the data received. A common check is to see if the data actually changed or meets some other criteria that you may use to validate the logic. A simple example is taking the header GUID of the business transaction and looking up the transaction type.

If the transaction type matches your criteria, then you'll continue processing. You can use the function module CRM_ORDERADM_H_READ_OW to determine the transaction type for your business transaction. This allows you to isolate your processing to a specific transaction type. You want to do this because, as you remember, the BTEs are at a business object level and not specified at the specific business transaction type level.

Basic structure of an event handler The coding example in Listing 4.1 shows the basic structure of an event handler minus the business logic. In Chapter 7, we'll examine specific business logic examples that can be coded by the event handler.

```
function Z_SCR_BTE_EC .
*"----------------------------------------------------------------
*"*"Local Interface:
*"  IMPORTING
*"     REFERENCE(IV_OBJECT_NAME) TYPE  CRMT_OBJECT_NAME
```

```
*"      REFERENCE(IV_EVENT_EXETIME) TYPE  CRMT_EVENT_EXETIME
*"      REFERENCE(IV_EVENT) TYPE  CRMT_EVENT
*"      REFERENCE(IV_ATTRIBUT) TYPE  CRMT_EVENT OPTIONAL
*"      REFERENCE(IV_HEADER_GUID) TYPE  CRMT_OBJECT_
GUID OPTIONAL
*"      REFERENCE(IV_OBJECT_GUID) TYPE  CRMT_OBJECT_
GUID OPTIONAL
*"      REFERENCE(IV_STRVAL_OLD) TYPE  ANY OPTIONAL
*"      REFERENCE(IV_STRVAL_NEW) TYPE  ANY OPTIONAL
*"      REFERENCE(IV_STRUC_NAME) TYPE  TABNAME OPTIONAL
*"  EXCEPTIONS
*"      ABORT
*"----------------------------------------------------------
  constants:
    lc_name_customer_h_wa type tabname value 'CRMT_CUSTOMER_
H_WRK'.

  field-symbols:
    <ls_customer_h_wrk> type crmt_customer_h_wrk,
    <lu_customer_h_wrk> type crmt_customer_h_wrk.
* // Check pre conditions
  if iv_header_guid is initial or ( iv_header_guid ne iv_
object_guid ).
    return.
  endif.
  if iv_struc_name ne lc_name_customer_h_wa.
    message e210(crm_order_misc) with lc_name_customer_h_wa
      raising abort.
  endif.

  assign  iv_strval_new to <ls_customer_h_wrk>.
  assign  iv_strval_old to <lu_activity_wrk>.

check <ls_customer_h_wrk> ne <lu_customer_h_wrk>.

check sy-subrc eq 0.
*    // Launch business logic

endfunction.
```

Listing 4.1 Example Code for Event Handler Z_SCR_BTE_EC

4.5.5 Registering the Function Module

Now that you've created the function module, you'll need to register it so that it will be called. To do this, you first must assign the function module to an object function by following these steps:

1. Go into Transaction CRMV_EVENT, and choose the OBJECT FUNCTION/CALLBACK option.

2. Add your function module to the object function. For this example, enter "Z_SCR_BTE_EC" for the FUNCTION MODULE and enter "CRM CUSTOMER_H" for the OBJECT FUNCTION as shown in Figure 4.25.

> **Note**
>
> As we discussed earlier in this chapter, any event handler function module should only be assigned once to a particular object function. The key for this customizing table is the function module name, so it prevents you from multiple uses. There never should be a need to reuse the same module across object functions because the physical data that will be processed and the business logic should be different between objects.

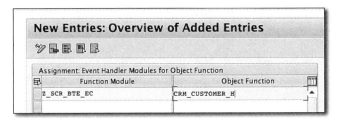

Figure 4.25 Assignment of Event Handler to Object Function

3. Now that the object is registered, register the function module in Table CRMV_EVENT_CUST to ensure that any entries created or changed by SAP during an upgrade won't overwrite the entries that you've created. To do this, either open the table for maintenance in Transaction SM30 or go into the IMG and choose CUSTOMER RELATIONSHIP MANAGEMENT • TRANSACTIONS • BASIC SETTINGS • EDIT EVENT HANDLER TABLE.

As seen in Figure 4.26, this table normally won't contain any entries in an SAP CRM system until the "SAP customer" adds the entries.

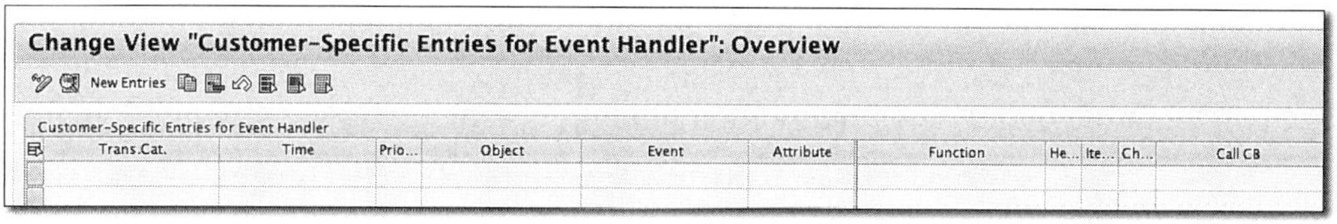

Figure 4.26 Customer-Specific Event Handler Entries

4. Choose NEW ENTRIES, and enter the following information for your function module: TRANS.CAT., EXECUTION TIME, PRIORITY, OBJECT NAME, EVENT, ATTRIBUTE, and FUNCTION.

5. Indicate whether the event is for the document header or document item and whether to process the event in case an error already occurred.

6. Specify the type of data that will be passed into your event handler function.

The TRANSACTION category corresponds to the logical business object type of the transaction. If your event should correspond to all business object types, you can use the BUS2001 type; otherwise, you can use a specific type such as BUS2000120 for complaints. One exception is that activities use BUS2000110 in the framework instead of BUS2000126.

As discussed earlier, the execution time indicates when the function module should be executed after the trigger of the event. It's possible to delay a function module execution until all processing is complete because, for example, the data needed for that logic isn't available yet in the business transaction.

Execution

To help you manage execution, note the following fields:

▶ The PRIORITY field specifies the order of execution for event handlers that match on the same transaction category, execution time, object name, event, and attribute. This allows you to add in additional logic as needed.

▶ The OBJECT NAME is the segment of data that will cause the corresponding event.

- The EVENT is the action that happens on the object name.
- The ATTRIBUTE is a value for certain segments that will provide further details on what has changed. You'll normally enter "<*>" for the attribute value if you don't want to restrict your event handler to a particular attribute value. The PARTNER segment uses this as way to communicate the partner function being created/changed in the business transaction and to allow different logic for a sold-to party versus a contact person.

In this example, you'll add a new entry in the customer-specific entries for event handler screen for the social media call report. You'll use the following settings:

- TRANS. CATEGORY: "BUS2001"
- EXECUTION TIME: "1" IMMEDIATELY
- PRIORITY: "99"
- OBJECT NAME: "CUSTOMER_H"
- EVENT: "AFTER_CHANGE"
- ATTRIBUTE: "<*>"
- FUNCTION MODULE: "Z_SCR_BTE_EC"

The completed entry should look similar to the entry in Figure 4.27. After this entry has been saved, test the completed event handler by editing data in the CUSTOMER_H segment of the social media call report. The event handler should trigger each time you make a change to any field that is stored on the CUSTOMER_H segment. As you can see, this works identically to the BAdI CRM_CUSTOMER_H_BADI with the exception that this is only called after data is changed and not during the initial creation of the segment because that event would normally not be triggered for the CUSTOMER_H BAdI.

After testing, you might note that AFTER_CREATE for the CUSTOMER_H segment might have been a more useful event because it can only be triggered once during processing. This is helpful for defaulting a value that you only want to be the default upon creation so that you don't have to build code that determines whether the user has already maintained the value in the CUSTOMER_H BAdI.

New Entries: Details of Added Entries

Trans. Category	BUS20001	CRM Bus Transactions
Execution Time	1	Immediately
Priority	99	
Object Name	CUSTOMER_H	Customer Header Data
Event	AFTER_CHANGE	
Attribute	<*>	
Function	Z_SCR_BTE_EC	

☑ Perform Function for Doc.Header
☐ Perform Function for Document Item
☐ Do Not Process Function If Event Error Occurs

Call Callback	Call to Header/Item, with Object, Event, Attr., Old/New Data

Figure 4.27 New Entry in CRMV_EVENT for Registration

Additionally, because the AFTER_CREATE event is only called once, you won't be calling the default logic every time you make a change to the segment. Other interesting uses for custom event handlers include updating data after a change in status on the business transaction and calculating durations on the business transaction if custom date rules don't meet your requirements.

In general, you can manipulate almost any piece of any information on the business transaction during the active processing of a business transaction by using the BTE framework. The only major exception to this is that document attachments normally don't trigger events because they are stored and saved separately from the actual business transaction. Long text, however, is included even though it's technically stored in the standard text management tables of SAP NetWeaver AS ABAP.

Does Standard SAP CRM Business Logic Exist?

Business requirements

If you haven't worked with sales and marketing business processes before, you may be asking why you need this framework in the first place. In an ideal world, processes such as tracking customer interactions should be standard, no matter what company is performing that action.

However, after many years of working with different businesses, we've found that even though the processes are similar, there tends to be different ideas for what is considered required and how data should default into the system, even for something as simple as recording a customer visit into an SAP CRM system. We used the customer visit because when you get into processes such as Complaint Management or Pipeline Management, the requirements tend to become even more complex.

When most people think of SAP CRM, they assume that Account and Contact Management is nothing more than a glorified electronic address book that doesn't require much effort or logic. We've found that for tracking call reports especially, it's just as important to have a process for when and how to enter that information even if no enhancements are required.

In the future, newer versions of SAP CRM will replace much of the coding with configuration for common requirements that tend to repeat at almost every implementation. Until that happens, there will never be a standard SAP CRM business logic that applies to all companies using an SAP CRM system.

In Chapter 7, we'll explain in further detail how you can use the BTE framework to meet some common requirements in sales and service. As you can see, the amount of effort to build your own event handler is only as complex as the business logic that is required. As a general reference, you should try to limit the size of the code that will be executed by your event handler.

As discussed earlier in this chapter, the framework for executing the event handler function modules is embedded within the standard function modules for updating the one order framework. We must repeat that it's important that your code is as optimized as possible and that you use this tool selectively to prevent potential performance issues.

4.6 Summary

The BTE framework is a complex, flexible, and powerful tool for adding custom business logic to business transactions in your SAP CRM system. You can use the BTE framework to meet almost any business requirement for business transaction processing logic when a BAdI isn't available.

In the next chapter, we'll examine how to use the XIF adapter to load and extract data from your SAP CRM system.

A complete view of the customer requires many different sources of data. Because not all of this data is found in the SAP ERP system or created from scratch in SAP CRM, the XIF adapter allows you to import the data needed to complete your view of the customer in SAP CRM.

5 Data Extraction and Loading with the XIF Adapter

In many SAP CRM implementation projects, you'll need to either convert customer data from legacy/external systems into SAP CRM or send SAP CRM data to other systems. SAP has provided a tool called the XIF adapter, which will allow you to perform this task.

In this chapter, we'll examine the XIF adapter and its benefits. You'll also learn two techniques for loading data into SAP CRM, as well as a technique you can use to extract data from SAP CRM using the XIF adapter.

5.1 Introduction to the XIF Adapter

The external interface adapter (XIF adapter) is a logical layer that is built on the SAP CRM Middleware to allow you to load and extract data from SAP CRM. The XIF adapter was introduced in SAP CRM version 3.X to meet common business requirements for SAP CRM to load legacy data from spreadsheets and other data sources into SAP CRM. The adapter allows for input and output via three primary methods: IDoc, Simple Object Access Protocol (SOAP), and remote function call (RFC). Each input and output method invokes the same core function modules contained in the SAP CRM system.

SAP CRM Middleware layer

In this section, we'll go over the different design benefits and structure of the XIF adapter function module and examine how to find the XIF adapter function in your SAP CRM system.

5.1.1 Design Benefits

By providing an interface exposure of the SAP CRM Middleware, the XIF adapter is capable of loading any data into the SAP CRM system that can be updated by a BDoc. This means all your business logic that was built into the SAP CRM system doesn't need to be recreated for external data loads. You also benefit from a consistent stable interface developed by SAP that was designed to handle large volumes of data being transferred to and from SAP CRM. You no longer need to worry about performance optimization of the data load itself because SAP has already optimized the inbound SAP CRM Middleware adapter.

This concept may seem logical to anyone designing a modern application. However, traditional applications such as SAP ERP didn't originally provide any type of external/internal application programming interface (API) as part of the system design. SAP CRM instead had an internal API that needed to be exposed via the XIF adapter. The XIF adapter didn't require the type of major overhaul seen in the Sales and Distribution (SD) module when Business Application Program Interfaces (BAPIs) were introduced in that system.

5.1.2 Structure of an XIF Remote-Enabled Function Module (RFC)

The code of an XIF RFC consists of the following series of steps that are used to import data into the SAP CRM system via the middleware:

Code steps
1. Determine how the XIF is being invoked via the `CRMXIF_SENDER_SITEID_GET` function module. As stated earlier, the XIF adapter can be invoked via IDoc, SOAP, or RFC.

2. Create the header of the inbound BDoc that will be used to post the data received by the RFC.

3. After the header is created, map the inbound XIF data structure to the body of the BDoc.

4. Submit the BDoc through the middleware validation service.

5. After the validation service has processed the BDoc, map the errors back to the XIF structure. If the XIF adapter is a SOAP or IDoc call with no errors, commit the message; otherwise, roll back the BDoc message.

For other processing scenarios, such as a synchronous direct call, you won't issue a commit work, and you'll let the calling program handle the commit/rollback process.

The function modules are structured this way because the XIF adapter only maps data and then invokes existing middleware logic. You can think of each adapter module as a basic mechanism to build a BDoc from a given set of data and then automatically submit the BDoc for processing. You shouldn't expect to find any business logic in the adapter function modules; instead, you'll only see data mapping logic from external to internal representation.

Data mapping

5.1.3 Finding an XIF Module

The function modules for reading and writing data via the XIF adapter follow the pattern

Read/write function modules

```
CRMXIF_<OBJECT>_SAVE
CRMXIF_<OBJECT>_EXTRACT
```

where <OBJECT> is the name of the object to be replaced. Table 5.1 provides a list of frequently used objects.

Object Name	Object Description
IBASE	Installed base
ORDER	Business transaction
PARTNER	Business partner
PARTNER_REL	Business partner relationship
PRODUCT_MATERIAL	Product: material
PRODUCT_SERVICE	Product: service

Table 5.1 Frequently Used Objects to Be Used as a Replacement

One important naming convention involves the product master object. The object name PRODUCT actually represents product catalog data in SAP CRM and not the SAP ERP equivalent of the material master or the SAP CRM product master.

To find these function modules, you can do a simple F4 lookup in the function module builder in Transaction SE37. Follow these steps:

1. Run Transaction SE37.

2. On the first screen, enter "CRMXIF_*_SAVE" in the FUNCTION MODULE NAME field, and press F4. You'll then see a list of all possible XIF adapter function modules in your system.

5.2 Loading Data via the XIF Adapter and the Legacy System Migration Workbench

The Legacy System Migration Workbench (LSMW) is a tool delivered by SAP that can be used to import data into an SAP NetWeaver AS ABAP system. The LSMW allows you to import data via batch/direct input, batch input recording, BAPI, or IDoc. You can also use the inbound IDoc interface with the LSMW to import data for the XIF adapter.

Import data steps To do this, follow these steps:

1. Create or find a source flat file that contains the data to be converted.

2. Identify the corresponding XIF adapter object type.

3. After you know the data type, set up a data conversion project in the LSMW.

4. Set up inbound IDoc processing for that object.

5. Map the file to the corresponding IDoc type using the LSMW toolset.

6. Run the generated conversion programs created by the LSMW to load the data in your SAP CRM system.

This process requires many steps but has the benefit of writing large conversion programs from scratch. We'll go over all of the necessary steps in the following sections (note that the first step is to create a flat file, which we don't discuss here).

5.2.1 Identifying the Target XIF Adapter

You first must determine what type of data you're converting before starting your conversion project. You can use the steps in Section 5.1.3 to determine the corresponding XIF adapter object for the data that needs to be converted. For this example, you want to convert a simple list of products contained in an Excel spreadsheet into the SAP CRM system.

5.2.2 Creating a New LSMW Data Conversion Project

You can access the LSMW via Transaction LSMW in your SAP CRM system. Once in the LSMW transaction, follow these steps:

1. Click the CREATE button to start the project creation. A popup window appears asking for the name of the project as shown in Figure 5.1.

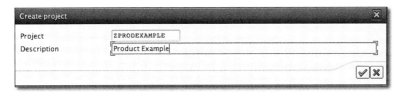

Figure 5.1 Create Project Popup Window

2. Give the project a short identifier and description, and then click the CHECKMARK button. Another popup appears asking for a subproject name, as shown in Figure 5.2.

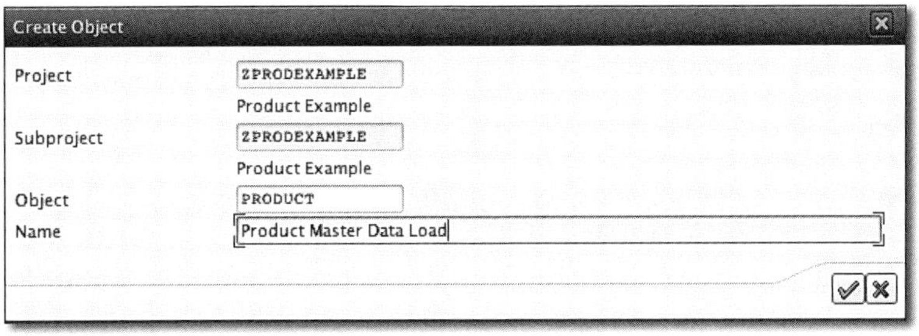

Figure 5.2 Create Subproject

The LSMW allows you to have a parent project that groups several related projects together. In our experience, we've found it's easier to keep these projects separate. Give the subproject a name and description, and then click the CHECKMARK button.

3. A popup appears asking you to create a new object for the project as shown in Figure 5.3.

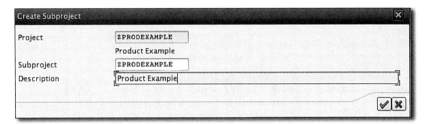

Figure 5.3 Create Subproject Popup

4. The object is the data type you're converting into your system. Enter a name and description, and click the CHECKMARK button to finish the process. Once complete, you should have a project available as shown in Figure 5.4.

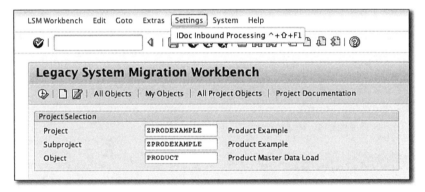

Figure 5.4 LSMW Project after Creation

Separate projects

Tips & Tricks

Normally when working with the LSMW, we recommend that you create a separate project for each data conversion project that you'll be working on, instead of trying to use several subprojects and products together when using the XIF adapter. The primary reason is that inbound IDoc processing settings are done at a project level, and this will allow you to use different settings for different data types as desired.

5.2.3 Setting Up the LSMW for Inbound IDoc Processing

A LSMW project must be configured for inbound IDoc processing. To do this, choose SETTINGS • IDOC INBOUND PROCESSING from the initial screen of the LSMW transaction while your project is displayed as shown in Figure 5.5.

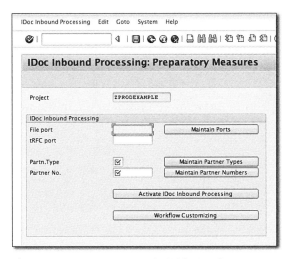

Figure 5.5 Settings Menu in LSMW Project Screen

You'll then see a screen that asks you to specify several settings for IDoc processing as shown in Figure 5.5. These settings include the file port definition and partner definition.

After these steps are complete, you need to activate the inbound processing. After this, you need to set up the SAP CRM Middleware for inbound XIF IDoc processing. These steps are explained in the following subsections.

File Port Definition

The file port definition is used to define where the IDocs that have been created by the LSMW conversion programs will reside on the application server of SAP CRM before being imported to the SAP CRM system. To set this up, you'll give a brief name for the port such as "XIF_INB", choose version 4.x IDoc record types for the version, and make sure to specify that your system is Unicode as shown in Figure 5.6.

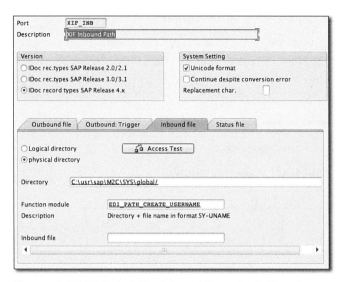

Figure 5.6 LSMW Project IDoc Inbound Processing Settings Screen

Inbound file path

Next, you set up the inbound file path for processing by choosing the INBOUND FILE tab. The system defaults a physical directory and normally suggests a function module for the file name of the generated files. If no value is present, use "EDI_PATH_CREATE_USERNAME". Figure 5.7 shows the port XIF_INB that you've created for this example.

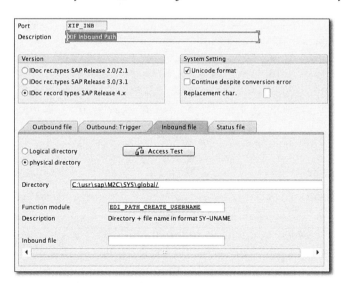

Figure 5.7 Port Definition for XIF Inbound IDoc Processing

Partner Definition

The partner definition is used to map the IDoc message type that will be used during inbound processing. To do this, you'll once again start in the SETTINGS • IDOC INBOUND PROCESSING of your project and then follow these steps:

Map IDoc message

1. Click the MAINTAIN PARTNER NUMBERS button shown previously in Figure 5.5.

2. Create a new partner of type user, and call this "XIF_INB" as shown in Figure 5.8.

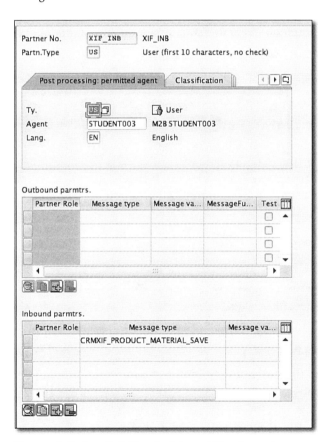

Figure 5.8 Partner Definition for Inbound IDoc Processing

3. On the POST PROCESSING: PERMITTED AGENT tab, assign your user ID as the permitted agent ("STUDENT003").

4. On the INBOUND PARMTRS. table, add the message type "CRMXIF_ PRODUCT_MATERIAL_SAVE". For product master data, the adapter object is PRODUCT_MATERIAL. The message type for this adapter object follows a pattern of CRMXIF_<adaptername>_SAVE, so that's why you use CRMXIF_PRODUCT_MATERIAL_SAVE as the message type.

5. In the expanded details for this message type for the partner, use the PROCESS CODE "APLI" as shown on Figure 5.9. It's important that you set the correct process code or the IDoc messages won't process in the SAP CRM system.

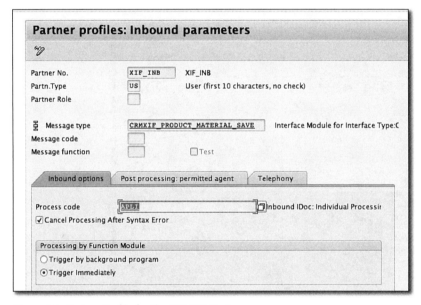

Figure 5.9 Partner Profile for the XIF_INB Partner

Activating Inbound Processing

After you've set up the file port definition and partner definition, your IDoc INBOUND PROCESSING: PREPARATORY MEASURES screen will contain an entry for the FILE PORT, PARTN. TYPE, and PARTNER NO. fields. After these are filled in, click on the ACTIVATE IDOC INBOUND PROCESSING button as shown in Figure 5.10, and click the YES button as shown in Figure 5.11.

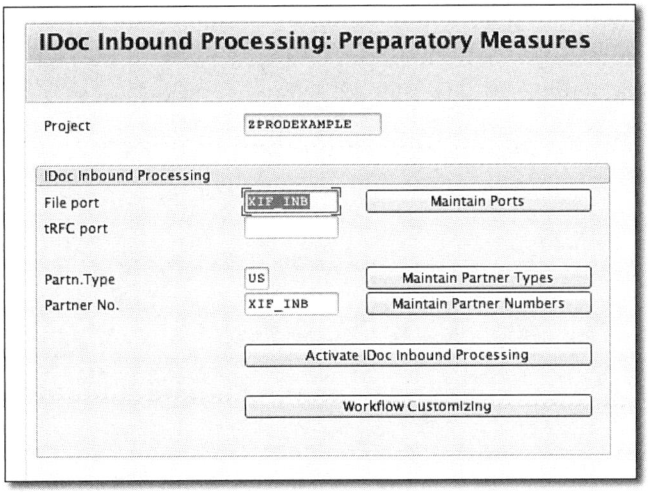

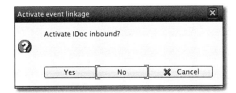

Figure 5.10 Completed IDoc Processing

Figure 5.11 Event Linkage Confirmation Popup

Setting Up the SAP CRM Middleware for XIF IDoc Processing

Now you need to configure the SAP CRM Middleware with a new
source site to process XIF IDocs. A *source site* in the middleware is a location that sends data to SAP CRM or receives data from SAP CRM. To use
the inbound XIF IDoc adapter, you must create a new site of type external interface for IDocs. Go to Transaction SMOEAC, and choose CREATE
NEW SITE to see the screen that's shown in Figure 5.12.

Source site

> **Note**
>
> It isn't necessary to have a fully set up SAP CRM Middleware connection to
> another system, such as SAP ERP, running to use the XIF adapter. However,
> we recommend that all middleware objects have been generated in your SAP
> CRM system by running Transaction SMOGTOTAL.

In addition, you should verify that the middleware is running in your system via Transaction MW_MODE. Performing these steps prior to running your first import of data with the XIF adapter should ensure the BDocs will be processed in your system.

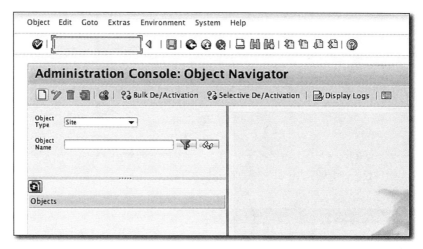

Figure 5.12 Transaction SMOEAC Start Screen

If you try to save the new site that you just created, the system warns that you need to maintain the EDI partner number for the site as shown in Figure 5.13. Depending on your requirements, you can choose to create one XIF adapter site for all data objects or create separate XIF adapter sites for each inbound data site. In this example, we'll create a separate XIF adapter site for each major data type being converted.

Click on the SITE ATTRIBUTES button, enter the partner number "XIF_INB" that you created during the partner definition step, and use partner type "US" as shown in Figure 5.14. Click the CHECKMARK to continue.

After you've made these settings, save the site. If you receive warnings about a "copy of" assignment, choose OK to continue and create the site as shown in Figure 5.15.

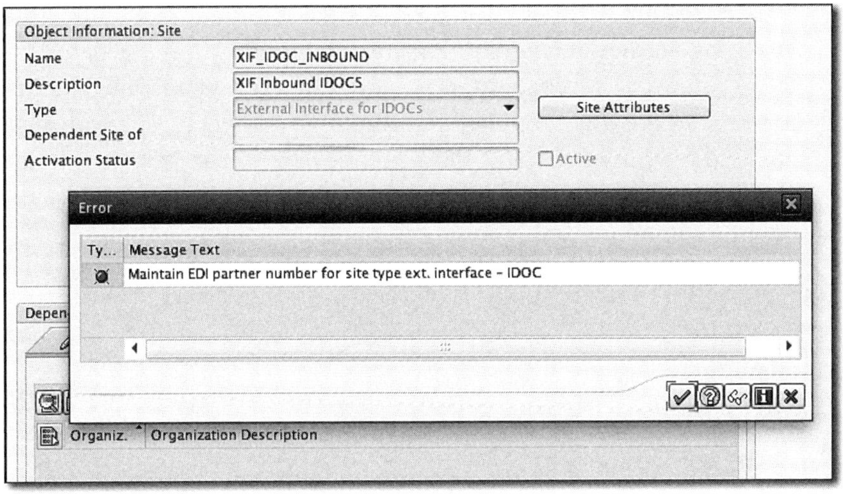

Figure 5.13 EDI Warning for XIF Inbound IDoc Site Type

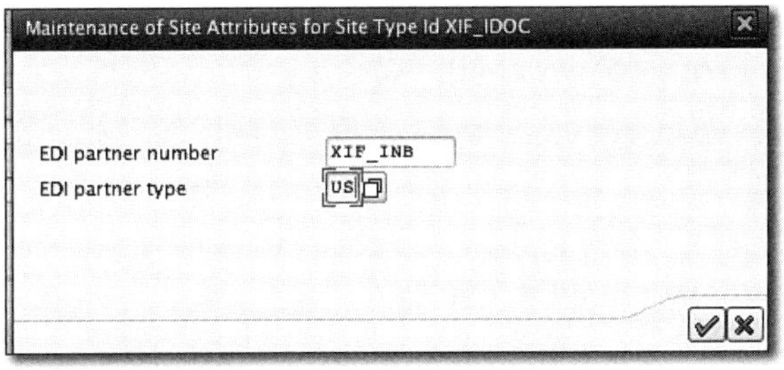

Figure 5.14 Site Attributes for XIF IDoc Site

Figure 5.15 Site Copy Warning for the XIF IDoc Site

This linkage via the XIF adapter is needed for the SAP CRM system to translate the XIF IDoc into a BDoc. As discussed earlier in this chapter,

Links

the XIF adapter module will process the received data differently depending on the source. Additionally, the SAP CRM Middleware normally requires a "source system" to properly process a BDoc. The XIF adapter sites are used to satisfy this requirement and avoid requiring a complete rewrite of the SAP CRM Middleware to support an external submission of BDoc data.

5.2.4 Mapping the Flat File in LSMW

Guided steps The LSMW provides a guided screen on the steps to convert data into the system:

1. The first step in this process is to maintain the attributes of the object that you're converting.

2. Next you need to define the source structures of the file that contains the data to be converted.

3. Then, for each source structure, you define the fields for those structures and map the source structures to the IDoc segments.

4. After the segments are mapped, you map each field to the corresponding field on the IDoc.

5. Finally, you specify the location and physical attributes of the source file as your last step of mapping the flat file.

You can find these steps in greater detail in the following subsections.

Define the Object Attributes

From the guided screen of your LSMW project, select the step MAINTAIN OBJECT ATTRIBUTES, and click on the EXECUTE button. This brings up the object attributes screen. Click on the DISPLAY <-> CHANGE toggle button to move the screen into change mode. Now that the screen is labeled CHANGE OBJECT ATTRIBUTES, choose IDOC (INTERMEDIATE DOCUMENT) as the object type. For this example of importing products, choose message type CRMXIF_PRODUCT_MATERIAL_SAVE and the basic type CRMXIF_PRODUCT_MATERIAL_SAVE02 as shown in Figure 5.16.

Note

For older SAP CRM systems, the basic type may be CRMXIF_PRODUCT_MATERIAL_SAVE01 instead.

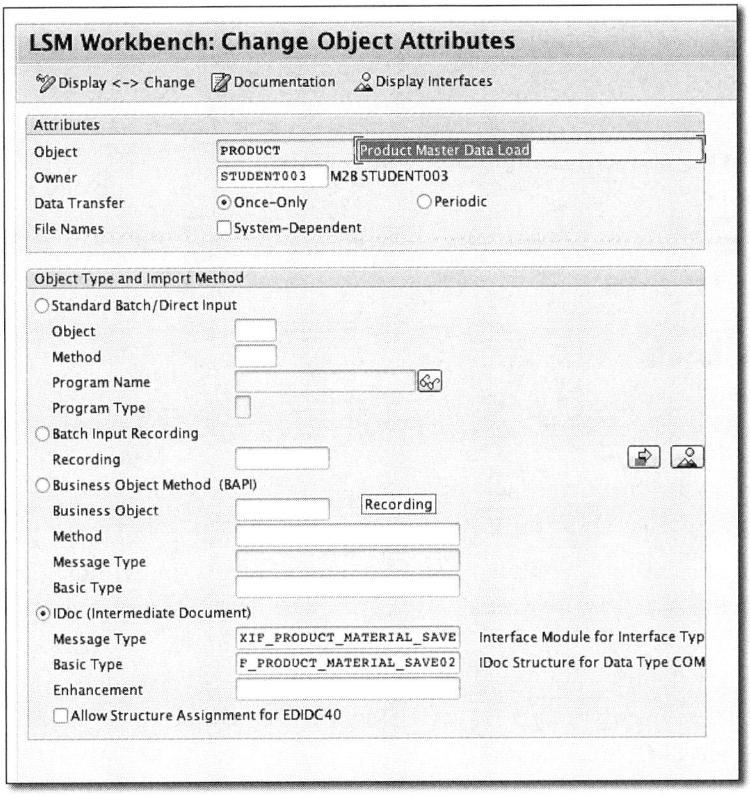

Figure 5.16 Object Attributes Screen for LSMW Project

After this is entered, save your settings, and go back to the guided processing screen for the project.

Define the Source Structures

For this example, you'll create your file containing one structure type. From the guided screen, choose the step CREATE SOURCE STRUCTURES, and then click EXECUTE. You can create this file by going into change mode on the source structure screens and clicking the CREATE icon. This source structure will be called "PRODUCT_DATA".

Multiple sources An entry appears under the source structure as shown in Figure 5.17. The LSMW allows you to have multiple source structures as needed. You might need to use this if you're importing the header of a business transaction along with the line items of that business transaction, for example.

Figure 5.17 Source Structure Screen for LSMW project

Define Source Structure Fields

In this example, you'll have a flat file containing three fields for the product: the ID, description, and UOM (unit of measure). Assume that the products will be created as product type material assigned to category MAT_FERT. We'll show how to fix those attributes when you map the source fields to the IDoc fields. Follow these steps to create the following three fields on the source structure: PRODUCT_ID, DESCRIPTION, and PRODUCT_UOM:

1. For PRODUCT_ID, enter the technical ID as "PRODUCT_ID" with no spaces, and then enter the description as "Product ID". Set the length of field to "40" and the data type to "C". This will correspond to the product ID found on Table COMM_PRODUCT of the product master. Your entry should look similar to what's shown in Figure 5.18.

2. For DESCRIPTION, enter the technical ID as "DESCRIPTION" with no spaces, and enter the description as "Short Description for Material". Set the length of field to "40" and the data type to "C". This will correspond to the short description of the product. Your entry should look similar to Figure 5.19.

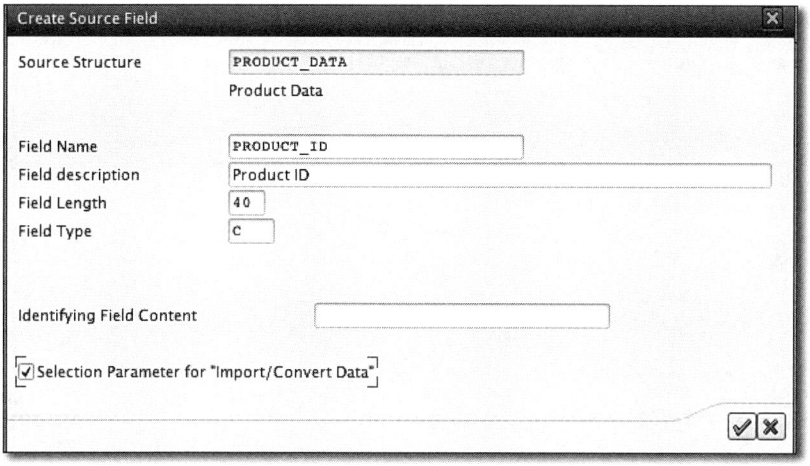

Figure 5.18 Source Field PRODUCT_ID Definition

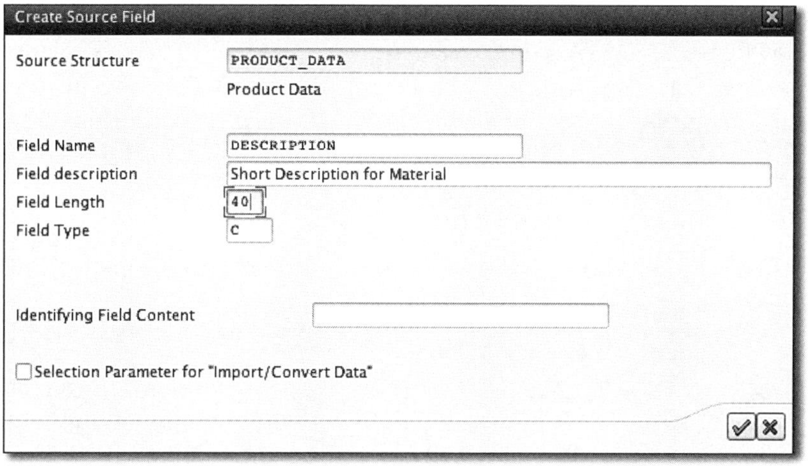

Figure 5.19 Source Field DESCRIPTION Definition

3. For PRODUCT_UOM, enter the technical ID as "PRODUCT_UOM" with no spaces, and enter the description as "Unit Of Measure". Set the length of the field to "3", and set the data type to "C". This will correspond to the UOM of the product. Your entry should look similar to Figure 5.20.

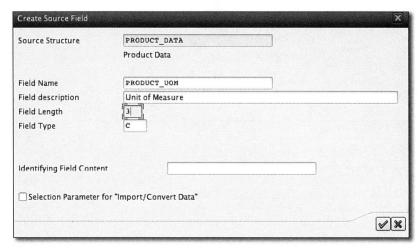

Figure 5.20 Source Field PRODUCT_UOM Definition

After you've created all three fields, you'll now see those listed under the PRODUCT_DATA structure as shown in Figure 5.21. This structure should correspond to the logical layout of your source flat file minus any field separators.

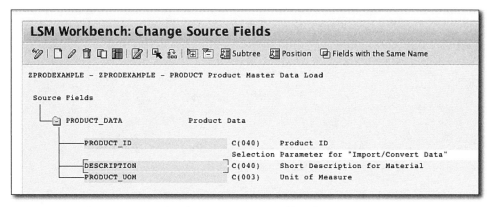

Figure 5.21 Completed Source Structure Field Definition

Map Source Structures to IDoc Structures

It's very important that you map your source structures to an IDoc structure because this mapping generates the segments of the created IDoc.

Because an IDoc has a hierarchy of segments, you must ensure that you map both parent and child segments in the IDoc structure.

In this example, you need to map the PRODUCT_DATA to the IDoc source structures listed in Listing 5.1 for the correct IDoc structure for the XIF adapter to be generated:

Code to generate Idoc structure

```
E101COMXIF_PRODUCT_MATERIAL
E101COMXIF_PR_S_COMM_PR_MAT
E116COMXIF_PRODUCT_S_ADMIN
E101OMXIF_PRD_S_COMM_PR_MAT
E101MXIF_PRD_SX_COMM_PR_MAT
E101COMXIF_PR_S_CATEGORIES
E101COMXIF_PRODUCT_S_ADMIN
E101COMXIF_PRD_S_CATEGORIES
E101COMXIF_PR_S_SHORT_TEXT
E102COMXIF_PRODUCT_S_ADMIN
E101COMXIF_PRD_S_SHORT_TEXT
E101COMXIF_PR_S_UNIT
E103COMXIF_PRODUCT_S_ADMIN
E101MXIF_PRD_S_COMM_PR_UNIT
E101XIF_PRD_SX_COMM_PR_UNIT
```

Listing 5.1 Required Segments of Product Master IDOC structure

To do this, follow these steps:

Mapping steps

1. Select the MAINTAIN STRUCTURE RELATIONSHIPS step from the guided screen of your project, and click EXECUTE. This takes you into the CHANGE STRUCTURE RELATIONSHIPS screen.

2. In this screen, click an IDoc structure to be mapped to bring the cursor focus to that segment.

3. Click on the CREATE RELATIONSHIP button, and choose your PRODUCT_DATA structure to be mapped to the segment.

For this example, you need to map the source structure against the following structures. Even though you may only need to fill a child node of the IDoc structure, you'll need to map against both the parent and child nodes to have your child node generated by the LSMW generated conversion program.

219

Once finished, save your work, and the result should look similar to what's shown in Figure 5.22.

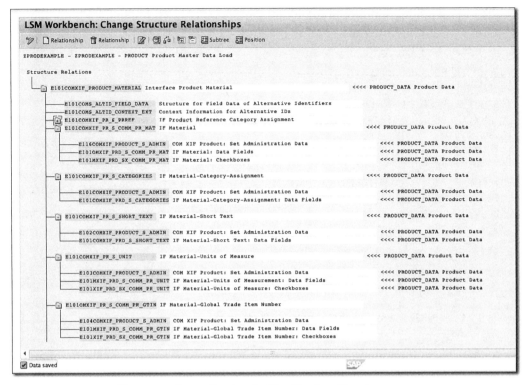

Figure 5.22 Source Structure to IDoc Structure Mapping

Map Source Fields to IDoc Fields

Products   Products in SAP CRM are different from your typical SAP R/3 material. A product in SAP CRM doesn't have any attributes until it's assigned to a category. Therefore, you need to assign your product to a category for it to load. The hierarchy commonly uses R3PRODSTYP and category ID MAT_FERT. This corresponds to the finished goods type of SAP R/3. If you aren't connected to an SAP R/3 system, you'll need to set up a product hierarchy and assign the basic product views to that category.

Another point to make is that all segments you map will require at least a logical system identifier. The easiest way to handle this is to retrieve the current logical system from Table T000 with a small mapping routine in LSMW. The logical system indicates where the data originated from, and, in this case, you want the logical system to show that SAP CRM is the origin of this data.

Logical system identifier

Specifying the Physical File

To specify the physical file, choose the step SPECIFY FILES in the guided processing screen of your project and click EXECUTE. This will then take you to the SPECIFY FILES screen in display mode. Click on the DISPLAY <-> CHANGE toggle button. When the screen is in change mode, position the cursor on the LEGACY DATA node of the screen, and click the CREATE button. In the popup that appears, enter a name for the file, and then specify that the file is data for one source structure. The delimiter will be the tabulator for this example; however, you may use any valid option presented, which includes semicolon, tabulator, comma, blanks, or a user-defined option.

> **Tips & Tricks**
>
> We recommend using the tabulator as the separator because you can easily create and maintain files of that type via spreadsheet programs such as Microsoft Excel.

For your file structure options, choose the options FIELD NAMES AT START OF FILE and FIELD ORDER MATCHES SOURCE STRUCTURE DEFINITION. Indicate that you're using a text file by selecting ASCII in the section labeled CODE PAGE. Your completed entry should look similar to Figure 5.23.

Then click the green check button to return the SPECIFY FILES screen and save your work by clicking the SAVE button. The saved file specification should look similar to what's shown in Figure 5.24.

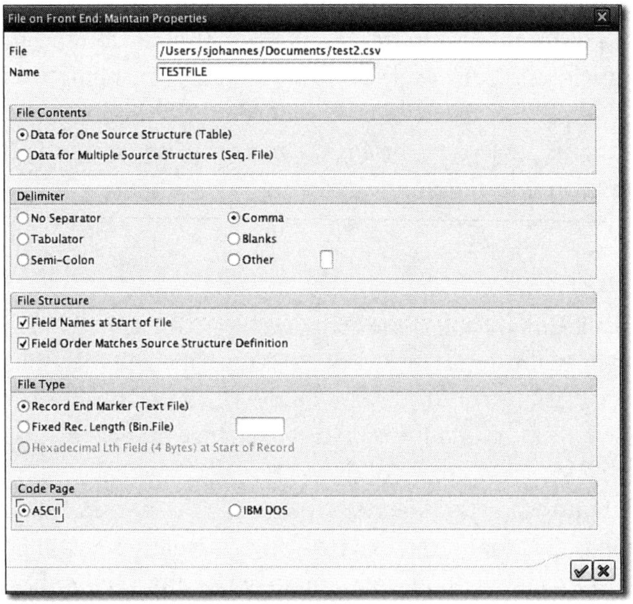

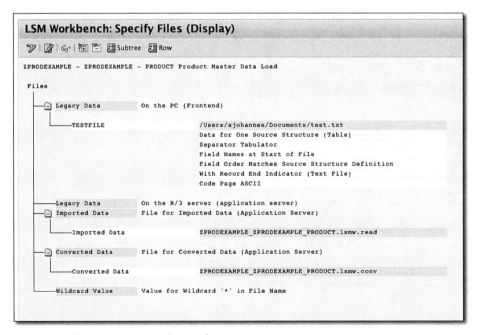

Figure 5.23 Maintain File Properties

Figure 5.24 Project File Specification

5.2.5   Running the Conversion Programs

After you've specified the file, you need to run the step READ DATA to load the file into your system. After the step is run, you can then choose to read the entire file or part of the contents.

Read data

After the file is read, review the contents to make sure the data was mapped from the physical layout into the correct import structure. You can use the step DISPLAY READ DATA to review the data that was read. Figure 5.25 shows the list of records by source structure type when viewing what data was imported into the system.

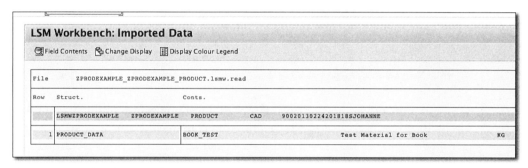

Figure 5.25 Display of Imported Data

After you've verified that the data imported is correct, you can convert the data by running the convert data step. You have the option to either convert the data to a file or create IDocs directly. If you choose to create IDocs directly, the records will start processing immediately in the background.

Convert data

You can then generate IDocs from your file by choosing the GENERATE IDOCS step. Afterward, you can start processing the IDocs generated through the step START IDOC PROCESSING.

5.2.6   Troubleshooting the Conversion Program

The most common error with the conversion program is incorrect mapping. To troubleshoot the conversion program, you can use the CREATE IDOC overview step in the LSMW project to see all of the IDocs that were processed and determine any issues with those IDocs. On the first screen, you can choose various selection criteria that allow you to

Error: incorrect mapping

restrict by date, time, message type, and EDI partner as shown in Figure 5.26. The message type corresponds to the type of the data you're loading such as products or business transactions.

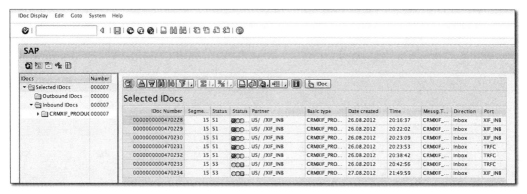

Figure 5.26 List of Processed IDocs

Depending on your selection criteria, you may get a single hit or a list of IDocs back from your query. When reviewing the list, you can see whether the IDoc is in error or posted successfully. IDocs with errors for the XIF adapter typically have a status code of 51, which indicates a validation issue. In addition to the status code, the system will display a red, yellow, or green symbol next to the error code to indicate the status. Red indicates errors have occurred, yellow indicates warnings, and green indicates processing without any errors.

IDoc error   You can drill into a single IDoc by clicking on the row and examining the errors during the posting of the IDoc. This will allow you to see if there were any mapping or posting issues that prevented the IDoc from being processed fully in the SAP CRM system. An example of an IDoc with errors is shown in Figure 5.27.

In most cases, the errors that you'll find will require mapping changes to your LSMW project, so you'll need to reload and run the conversion program again and post new IDocs into the system. However, it's possible to reprocess IDocs with errors in your system if the error wasn't related to a mapping issue but rather some other technical issue such as missing business configuration in your system. Use the project step START IDOC FOLLOW-UP to fix any errors that you may encounter that fall into this category.

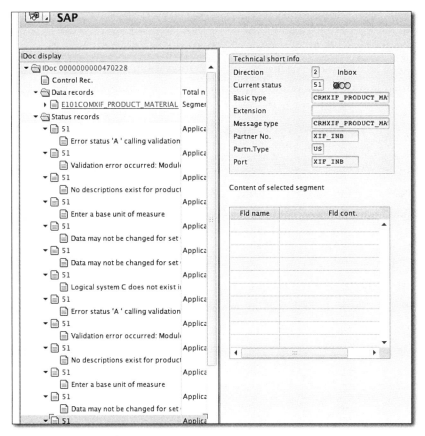

Figure 5.27 Error List for a Single IDoc

5.3 Loading Data via XIF and Custom Code

As you discovered in Section 5.1.3, the XIF adapter consists of several remote-enabled function modules. These function modules are used in IDoc processing and can be used as an application programming interface (API) for SAP CRM. In many cases, you may need more flexibility than the LSMW provides when saving data into SAP CRM.

For example, a common business requirement is converting or loading transactional data into SAP CRM. To do this, you can use the XIF adapter function module CRMXIF_ORDER_SAVE. In using the function module, you

CRMXIF_ORDER_
SAVE

need to pack and prepare the input parameters for the call. This mapping is the most difficult part, as the call itself is a simple execution. In the following sections, we'll examine the data that's required to create a business activity, as well as the custom code you'll need to build into the program.

5.3.1 Required Data Segments

In certain cases, you may be asked to load a flat file of data that contains information corresponding to transactional data in SAP CRM. For this example, you'll look at loading a business activity into your SAP CRM system. If you recall from Chapter 2, Section 2.4, a business activity is a type of business transaction. For a business transaction to be created, certain fields are required. As you also recall from Section 2.4 in Chapter 2, the data in the business transaction is stored in several different segments. Let's review the segments that are required to create a business transaction with meaningful data.

Activity transaction

When creating an activity transaction manually through the SAP Web Client, the system prompts you to enter several different pieces of information in creating the activity. Depending on how your system is configured, you might be prompted to select the transaction type you're creating. After this is selected, you then start entering the details of the transaction. In the details of the transaction, you need to enter a description of the transaction. Next, you have to select the activity partner associated with the transaction, and finally enter some long notes on the details of the interaction. If you don't enter all of this data, the system may issue an error, or you'll end up with a transaction that doesn't have enough information to provide value to your business.

Header Data

The header data of a business activity requires PROCESS TYPE, BUSINESS OBJECT TYPE, POSTING DATE, CREATED BY, and DESCRIPTION field information to be provided to the XIF adaptor function module. The coding example in Listing 5.2 shows how to build that data into your program. Note that you'll hardcode the value of the object type to BUS2000126. You may instead choose to include the process type as a value in your source data file. You can then derive the value of the object type by reading Table CRMC_PROC_TYPE.

```
*PrepareHeader
ls_xif_data-object_task  = 'I'.
ls_xif_data-process_type = '0001'.
ls_xif_data-object_type = "BUS2000126'.
ls_xif_data-posting_date = lv_created_on.
ls_xif_data-created_by = lv_created_by.
ls_xif_data-description   = lv_description.

ls_xif_data-input_fields-process_type  = 'X'.
ls_xif_data-input_fields-object_type   = 'X'.
ls_xif_data-input_fields-posting_date  = 'X'.
ls_xif_data-input_fields-created_by    = 'X'.
ls_xif_data-input_fields-description   = 'X'.
```

Listing 5.2 Prepare Header Data for XIF Function Call

Partner Data

The partner data that needs to be prepared is normally the primary partner of the activity along with the any related partners, such as a contact partner. The segment of code in Listing 5.3 shows how to add an entry for a single partner; this code can be repeated or developed as a method call as needed.

Add entry for single partner

```
CALL FUNCTION 'CONVERSION_EXIT_ALPHA_INPUT'
  EXPORTING
    input         = lv_partner
  IMPORTING
    OUTPUT        = lv_partner.

ls_partner_xif_data-partner_no   = lv_partner.
SELECT SINGLE partner_guid INTO lv_partner_guid
      FROM but000 WHERE partner = lv_partner.

CHECK sy-subrc = 0.

ls_partner_xif_data-partner_guid = lv_partner_guid.
ls_partner_xif_data-partner_fct  = lv_partner_fct.
ls_partner_xif_data-mainpartner = 'X'.
```

```
ls_partner_xif_data-input_fields-partner_no = 'X'.
ls_partner_xif_data-input_fields-partner_guid = 'X'.
ls_partner_xif_data-input_fields-partner_fct = 'X'.
ls_partner_xif_data-input_fields-mainpartner = 'X'.

INSERT ls_partner_xif_data INTO TABLE lt_partner_xif_data.
```

Listing 5.3 Prepare Partner Data for XIF Call

Partner GUID   A key issue in converted partner data is that you need to provide the GUID of an existing partner. As you may realize, if you don't have the partner number stored in the zero-filled database format used by SAP for the partner ID, you need to invoke the function module CONVERSION_ EXIT_ALPHA_INPUT to properly retrieve the GUID of the business partner.

Preparing Long Text Data

Tabular ITF format   Long text data can be difficult to load because your source file may contain the data in a single string, while SAP CRM expects the data formatted as a tabular text table or SAPscript Interchange Text Format (ITF) . The following example takes a string of data and converts it into a tabular ITF format. Please keep in mind that the code in Listing 5.4 is only needed if you don't already have the data stored as ITF. In your flat file, you can store the long text as a valid string as needed.

```
DATA: LT_LINE(3000)    TYPE C OCCURS 10 WITH HEADER LINE.

  DATA:LS_TEXT_XIF_DATA  TYPE CRMXIF_TEXT,
       LT_TEXT_LINES     TYPE CRMXIF_TLINE_T,
       LS_TEXT_LINES     TYPE CRMXIF_TLINE,
       LT_TEXT           TYPE COMT_TEXT_LINES_T,
       LS_TEXT           TYPE TLINE,
       LV_STRING         TYPE STRING,
       ILEN              TYPE I.

  CLEAR: LS_TEXT_XIF_DATA,LT_TEXT_LINES,LS_TEXT_LINES, LT_
TEXT.

  LV_STRING = LV_TEXT.
  CHECK LV_STRING IS NOT INITIAL.
```

```
CALL FUNCTION 'CONV_TEXTSTRING_TO_ITF'
  EXPORTING
    IV_TEXTSTRING = LV_STRING
  IMPORTING
    ET_ITF        = LT_TEXT.
LS_TEXT_XIF_DATA-TEXT_ID = LV_TEXTID.
LS_TEXT_XIF_DATA-INPUT_FIELDS-TEXT_ID = 'X'.
LOOP AT LT_TEXT INTO LS_TEXT.
  CLEAR LS_TEXT_LINES.
  IF SY-TABIX = 1.
    LS_TEXT_LINES-FORMAT_
COL = '*'.  "New Line Indicator    ENDIF.
  LS_TEXT_LINES-TEXT_LINE = LS_TEXT-TDLINE.
  LS_TEXT_LINES-INPUT_FIELDS-TEXT_LINE = 'X'.

  INSERT LS_TEXT_LINES INTO TABLE LT_TEXT_LINES.

ENDLOOP.

LS_TEXT_XIF_DATA-TEXT_LINES = LT_TEXT_LINES.

INSERT LS_TEXT_XIF_DATA INTO TABLE LT_TEXT_XIF_DATA.
```

Listing 5.4 Preparing Long Text Data

5.3.2 Putting It All Together

Now that we've reviewed several techniques for formatting the input data into the format required by the XIF adapter, let's look at an example program that loads the data from a flat file stored on a local desktop (PC or Mac). In this example shown in Listing 5.5, the data is contained in a tab-delimited file stored on a Mac. If you're using a Windows machine, you just need to change the path to your familiar C:\ path structure.

Load data from flat file

```
REPORT  zcrm_tpp_xif_btx_load.

DATA: lv_created_on TYPE datum,
      lv_created_by TYPE uname,
      lv_description TYPE string,
      lv_partner_fct TYPE string,
      lv_text TYPE string,
      lv_textid TYPE string.
```

```
DATA:
      lv_partner TYPE bu_partner,
      lv_partner_guid TYPE bu_partner_guid.
DATA: lt_data TYPE crmxif_bustrans_t,
      ls_xif_data TYPE crmxif_bustrans,
      lt_return TYPE bapiretm,
      ls_return type bapireti.
DATA:  ls_partner_xif_data TYPE crmxif_partner,
        lt_partner_xif_data TYPE crmxif_partner_t.
DATA: lt_line(3000)    TYPE c OCCURS 10 WITH HEADER LINE.
DATA:  lt_text_xif_data  TYPE crmxif_text_t,
       ls_text_xif_data  TYPE crmxif_text,
       lt_text_lines     TYPE crmxif_tline_t,
       ls_text_lines     TYPE crmxif_tline,
       lt_text           TYPE comt_text_lines_t,
       ls_text           TYPE tline,
       lv_string         TYPE string,
       ilen              TYPE i.
data: lv_loc_filename type string,
      lv_separator type c,
      lv_length type i,
      lt_file_content type table of string,
      ls_file_content type string.

  lv_separator = CL_ABAP_CHAR_UTILITIES=>HORIZONTAL_TAB.
  lv_loc_filename = '/Users/sjohannes/Documents/
callreports.txt'.

  CALL FUNCTION 'GUI_UPLOAD'
    exporting
      filetype =  'TXT'
      filename =  lv_loc_filename
    importing
      filelength = lv_length
    tables
      data_tab = lt_file_content.

* Skip the first line as it has file description
loop at lt_file_content into ls_file_content from 2.

  split ls_file_content at lv_separator into
          lv_created_on
          lv_created_by
```

```
            lv_description
            lv_text
            lv_partner.
*You may want to include any validation routines on the
*imported data before completing the mapping structure

*Need to provide which type of text will be updated
lv_textid = 'A002'.
*We will need to specify which partner function is being
*updated
lv_partner_fct = '00000009'.

*PrepareHeader
ls_xif_data-object_task  = 'I'.
ls_xif_data-process_type = '0001'.
ls_xif_data-object_type  = "BUS2000126".
ls_xif_data-posting_date = lv_created_on.
ls_xif_data-created_by   = lv_created_by.
ls_xif_data-description   = lv_description.

ls_xif_data-input_fields-process_type  = 'X'.
ls_xif_data-input_fields-object_type   = 'X'.
ls_xif_data-input_fields-posting_date  = 'X'.
ls_xif_data-input_fields-created_by    = 'X'.
ls_xif_data-input_fields-description   = 'X'.

CLEAR: lv_partner_guid, ls_partner_xif_data.
CHECK lv_partner IS NOT INITIAL.
CALL FUNCTION 'CONVERSION_EXIT_ALPHA_INPUT'
  EXPORTING
    input        = lv_partner
  IMPORTING
    OUTPUT       = lv_partner.

ls_partner_xif_data-partner_no   = lv_partner.
SELECT SINGLE partner_guid INTO lv_partner_guid
       FROM but000 WHERE partner = lv_partner.

CHECK sy-subrc = 0.

ls_partner_xif_data-partner_guid = lv_partner_guid.
ls_partner_xif_data-partner_fct  = lv_partner_fct.
ls_partner_xif_data-mainpartner = 'X'.
```

```
ls_partner_xif_data-input_fields-partner_no = 'X'.
ls_partner_xif_data-input_fields-partner_guid = 'X'.
ls_partner_xif_data-input_fields-partner_fct = 'X'.
ls_partner_xif_data-input_fields-mainpartner = 'X'.

INSERT ls_partner_xif_data INTO TABLE lt_partner_xif_data.
CLEAR: ls_text_xif_data,lt_text_lines,ls_text_lines, lt_text.

lv_string = lv_text.
CHECK lv_string IS NOT INITIAL.
CALL FUNCTION 'CONV_TEXTSTRING_TO_ITF'
  EXPORTING
    iv_textstring = lv_string
  IMPORTING
    et_itf        = lt_text.

ls_text_xif_data-text_id = lv_textid.
ls_text_xif_data-input_fields-text_id = 'X'.
LOOP AT lt_text INTO ls_text.
  CLEAR ls_text_lines.
  IF sy-tabix = 1.
    ls_text_lines-format_col = '*'.   "New Line Indicator
  ENDIF.
  ls_text_lines-text_line = ls_text-tdline.
  ls_text_lines-input_fields-text_line = 'X'.

  INSERT ls_text_lines INTO TABLE lt_text_lines.

ENDLOOP.

ls_text_xif_data-text_lines = lt_text_lines.

INSERT ls_text_xif_data INTO TABLE lt_text_xif_data.
INSERT ls_xif_data INTO TABLE lt_data.

CALL FUNCTION 'CRMXIF_ORDER_SAVE'
  EXPORTING
    data   = lt_data
  IMPORTING
    return = lt_return.
*You can check the results of lt_return
*If an error is found then you will want to rollback work
```

```
read table lt_return into ls_return index 1.

read table ls_return-object_msg transporting no fields
    with key type = 'E'.
if sy-subrc ne 0.

 COMMIT WORK.
else.
  rollback work.
endif.
ENDLOOP.
```

Listing 5.5 Example XIF Business Transaction Load Program

5.3.3 Example: Creating a Product

In Section 5.2, you created a product using the LSMW and XIF adapter. As a comparison, Listing 5.6 shows a sample program that creates a very basic product using a direct function module call to CRMXIF_PRODUCT_ MATERIAL_SAVE instead.

Create product with function module call

```
REPORT  zcrm_tpp_xif_load_prod.

DATA: lv_product_id TYPE string,
      lv_description TYPE string,
      lv_uom TYPE string.


DATA: lt_data TYPE comxif_product_material_t,
      ls_xif_data TYPE comxif_product_material,
      lt_return TYPE bapiretm,
      ls_return TYPE bapireti.

DATA: lt_categories TYPE comxif_pr_s_categories_t,
      ls_categories TYPE comxif_pr_s_categories,
      lt_short_description TYPE comxif_pr_s_short_text_t,
      ls_short_description TYPE comxif_pr_s_short_text,
      lt_unit TYPE comxif_pr_s_unit_t,
      ls_unit TYPE comxif_pr_s_unit.

DATA: lv_logsys TYPE logsys.

DATA: lv_loc_filename TYPE string,
```

```
            lv_separator TYPE c,
            lv_length TYPE i,
            lt_file_content TYPE TABLE OF string,
            ls_file_content TYPE string.

START-OF-SELECTION.

  lv_logsys = 'DTZ_800'.

  lv_separator = cl_abap_char_utilities=>horizontal_tab.

  lv_loc_filename = '/Users/sjohannes/Documents/
products.txt'.

  CALL FUNCTION 'GUI_UPLOAD'
    EXPORTING
      filetype   = 'TXT'
      filename   = lv_loc_filename
    IMPORTING
      filelength = lv_length
    TABLES
      data_tab   = lt_file_content.

END-OF-SELECTION.

* Skip the first line as it has file description
  LOOP AT lt_file_content INTO ls_file_content FROM 2.

    SPLIT ls_file_content AT lv_separator INTO
           lv_product_id
           lv_description
           lv_uom.

*PrepareHeader
    ls_xif_data-task  = 'I'.
    ls_xif_data-product_id = lv_product_id.
    ls_xif_data-logsys = lv_logsys.

    ls_categories-s_admin-task = 'I'.
    ls_categories-s_admin-logsys = 'DTZ_800'.
    ls_categories-data-category_id = 'MAT_FERT'.
    ls_categories-data-hierarchy_id = 'R3PRODSTYP'.
    ls_categories-data-logsys = lv_logsys.
```

```
    APPEND ls_categories TO lt_categories.

    ls_short_description-s_admin-task = 'I'.
    ls_short_description-s_admin-logsys = lv_logsys.
    ls_short_description-data-language = sy-langu.
    ls_short_description-data-short_text = lv_description.

    APPEND ls_short_description TO lt_short_description.

    ls_xif_data-common_material-s_admin-task = 'I'.
    ls_xif_data-common_material-s_admin-logsys = lv_logsys.
    ls_xif_data-common_material-data-base_uom = lv_uom.
    ls_xif_data-common_material-datax-base_uom = 'X'.


    ls_xif_data-categories = lt_categories.
    ls_xif_data-unit = lt_unit.
    ls_xif_data-short_description = lt_short_description.


    INSERT ls_xif_data INTO TABLE lt_data.
    CALL FUNCTION 'CRMXIF_PRODUCT_MATERIAL_SAVE'
      EXPORTING
        data   = lt_data
      IMPORTING
        return = lt_return.

    READ TABLE lt_return INTO ls_return INDEX 1.

    READ TABLE ls_return-object_msg TRANSPORTING NO FIELDS
        WITH KEY type = 'E'.
    IF sy-subrc NE 0.

      COMMIT WORK.
    ELSE.
      ROLLBACK WORK.
    ENDIF.
  ENDLOOP.
```

Listing 5.6 Example XIF Load Product Program

5.3.4 Example: Creating a Business Partner

The program in Listing 5.7 creates a new business partner, which is of type organization, in your SAP CRM system by executing the XIF adaptor function module CRMXIF_PARTNER_SAVE. The program uses a flat tab-delimited text file consisting of the name1, name2, street, city, country, region, and postal code of the business partner.

```
REPORT  ZCRM_TPP_XIF_BP_LOAD.

data: lv_bp_guid type bu_partner_guid,
      lv_addr_guid type SYSUUID_C.
data: lt_bp_data type CRMXIF_PARTNER_COMPLEX_T,
      ls_bp_data type CRMXIF_PARTNER_COMPLEX.
data: ls_central_data type BUS_EI_BUPA_CENTRAL_DATA,
      ls_central_datax type BUS_EI_BUPA_CENTRAL_DATA_XFLAG.
data: lt_addresses type BUS_EI_BUPA_ADDRESS_T,
      ls_addresses type BUS_EI_BUPA_ADDRESS.
data: ls_postal_data type BUS_EI_STRUC_ADDRESS,
      ls_postal_datax type BUS_EI_STRUC_ADDRESS_X.
data: lt_return type BAPIRETM,
      ls_return type BAPIRETI.
data: lv_name1 type string,
      lv_name2 type string,
      lv_street type string,
      lv_city type string,
      lv_region type string,
      lv_postal type string,
      lv_country type string.

data: lv_loc_filename type string,
      lv_separator type c,
      lv_length type i,
      lt_file_content type table of string,
      ls_file_content type string.

lv_separator = CL_ABAP_CHAR_UTILITIES=>HORIZONTAL_TAB.
lv_loc_filename = '/Users/sjohannes/Documents/bporgs.txt'.

CALL FUNCTION 'GUI_UPLOAD'
  EXPORTING
    filetype   = 'TXT'
    filename   = lv_loc_filename
```

```
  IMPORTING
    filelength = lv_length
  TABLES
    data_tab   = lt_file_content.

* Skip the first line as it has file description
loop at lt_file_content into ls_file_content from 2.
  clear: lv_bp_guid, lv_addr_guid.
  clear: ls_bp_data, ls_central_data,
         ls_postal_data, ls_addresses.
  refresh: lt_bp_data, lt_return.

  split ls_file_content at lv_separator into
          lv_name1
          lv_name2
          lv_street
          lv_city
          lv_region
          lv_postal
          lv_country.

  lv_bp_guid = cl_system_uuid=>create_uuid_x16_static( ).
  lv_addr_guid = cl_system_uuid=>create_uuid_c32_static( ).

  ls_bp_data-header-object_task = 'I'.
  ls_bp_data-header-object_instance-partner_guid = lv_bp_
guid.

  ls_central_data-bp_control-category = '2'.
  ls_central_data-bp_control-grouping = '0001'.
  ls_central_data-bp_organization-name1 = lv_name1.
  ls_central_data-bp_organization-name2 =  lv_name2.
  ls_central_datax-bp_organization-name1 = 'X'.
  ls_central_datax-bp_organization-name2 = 'X'.

  ls_bp_data-central_data-common-data = ls_central_data.
  ls_bp_data-central_data-common-datax = ls_central_datax.

  ls_postal_data-street = lv_street.
  ls_postal_data-region = lv_region.
  ls_postal_data-country = lv_country.
  ls_postal_data-POSTL_COD1 = lv_postal.
  ls_postal_data-city = lv_city.
```

```
ls_postal_data-standardaddress = 'X'.

ls_postal_datax-street = 'X'.
ls_postal_datax-region = 'X'.
ls_postal_datax-country = 'X'.
ls_postal_datax-POSTL_COD1 = 'X'.
ls_postal_datax-city = 'X'.
ls_postal_datax-standardaddress = 'X'.

ls_addresses-data-postal-data = ls_postal_data.
ls_addresses-data-postal-datax = ls_postal_datax.
ls_addresses-currently_valid = 'I'.
ls_addresses-data_key-guid = lv_addr_guid.
ls_addresses-task = 'I'.
insert ls_addresses into table lt_addresses.

ls_bp_data-central_data-address-addresses[] = lt_
addresses[].
insert ls_bp_data into table lt_bp_data.

CALL FUNCTION 'CRMXIF_PARTNER_SAVE'
  EXPORTING
    DATA  = lt_bp_data
  IMPORTING
    RETURN = lt_return.
read table lt_return into ls_return index 1.
read table ls_return-object_msg transporting no fields
  with key type = 'E'.
if sy-subrc ne 0.
  COMMIT WORK.
else.
  rollback work.
endif.
endloop.
```

Listing 5.7 Example XIF Business Partner Program

5.4 Extracting Data via the XIF Adapter

In the previous sections of this chapter, we've shown how the XIF adapter can be used to import data into SAP CRM. However, that isn't the only purpose for which you can use the XIF adapter. In some situations, you may need to extract and send data from SAP CRM to an external source. We'll show you how the outbound XIF adapter can accomplish this task in the following sections. You can either output the data via XML or via IDoc.

To set up the XIF adapter for outbound IDoc processing, you need to determine what data needs to be transferred and whether the existing IDoc structure meets your needs. Then, follow these steps to configure the system:

Outbound IDoc
Processing

1. Configure an RFC destination that will receive your outbound IDocs. In addition to the RFC destination, you need to create a logical system for that outbound destination.

2. Create a receiver port for outbound IDoc processing.

3. Create an IDoc partner profile that will use the receiver port created in your previous steps.

4. After the IDoc basis configuration is complete, configure the XIF adapter to use your IDoc outbound configuration.

5. Create a new outbound XIF adapter site that will use the partner profile.

6. Assign a subscription of outbound BDoc data to this site.

7. Link the outbound site with the corresponding outbound BDoc type.

The following sections provide the technical details to complete these steps.

5.4.1 Create a Logical System

To create a logical system, use Transaction SM30 to maintain the view V_TBDLS. Launch Transaction SM30, and then open this table in maintenance mode. For this example, name your logical system "CADCLNT900" and enter the description "Development/Test Client" as shown in Figure 5.28. Keep in mind the definition of logical systems is usually set up by your SAP NetWeaver administrator. If you don't have another SAP CRM system to receive the IDoc, you can instead use the logical system name of your current SAP CRM system for this exercise.

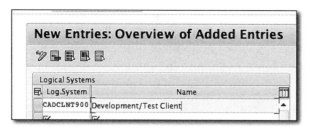

Figure 5.28 New Logical System CADCLNT900

5.4.2 Create Receiver Port

The receiver port in IDoc customizing defines the transactional RFC (tRFC) destination that will receive the IDocs generated by your interface.

To set this up, use Transaction WE21. Once in Transaction WE21, expand the left-hand menu tree of ports, and choose the TRANSACTIONAL RFC node. Click the CREATE button.

RFC A popup window appears asking you to either choose a generated name or enter your own port name. In this example, let the system generate the port name. Click the CHECKMARK button when you're finished.

Now enter a description for your receiver port such as "XIF Outbound Port". Select IDoc RECORD TYPES SAP RELEASE 4.x as the VERSION. Finally, enter the name of the RFC destination that you'll use (see Figure 5.29).

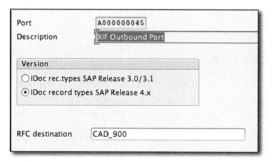

Figure 5.29 Outbound Receiver Port

5.4.3   Create Partner Profile

The partner profile tells the system what type of IDoc messages you're transferring out of the system and to what destination. To set up the partner profile, use Transaction WE20. Once in Transaction WE20, expand the PARTNER PROFILE left-hand navigation tree. Select the PARTNER TYPE LS node, and click the CREATE button. Name this partner number "DTZ_800", which was the logical system of your outbound client. In the POST PROCESSING: PERMITTED AGENT tab, enter the type as "US" and the agent as your user ID. Your local language such as "EN" for English is defaulted in the LANG. field. The screen should look like the one shown in Figure 5.30. Click SAVE when you're finished.

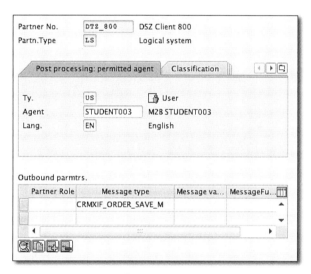

Figure 5.30 Partner Profile

After this data has been successfully saved, you'll add a new entry under outbound parameters. For this example, choose the message type CRMXIF_ORDER_SAVE_M. For the receiver port, choose the port that you created in the previous step. The package size should be a reasonable number of outbound entries that should be processed together. In this case, set this to "100". For the OUTPUT MODE, choose COLLECT IDOCS. Next, choose the IDoc type as CRMXIF_ORDER_SAVE_M02, and make sure CANCEL PROCESSING AFTER SYNTAX ERROR is checked. After this information is entered and looks like the screen shown in Figure 5.31, click SAVE.

Outbound parameters

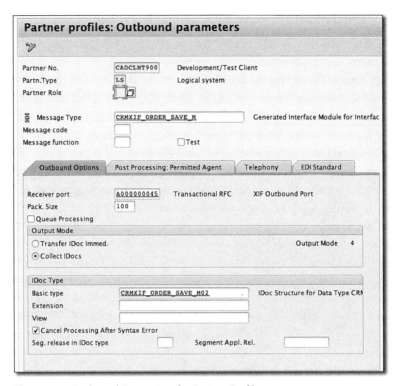

Figure 5.31 Outbound Parameters for Partner Profile

5.4.4 Create an XIF Adapter Site

Outbound processing

As shown earlier in Section 5.2.3 with inbound IDoc processing for the XIF adapter, you need to create an SAP CRM Middleware site for XIF processing for XIF outbound processing. To do this, launch Transaction SMOEAC. Once in Transaction SMOEAC, select SITE as the object type, and then click the CREATE button. Give the site a name such as "XIF_OUTBOUND_IDOC", and choose the external interface for IDocs. Click on the site attributes, enter the name of the partner profile you created—"CADCLNT900"—and enter the partner profile type as "LS" for logical system.

This setting connects the XIF adapter outbound to the IDoc configuration that you created. Unlike inbound processing where you are instantly ready to start transferring data into SAP CRM, there are additional steps required to start transferring the data from your system.

Create a Subscription

The SAP CRM Middleware requires you to set up a subscription for every outbound site that you'll be using. These subscriptions specify what type of BDoc messages should be sent to your external site via the middleware. You'll then assign to the subscription all of the business transactions to your site.

Maintain Settings in Transaction CRMXIF_C1

In this step, you link the BDoc structure to your outbound site by launching Transaction CRMXIF_C1. Once in Transaction CRMXIF_C1, you'll choose XIF_OUTBOUND_IDOC as your site name, BUS_TRANS_MSG as the BDoc Type, and CRMXIF_ORDER_SAVE as the Interface Name. Finally, you need to make sure the flags Complete and Return are checked. Save your work. Your completed entry should look similar to Figure 5.32.

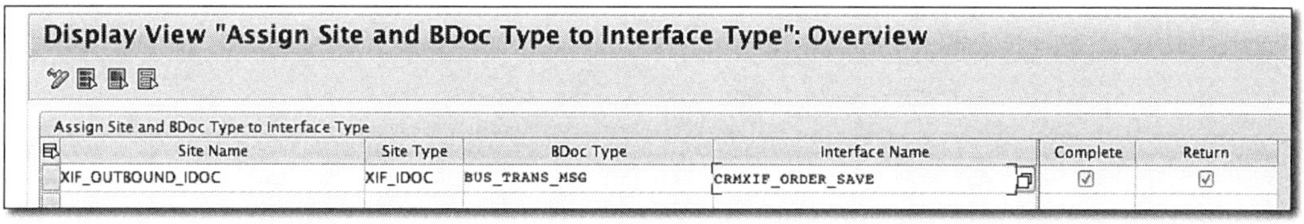

Figure 5.32 Completed Entry in Transaction CRMXIF_C1

You've now completed your setup for the XIF adapter for outbound IDoc processing. This allows you to send data to another system capable of processing and receiving IDoc information from an SAP NetWeaver ABAP-based system.

5.5 Summary

As you've discovered in this chapter, the XIF adapter provides a powerful means of importing data into and exporting data out of an SAP CRM system. The XIF adapter supports the most common business objects in an SAP CRM system by exposing the SAP CRM Middleware through an IDoc or RFC interface. The IDoc interface of the XIF adapter can leverage the LSMW to allow for conversion of data into SAP CRM with minimal coding required. For more complicated requirements, you can use the function module interface of the XIF adapter to build complex data load programs or even call those via tools that speak RFC to load data into SAP CRM.

Although the most common use of the XIF adapter is converting data into SAP CRM, the XIF adapter can also extract and send data to external systems. This data can be sent via XML or IDocs and can be exported to a either an RFC-compatible middleware or a flat file system.

Due to the broad range of capabilities provided by the XIF adapter, it remains a powerful tool for SAP CRM technical developers who need to import or update data in an SAP CRM system since its release in version 3.X of SAP CRM.

In the next chapter, we'll examine how the Post Processing Framework in SAP CRM can be used for both output determination and business logic execution.

Even though a central electronic repository should replace the need for print outputs, they still exist. A modern output system should be capable of multiple forms of communication, and not just printing. The Post Processing Framework redefines the concept of output beyond print.

6   The Post Processing Framework: Output and Actions

The Post Processing Framework (PPF) is used in SAP CRM to generate output from business transactions. In this chapter, we'll provide an introduction to the framework, and then explain how to customize the framework to meet your needs, how to schedule automatic processing of outputs, and how to use the framework for tasks that don't necessarily entail output, but rather involve the update of business transaction data.

6.1   Introduction to the Post Processing Framework (PPF)

The PPF is a generic framework built in SAP CRM to handle the execution of business logic, including, but not limited to, output control. This framework allows for the creation of output from a business transaction that can include print, fax, and email. In addition to this standard type of output, the PPF provides the ability to execute methods that contain business logic. This business logic can create, change, or copy the business transaction and other data contained in the SAP CRM system.

Business logic execution

Framework: three parts
The framework consists of three parts: framework one order application code, customizing definitions, and application-/user-defined processing logic:

▶ The one order application code refers to the embedded calls to the PPF found inside the code that creates and maintains business transaction data.

▶ The framework customizing definition consists of a series of actions that are grouped together in an action profile that will execute one or more processing methods. An *action* is either an output execution or code execution that can be scheduled or triggered immediately. In addition, the processing of the action can be restricted to only start after a logical condition is met, even though the action has been scheduled for processing.

▶ The application-/user-defined processing logic is the code that will execute the business logic defined in customizing. This includes standard code delivered by SAP and custom code created on your system.

PPF: Beyond output control
The PPF can be used for activities beyond document outputs. In past projects, it has been used as a poor-man's version of SAP Business Workflow because it can trigger email notifications and perform transaction updates based on certain conditions being met. It can also be used to create reminders or follow-up activities from an existing transaction when certain logic is met. For example, in complaint processing when a complaint is set to IN PROCESS, you may want to assign a task to a partner in the complaint to perform an investigation. You can use the PPF to create a follow-up task from the complaint without using any code.

As we go further through this chapter, we'll take a look at the options available and provide some ideas on how they are commonly used.

However, we strongly stress that this dive into the PPF should serve as a starting point for you to come up with new creative ideas to meet business requirements in your SAP CRM system for business transactions.

6.2   Customizing

You'll need to set up the PPF through a series of customizing steps. These customizing steps define an *action profile* that will be associated with your business transaction type. To better understand how the customizing works, we'll review a simple example of a standard delivered action profile, and then discuss all of the different options that are available for actions. We'll also look at the steps you'll follow to create a new action profile using a system wizard.

Action profile

6.2.1   Standard Delivered Action Profiles

SAP delivers several standard profiles for the standard business transactions delivered in SAP CRM. You can use these profiles as a template for your own custom process types. We recommend that you never change the standard delivered profiles, but rather either copy those to your version or build action profiles based on that.

SAP standard profiles as a template

To view an existing action profile, run Transaction SPPFCADM. On the main screen shown in Figure 6.1, choose an application. The application for business transactions is CRM_ORDER. After you've selected the CRM_ORDER application, you can then click the DEFINE ACTION PROFILE AND ACTIONS button from the main screen. This will bring up a list of action profiles defined for business transaction types. Each action profile contains one or more actions associated with it. The action profile defines what will be executed but not when. This is important to keep in mind because you'll have a separate customizing step that defines when the actions will be executed.

Bring up existing action profile

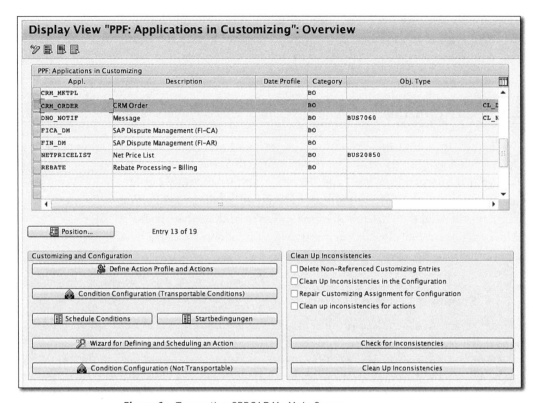

Figure 6.1 Transaction SPPCADM: Main Screen

Basic Attributes

If you take a look at the definition of the action profile name ACTIVITY as shown in Figure 6.2, you'll notice that you need to define several basic attributes. These include the technical name, DESCRIPTION, CATEGORY OF OBJECT TYPE, OBJECT TYPE NAME, DATE PROFILE, and CONTEXT CLASS.

The CATEGORY OF OBJECT TYPE can be either a business repository object or persistent class. For usage within the SAP CRM business transaction, you'll always choose the BUSINESS OBJECT REPOSITORY as your type. The OBJECT TYPE name corresponds to the BOR object that corresponds to the transaction type using the action profile.

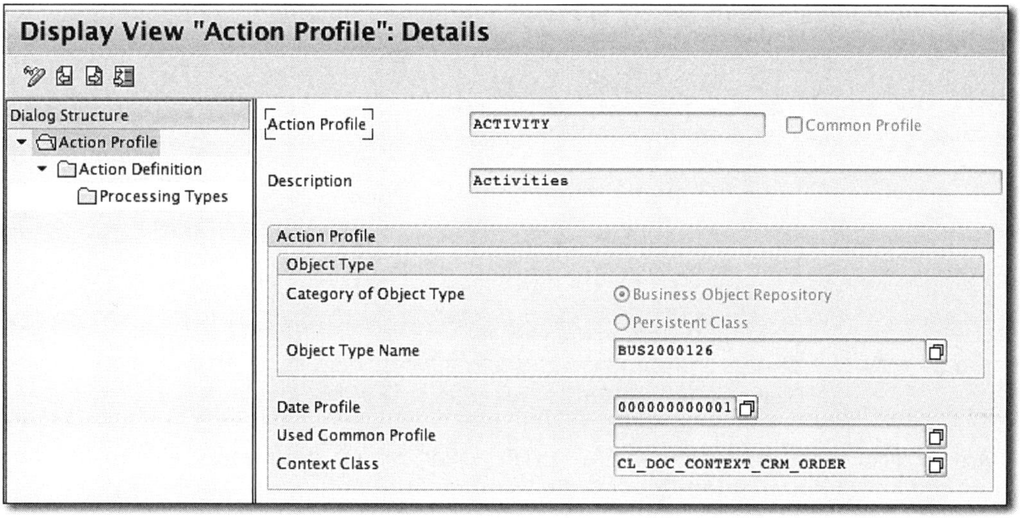

Display View "Action Profile": Details

Dialog Structure
- ▾ Action Profile
  - ▾ Action Definition
    - Processing Types

Action Profile: ACTIVITY   ☐ Common Profile

Description: Activities

Action Profile

Object Type

Category of Object Type: ⦿ Business Object Repository
     ○ Persistent Class

Object Type Name: BUS2000126

Date Profile: 000000000001

Used Common Profile:

Context Class: CL_DOC_CONTEXT_CRM_ORDER

Figure 6.2 Standard Profile Activity

In your standard SAP CRM system, the BUS2000126 object type is the standard business object type for activity transactions. This use of business object types is quite common throughout SAP CRM. In fact, in the Web Client, the UI components are named in a similar fashion.

Business object type

The final attribute is the context class. This should always default to CL_DOC_CONTEXT_CRM_ORDER. This class acts a data handler that provides information about the transaction being processed to the action.

Context class

6.2.2 Actions

Each action profile contains one or more actions defined as shown in Figure 6.3. Actions must always exist within a profile to be used. These actions can perform various tasks such as create a print output, send an email, send a fax, copy the document to a new transaction, or call custom logic. In the activity profile, actions are defined for creating a follow-up transaction, sending a reminder email, and printing a copy of the activity.

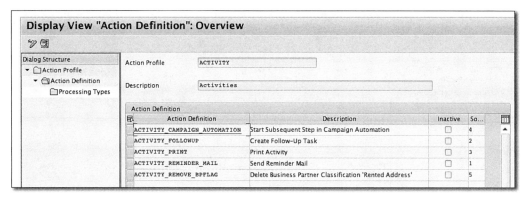

Display View "Action Definition": Overview

Dialog Structure				
▼ ☐ Action Profile	Action Profile	ACTIVITY		
▼ ☐ Action Definition	Description	Activities		
☐ Processing Types				

Action Definition

Action Definition	Description	Inactive	So...
ACTIVITY_CAMPAIGN_AUTOMATION	Start Subsequent Step in Campaign Automation	☐	4
ACTIVITY_FOLLOWUP	Create Follow-Up Task	☐	2
ACTIVITY_PRINT	Print Activity	☐	3
ACTIVITY_REMINDER_MAIL	Send Reminder Mail	☐	1
ACTIVITY_REMOVE_BPFLAG	Delete Business Partner Classification 'Rented Address'	☐	5

Figure 6.3 Standard Profile Activity Action Overview Screen

Action definition   If you look at the ACTIVITY_PRINT action definition as shown in Figure 6.4, you'll see the definition of the action. The processing types are defined on a further drilldown in a separate screen. The action definition defines when the action will be executed, whether output should be based on a particular partner, and how many times can it be executed. The processing type defines what type of processing will be performed by the action.

Several options are defined in the action definition, including:

► PROCESSING TIME

► PROCESSING TIMES NOT PERMITTED

► SORT ORDER FOR DISPLAY

► SCHEDULE AUTOMATICALLY

► DELETE AFTER PROCESSING

► CHANGEABLE IN DIALOG

► EXECUTABLE IN DIALOG

► DISPLAY IN TOOLBOX

► PARTNER-DEPENDENT

► PARTNER FUNC.

► DETERMINATION TECHNOLOGY

► RULE TYPE

► ACTION MERGING

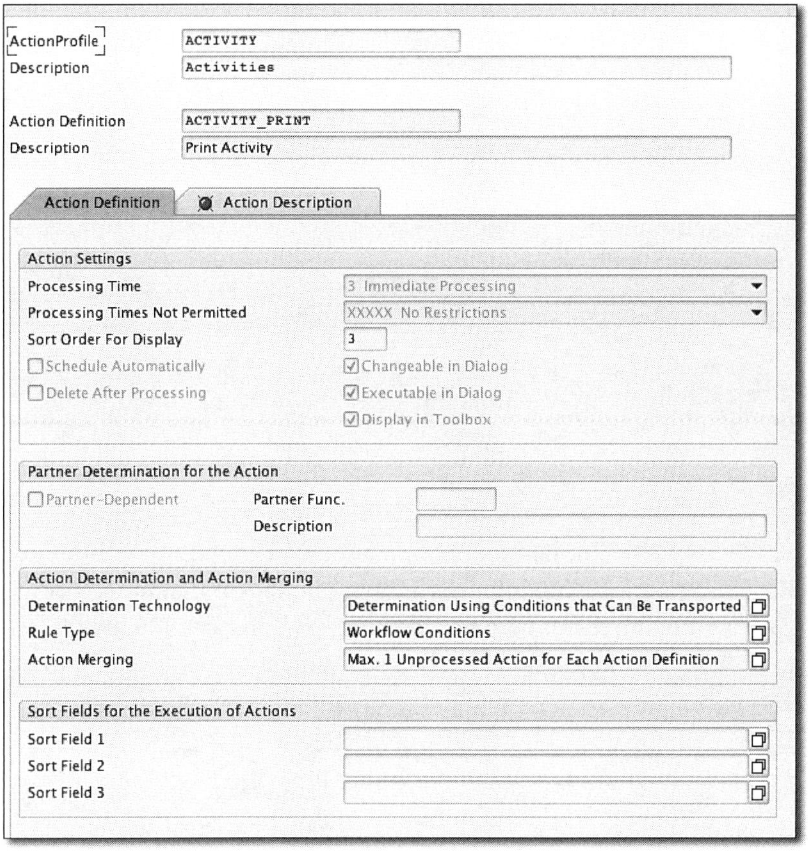

ActionProfile	ACTIVITY
Description	Activities

Action Definition	ACTIVITY_PRINT
Description	Print Activity

Action Definition | **Action Description**

Action Settings

Processing Time	3 Immediate Processing
Processing Times Not Permitted	XXXXX No Restrictions
Sort Order For Display	3

☐ Schedule Automatically   ☑ Changeable in Dialog
☐ Delete After Processing   ☑ Executable in Dialog
        ☑ Display in Toolbox

Partner Determination for the Action

☐ Partner-Dependent   Partner Func.   [ ]
        Description

Action Determination and Action Merging

Determination Technology	Determination Using Conditions that Can Be Transported
Rule Type	Workflow Conditions
Action Merging	Max. 1 Unprocessed Action for Each Action Definition

Sort Fields for the Execution of Actions

Sort Field 1	
Sort Field 2	
Sort Field 3	

Figure 6.4 Standard Activity Print Action

We'll describe the options shown in Figure 6.4 in more detail in the following subsections. Understanding the options on this screen is key to understanding how to customize the PPF to meet your business needs.

Action definition options

Processing Time

For all actions, there are normally three possible times when the action will be processed as shown in Figure 6.5: PROCESSING USING SELECTION REPORT, IMMEDIATE PROCESSING, and PROCESSING WHEN SAVING DOCUMENT.

Selection report   PROCESSING USING SELECTION REPORT causes the action to be scheduled for later processing. The action will then only run when the selection report for processing action is running. This report is called RSPPFPRO-CESS, and we'll examine how to run and schedule this report in Section 6.3 of this chapter.

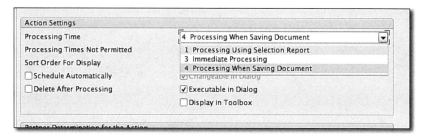

Figure 6.5 Processing Times for Action

Immediate   IMMEDIATE PROCESSING means that the logic of the action will be executed at the time of scheduling or trigger. This means that the action will normally use the current state of the business transaction to generate its result. You'll normally use this if say you wanted an immediate printout through an action.

When saving document   PROCESSING WHEN SAVING DOCUMENT waits to trigger the output after the user saves the changes to the business transaction. This option is useful in cases where say an action should trigger an email when a status has been changed. However, if the user decides not to save his work, then the email shouldn't be sent. By scheduling the action to only be processed upon a save, this allows the action to only be processed when a change is committed to the document instead of immediately.

Processing Times Not Permitted

Prevent action   The PROCESSING TIMES NOT PERMITTED options allow you to prevent the action from being scheduled manually or from executing in a way that isn't intended. In most cases, you'll always use NO RESTRICTIONS. For this setting, you can see the other options as shown in Figure 6.6.

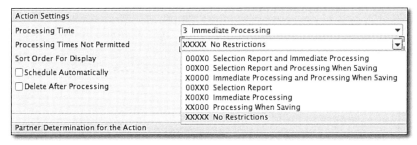

Figure 6.6 Processing Times Not Permitted

Sort Order for Display

The Sort Order For Display option refers to how the list of actions should be displayed to your end user from the Web Client of those available to schedule.

Schedule Automatically

This flag tells the system that this action should always be scheduled regardless.

Delete After Processing

If the Delete After Processing flag is set, then the record of the action will be deleted from the transaction history after the action is executed.

Changeable in Dialog

This allows the user to change the output parameters of the action before the action is scheduled.

Executable in Dialog

This allows the user to execute/schedule an action in the Web Client, instead of it having to be generated through conditional output. A common example of why not to check this flag is that you may not want your users to also be able to generate the automatic notifications and you may want to only allow them to generate manual printouts.

Display in Toolbox

The DISPLAY IN TOOLBOX option lists the action as available for the user to schedule from the Web Client.

Partner Determination

Deliver output of actions to specific partner functions

In some cases, you'll only want the output of an action to be sent to a particular partner function. To do this, mark the action as PARTNER-DEPENDENT. This tells the system that the action can only be scheduled when a partner function has been maintained on the business transaction.

Also, you need to specify the partner function that the results of the action will be sent to by entering the partner function in the PARTNER FUNC. field next to the PARTNER-DEPENDENT checkbox. A perfect example is sending an email to a particular partner listed on your business transaction.

Determination Technology

The DETERMINATION TECHNOLOGY option defines how an action should be determined for scheduling by the system. Even though there are several options, you'll normally use the DETERMINATION USING CONDITIONS for all of your customizing. By selecting this option, you're indicating that the action may be conditionally scheduled and executed. This means that even though the action may be assigned to a profile that is assigned to your business transaction, it won't guarantee unconditional execution unless you specify that to be the case. The other possible values are shown in Figure 6.7.

Select rules

After you've defined the determination technology, select the type of rules used to define whether an action should be started and/or scheduled. The two options are CONDITIONS USING BUSINESS ADDIN (BAdI) or WORKFLOW CONDITIONS as shown in Figure 6.8. The easiest and most commonly used option is WORKFLOW CONDITIONS. We don't recommend using the BAdI option.

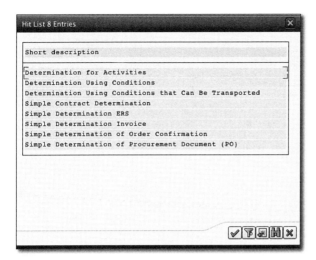

Figure 6.7 Determination Popup Screen

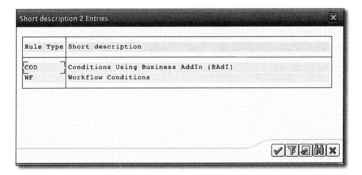

Figure 6.8 Condition Types for Actions

Action merging

The ACTION MERGING field, as shown earlier in Figure 6.4, defines how often an action can be executed for your transaction. The possible values that are normally used include MAX. 1 ACTION FOR EACH ACTION DEFINITION, MAX. 1 UNPROCESSED ACTION FOR EACH ACTION DEFINITION, and MAX. 1 UNPROCESSED ACTION FOR EACH PROCESSING TYPE, as shown in Figure 6.9.

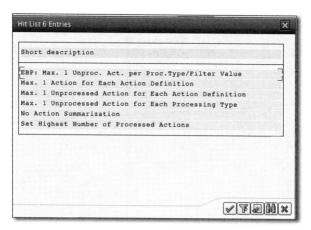

Figure 6.9 Number of Actions Possible Options

Processing Types

On the left-hand navigation bar shown previously in Figure 6.3, you see a section underneath the ACTION DEFINITION called PROCESSING TYPES. This section is where you define the types of processing that an action will perform. These processing types can be print, email, or method calls. Under PROCESSING TYPE, there is usually just one entry associated per action; you can have multiple entries, but it isn't recommended.

Each processing type has unique attribute definitions, which require different entry screens. Let's review these options in the following subsections. The technical names of the options are SMART FORMS PRINT, SMART FORMS MAIL, and METHOD CALL. When you click on the processing types, a screen appears that contains a list of processing types for the action and the attributes for the processing type selected.

Smart Forms

Smart Forms Print option

For the SMART FORMS PRINT option, you'll maintain the following attributes: FORM NAME, PROCESSING CLASS, PROCESSING METHOD, and ARCHIVE MODE, as shown in Figure 6.10:

▶ FORM NAME is a name of a valid smart form in your system. In the standard delivered SAP CRM system, the class CL_DOC_PROCESSING_ CRM_ORDER has been delivered to handle the print output needs of the standard smart forms delivered in the SAP CRM system for various business transaction types.

▶ The PROCESSING CLASS is the name of an ABAP Objects class that contains a method to process the smart form.

▶ The PROCESSING METHOD is a method of the processing class that will perform the processing of the smart form specified.

▶ The ARCHIVE MODE determines whether the results of the output should be stored.

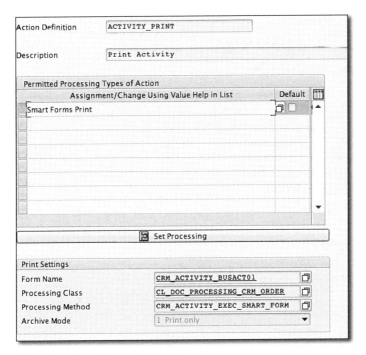

Figure 6.10 Smart Forms Print Settings

For the SMART FORMS MAIL option, you have the following fields: FORM NAME, FORM TYPE, FORMAT, and PERSONALIZATION TYPE, as shown in Figure 6.11.

Smart Forms Mail option

For the METHOD CALL action, you have the METHOD and PROCESSING PARAMETERS settings, as shown in Figure 6.12.

Method Call options

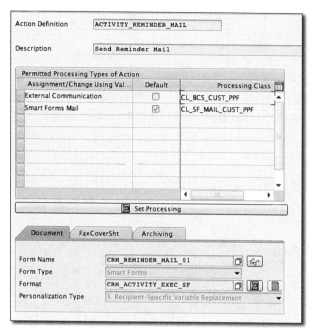

Figure 6.11 Smart Forms Mail Options

Figure 6.12 Method Call Processing Options

6.2.3 Condition Configuration for Actions

Up to this point, you've explored how actions are defined in terms of what will be executed and how they can be processed. For those actions that you want the system to schedule and/or only start after certain criteria, the system provides the *condition configuration concept* to allow you to control how actions are triggered. The idea behind conditions is that not all of the actions that may be associated with a business transaction should be scheduled and/or executed at the same time. A classic example is sending out an order confirmation, which should only be sent when the order status has been sent to be confirmed and free of errors. If you didn't have conditions, then the system would always execute your action or schedule it for processing regardless of its status.

Control how actions are triggered

To access condition configuration, you'll once again execute Transaction SPPFCADM and then follow these steps:

Condition configuration

1. From the main screen, select the CRM_ORDER line in the table, and then click on CONDITION CONFIGURATION (TRANSPORTABLE CONDITIONS) as show earlier in Figure 6.1. This brings you into the CONDITIONS FOR ACTIONS: DISPLAY overview screen as shown in Figure 6.13.

2. To view the conditions for a particular action, select the action profile in the upper-left corner. For this review, select the ACTIVITY profile.

3. Now choose the action to review by selecting from the list in the upper-right portion of your screen. For this review of the customizing, select ACTIVITY_REMINDER_EMAIL.

4. In the lower section of the screen, you can now see the OVERVIEW tab, which shows part of the action definition. Click the PROCESSING DETAILS tab to open a screen similar to Figure 6.14. The information contained here is the processing type information defined for the action. The remaining two tabs allow you to define two different sets of conditions for an action: the schedule conditions and start conditions.

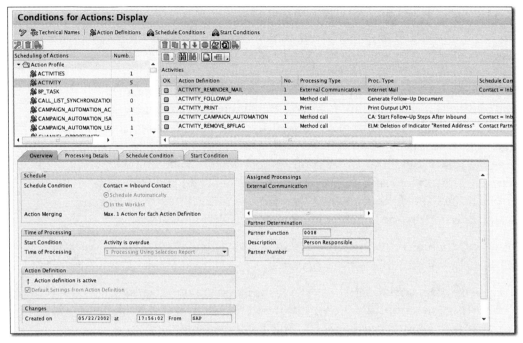

Figure 6.13 Overview Screen for Condition Configuration

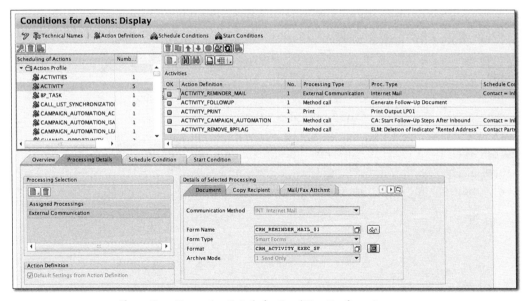

Figure 6.14 Processing Details for Condition Configuration

If you click on the SCHEDULE CONDITION tab in the lower part of the screen you'll bring up the first condition type you can customize—the schedule condition—as shown in Figure 6.15. The schedule condition defines when an action should be raised or scheduled by the system for processing. If there are no schedule conditions for an action, and the action hasn't been defined as scheduled automatically, then the action won't be scheduled for processing unless explicitly scheduled by a user.

First condition type: schedule condition

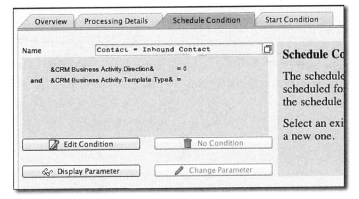

Figure 6.15 Schedule Condition Logic

The second condition type is the start condition as shown in the START CONDITION tab in Figure 6.16.

Second condition type: start condition

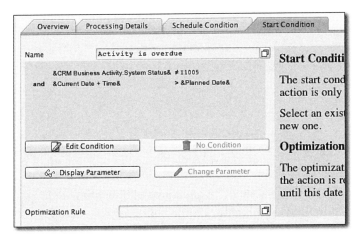

Figure 6.16 Start Condition Logic

This is used to define when an action should be processed. Normally, you use this when an action is set for batch processing. A classic example is sending a user a notice that something is overdue. You would have the system schedule the action automatically or based on a business transaction status being met such as IN PROCESS. The start condition would then be based on a combination of date criteria such as today's date being greater than the creation date of the transaction + 30 days. When this is met, the system would execute your action and send an email message to the employee responsible. This type of action condition is found for the action ACTIVITY_REMINDER_EMAIL found in the standard action profile called ACTIVITY.

Condition definition

The mechanism to define conditions was specified earlier in your action definition. If you recall, you normally use business workflow-based conditions for this task. This means that the conditions will use the same rule editor found in SAP Business Workflow, and the data available in the rule editor will be based on the BOR definition of the business transaction. This is important to remember because if you've extended your business transaction, the custom fields created via the Application Enhancement Tool (AET) or Easy Enhancement Workbench (EEWB) won't be present in the standard delivered BOR object created by SAP.

Business Object Builder

To see what fields are available for condition logic, you'll need to use the Business Object Builder, which you access with Transaction SWO1. (Note this is Transaction Sierra Whiskey Oscar One and not Sierra Whiskey Zero One.) On the initial screen of the transaction, enter the business object type that corresponds to the transaction. For business activities, this is "BUS2000126". Choose DISPLAY, and you'll see a tree view of the object.

You can expand the KEY FIELDS and ATTRIBUTES nodes of the tree. This shows all data that is available. In addition, there is a list of methods for that business object. In the standard system, you can use the result data of any method call as a comparison value for conditions.

Make custom business transaction fields available

Now if you aren't familiar with SAP Business Workflow or the BOR, you may be wondering how to get your custom business transaction fields available for comparison within your condition. The good news is that this isn't complicated, but does require some additional work. To make your fields available, you need to create a subtype of the standard object, delegate the standard business object type to your subtype, and then add the custom attributes to your business object subtype.

> **Note**
>
> For this book, we'll cover the basics of this extension; however, for more in-depth explanation, we recommend that you review the second edition of *Practical Workflow for SAP* by Ginger Gatling et al. (SAP PRESS 2009).

We'll go over the basics in the following subsections.

Creating the Subtype

The first step you need to take when making your custom business Delegation transaction fields available is to create the subtype of a standard business object type. To create the subtype, you first must verify that the business object type hasn't been delegated. The reason for this is that the standard SAP CRM system only allows one delegation per standard business object type. To do this, open Transaction SWO1, and then choose SETTINGS • DELEGATE. On this screen, you shouldn't see an entry for your business object.

> **Note**
>
> If you see an entry on this screen, then you should skip ahead to add the attribute to your business object subtype.

Now that you've verified that an entry doesn't exist, you can return to the initial screen of Transaction SWO1. Enter the business object that you want to extend; for this example enter "BUS2000126". Choose the CREATE SUBTYPE button, and a popup appears as shown in Figure 6.17. Enter the following information:

▶ OBJECT TYPE: "ZBS2000126"

▶ OBJECT NAME: "ZBS2000126"

▶ NAME: "Business Activity"

▶ DESCRIPTION: "Extended Business Activity"

▶ Program: ZBUS2000126

▶ Application: "Z"

Figure 6.17 Create a New Business Object Subtype

Create and release the object

After you've entered these settings, click the Execute button to create the object. Click Save on the next screen. The object can't be used until you release it and generate the object.

To release the object, choose the Edit • Change Release Status • Object Type • To Implemented menu option. Next, generate the object by clicking the beach ball icon.

Once you've finished, you can delegate the standard business object to use your subtype.

Delegating the Subtype

Go to the main screen of Transaction SWO1 and choose the Settings • Delegate menu option. Change the screen to edit mode, and choose the New Entries option. Enter "BUS2000126" as the Object type, enter your user ID in the Person Responsible field, and ZBS2000126 should be in the Delegation type field, as shown in Figure 6.18.

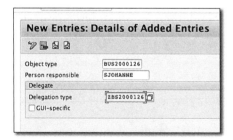

Figure 6.18 Delegate Object Type

Click SAVE, and you may be prompted for a transport request. If this happens, use an existing transport or create a new one as appropriate.

Now that the delegation has been defined, the system will use your subtype as a run-time definition for the BUS2000126 object. The subtype you created will inherit all standard attributes of the BUS2000126 object, but you'll be able to add additional attributes to that object without modifying the standard SAP business object. This technique is similar to how inheritance works in standard object-oriented programming methods.

Use subtype as a run-time definition

Adding the Additional Attribute

Now, go back to the start screen of Transaction SWO1. Enter your subtype type as "ZBS2000126", and click on the CHANGE button. On the next screen, move your mouse cursor to highlight the ATTRIBUTES node, and then click the CREATE button. The system asks you to create with ABAP dictionary field proposals; choose No. In the next popup screen, fill out the values as illustrated in Figure 6.19 with the information from Table 6.1, and then click the CHECKMARK button to continue.

Field Name	Value/Option
ATTRIBUTE	ZZHASHTAG
NAME	Hashtag
DESCRIPTION	Hashtag
SOURCE	VIRTUAL
ATTRIBUTE PROPERTIES	(none checked)
DATA TYPE REFERENCE	ABAP DICTIONARY
REFERENCE TABLE	CRMD_CUSTOMER_H
REFERENCE FIELD	ZZHASHTAG

Table 6.1 Field Values for Change Object Type

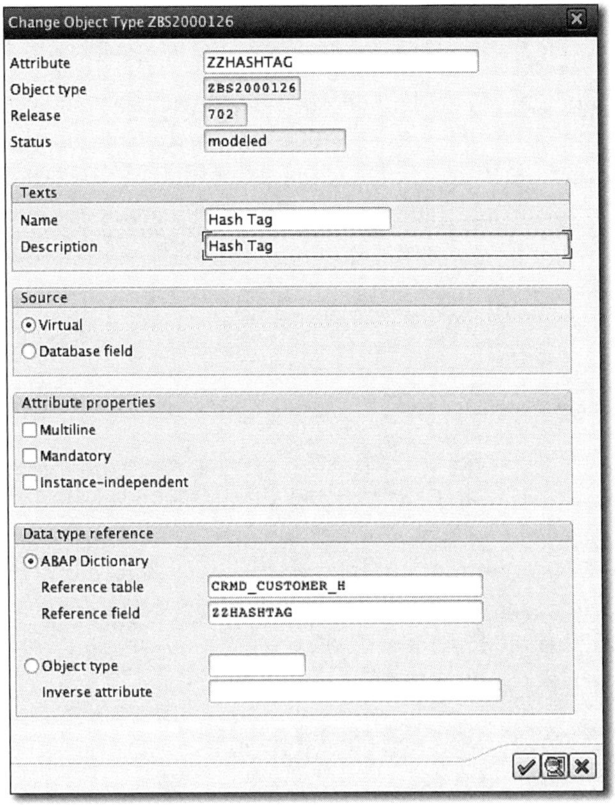

Figure 6.19 Create a New Attribute for Business Object

Code logic for attribute

You'll now see your hashtag attribute listed under ATTRIBUTES. You need to code the logic to retrieve this by highlighting the attribute and choosing the PROGRAM option. The system then warns you that the attribute isn't implemented, and asks if you want to generate a template of the missing section. Choose YES to code your logic. You'll need to implement the program section as shown in Listing 6.1.

```
GET_PROPERTY ZZHASHTAG CHANGING CONTAINER.
  data: lv_object_guid type crmt_object_guid,
        ls_customer_h_wrk type CRMT_CUSTOMER_H_WRK.

  lv_object_guid = object-key-businessprocess.
  CALL FUNCTION 'CRM_CUSTOMER_H_READ_OW'
    EXPORTING
      IV_GUID                    = lv_object_guid
```

```
  IMPORTING
    ES_CUSTOMER_H_WRK        = ls_customer_h_wrk
  EXCEPTIONS
    HEADER_NOT_FOUND         = 1
    OTHERS                   = 2.

 object-zzhashtag = ls_customer_h_wrk-zzhashtag.
  SWC_SET_ELEMENT CONTAINER 'ZZHASHSTAG' OBJECT-ZZHASHTAG.
END_PROPERTY.
```

Listing 6.1 GET_PROPERTY ZZHASHTAG Routine

After you've saved your code, you need to change the status of the attribute to IMPLEMENTED by highlighting the row and choosing the menu option EDIT • CHANGE RELEASE STATUS • OBJECT TYPE COMPONENT • TO IMPLEMENTED. Then, choose GENERATED. You can now use the custom attribute in the schedule or start conditions for your action. In addition, this attribute can be used by any other application that utilizes the BOR objects of the system.

Change the status of the attribute

6.2.4 Creating a New Action Profile

If you choose not to use an existing action profile or copy an existing one, you can instead use the wizard to create your profile. The wizard guides you through the creation of a new action profile. The basic steps are listed in Figure 6.20.

Wizard for new action profile

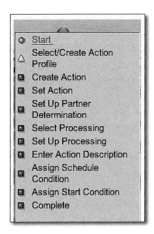

Figure 6.20 Wizard Start Create Action

For this section, we'll look at how to set up a new action profile for the social media call report transaction that you've been building enhancements for throughout this book. In this example, you want to give your users the chance to create a hard copy printout of the call report. To do this, first launch Transaction SPPFCADM. On the initial screen, select the application entry for CRM_ORDER, and then click the WIZARD FOR DEFINING AND SCHEDULING ACTIONS button to bring up the initial screen of the wizard.

In the first step, you can either choose to create a new profile or add to an existing profile as shown in Figure 6.21. In this screen, you'll need to provide entries for these fields: ACTION PROFILE technical name, DESCRIPTION, DATE PROFILE, CATEGORY OF OBJECT TYPE, and OBJECT TYPE NAME. For this example, choose to create a new action profile. Call the action profile "ZSCR", with a description of "Social Media Call Report". Use the default date profile for your action. The category of the object type will be "BUS2000126". This will allow you to assign this profile to business transactions, which are activities. After you've provided the information, click CONTINUE.

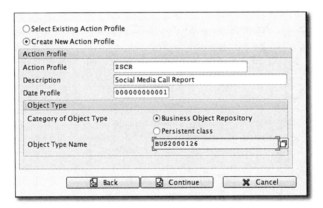

Figure 6.21 Create New Action Profile Screen

In the second step, you start defining the individual action. Here, you need to provide a technical name of the action and description. The technical name is a unique identifier for the action in your profile. The description should be a business-friendly short description of what the action is doing. A normal SAP CRM business user will be able to see this description, so please keep that in mind when providing the description. For this example, call the action "ZZPRINT_REPORT" and enter the DESCRIPTION as "Print Social Call Report" as shown in Figure 6.22.

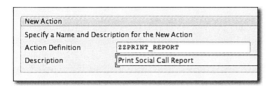

Figure 6.22 Define New Action Name

In the third step, you define the processing attributes of the action as shown in Figure 6.23. The first part defines when the action should be processed. The PROCESSING TIME is processing using SELECTION REPORT, IMMEDIATE PROCESSING, or PROCESSING WHEN SAVING DOCUMENT. PROCESSING USING SELECTION REPORT is typically used for those actions that should be handled as part of a batch update process. For example, you may only want to send out notifications for all transactions that are past a deadline criterion on a daily basis.

Step 3: Define processing attributes of the action

IMMEDIATE PROCESSING causes the action, when executed/scheduled from the foreground, to execute immediately in the system without waiting for the document to be saved to the database.

PROCESSING WHEN SAVING DOCUMENT causes the action to be processed after the document is saved. For example, when a sales order is confirmed by a customer service representative, you might want to send a confirmation notice to your customer.

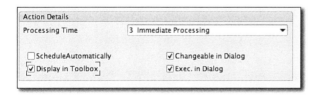

Figure 6.23 Define Action Details

After you select the processing time, you can then choose different execution options:

Choose execution options

▶ The SCHEDULEAUTOMATICALLY checkbox automatically triggers the action regardless of any schedule conditions.

▶ The DISPLAY IN TOOLBOX checkbox shows the action in the list of possible actions in Transaction CRMD_ORDER.

▶ The CHANGEABLE IN DIALOG checkbox allows you to reprocess the action again if it fails.

▶ The EXEC. IN DIALOG checkbox allows you to manually process an action in the foreground without the need for the selection report.

For this example, select the processing time as IMMEDIATE PROCESSING so that the printout will be triggered upon demand. Also check the DISPLAY IN TOOLBOX, CHANGEABLE IN DIALOG, and EXECUTABLE IN DIALOG options. This will allow the end user to select this action from the PRINT button or through a button coded on the Web Client screen that executes the action.

Step 4: Partner determination

The next step is the partner determination for your action as shown in Figure 6.24. Your actions can be set up to only send the information to a particular partner function on the transaction. If that partner doesn't exist, then the action won't be executed. For this example, you won't make this action partner dependent, so you don't need to enter any data on the fields on the screen. You want your action to be sent regardless of whether a particular partner exists on your business transaction.

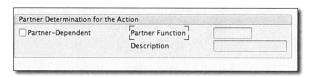

Figure 6.24 Partner Determination for the Action

Step 5: Select processing type

Next you'll need to select the processing type of the action as shown in Figure 6.25. The processing type defines what the action will be doing. The possible options include TRIGGER ALERT, EXTERNAL COMMUNICATIONS, METHOD CALL, SMART FORMS FAX, SMART FORMS MAIL, SMART FORMS PRINT, and WORKFLOW. For this book, we'll look at METHOD CALL, SMART FORMS MAIL, and SMART FORMS PRINT, which are the most common use case scenarios.

For this example, choose SMART FORMS PRINT. As you can imagine, SMART FORMS PRINT will create a print output for the transaction type.

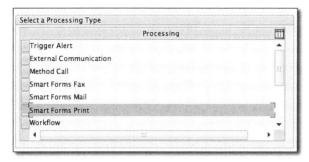

Figure 6.25 Processing Type for the Action

After choosing SMART FORMS PRINT, PRINT SETTINGS will appear as shown in Figure 6.26. You'll need to provide a valid FORM NAME, PROCESSING CLASS, and PROCESSING METHOD for the smart form. In addition, you can specify a default OUTPUT DEVICE for the printout. For this example, use the standard delivered smart form for printing out activities from SAP CRM. Your FORM NAME should be "CRM_ACTVITIY_BUSACT01", PROCESSING CLASS should be "CL_DOC_PROCESSING_CRM_ORDER", and PROCESSING METHOD should be "CRM_ACTIVITY_EXEC_SMART_FORM".

Printing options

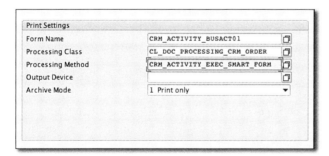

Figure 6.26 Print Settings for the Smart Form's Print Action Type

For this example, you won't specify any start or schedule conditions for your action. This action you created will allow a user to generate a print output of your business transaction on demand as needed. Even though you didn't specify any conditions, the system still creates the appropriate action condition configuration for you.

6.2.5 Assigning the Profile to a Business Transaction

After the wizard has created the profile, it still needs to be assigned to your business transaction type. Go into the IMG and choose the menu path CUSTOMER RELATIONSHIP MANAGEMENT • TRANSACTIONS • BASIC SETTINGS • DEFINE TRANSACTION TYPE. Select the business transaction that you want to assign the profile to, and then drill into the details of that transaction. On the details screen, specify the action profile in the ACTION PROFILE field, and click SAVE.

6.3   Action Scheduling

As you learned in the previous sections, not all actions are processed immediately, and they can be scheduled for later processing. This is useful for actions that may require intense processing or that should be done in batch fashion, such as creating mailing printouts from your system. The only drawback to this approach is that SAP CRM doesn't automatically process those actions scheduled for later, so you must set up a batch job to handle this process. SAP has provided a program called RSP-PFPROCESS, which can also be reached by Transaction CRMC_ACTION_JOB. This program can be set up as a batch job in Transaction SM37 to run on a regular basis to handle your scheduled action processing.

Schedule batch job   To set up a batch job, you first run program RSPPFPROCESS to bring up the parameter screen. This screen allows you to create a variant on what actions should be processed. You need to create a variant because you may not want to process all types of schedule actions at the same time, and it also prevents any actions that you don't want to be processed automatically from being processed. Technically, you could run this job on demand in the foreground to process any actions scheduled in the system if desired. However, you should normally just set up a batch job to handle this task.

Parameter selection

As you can see form the selection screen of the program in Figure 6.27, you have several options that are available to pick which actions should be processed by the program.

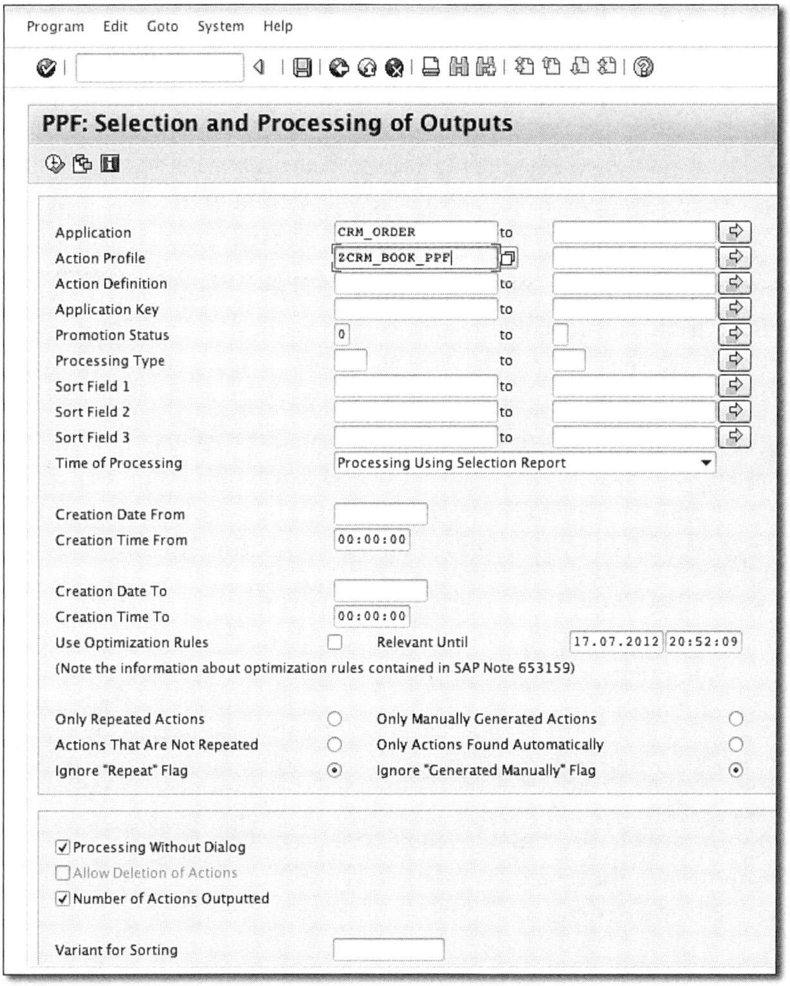

Figure 6.27 Selection Report Screen

The following are the most important screen fields:

- The Application for business transaction based actions should always be "CRM_ORDER".

▶ The ACTION PROFILE should correspond to the action profile that contains the action that you want to be processed in batch.

▶ The ACTION DEFINITION allows you to specify a name of a specific action that you want to process.

The other selection parameters allow you to filter this further if needed, but normally you should only need to specify the action profile and action definition to restrict the processing to a specific action. In general, you'll want the TIME OF PROCESSING to always be PROCESSING USING SELECTION REPORT. It doesn't make sense to attempt to have the program process actions that run at other times such as IMMEDIATELY.

Restrict report via the parameters In addition to defining which actions should be processed by name or profile attributes, you can also restrict the report to only pick those created during a certain time frame. This feature is generally more useful for a test or development environment because in a production environment, you usually want to process everything that is outstanding, regardless of the creation date. You can also restrict the report to process actions based on whether they were repeated before or whether they were generated manually or based on a schedule condition.

It's also important when setting up this report that you ensure that the PROCESSING WITHOUT DIALOG option is checked because you'll be running this in the background.

Create the variant After inputting the appropriate selection options for running the report, click the SAVE button to create a variant. If you aren't familiar with SAP batch processing, a *variant* is used to tell a batch program inside of the ABAP system what parameters should be used. You don't want to run this report with the default parameters in the background, so you should always create a variant.

A screen appears asking you to give the variant a technical name and description as shown in Figure 6.28. For this example, call the variant "CRM_BOOK", and click SAVE. Now that the variant has been saved, you can use Transaction SM37 to schedule the job, which will process your actions by running the program RSPPFPROCESS.

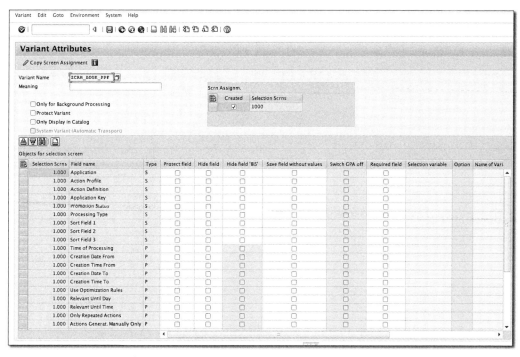

Figure 6.28 Variant Setup for Program RSPPFPROCESS

To create the job, run Transaction SM37. The DEFINE BACKGROUND JOB screen appears as shown in Figure 6.29. Give the job a technical name, and choose the default JOB CLASS C.

Create the job

Next you'll need to define a step for the job. The *step definition* of a job is where you define the execution of various programs by a job in batch processing. It's possible to run more than one program in a single job through a series of steps defined for the job. This might be useful if you want to process separate types of actions that need to be processed in batch but you require a set of actions to be processed first before the second set. Keep in mind that you'll still need to create separate variants for each set of actions that you want to process to separate out the processing of the actions that were scheduled.

Step definition

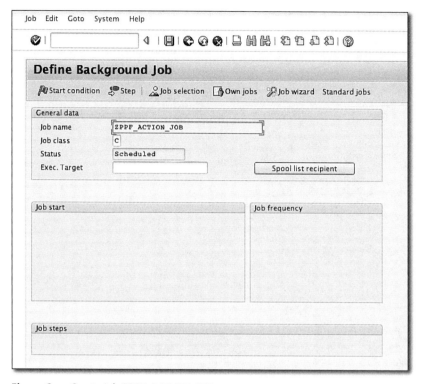

Figure 6.29 Create Job ZPPF_ACTION_JOB

Create step   To create the step, choose the STEP button, which launches a popup screen to create a new step as shown in Figure 6.30. On this step, you'll need to specify the user name in which the action is running, the type of work being processed, and the details for that type of work. When you specify a user to run the job, it's important that the user has sufficient security to read and update all transaction data that will be processed by that action. For this situation, you should create a background user with sufficient security that is separate from your end-user and support accounts on your SAP CRM system.

Choose the ABAP PROGRAM button, and then provide the name of the ABAP program, which for action processing will always be "RSPPFPRO-CESS", the name of the variant that you set up in the system ("CRM_BOOK"), and the runtime language of the job. Choose EN for English as the runtime language for this batch job.

The complete entry should look similar to Figure 6.30. After you specify which program will be run, save your work. You can also specify the print output destination of the job if needed.

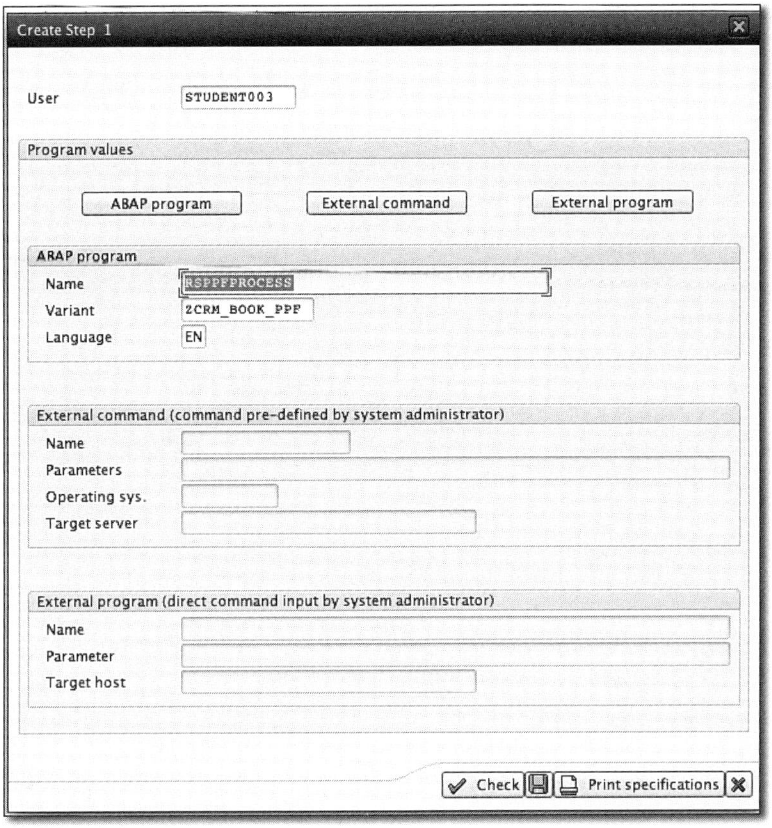

Figure 6.30 Create Job Step

You'll then be back on the job definition screen and now need to specify when this job should run. Click on the START CONDITION button and another popup appears, as shown in Figure 6.31, asking you when this job should be run. For scheduled actions, schedule the job during a period when your users won't be working with the system, especially if the actions perform updates on data in the system. The time period options allow you to set up the job on a periodic basis if desired or needed. After you've defined when the job should be run, click SAVE to go back to the job definition screen again. Click SAVE once more. Now

Choose a time for the job to run

that the job is scheduled, you can review the progress and logs of the jobs through Transaction SM38, which is the standard method for all ABAP batch processing.

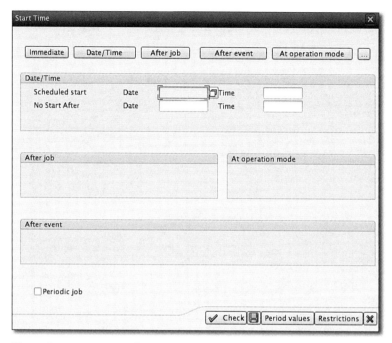

Figure 6.31 Time Options for Job Processing

Based on this example, you can see that it's a straightforward task to set up the SAP CRM system to process scheduled actions that have been defined to be processed later. However, remember that you must schedule this job as part of your setup for your action profile, which contains actions that have the processing time set to process via selection report, or otherwise they won't be executed in your system.

6.4 Using Actions for Nonoutput Tasks

Update data A key difference between the PPF and output control found in SAP ERP is the ability to create actions that update data but don't generate a document output. One primary way to achieve this is to use the method call of the PPF. A *method call* is the execution of a unit of code by the PPF that may not generate any output but rather updates data within the business transaction or creates a new business transaction. Method calls of the PPF are implemented using the BAdI `EXEC_METHODCALL_PPF`. All method calls include those delivered as part of the standard SAP code.

In the following sections, we'll explain what a standard method call is and then show you how to create your own. As part of creating your method call, you'll see how to create an implementation of the BAdI `EXEC_METHODCALL_PPF` and how to include that method call as a processing type of an action in a new action profile.

6.4.1 Standard Delivered Method Calls

SAP provides many standard method calls for business transactions. These method calls can be used to perform some very common types of updates within the SAP CRM system. A few of the more useful include:

▶ `COPY_DOCUMENT`

Standard method calls

Generates a follow-up document in reference to the existing business transaction. You provide the target business transaction as a parameter to the method. The system then copies the data from the existing business transaction to the new document using the copy control procedure that you've defined for the document.

▶ `COMPLETE_DOCUMENT`

Sets the status of the existing business transaction to "complete." This is useful if you want to have documents marked as "complete" when certain values are reached within your business transaction automatically.

▶ `TRIGGER_ALERT`

Raises an alert in the SAP CRM Alert Framework. This method requires you to set the alert type to be raised as a parameter in the transaction. This is one way of raising alerts if certain criteria are met.

6.4.2 Creating a New Method Call

To create a new method call that can be used as part of a scheduled action, you need to implement the BAdI `EXEC_METHODCALL_PPF` first. Go to Transaction SE18, enter "EXEC_METHODCALL_PPF" as the BAdI name, and click DISPLAY.

Create filter value

You now need to create a new filter value for this BAdI. This filter value will be the technical name of the method call that will be referenced when you create the action definition that executes this method call. Choose the menu FILTER VALUE • CREATE to open the popup shown in Figure 6.32.

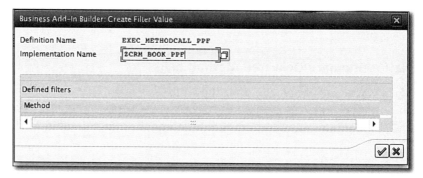

Figure 6.32 Create Filter Value for EXEC_METHODCALL_PPF

Create implementation

After you've created a filter value, you need to create an implementation that corresponds to your filter value. Follow these steps:

1. Choose the CREATE IMPLEMENTATION menu option from the overview screen of the BAdI EXEC_METHODCALL_PPF in Transaction SE18, and enter the technical name of your implementation, along with a description. For this example, enter "ZCRM_BOOK".

2. Assign the filter value ZCRM_BOOK to your BAdI as part of the definition process.

3. Click SAVE, and you'll be prompted to assign the BAdI implementation to a package. If you choose a transportable package, you'll need to pick a workbench request to assign your work. After this has been assigned, the BAdI implementation is inactive in your system as shown in Figure 6.33.

4. Verify the class used to implement the BAdI by selecting the INTERFACE tab as shown in Figure 6.34.

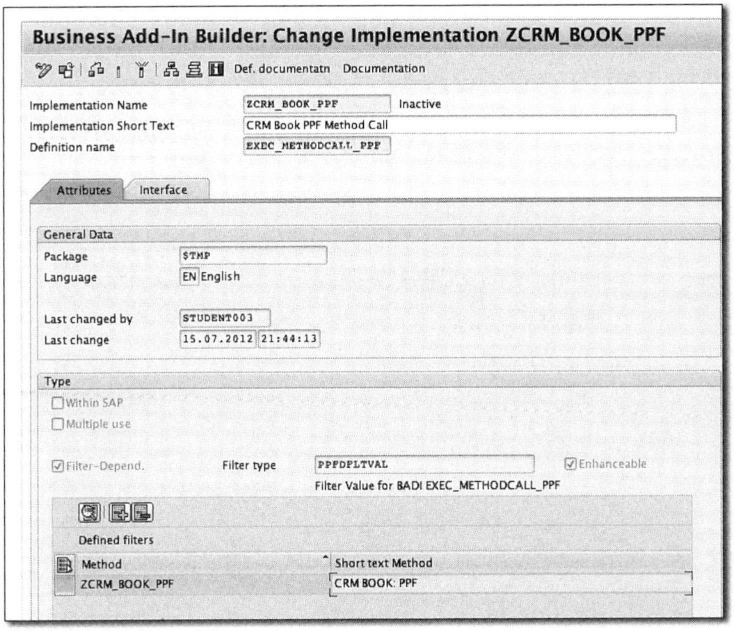

Figure 6.33 BAdI Implementation for the Filter Value

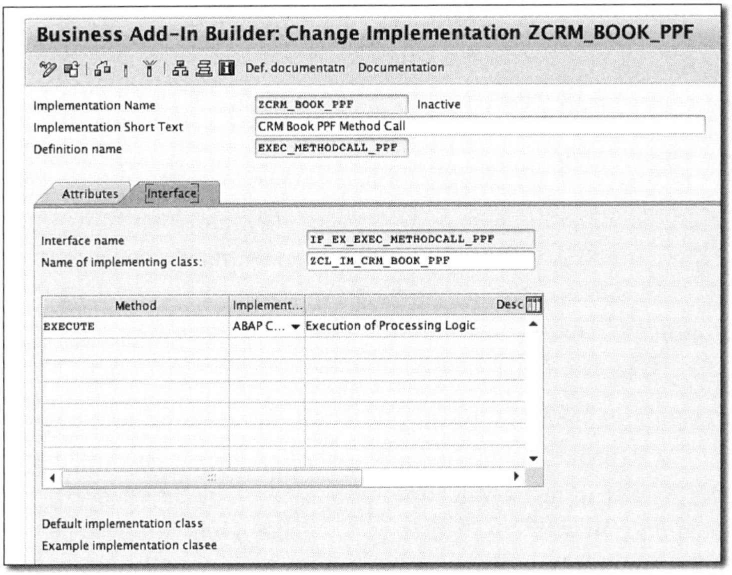

Figure 6.34 Define the Class for Implementation

5. Activate the BAdI implementation to use in your action customizing by clicking on the ACTIVATE BADI button, and the BAdI implementation should appear active as shown in Figure 6.35. However, at this point you now must implement code in your BAdI implementation for it to execute any type of logic when executed as an action in your system.

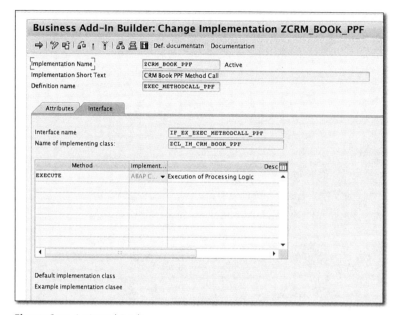

Figure 6.35 Activated BAdI

The BAdI implementation creates a new class that implements the interface IF_EXEC_METHODCALL_PPF. This interface has one primary method called EXECUTE that has the parameters as shown in Figure 6.36. One interesting reference implementation of the BAdI can be found by looking at the class CL_IM_CRM_MKTCA_PROC_INB.

If you examine the code of this implementation, you can find usage of the class CL_ACTION_EXECUTE. This class is used by the standard delivered SAP method calls to manage business transactions within actions. The most commonly used method that you'll need is the GET_REF_OBJECT method. This method translates the abstract object provided by the PPF into a one order object. By performing this translation, you can get the GUID of the object and the type of object being used.

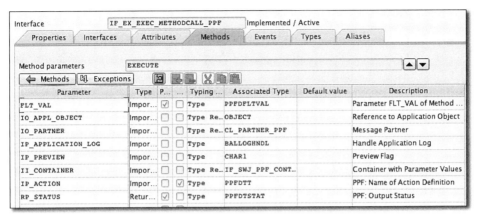

Figure 6.36 Interface IF_EX_EXEC_METHODCALL_PPF

6.4.3 Implementing the IF_EX_EXEC_METHODCALL_PFF Interface

The interface of the method call execution provides an abstract reference to the business object being processed.

To get the exact details of that object, you need to use a method in the CL_ACTION_EXECUTE class by using the code from Listing 6.2.

```
DATA:   lr_action_execute  TYPE REF TO cl_action_execute.      Retrieve
CREATE OBJECT lr_action_execute.                               class details
* get parameter from reference object
CALL METHOD lr_action_execute->get_ref_object
  EXPORTING
     io_appl_object = io_appl_object
     ip_action      = ip_action
     ip_preview     = ip_preview
     ii_container   = ii_container
  IMPORTING
     ev_guid_ref    = lv_guid_ref
     ev_kind_ref    = lv_kind_ref
     et_container   = lt_container
     ev_preview     = lv_preview.
```

Listing 6.2 GET_REF_OBJECT Method of CL_ACTION_EXECUTE Class

The parameter EV_GUID_REF returns the GUID of the header of the business transaction. With this GUID, you now can retrieve any information

283

about the business transaction using the one order API function modules that we discussed in Chapter 2.

For your full example, you can then read the business transaction data using the function module CRM_ORDER_READ via the logic in Listing 6.3.

```
* only relevant on header level
  CHECK: lv_kind_ref EQ gc_object_kind-orderadm_h.

* fill GUID of the source document
  INSERT lv_guid_ref INTO TABLE lt_guids.

* fill requested object
  INSERT gc_object_name-orderadm_h INTO TABLE lt_req_obj.
  INSERT gc_object_name-doc_flow   INTO TABLE lt_req_obj.
  INSERT gc_object_name-partner    INTO TABLE lt_req_obj.

* read source document
  CALL FUNCTION 'CRM_ORDER_READ'
    EXPORTING
       it_header_guid      = lt_guids
       it_requested_objects = lt_req_obj
       iv_only_spec_items   = false
    IMPORTING
       et_orderadm_h        = lt_orderadm_h_ref
       et_partner           = lt_partner
       et_doc_flow          = lt_doc_flow
EXCEPTIONS
       document_not_found   = 1
       error_occurred       = 2
       document_locked      = 3
       no_change_authority  = 4
       no_display_authority = 5
       OTHERS               = 6.
```

Listing 6.3 Retrieve Data through CRM_ORDER_READ

After you've retrieved the data to perform the update, you need to follow a few rules. These include no commit work and not performing any coding that would trigger a user dialog.

Based on the results of the action, you now need to let the system know whether the action was successful and provide any related processing messages for viewing by the users. First, add any messages to the log about the action using the static method `CL_LOG_PFF=>ADD_MESSAGE` (see Listing 6.4).

```
MESSAGE w001(zmesgclass)
  INTO lv_dummy.
CALL METHOD cl_log_ppf=>add_message
  EXPORTING
    ip_problemclass = '2'
    ip_handle       = ip_application_log.
```

Listing 6.4 Method ADD_MESSAGE for Class CL_LOG_PPF

The return variable `RP_STATUS` is used to indicate whether processing was successful or not. If not successful, set this value to `0`. If successful, then set the value of `RP_STATUS` to `1`.

6.4.4 Method Action Customizing

Now that you've created the action, you need to create a new action that will use the method call that you just created. The customizing steps follow similar steps to what was reviewed in Section 6.2.

Create new action

1. Start once again by running Transaction SPPFCADM.

2. Choose the row CRM_ORDER, and click on the WIZARD FOR DEFINING AND SCHEDULING AN ACTION button.

3. When prompted, provide a new name for the action profile, description, and business object type as shown in Figure 6.37.

4. Provide a technical name and description for the new object. For this example, enter "ZCRM_BOOK_PPF_METHOD" for the ACTION DEFINITION field and "PPF Method Example" for the DESCRIPTION field, as shown in Figure 6.38.

5. Click the CONTINUE button.

6. You now need to define the processing time and options for the action as shown in Figure 6.39. Set the processing time as PROCESSING USING SELECTION REPORT.

7. Select CHANGEABLE IN DIALOG and EXEC. IN DIALOG.

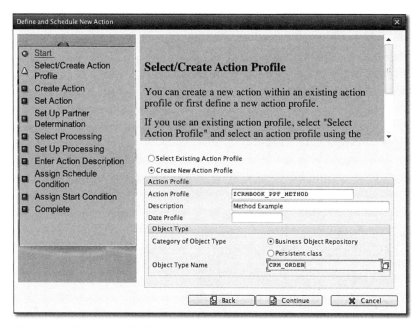

Figure 6.37 New Action Profile

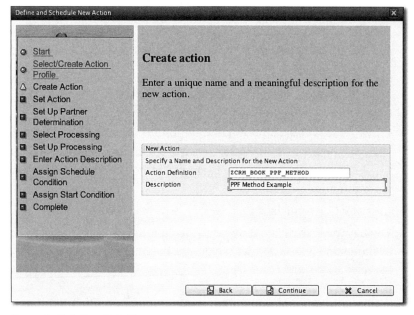

Figure 6.38 Action Definition

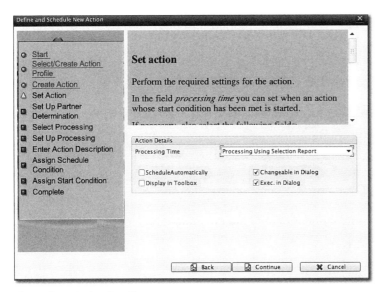

Figure 6.39 Action Details

8. For partner determination in this example, choose PARTNER-DEPEN-
   DENT, and then choose the PARTNER FUNCTION 00000001 (sold-to
   party) for this action as shown in Figure 6.40.

Partner
determination

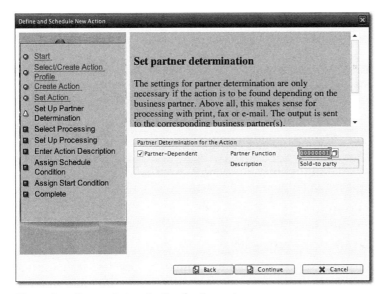

Figure 6.40 Partner Determination for Processing

9. Define the type of processing for your action as shown in Figure 6.41. Choose METHOD CALL, which will allow the method call that you created to be used by your action.

10. Click CONTINUE to move to the next step.

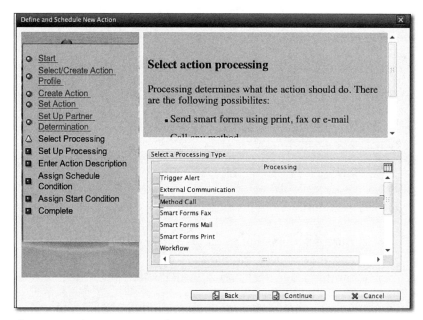

Figure 6.41 Select Process Type for Action

11. In the SET UP PROCESSING step (see Figure 6.42), pick your method call by clicking the SEARCH HELP icon and then choosing the ZCRM_BOOK_PPF method from the options available as shown in Figure 6.43.

12. Click CONTINUE to move to the next step.

13. Enter a description for the action as shown in Figure 6.44. For this example, enter "Method Call Example for PPF Book".

14. Click CONTINUE to go to the ASSIGN SCHEDULE CONDITION step. Skip defining any schedule conditions and click CONTINUE to move to the ASSIGN START CONDITION step.

15. Do not assign any start conditions and then complete the wizard by clicking on the green check button on the last review screen of the wizard.

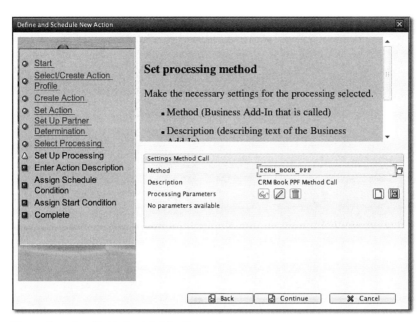

Figure 6.42 Specify Method Call for Processing

Figure 6.43 Choose Available Method Calls

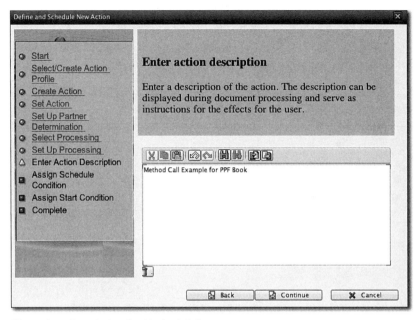

Figure 6.44 Description for Method Call

The system now generates your action that will use your method call. You can assign this action profile to your business transaction type as explored earlier in this chapter.

As you've learned, the method calls can be created to execute custom logic. The logic can be triggered in the exact same fashion as you might trigger a print output or email notification. The flexibility of method calls gives you another option for performing conditional updates of business transactions and/or dependent data without the need for creating BTEs or BAdI implementations within the internal framework of the business transaction.

6.5 Summary

The PPF allows you to define both possible output and business logic execution for a business transaction. The customizing for the framework is maintained through Transaction SPPFCADM in your SAP CRM system. The building blocks of this customizing consist of action profiles, which will be assigned to a particular transaction type. The action profile consists of a series of actions, which can be either scheduled manually or automatically when a particular condition is met.

The execution of those actions can happen either immediately, upon the save of the business transaction, or through batch processing. Batch processing of the actions is controlled through a batch job that can be scheduled as needed or run on demand if desired. The actions can generate a print output, email, or fax. In addition, the actions can execute standard or custom logic that can generate a new business transaction logic or update data in the SAP CRM system. The system provides the capability for you to build custom logic using a BAdI implementation. The action framework is quite flexible and can be used to meet different types of business requirements beyond output control without having to implement exit logic within the framework of the business transaction.

Although the initial setup of the action profile customizing can be somewhat complicated, its capability to be extended to meet many different requirements when it comes to notifications and other types of outputs is quite powerful. The PPF should always be considered whenever you have any business requirement that involves sending an email from a business transaction contained within SAP CRM.

In the next chapter, we'll discuss common enhancement requests for sales and services processes in SAP CRM.

*Because no two businesses will have exactly the same require-
ments, this chapter provides the most common sales and service
enhancements you can use to make your SAP CRM system
unique.*

7   Common Enhancement Requests in Sales and Service

No two snowflakes are exactly identical, and this is also true for the implementation of SAP CRM business processes. Even though the out-of-the-box SAP CRM system can be configured to meet the needs of most businesses, there are times where you need to go beyond the standard delivered features. The SAP CRM system provides the flexibility to allow you to turn it into that unique, one-of-a-kind "snowflake" by implementing enhancements in your system. The most common enhancements may not be as unique as a snowflake, but they allow the business to feel like its SAP CRM system is one of kind.

SAP CRM provides the capability to enhance the business logic of the system using different techniques. In this chapter, we'll examine common requests that you may receive when implementing a process in SAP CRM Sales or SAP CRM Service. We'll present each request with the typical business case behind the request and the technical options to solve the problem.

Enhance business logic

> **Note**
>
> Keep in mind that the options we'll present aren't your only options, but rather they are the most common choices. For the purpose of this chapter, we'll only focus on the most common requests found in an SAP CRM project. Those include making fields required in a business transaction, defaulting values in a business transaction, updating values in another transaction based on a valued entered in the first, using custom date rules, performing partner determination, and determining organizational models.

Configuration +
ABAP development
In this chapter, you'll use a combination of SAP configuration and ABAP development to implement a business requirement. To simplify the instructions, we'll use a common notation of referring to the standard SAP IMG. If you're not familiar with SAP functional configuration, the IMG can be found in the SAP CRM system by executing Transaction SPRO. In Transaction SPRO, there is an option to view the SAP Reference IMG. The IMG locations that we'll refer to are based on SAP Reference IMG for SAP CRM 7.0. Because SAP may change the IMG structure when releasing a newer version of SAP CRM, these locations may not match your system exactly.

> **Why Implement Logic in the Business Logic Layer instead of the UI Layer?**
>
> Those of you familiar with the Web Client may be asking why you should be implementing any of the enhancement requests in the business logic layer of SAP CRM, when many of these can be done in the UI layer.
>
> The simple answer is that business logic should always be separated from the UI when designing an application. After many years of working with SAP CRM, we've seen the UI layer switched between technologies several times over the various releases of SAP CRM. If we had coded all of our business logic in the UI layer, we would have had to rebuild that logic each time we upgraded to a new release of the SAP CRM that contains the new UI technology.
>
> By placing our business logic in the correct place, we can survive a UI upgrade with less pain. During an upgrade project from PCUI to the Web Client, we didn't have to recode any of the segment BAdIs or BTE function modules because we had built them in a UI-independent fashion. This saved a lot of work because our business logic still worked as expected. If we had put the logic in the PCUI, it would have meant a longer upgrade and more work for us. The ability to create "timeless" business logic independent of the UI is a testament to the design of SAP CRM.

7.1   Requiring Fields in a Business Transaction

In almost every SAP CRM project on which we've worked, we always encounter the requirement to make a field required regardless of the type of business transaction. In SAP CRM, most fields aren't required to be entered on a business transaction, so to meet the business requirement, you need to either configure or add additional logic into your system to make sure that a transaction doesn't save without errors when required data is missing.

To achieve this, we'll look at four common techniques that will make fields required in your SAP CRM system:

Common techniques

- ▶ Incompletion procedure
- ▶ Segment BAdIs
- ▶ Business transaction events (BTEs)
- ▶ ORDER_SAVE BAdI

These techniques are complementary, as you may need to use a different technique depending on your requirements.

7.1.1 Business Scenario

In this example scenario, your business wants to use SAP CRM to track new social media interactions. To do this, the standard interaction log business transaction 0001 has been copied to a custom business transaction process type known as a *social call report* or ZSCR.

Social call report

To make things easier on end users, you'll make some of the social call report fields required. For your social call report transaction, you'll make the hashtag that corresponds to the conversation recorded so that you can use that information to find other similar conversations on Twitter. The Twitter service uses a concept of hashtags to allow people to group messages together as part of a larger conversation. The hashtag in this case will be a 60-character field that created on the CUSTOMER_H segment of the business transaction, which has a technical name of ZZHASHTAG.

7.1.2 Incompletion Procedure

In SAP CRM, there is standard functionality to make certain fields required to have a complete document through the *incompleteness function*, which is also known as an *incompletion procedure*. The incompletion procedure allows you to configure a list of fields for a given business

Configure required list of fields

transaction that must be maintained for a document to be considered complete. It's important that a document is complete and without errors because if it's replicated to another system, there could be problems in the actual replication.

In the case of sales orders being created in SAP CRM and sent to SAP ERP, the orders created in SAP CRM won't replicate unless they are error-free. Thus, if you do need a particular field to be filled in before replicating to SAP ERP, you'll need to raise an error message to block the replication.

This is only one example, as you may need certain fields to be required in other types of transactions such as activities, which also are commonly referred to as call reports. For this chapter, we'll use a call report as the example.

Pros/cons   The primary advantages of using the incompletion procedure are that no coding is required, and all fields of the business transaction are available. The major drawback of this technique is that you can't use it to require a value in one field when another field is present. In addition, this technique only checks for data being entered, rather than a particular value being present in the field. The incompletion procedure should, however, be your first choice in making a field required unless you have more complex requirements.

Configuration   To configure the incompletion procedure, follow these steps:

1. Open the IMG, and navigate to the location via the path: Customer Relationship Management • Basic Functions • Incompleteness • Define Incompleteness Procedure.

2. Click the Execute button next to the Define Incompleteness Procedure to open a window that is first focused on Change View "Incompleteness Group: Transaction/Item."

3. Click on the Incompleteness Procedure node on the left-hand side of the dialog structure.

4. Choose the New Entry button to open the screen shown in Figure 7.1. On this screen, you'll provide a four-digit technical code for your procedure and a description of the purpose of the procedure. This information is considered the *header* of the procedure. For this

example, enter "ZEX1" as the technical code and "CRM Book" as the description.

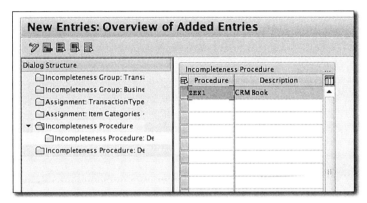

Figure 7.1 New Incompleteness Procedure Header

5. Assign the fields that will be required by choosing the INCOMPLETE-NESS PROCEDURE DETAIL subnode. You'll then see the screen shown in Figure 7.2. At this point, because you've only created the header of the incompleteness procedure, there will be no entries listed.

6. To create entries for each field that you want to make required, click on the NEW ENTRIES button, and enter the information about the field that you want to make required.

Required field

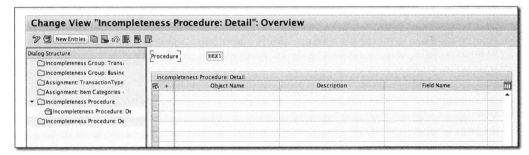

Figure 7.2 Incompleteness Procedure Detail Screen

Provide several pieces of information to specify that a field is required:

▶ OBJECT NAME: The segment that contains the field in the business transaction. For this example, enter "SALES".

297

▶ FIELD NAME: The technical name of the field in that segment. Enter "PO_NUMBER_SOLD", which is the technical name for the external reference number on the business transaction.

▶ RELEVANCE: Indicates the type of check at the header or item level of the business transaction. Choose HEADER.

▶ MESSAGE CATEGORY: Allows you to either issue a warning or an error message.

▶ BUS. TRANSACTION: Used to trigger certain system status events when the transaction meets this condition of missing data. The system defaults a value into this field for you.

7. After you've entered the data as shown in Figure 7.3, click SAVE.

Figure 7.3 Example Entry for PO_NUMBER Field in Incompleteness Routine

Additional fields   If you want to require additional fields in your business transaction, you must go back, click the NEW ENTRIES button, and add in the additional fields that you need to be required. Keep in mind that listing these fields together doesn't imply that if one field is maintained, then the other field must be maintained. Instead, it means that all fields that are listed in the incompletion procedure must have values entered for the transaction to be complete without warnings or errors present. This is one major limitation of the incompletion procedure, which will require you to look at different techniques when you want to make one field required when another value is maintained in another field.

Incompleteness Groups

Now that the incompleteness procedure is defined, there are additional steps to have your transaction use this procedure. Commonly in SAP CRM, there are times when the system design is more complex than needed. This is the case with incompleteness groups that allow you to have multiple incompletion procedures for a transaction and then select the correct procedure based on certain criteria.

Follow these steps to create a new group: New group

1. Click on the Incompleteness Group: Transaction/Item node, and then choose New Entries as shown in Figure 7.4.

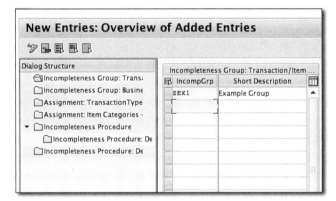

Figure 7.4 Incompleteness Groups

2. Enter a four-character technical code for the group, along with a description of the group as shown in Figure 7.5. For this example, enter a technical code of "ZEX1" and a description of "Example Group".

3. Now assign your incompletion procedure to the group by clicking on the Incompleteness Procedure Details node and then clicking on New Entries. Enter the Incompleteness Group as "ZEX1" and the Procedure assigned as "ZEX1", as shown in Figure 7.5.

4. Assign the incompleteness group to your transaction by clicking on the Assignment: Transaction Type node.

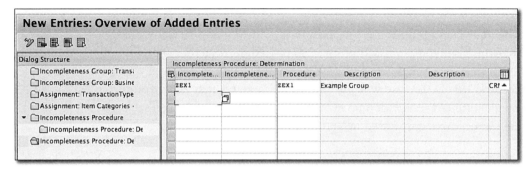

Figure 7.5 Incompleteness Procedure Determination from Group

5. Scroll down until you see the transaction type, and then enter the incompleteness group "ZEX1" next to your transaction type as shown in Figure 7.6.

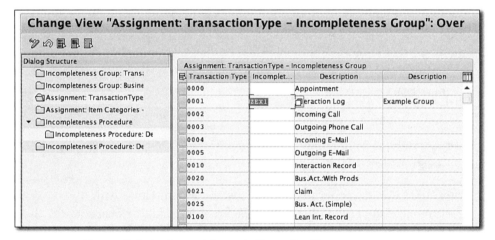

Figure 7.6 Assign Incompleteness to Transaction Type

Test   Now that you've assigned the incompleteness procedure to your transaction, you can test your work. To do this, create a new transaction, and then either click SAVE or press Enter when you're in create mode. You then should receive an error message indicating that the field you listed in your incompleteness procedure is a required field. You'll still be able to save the transaction with this error, but the transaction will no longer be error-free until you entered a value for that particular field.

As you've seen through this example, you can make a field on the SAP CRM business transaction required without having to write any ABAP code. This technique can handle simple requirements for required fields. As this only requires configuration, the amount of time to implement is quite small. This should always be your first choice because it requires the least amount of effort.

7.1.3   Using Segment BAdIs

One of the primary drawbacks of using the incompleteness procedure is that you can't make a field required based on a value entered in another field. To do this, you need to use segment BAdIs.

As you learned earlier in Chapter 2, Section 2.4, the business transaction consists of several segments. For each segment in the business transaction, there is a BAdI available that allows you to develop specific logic based on your business needs. These BAdIs are normally named CRM_<SEGMENTNAME>_BADI. Where <SEGMENTNAME> is the name of the segment that you want to perform your custom logic.

For this example, let's take a look at the ACTIVITY_H BAdI. The interface of the ACTIVITY_H BAdI contains two methods: CRM_ACTIVITY_H_CHECK and CRM_ACTIVITY_H_MERGE. To implement this example, you'll use the CRM_ACTIVITY_H_CHECK method to raise the error message.

Raise error message

Determine the Timing

Before you implement the segment BAdI, you must first determine the correct timing of when it will be called. One drawback about using segment BAdIs is that they are only called when the segment is maintained; that is, a value is entered in any field that is contained on that segment. Thus, you must choose the correct segment when designing a check such as "field A is required when field B...".

If field A and field B both exist on the same segment, then you don't need to worry about the correct segment. However, if field A and field B are on separate segments, then you must use the BAdI for the segment that contains field B. For example, if you created the ZZHASHTAG field on CUSTOMER_H, and your business requirement is "when the PRIORITY field on ACTIVITY_H is High, a value must be entered in the ZZHASHTAG field," you would then need to use the segment BAdI for ACTIVITY_H to validate that the field on CUSTOMER_H was maintained.

Implement Logic

After you've identified the correct segment, you can implement the logic as follows:

CRM_ACTIVITY_
H_BADI
1. Go to Transaction SE18 and bring up the appropriate BAdI in display mode. In this case, use the CRM_ACTIVITY_H_BADI.

2. Choose IMPLEMENTATION • CREATE to create a new implementation for your BAdI as shown in Figure 7.7.

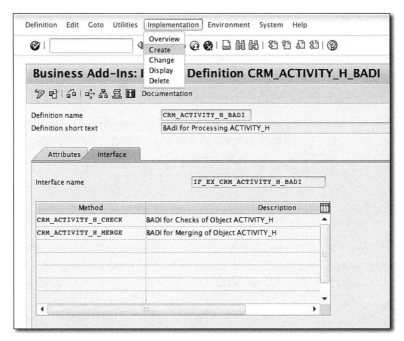

Figure 7.7 Display BAdI CRM_ACTIVITY_H_BADI

3. A popup appears as shown in Figure 7.8 that will ask for a name of your BAdI implementation. For this example, use "ZTPP_BOOK_REQ_FIELD" as the name. The name can be any valid name that conforms to your system naming convention.

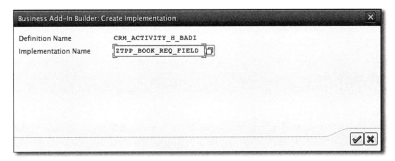

Figure 7.8 Create Implementation Popup

4. Upon clicking the CONTINUE button, the details of the BAdI implementation are provided. Enter a description for the BAdI implementation, and change the name of the implementing class if desired as
   shown in Figure 7.9.

Business Add-In Builder: Change Implementation ZTPP_BOOK_REQ_FIELD

⬅ | 🖉 🗂 | 🗂 ¦ 🍴 | 品 昌 🔲 Definition Documenta Documentation

Implementation Name	ZTPP_BOOK_REQ_FIELD Inactive
Implementation Short Text	Required Field Example
Definition Name	CRM_ACTIVITY_H_BADI
Runtime Behavior	Implementation will not be called

　　Properties / Interface

Interface name	IF_EX_CRM_ACTIVITY_H_BADI
Name of implementing class:	ZCL_IM_TPP_BOOK_REQ_FIELD

Method	Implement...	Desc 🎟
CRM_ACTIVITY_H_CHECK	ABAP A.. ▾	BADI for Checks of Object ACTIVITY_H ▲
CRM_ACTIVITY_H_MERGE	ABAP A.. ▾	BADI for Merging of Object ACTIVITY_H
		▼

Default implementation class

Example implementation clasee

Figure 7.9 Inactive BAdI Implementation Screen

Code implementation

5. After you save the BAdI implementation, you can start to code the implementation. Drill down into the name of the method you want to implement, which for this example is the CRM_ACTIVITY_H_CHECK method. This brings up a source code editor as shown in Figure 7.10.

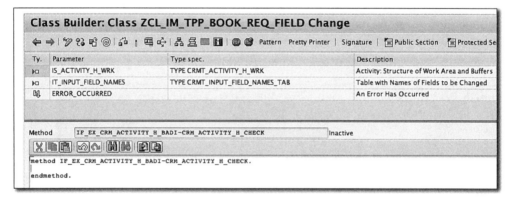

Figure 7.10 CRM_ACTIVITY_H_CHECK Method

can't raise error messages using the message statement directly without causing a technical short dump in your system.

The problem is that you still need to raise error messages but don't want to recreate the standard error functionality of the ABAP system. To solve this problem, SAP allows you to send the results of the message statement into a variable. You then can collect the results of these errors and pass them along at a later date for display. The SAP CRM business transaction achieves this by using the function module `CRM_MESSAGE_COLLECT` to display error messages. However, if an error has been cleared, you also need a way to remove these error messages. You can use the function module `CRM_MESSAGES_DELETE` to remove those error messages. These two function modules are part of a function group called `CRM_MESSAGES`, which supports the error message handling in the business transaction.

6. Insert the code from Listing 7.1, which will determine whether the logic should be executed for your transaction type, determine whether the priority field is filled in, read the value of your custom field, and raise an error message if your custom field is initial.

```
method IF_EX_CRM_ACTIVITY_H_BADI~CRM_ACTIVITY_H_CHECK.
  data: lv_orderadm_h_guid type crmt_object_guid,
      lv_process_type type crmt_process_type,
      ls_customer_h_wrk type CRMT_CUSTOMER_H_WRK.

  include crm_direct.

  CALL FUNCTION 'CRM_ORDERADM_H_READ_OW'
    EXPORTING
      iv_orderadm_h_guid              = lv_orderadm_h_guid
    IMPORTING
      EV_PROCESS_TYPE                 = lv_process_type
    EXCEPTIONS
      ADMIN_HEADER_NOT_FOUND          = 1
      OTHERS                          = 2.

  check lv_process_type eq 'ZSCR'.

  if is_activity_h_wrk-priority eq '1'.
    CALL FUNCTION 'CRM_CUSTOMER_H_READ_OW'
      EXPORTING
        IV_GUID                 = lv_orderadm_h_guid
```

```
      IMPORTING
        ES_CUSTOMER_H_WRK          = ls_customer_h_wrk
      EXCEPTIONS
        HEADER_NOT_FOUND           = 1
        OTHERS                     = 2.
    if ls_customer_h_wrk-zzhastag is initial.
*raise error
    MESSAGE I001(ZCRMBOOK) INTO LV_DUMMY.
    CALL FUNCTION 'CRM_MESSAGE_COLLECT'
        EXPORTING
          IV_CALLER_NAME = GC_OBJECT_NAME-activity_h
          IV_REF_OBJECT  = IV_GUID
          IV_REF_KIND    = 'A'.
    endif.
  endif.
endmethod.
```

Listing 7.1 IF_EX_CRM_ACTIVITY_H~CRM_ACTIVITY_H_CHECK Implementation

As you can see, the code for validating the field was quite simple for this example. You could put in much more complex validation logic as needed for the field, such as certain thresholds being met if the field was numeric or restricting the field to certain possible values. The only drawback if you make your logic too complex is that the system will need to run through your logic every time the user presses the [Enter] key or clicks the SAVE button from the data entry screen.

Minimize validations For performance reasons, you'll want to make sure that you minimize the number of needed validations. For the validations you do include, keep them as simple as possible. That isn't always feasible, however, so when discussing the business process requirements with your business users, you should always validate the need for making fields required based on another field.

> **Naming Conventions in SAP CRM ABAP Code**
>
> As you may have noticed from working with an SAP CRM system, there is a logical naming convention for variables and parameters within the ABAP code. To better examine the standard SAP-delivered code and these examples, let's take a look at the naming conventions.
>
> For variables, the convention is `<prefix>_<description>`.

<prefix> is a two-character code, and <description> describes the variable. The first character is normally either l for local scope or g for global scope. The second character represents the type of variable:

- c: Constant
- v: Single field
- s: Structure
- t: Table
- r: Reference and/or range

For import and export parameters in either function modules or method calls, the naming convention also follows the pattern <prefix>_<description>.

<prefix> is a two-character code, and <description> describes the parameter. The first character is normally one of the following:

- I: Importing
- E: Exporting
- C: Changing
- R: Returning

The second character is the same as for variables.

Knowing this convention makes the ABAP code in SAP CRM much more understandable. In this chapter and other parts of this book, we've tried to follow this naming pattern as much as possible.

7.1.4   ORDER_SAVE BAdI

The preceding three methods have provided different technical techniques in requiring a field on a business transaction. Common to all three techniques is that you were still able to save a business transaction with errors even though you issued the error message. The SAP CRM system is designed to allow you to save a business transaction with errors; however, for some business processes, you may not want to allow that.

In earlier versions of SAP CRM and even today, there is a strong argument against stopping the save of the business transaction when there are errors. SAP CRM uses the Web Client, which uses a web browser to access SAP CRM. As you may encounter, many SAP CRM end users are working on the system outside of an office environment on a virtual

Stop the save

private network (VPN) with less than stellar access to their corporate VPN. If you require that a business transaction must be in correct fashion before saving to the database, then a user could lose all his work due to a network issue. Even though Internet access is available in most countries, the quality of the access varies from location. Nothing is more frustrating than having to start over again because you lost all your work due to a simple outage on your Internet connection. Thus we strongly recommend that before implementing this requirement, you consider whether you will have remote users using the system if you require fields to be entered before physically saving the business transaction.

Physical save control

To overcome this limitation, you can use the ORDER_SAVE BAdI. This BAdI allows the system to control whether a business transaction will be physically saved to the SAP CRM database level. This coding example once again reflects that when the priority of the social call report business transaction is set to high, you must have a hashtag maintained or you won't be able to save the transaction in the SAP CRM system.

Implement the BAdI

New implementation

To implement this, you need to create a new implementation of the ORDER_SAVE BAdI by following these steps:

1. Go to Transaction SE18, and bring up the definition of ORDER_SAVE_BADI in display mode.

2. Choose IMPLEMENTATION • CREATE as shown in Figure 7.11.

3. Enter a new name for the implementation. This example uses "ZTPP_ORDER_SAVE" as shown in Figure 7.12; however, you can choose any valid name starting with "Y" or "Z" or within a customer namespace.

4. Enter a description for the BAdI, and change the name of the class that will be used to physically implement the interface of the BAdI if needed as shown in Figure 7.13.

5. Save the BAdI implementation. You are prompted for a transport request; as always, you can choose to use an existing transport request or create a new request.

Figure 7.11 Order Save BAdI

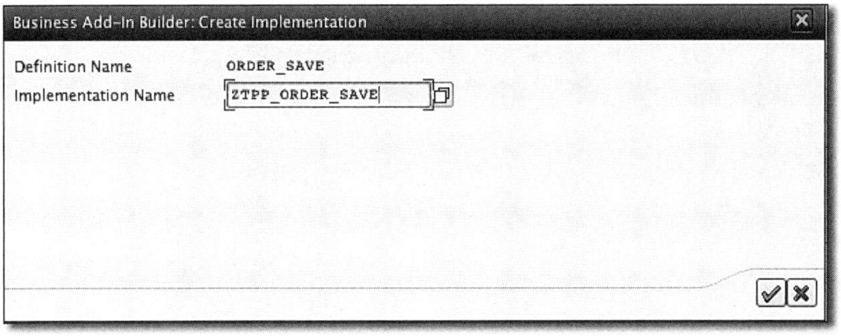

Figure 7.12 Enter an Implementation Name for ORDER_SAVE

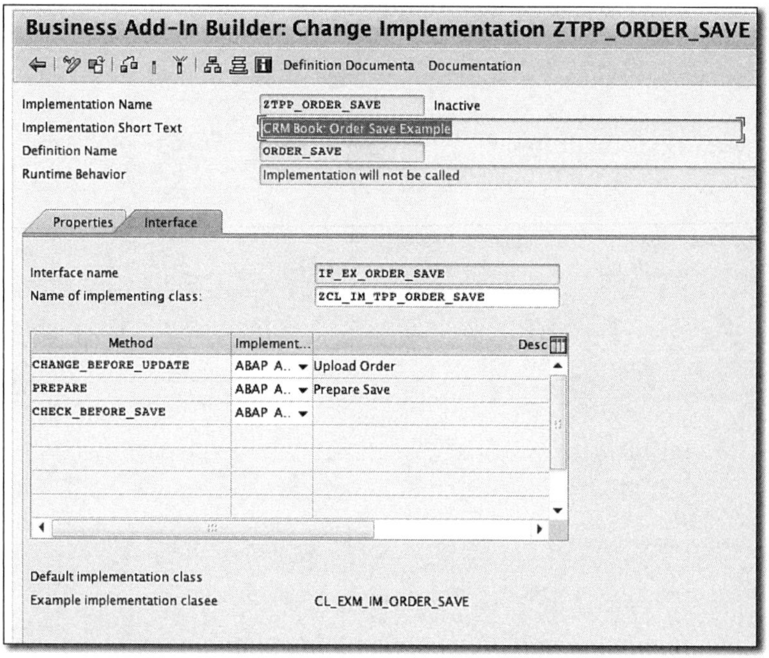

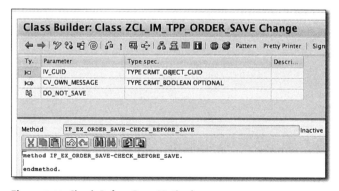

Figure 7.13 Order Save Inactive

Implement CHECK_BEFORE_SAVE

The next step is to implement the CHECK_BEFORE_SAVE method of the BAdI interface, which is shown in Figure 7.14. The method has a primary import parameter of IV_GUID, which is the GUID of the current business transaction.

Figure 7.14 Check Before Save Method

In addition to the primary import parameter, there is a single exception called DO_NOT_SAVE that can be raised. To do this, drill into the CHECK_ BEFORE_SAVE method by double-clicking it under the method listing or drilling into the class definition and going into the method screen to edit the code. You'll then need to add the code from Listing 7.2 to your method.

Exception
DO_NOT_SAVE

```
method IF_EX_ORDER_SAVE~CHECK_BEFORE_SAVE.

  include crm_direct.

  DATA:     LS_MSGIDNO              TYPE BAL_S_IDNO,
            LT_MSGIDNO              TYPE BAL_R_IDNO.

  data: lv_process_type type crmt_process_type,
        ls_orderadm_h_wrk type CRMT_ORDERADM_H_WRK,
        lv_error type c,
        lv_dummy type string.

  CALL FUNCTION 'CRM_ORDERADM_H_READ_OW'
    EXPORTING
      IV_ORDERADM_H_GUID      = iv_guid
    IMPORTING
      EV_PROCESS_TYPE         = lv_process_type
      ES_ORDERADM_H_WRK       = ls_orderadm_h_wrk
    EXCEPTIONS
      ADMIN_HEADER_NOT_FOUND = 1
      OTHERS                  = 2.

  check ( lv_process_type eq 'ZSCR' ) .

* Delete error messages raised in this BADI
  LS_MSGIDNO-SIGN       = 'I'.
  LS_MSGIDNO-OPTION     = 'EQ'.
  LS_MSGIDNO-LOW-MSGID  = 'ZCRMBOOK'.
  LS_MSGIDNO-LOW-MSGNO  = '001'.
  APPEND LS_MSGIDNO TO LT_MSGIDNO.

* Delete the messages @ header level
  CALL FUNCTION 'CRM_MESSAGES_DELETE'
    EXPORTING
      IT_R_MSGIDNO   = LT_MSGIDNO
      IV_REF_OBJECT  = IV_GUID
```

```
        IV_REF_KIND    = 'A'
    EXCEPTIONS
      APPL_LOG_ERROR = 1
      OTHERS         = 2.

  if ls_customer_h_wrk-zzhashtag is initial.
    lv_error = abap_true.
  endif.

  if lv_error eq abap_true.
* Raise our error message
    MESSAGE I001(ZCRMBOOK) INTO LV_DUMMY.
    CALL FUNCTION 'CRM_MESSAGE_COLLECT'
          EXPORTING
            IV_CALLER_NAME = GC_OBJECT_NAME-orderadm_h
            IV_REF_OBJECT  = IV_GUID
            IV_REF_KIND    = 'A'.

    raise do_not_save.
  endif.
endmethod.
```

Listing 7.2 Method IF_EX_ORDER_SAVE~CHECK_SAVE Implementation

The code is very similar to the previous examples. However, note that the key difference is that the ORDER_SAVE BAdI only provides the GUID of the business transaction, so you must read both the ACTIVITY_H and CUSTOMER_H segments via the one order API function modules. After you have the values, then you still raise the error message in the same fashion using the CRM_MESSAGES_COLLECT function module, but then you need to add one more extra step to prevent the save.

You prevent the save of the actual transaction by raising the exception of this method called DO_NOT_SAVE. This raising of the DO_NOT_SAVE exception is what causes the SAP CRM system not to save the business transaction to the database when using the ORDER_SAVE BAdI.

7.2 Defaulting Values in a Business Transaction

The next most common request that we've received in many SAP CRM projects is to have the system default values into the business transaction when creating or maintaining a business transaction. The common business driver is either to prevent errors or to automatically classify the data entered on a business transaction via a predetermined attribute. To achieve this, you can use the segment BAdI technique and the BTEs technique. As you learned with making fields required in the business transaction, the use of these techniques will depend on your requirements. Both techniques are described in the following sections.

Prevent errors/
classify data

7.2.1 Business Scenario

In this business scenario, your business receives interactions from customers who don't use a hashtag as part of the social media interaction. The social media service Twitter doesn't require the use of hashtags in messages that are sent. You want to default a suggested hashtag of #sapcrm in your social call report so that you can report off of this value as needed. If the user has already provided a hashtag, then you don't want to override this value.

#sapcrm

7.2.2 Segment BAdI

As we discussed earlier in this chapter, the business transaction consists of several segments. For each segment in the business transaction, there is a BAdI available that allows you to specify logic based on your business needs. These BAdIs are normally named CRM_<SEGMENTNAME>_BADI, where <SEGMENTNAME> is the name of the segment that you want to perform your custom logic. For this example, let's take a look at the CUSTOMER_H BAdI.

The interface of the CUSTOMER_H BAdI contains four methods:

CUSTOMER_H
BAdI methods

- CRM_CUSTOMER_H_CHECK
- CRM_CUSTOMER_H_MERGE
- CRM_CUSTOMER_H_SET_SCREEN
- CRM_CUSTOMER_H_SET_TITLE

You can use the MERGE method found in each segment BAdI to set default values for that segment or you can set values for other attributes via the one order object layer API function modules.

To do this, you need to create a new implementation of the CUSTOMER_H BAdI because in the previous section you only had implemented the ACTVITY_H BAdI. Follow these steps:

1. Go to Transaction SE18, and bring up the CRM_CUSTOMER_H_BADI in display mode.

2. From the display screen, choose the menu option IMPLEMENTATION • CREATE. A popup appears once again asking for you to enter a name for your implementation.

3. Name the implementation "Z_DEFAULT_HASHTAG", and click CHECKMARK button.

4. Enter a description for the BAdI, and change the name of the implementing class as necessary.

5. Click SAVE. Drill into the CRM_CUSTOMER_H_MERGE method of the BAdI interface, and insert the code shown in Listing 7.3.

```
method IF_EX_CRM_CUSTOMER_H_BADI~CRM_CUSTOMER_H_MERGE.
    DATA: LV_PROC_TYPE TYPE CRMT_PROCESS_TYPE,
          LV_INPUT_FIELD_NAME type CRMT_INPUT_FIELD_NAMES.

    CALL FUNCTION 'CRM_ORDERADM_H_READ_OW'
      EXPORTING
        IV_ORDERADM_H_GUID                = IS_CUSTOMER_H_WRK-
GUID
      IMPORTING
        EV_PROCESS_TYPE                   = LV_PROC_TYPE
      EXCEPTIONS
        ADMIN_HEADER_NOT_FOUND            = 1
        OTHERS                            = 2.

    IF SY-SUBRC <> 0.
      EXIT.
    ENDIF.

    CHECK LV_PROC_TYPE EQ 'ZSCR'.

    if IS_CUSTOMER_H_WRK-ZZHASHTAG is INITIAL.
```

```
      CS_CUSTOMER_H_BADI-ZZHASHTAG = '#sapcrm'.
   ENDIF.

endmethod.
```
Listing 7.3 CRM_CUSTOMER_H_MERGE Implementation

The BAdI interface provides an IS_CUSTOMER_H_WRK structure containing the current values of the field and the CS_CUSTOMER_H_BADI, which can be used to update the values that were maintained. For this BAdI, all you need to do is update the appropriate field in the CS_CUSTOMER_BADI structure.

7.2.3 Business Transaction Events

As we discussed earlier, the drawback of segment BAdIs is the fact that they are triggered only when data is maintained in the transaction. You may, however, want to have data defaulted before the user inputs any data in a transaction or only once during the lifetime of the transaction.

If this is the case, then you'll need to use the business transaction events (BTEs) to default the values in. As we discussed earlier, it's even more important during the maintenance of data via BTEs that you avoid recursive call loops. Because we've already studied the use of BTEs in detail in Chapter 4, we'll just focus on the function module code to default a value via a BTE. To do this, you'll create a new function module Z_CRM_HASHTAG_DEFAULT in Transaction SE37. The function module should contain the interface and coding as shown in Listing 7.4.

Default values

```
FUNCTION z_crm_hashtag_default.
*"----------------------------------------------------------
*"*"Local Interface:
*"  IMPORTING
*"   REFERENCE(IV_HEADER_GUID) TYPE  CRMT_OBJECT_GUID
*"   REFERENCE(IV_OBJECT_GUID) TYPE  CRMT_OBJECT_GUID
*"   REFERENCE(IV_OBJECT_NAME) TYPE  CRMT_OBJECT_NAME
*"   REFERENCE(IV_EVENT_EXETIME) TYPE  CRMT_EVENT_EXETIME
*"   REFERENCE(IV_EVENT) TYPE  CRMT_EVENT
*"   REFERENCE(IV_STRVAL_OLD) TYPE  ANY OPTIONAL
*"   REFERENCE(IV_STRVAL_NEW) TYPE  ANY OPTIONAL
```

```
*"  REFERENCE(IV_STRUC_NAME) TYPE  CRMC_EVENT_STRUC-
STRUC OPTIONAL
*"  REFERENCE(IV_ATTRIBUT) TYPE  CRMT_EVENT_ATTRIBUT OPTIONAL
*"------------------------------------------------------------
  DATA: ls_customer_h_wrk TYPE crmt_customer_h_wrk,
        ls_customer_h_com TYPE crmt_customer_h_com,
        lt_input_field_names TYPE crmt_input_field_names_tab,
        ls_input_field_names TYPE crmt_input_field_names.

  FIELD-SYMBOLS: <ls_activity_h_wrk> TYPE crmt_activity_h_
wrk,
                 <lu_activity_h_wrk> TYPE crmt_activity_h_
wrk.

  ASSIGN iv_strval_new TO <ls_activity_h_wrk>.
  ASSIGN iv_strval_old TO <lu_activity_h_wrk>.

  CHECK <ls_activity_h_wrk> NE <lu_activity_h_wrk>.

  CHECK <ls_activity_h_wrk>-priority EQ '1'.
  CALL FUNCTION 'CRM_CUSTOMER_H_READ_OW'
    EXPORTING
      iv_guid           = iv_header_guid
    IMPORTING
      es_customer_h_wrk = ls_customer_h_wrk
    EXCEPTIONS
      header_not_found  = 1
      OTHERS            = 2.

  ls_customer_h_wrk-ZZHASHTAG = '#sapcrm'.
  ls_input_field_names-fieldname = 'ZZHASHTAG'.
  INSERT ls_input_field_names INTO TABLE lt_input_field_
names.

  MOVE-CORRESPONDING ls_customer_h_wrk TO ls_customer_h_com.

  IF ls_customer_h_com-ref_guid IS INITIAL.
    ls_customer_h_com-ref_guid = iv_header_guid.
  ENDIF.

  CALL FUNCTION 'CRM_CUSTOMER_H_MAINTAIN_OW'
    EXPORTING
      is_customer_h_com         = ls_customer_h_com
```

```
    CHANGING
      ct_input_field_names        = lt_input_field_names
    EXCEPTIONS
      header_change_error         = 1
      header_create_error         = 2
      error_occurred              = 3
      OTHERS                      = 4.
ENDFUNCTION.
```

Listing 7.4 Function Module Z_CRM_HASHTAG_DEFAULT

In this coding example, you first determined whether the value had changed for priority. You only want to update the hashtag field when the priority has been set to high or "1". After you determine that the priority is high, you need to read the existing values of the current hashtag field using the `CRM_CUSTOMER_H_READ_OW` function module.

If the field is currently blank, then you default to the #sapcrm hashtag and call the function module `CRM_CUSTOMER_H_MAINTAIN_OW` to update the value. Notice that you won't issue a `commit work` in this logic to save your changes because the overall one order framework for the SAP CRM business transaction is responsible for managing the commit of the data.

7.3   Custom Date Rules

In many business processes, there is a need to calculate metrics or suggest deadline dates based on current values. SAP CRM allows you to calculate dates on a transaction using a set of delivered date rules. Most of the predelivered rules perform a simple addition on a source date to provide a future date.

7.3.1   Business Scenario

This might be fine when you only want to increment a date by a time frame such as 30 days, but it won't work when the date should only be incremented when the transaction meets certain criteria. To get around this limitation, you can create a new date rule that executes an ABAP function module that accepts a predefined set of import parameters and returns a certain set of export parameters that will calculate the date based on your needs. For example, the expected completed date for a complaint should be based on the type of customer or severity of the complaint.

7.3.2 Create New Date Rule

To create a new date rule, you need to perform a series of configuration and development steps:

1. Open the DATE RULE customizing screen by going into the IMG and following the menu path: CUSTOMER RELATIONSHIP MANAGEMENT • BASIC FUNCTIONS • DATE MANAGEMENT • DEFINE DATE TYPES, DURATION TYPES AND DATE RULES.

2. In the dialog structure that appears, select DATE RULES, and then click the NEW ENTRIES button. The screen shown in Figure 7.15 appears.

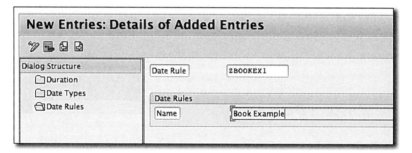

Figure 7.15 New Date Rule

3. Enter a technical name for the rule such as "ZBOOKEX1", and then enter a description such as "Book Example".

4. Click SAVE, and you are prompted for a customizing request. If you don't have an existing customizing request, you'll create a new one; otherwise, you'll select one for your work.

5. Go back to the overview screen of all existing date rules as shown in Figure 7.16, select the date rule that you created, and then click the DETAILS icon.

Figure 7.16 Date Rule Overview

6. An overview screen appears showing all of the versions of the under-lying XML that makes up the date rule as shown in Figure 7.17. Double-click on the only row, and then you're ready to start editing the XML of the date rule. There isn't much documentation on this format, but to invoke an ABAP function module for date rules, you can enter a certain pattern as shown in Figure 7.18 and Listing 7.5.

Underlying XML

7. When you first open the editor, it will be in display mode. Click the CHANGE button to insert the necessary XML code.

Date Rules: Version Selection

In Transport Order

| Date Rule | Book Example |
| Key | ZBOOKEX1 |

Version	Creat.by	Created on	Changed by	Changed on	ID for Date Rule	...
Standard	SJOHANNE	SU 02/24/2013 17:10:10 CET	SJOHANNE	SU 02/24/2013 17:10:11 CET	001E4F2D28891ED29FD394CDF6A1301C	

Figure 7.17 Date Rule Versioning

The EDITOR FOR DATE RULES screen expects a certain pattern of XML to be entered that specifies the date rule as shown in Listing 7.5. The pattern has been derived by examining the delivered date rule in the system called "Planned Date (Activities)" with a technical key of "000000000002".

XML pattern

```xml
<?xml version="1.0"?>
<SAPTimeRule>
  <ABAPTimeRule function="Z_CRM_DATE_CALC"/>
</SAPTimeRule>
```

Listing 7.5 XML for Date Rule ZBOOKEX1

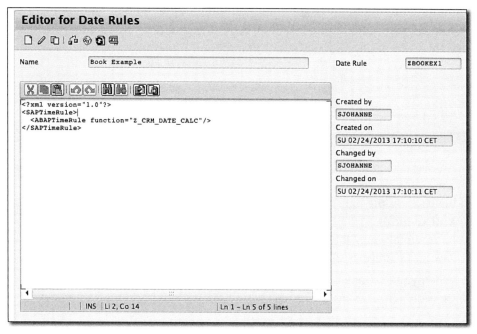

Figure 7.18 Date Rule XML Code

8. After you've created the XML for the date rule that calls the ABAP function module you'll create in the next step, save your work.

Code ABAP logic   9. Before you can use this date rule in a date profile, you now must code the ABAP logic that will evaluate the date passed and return a result. Create a function module that has two importing parameters:

- ▶ CONTEXT
  A type reference to IF_TIMECONTEXT.

- ▶ TIMEMESSAGE
  A type reference to CL_TIMEMESSAGE.

Your function module also must return a reference value named ERROR that is of type XFLAG.

The context reference provides you access to the date data being manipulated in your function module. The interface allows you to retrieve the list of time events and then add back a special time event called the *result*, which is the result of your calculation and will populate the date type that will use this rule.

Function Module Logic: Date Context

To better understand this logic, let's take a look at the following function module that calculates your date. The first call will be to get the event set from the context as shown in the code fragment: — Event set

```
li_eventset = context->get_eventset( ).
```

This is always needed to provide the result back and calculate any dates you may encounter.

Next you'll get the GUID of the current transaction you're processing so you can access any data needed for the calculation via the one order API. You'll use the function module CRM_CONTEXT_GET_ACTUALGUID_OW to get this GUID. — Calculation data

After you have the GUID, you retrieve any other data from the business transaction using the one order OW function modules by passing in the header GUID. As you might have noticed, your function module doesn't provide any data about the business transaction you're working with directly.

If your calculation is based on another date, you first need to retrieve the value of that date by retrieving it from the event set. The following code fragment can be used to achieve this in your date rule function module: — Find date value

```
li_tns_zfirstcont ?= li_eventset->get_by_name( lv_name ).

 if li_tns_zfirstcont is initial.
   exit.
 endif.
```

Note that you won't want to process the date rule if the date you need to calculate hasn't been entered or already calculated. Thus, you'll exit the function module to prevent any short dumps with improper date calls.

One big difference of working with a date context as compared to standard ABAP time and date types is that you can't perform simple add or subtract functions on the dates themselves. You instead need to create a duration that corresponds to how much you want to increment or decrement the date and then apply the duration to the date itself. To do this, create a new duration object using the class CL_TIMEDURA. You can then calculate the new date by using the static method CL_TIMECALC. — New duration object

7.3.3 Store the Result

The final part of working with custom date rules is to store the result. For date calculation rules, you need to change the event called RESULT in your event set. You first must check to see if it exists; if so, you remove the previous result and then insert and create your new result in the event set. After this is done, your function module is complete, and there is no more logic that you need to build within the function module.

Built function module

Listing 7.6 shows the completed function module, which you can build in Transaction SE37 for your date rule. For this example, you'll call the function module "Z_CRM_DATE_CALC".

```
FUNCTION Z_CRM_DATE_CALC.
*"----------------------------------------------------------------
*"*"Local Interface:
*"  IMPORTING
*"     REFERENCE(CONTEXT) TYPE REF TO  IF_TIMECONTEXT
*"     REFERENCE(TIMEMESSAGE) TYPE REF TO  CL_TIMEMESSAGE
*"  EXPORTING
*"     REFERENCE(ERROR) TYPE  XFLAG
*"----------------------------------------------------------------

  CLASS cl_timecalc DEFINITION LOAD.

  CLASS cl_timeunit_broker DEFINITION LOAD.

  INCLUDE timecalc_const.

  data:
    li_tns_zfirstcont      type ref to cl_timeevent,
    li_time_tns_zfirstcont type ref to cl_timetime,
    li_time_result         type ref to cl_timetime,
    li_time_start          type ref to cl_timetime,
    li_result              type ref to cl_timeevent,
    li_eventset            type ref to CL_TIMESET_GENERIC,
    li_duraset             type ref to cl_timeset_generic,
    dura                   TYPE timedura value '120',
    li_dura                TYPE REF TO cl_timedura,
    li_dura_start          type ref to cl_timedura,
    li_duraunit            TYPE REF TO cl_timeunit,
```

```
      li_timeunit            TYPE REF TO cl_timeunit,
      lv_object_guid         type crmt_object_guid,
      ls_customer_h_wrk      type CRMT_CUSTOMER_H_WRK.

   data: lv_name type timename.


* get contstart from context
   lv_event = 'LASTTWEET'.
   li_eventset = context->get_eventset( ).

   CALL FUNCTION 'CRM_CONTEXT_GET_ACTUALGUID_OW'
     IMPORTING
       EV_REF_GUID = lv_object_guid.

   CALL FUNCTION 'CRM_CUSTOMER_H_READ_OW'
     EXPORTING
       IV_GUID            = lv_object_guid
     IMPORTING
       ES_CUSTOMER_H_WRK = ls_customer_h_wrk
     EXCEPTIONS
       HEADER_NOT_FOUND  = 1.

   IF ls_customer_h_wrk-zzhashstag eq '#sapcrm'.
     dura = 15.
   ELSE.
     dura = 33.
   ENDIF.

   li_tns_zfirstcont ?= li_eventset->get_by_name( lv_name ).

   if li_tns_zfirstcont is initial.
     exit.
   endif.

* now that we have final keys for calculation then get
* the values * needed

   if li_tns_zfirstcont->m_time_to is not initial.
     li_time_tns_zfirstcont ?= li_tns_zfirstcont->m_time_to.
   else.
     li_time_tns_zfirstcont ?= li_tns_zfirstcont->m_time_from.
   endif.
```

```
    li_timeunit = cl_timeunit_broker=>get_unit( gc_timeunit_
day ).

* Create Object Duration
  CREATE OBJECT li_dura
    EXPORTING
      NAME        = 'DURA'
      DURA        = dura
      TIMEUNIT    = li_timeunit
      TIMEOBJECT  = li_time_tns_zfirstcont->M_TIMEOBJECT
    EXCEPTIONS
      FATAL_ERROR = 1
      others      = 2.

  CREATE OBJECT li_dura_start
    EXPORTING
      NAME        = 'DURA'
      DURA        = '1'
      TIMEUNIT    = li_timeunit
      TIMEOBJECT  = li_time_tns_zfirstcont->M_TIMEOBJECT
    EXCEPTIONS
      FATAL_ERROR = 1
      others      = 2.

  CALL METHOD li_dura->SET_DURA
    EXPORTING
      DURA     = dura
      TIMEUNIT = li_timeunit.

  call method li_dura_start->set_dura
    exporting
      dura = '1'
      timeunit = li_timeunit.

  cALL METHOD CL_TIMECALC=>MOVE
    EXPORTING
      TIME      = li_time_tns_zfirstcont
      DURA      = li_dura_start
      DIRECTION = '+'
    RECEIVING
      RESULT    = li_time_start.

  cALL METHOD CL_TIMECALC=>MOVE
```

```
    EXPORTING
      TIME       = li_time_tns_zfirstcont
      DURA       = li_dura
      DIRECTION = '+'
    RECEIVING
      RESULT     = li_time_result.

  li_result ?= li_eventset->get_by_name( 'RESULT' ).

  if li_result is not initial.

    CALL METHOD li_eventset->REMOVE_BY_NAME
      EXPORTING
        NAME             = 'RESULT'
      EXCEPTIONS
        ITEM_NOT_FOUND = 1
        OTHERS         = 2.

  endif.

  clear: li_result.

  create object li_result
    EXPORTING
      name       = 'RESULT'
      time_to    = li_time_result
      time_from = li_time_start.

  CALL METHOD li_eventset->INSERT
    EXPORTING
      ITEM           = li_result
    EXCEPTIONS
      FATAL_ERROR = 1
      OTHERS      = 2.

ENDFUNCTION.
```

Listing 7.6 Function Module Z_CRM_DATE_CALC

As you can see, the coding for a custom date appears complicated due to the indirect access and update of the date information. Once created, though, it's quite possible to reuse the date rule across one date type or several transactions as needed.

Use new date rule   To use the new date rule in your transaction, you'll need to add the date rule to a date rule profile, assign the date rule to date in the profile, and then assign the profile to your transaction type. To do this, follow these steps:

1. Go to the following path in the IMG: CRM • BASIC FUNCTIONS • DATE MANAGEMENT • DEFINE DATE PROFILE.

2. Select DATE PROFILE 000000000001, and then choose COPY. Use "ZSCR" as the technical name and "Social Call Report" as the description for the copied entry.

3. Go to DATE RULES FOR THE COPIED PROFILE. Select NEW ENTRIES, and the ZBOOKEX1 rule to the list data rules for the profile.

4. Go to the date types for your date profile. Choose the ORDER-PLANNED date, and click on the DETAILS button. Assign the date rule to this date as shown in Figure 7.19.

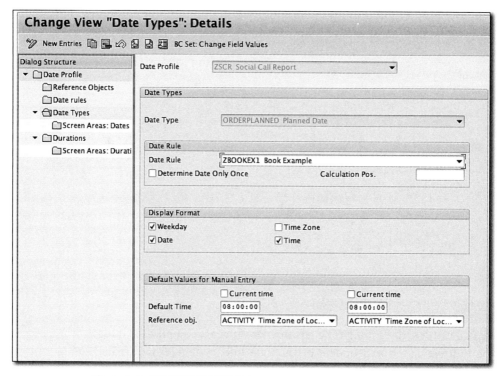

Figure 7.19 ORDERPLANNED Date

5. Assign the ZSCR date profile to your ZSCR transaction type by going to the IMG path: CRM • Basic Functions • Assign Date Profile to Transaction Type. Select the ZSCR business transaction type, and choose Details.

6. In the Details screen under Profiles, change the entry for date profile to ZSCR. This will now take effect the next time you create a new social call report business transaction.

> **Caution**
>
> One important thing to remember is that date rule changes to business transactions don't always work correctly with existing business transactions. This means if you do change the date profile for a business transaction type, the changes won't work correctly until a new transaction is created, especially with date rule calculations.

As you've learned, custom date rules can be set up with a combination of configuration and development. The calculations allow your business users to see plan dates based on the data provided in the business transaction. This is quite useful for processes where there is a need to track against plan and actual, and for this tracking to be visible within the details of a transaction instead of having to refer to a separate report to view this information for a given business transaction.

7.4   Partner Determination Access Rules

There are several situations in which you'll want to automatically determine a partner in a business transaction based on another partner. A common example would be in a sales order, where you may want to provide the list of available ship-to parties that are related to the sold-to party entered on a sales order. Another example is that you may want to determine the contacts related to the primary partner entered on an activity transaction. Most of the time, you can use the pre-delivered access rules from SAP to determine the partner.

Automatically determine partner

7.4.1 Business Scenario

However, a business may want to add a new type of relationship or partner type for a transaction, which means that the standard delivered access rules for partner determination won't meet the need. The standard delivered access rules don't cover custom relationship types. It may be common for a business to track relationships between partners whose descriptions don't match those delivered in the standard system. To track these relationships, you can create new relationship types. In the following sections, we'll examine two different scenarios of creating custom partner determination rules. One doesn't involve code, but rather configuration, and the other involves using the BAdI COM_PARTNER_BADI.

7.4.2 Configuration Only Method

In this example, the business wants to track the social influencers that were part of a customer interaction. A social influencer has been modeled in the SAP CRM system as a new partner function called YTWEETER, which is based on the relationship type ZTWEET "is the social influencer for." The business wants its copy of the standard activity transaction type "0001," which is called "ZSCR" for social call report, to automatically suggest the related social influencers for a customer when the social call report transaction is created. To do this, the business needs to configure the social call report with a new partner determination procedure, which will be a copy of the standard procedure used by transaction type "0001" and will now include the YTWEETER partner function.

To implement this, follow these steps:

1. Create the relationship category ZTWEET.
2. Create a new partner function called YTWEETER.
3. Create a new access sequence called YSMI.
4. Copy the existing procedure used by the "0001," and then add the YTWEETER partner function to the procedure.
5. Add the procedure to the YSCR transaction.

We'll go over each of these steps in greater detail in the following subsections.

Create a Relationship Category

To create a new relationship type, follow these steps:

1. Use Transaction BUBA.

2. In the screen that pops up, choose the entry RELATIONSHIP CATEGORIES. From this list, pick a relationship category that most closely matches the type of new relationship you're creating.

3. In this example, copy the BUR001 Contact Person type as the basis for your ZTWEET relationship category as shown in Figure 7.20. Select the entry BUR001, and then choose the COPY ENTRY icon. You'll then get a screen to change the copy that was made to a new target entry.

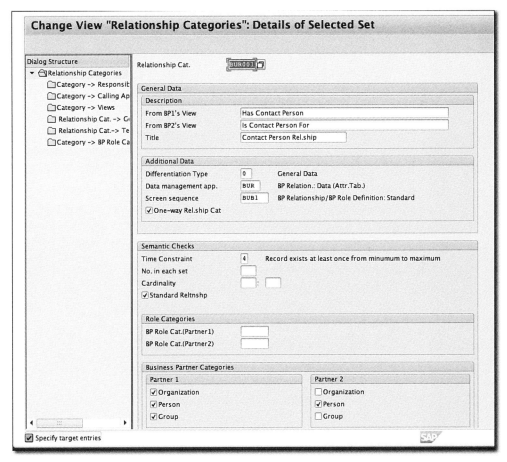

Figure 7.20 Entry to Modify in Copy

4. Change the RELATIONSHIP CAT. code to "ZTWEET" as shown in Figure 7.21.

5. For the description from the view of the primary business partner (FROM BP1'S VIEW), enter "Has Social Influencer", and for the description from the view of the related business partner (FROM BP2'S VIEW), enter "Is Social Influencer For". Enter the TITLE of this relationship as "Social Influence Relshp" (see Figure 7.22). Leave all other settings unchanged.

6. Press ⌷Enter⌷, and a popup appears asking if you want to copy the dependent entries. Choose the COPY ALL button as shown in Figure 7.23.

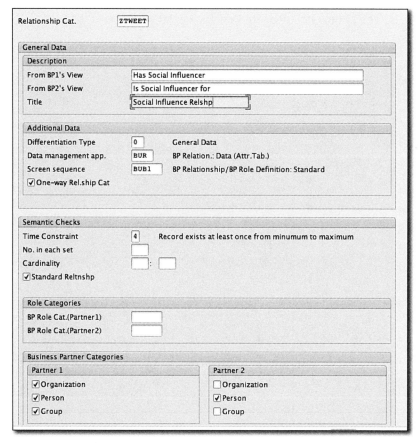

Figure 7.21 Modified Entry

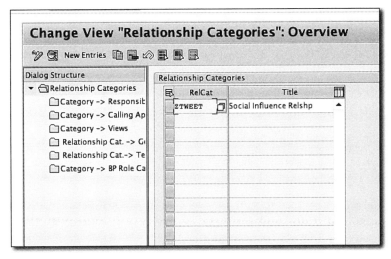

Figure 7.22 Entry Finish

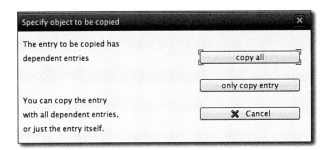

Figure 7.23 Copy Dependent Entries

7. Another message appears telling you the number of entries that were copied. Click the checkmark button to continue.

8. After this is complete, click SAVE, and then once again you can either use an existing transport request or create a new transport request to save your work.

Partner Function Creation

Now that you have a relationship category created, you can create a new partner function that will be used in your business transaction and is based on your relationship category. To do this, follow these steps:

1. Go to the path in the IMG: CUSTOMER RELATIONSHIP MANAGEMENT •
   BASIC FUNCTIONS • PARTNER PROCESSING • DEFINE PARTNER FUNCTIONS.

2. Click on the NEW ENTRIES button, and enter a new entry for your partner function. Make these settings on the screen:

   ▶ FUNCTION: "YTWEETER".

   ▶ TEXT: "Social Influencer".

   ▶ ABBREV.: "YSMI".

   ▶ FUNCTION CATEGORY: Choose CONTACT PERSON to correspond to
   the type of relationship category you've built.

   ▶ USAGE: Choose CRM. You have to choose a usage because at one
   point SAP CRM and Business to Business Procurement (now
   known as SAP Supplier Relationship Management) used a common SAP code base.

   ▶ RELATIONSHIP CAT.: "ZTWEET".

3. Your completed entry will appear similar to Figure 7.24. Click SAVE,
   and when prompted for a transport, choose either an existing transport or create a new own for this work.

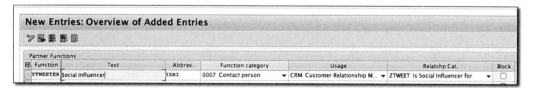

Figure 7.24 New YTWEETER Partner Function

Access Sequence Creation

Configure logic Now that you've configured a new partner function and relationship category, you need to configure logic that will find all partners based on
your relationship category. The access sequence in partner determination is a tool that you can use to define this logic. Follow these steps:

1. Go to the following path in the IMG: CUSTOMER RELATIONSHIP
   MANAGEMENT • BASIC FUNCTIONS • PARTNER PROCESSING • DEFINE
   ACCESS SEQUENCES.

2. From the first screen, click on NEW ENTRIES.

3. Enter "YSMI" as the technical code for your entry, and enter "Proceeding Document ->ACTIVITY PARTNER -> Social Influencer" as the description.

4. Click SAVE; you'll be prompted for a transport request. Use an existing request or create a new one.

5. Select the entry you created, and then choose INDIVIDUAL ACCESS DIALOG on the left-hand side.

6. Choose CREATE NEW ENTRIES. The first entry you'll create will allow you to copy the partner from a previous document as needed. This entry is important if you want to allow for the copy of partners between business transactions. For this entry, configure it with BATCH SEQ. equal to "10", DIALOG SEQ. equal to "10", and a SOURCE of "COM_PARTNER_A Preceding Document". Your entry for this step should look like Figure 7.25.

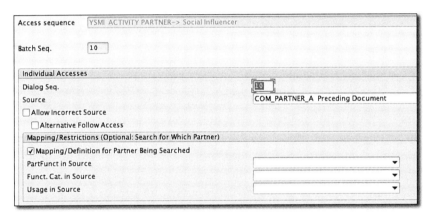

Figure 7.25 Access Sequence YSMI Step 10

7. For the second entry, configure it with the BATCH SEQ. equal to "20", DIALOG SEQ. equal to "20", and SOURCE as "CRM_PARTNER_C Business Partner Relationships".

8. Check the WAIT UNTIL SOURCE IS AVAILABLE and DETERMINATION AS BUSINESS PARTNER flags.

9. Specify the activity partner as the source to find the related partners.

10. Search for partners that were related as YTWEETER partner function with the activity partner as shown in Figure 7.26.

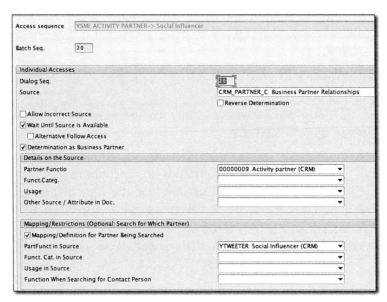

Figure 7.26 Access Sequence YSMI Step 20

Determination Procedure Copy and Modification

Partner determination procedure

Now that the access sequence is defined, you can use it in your business transaction to find the related partners. You define this use by a *partner determination procedure*. A partner determination procedure defines the possible business partners recorded in a business transaction and how they are entered or found for the business transaction. Each and every business transaction is assigned to exactly one partner determination procedure.

For the social call report example, you'll use a copy of a standard delivered partner determination procedure and then add your new YTWEETER partner function to the transaction.

Follow these steps:

1. Choose DEFINE PARTNER DETERMINATION PROCEDURE in the IMG.

2. Select the entry with key 00000002, and choose COPY.

3. Modify the technical code of the procedure to be "ZSCR". For the description, enter "Social Call Report", and then leave all the other settings the same.

4. Press ⌈Enter⌉; the system will ask you if you want to copy the dependent entries as shown in Figure 7.27. Choose the COPY ALL button.

5. Click SAVE, and assign to an appropriate transport as needed.

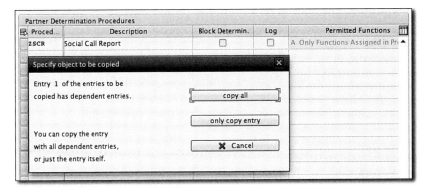

Figure 7.27 Copy-Dependent Entries for Procedure

6. Select your newly created procedure, and then choose PARTNER FUNCTIONS IN PROCEDURE. You can now see a list of the existing partner functions that came from the copy of the partner procedure you copied as shown in Figure 7.28. You can see that one of options displayed shows the minimum and maximum number of partners available.

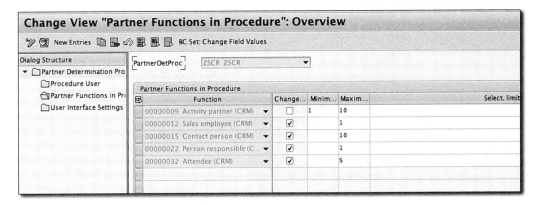

Figure 7.28 Existing Functions in Procedure

7. Choose NEW ENTRIES, and insert your "YTWEETER" partner function into the partner determination procedure. Choose the partner function to be YTWEETER SOCIAL INFLUENCER.

8. Check the CHANGEABLE flag. For the lowest number of occurrences, leave the NO. OF OCCURRENCES (LOWEST) field blank. This makes the partner function optional in your transaction. If you always require a certain number of influencers to be recorded, you can enter a value in this field.

9. Enter the maximum number of occurrences as "10". This restricts how many social influencers can be recorded in the transaction.

10. Enter "2" for the SELECTION LIMIT field. The SELECTION LIMIT field allows you to require the user to choose a particular partner from a list when receiving multiple possible values as a result of the access sequence. By setting the SELECTION LIMIT at "2", you require the user to pick one value and only put one partner in the transaction instead of all possible values.

11. In the PARTNER DETERMINATION section, assign the access sequence YSMI that you created to have this partner be determined from the business partner relationship you created. After you've made your changes, the screen should be similar to Figure 7.29.

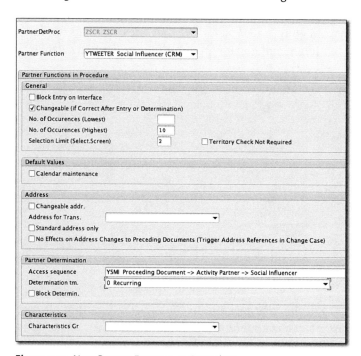

Figure 7.29 New Partner Function in Procedure

Assignment to the Business Transaction

In the last step, you have to assign the partner determination to your social call report activity by following these steps:

1. Go to the IMG menu path: CRM • BASIC FUNCTIONS • TRANSACTIONS • BASIC SETTINGS • DEFINE TRANSACTION TYPES.

2. Select your ZSCR transaction type, and then choose the DETAILS button. In the PROFILES block, enter the technical code of your partner determination procedure "ZSCR" in the PARTNER DETERM. PROC. field (see Figure 7.30).

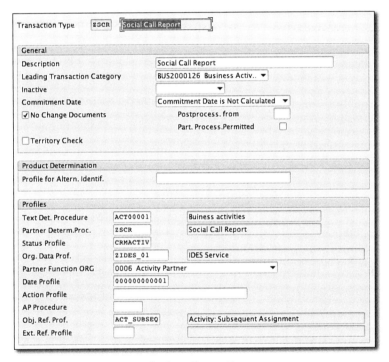

Figure 7.30 Assignment to a Business Transaction

Testing Your Work

Now that you've completed the configuration of the partner determination procedure, you need to test your work. Follow these steps for the test:

1. Create a new contact person in your SAP CRM system independent of any business partner.

2. Assign that contact person to a corporate account in your system.

3. Create a new social call report using the business partner that you set up to verify that the partner determination procedure will populate the partner function field into your business transaction.

7.4.3 Configuration and BAdI Implementation Method

For those rare cases where business partner relationships aren't sufficient, and you need more complex logic based on the organization model or other logic, you can use a combination of configuration and a BAdI implementation. The COM_PARTNER_BADI allows you to create three new sources for access sequences. Implementing the DETERMINATION_ADD_IN_1, DETERMINATION_ADD_IN_2, and DETERMINATION_ADD_IN_3 methods can create these sources. These methods correspond to the COM_PARTNER_X, COM_PARTNER_Y, and COM_PARTNER_Z data sources.

COM_PARTNER_BADI

To use these sources, you'll need to first implement the COM_PARTNER_BADI:

1. Access Transaction SE18 and display the COM_PARTNER_BADI.

2. Choose IMPLEMENTATION • CREATE, enter the name of your implementation, and click the checkmark button.

3. Enter a description for your implementation, and change the implementing class name as needed as shown in Figure 7.31.

4. Drill into the DETERMINATION_ADD_IN_1 method, and insert the code from Listing 7.7.

```
method IF_EX_COM_PARTNER_BADI~DETERMINATION_ADD_IN_1.
 data: is_existing_partner type COMT_PARTNER_WRK,
       lt_found_badi_partner type comt_partner_found_via_
badi_t,
       requester_guid type CRMT_PARTNER_GUID.
check is_determination_step-partner_fct = '000000001'.
* Depends on the existence of the requestor partner in the
* partners
```

```
* Org model code insert here.
  et_found_partners = lt_found_badi_partner.
endmethod.
```

Listing 7.7 DETERMINATION_ADD_IN_1

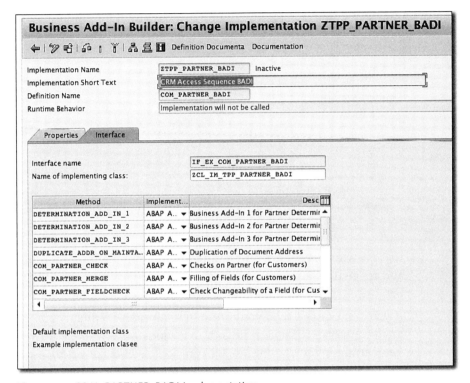

Figure 7.31 COM_PARTNER_BADI Implementation

After you've created your BAdI implementation, you can use the source in an access sequence:

Use source in access sequence

1. Create a new access sequence similar to YSMI, which we defined previously. You may copy access sequence YSMI to a new sequence.
2. You will now need to change the definition of step 20 of the access sequence in order to use the BADI implementation. Change the source of step 20 to be "Business Add-In 1", and then specify the partner function as shown in Figure 7.32. Specifying the partner function provides the input source for determination and offers a way to create

multiple implementations of the COM_PARTNER_BADI for the same source because you can filter on the partner function within the BAdI code.

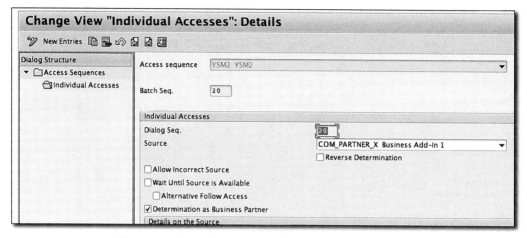

Figure 7.32 Access Sequence Step for BAdI Source

3. Use the access sequence within a partner determination procedure, and assign that procedure to your business transaction as you did earlier.

4. If you want to test this, you can switch the access sequence for the YTWEETER partner function in your determination and then create a new business transaction to see if your logic works correctly.

As a reminder, you can insert an external breakpoint into the code of your BAdI implementation to debug any flaws in the logic that you implemented.

7.5   Organization Model Access Rules

For most businesses, the standard determination rules used to determine the responsible sales or service organization will suffice. However, there are cases where you may want to determine the organizational unit through nonstandard criteria to meet a particular business requirement.

7.5.1 Standard Delivered Rules

In this section, we'll take a look at how the standard delivered rule is built by SAP. The rules are maintained by going to the following path in the IMG: CUSTOMER RELATIONSHIP MANAGEMENT • MASTER DATA • ORGANIZATIONAL MANAGEMENT • ORGANIZATIONAL DATA DETERMINATION • CHANGE RULES AND PROFILES • MAINTAIN DETERMINATION RULES. We'll look at the ACT_REASON_A rule. Search for the rule using the F4 search help with "ACT_REASON_A" as the search term.

When the one result is returned, click the DISPLAY button on the MAINTAIN RULE screen. You can now see a screen similar to Figure 7.33, which shows the rule's technical abbreviation, description, and definition. The definition consists of the category, scenario, and corresponding function module. The category defines that the rule will use the organizational model to find the corresponding organizational unit based on the container passed to the rule.

Result

Rule: Display

Rule	10000146	ACT_REASON_A
Name	Processor:Detrm.ActvyReasn	
Pack.	CRM_ORGMAN	Appl. Component	CRM-MD-ORG

Rule definition | Description | Container

Basic data

Abbr.	ACT_REASON_A
Name	Processor:Detrm.ActvyReasn

Rule definition

Category	A Agent Determination: Organization Model
Scenario	SERVICE Service
Function Module	CRM_ORGMAN_ORGOBJECTS_FIND_5

☑ Terminate If Rule Resolution Without Result

Figure 7.33 Example Rule Definition

Searching through Attributes

Hierarchy The container contains the attributes that will be searched for in the organizational model. The SAP CRM organizational model is a hierarchal structure of organizational units, positions, and position holders. The highest level is an organizational unit, which represents a department or organization within a company. The organizational unit contains positions, which are held by employees within the company.

For all positions and organizational units, there can be attributes assigned that designate whether the organization is responsible for a particular area of sales or service. In most SAP CRM implementations, a business partner record represents each user of the system. These business partners are then assigned positions in the organizational model that normally correspond to their area of responsibility in the business.

Organization

Primary partner You typically determine the sales or service organization based on the primary partner of the business transaction. This partner then is related to the sales organization or service organization through sales area data or master data relationships. You can also specify on which organizational unit attributes that certain number ranges of customers or regions are directly responsible for a business partner.

If you look at the standard delivered function module CRM_ORGMAN_ ORGOBJECTS_FIND_5, you can see that it calls the standard SAP function module CRM_ORGMAN_ORGOBJECTS_FIND_1 for the service-related organization. It then filters out any objects that aren't organizational units and returns those back in the ACTOR_TAB.

7.5.2 Creating a Custom Rule

Now that we've examined how the standard delivered rules work, let's review how to create a custom rule. To do this, go to the following path in the IMG: CUSTOMER RELATIONSHIP MANAGEMENT • MASTER DATA • ORGANIZATIONAL MANAGEMENT • ORGANIZATIONAL DATA DETERMINA-TION • WIZARD FOR ORGANIZATIONAL DATA DETERMINATION • CREATE DETERMINATION RULE FROM ORGANIZATIONAL MODEL.

You'll then see a wizard pop up that will guide you through creating your rule. Follow these steps: Rule wizard

1. On the first screen, enter a technical SHORT DESCRIPTION for the rule. Choose an abbreviation that either starts with "Z" or "Y" and doesn't already exist in your system. For this example, enter "ZBOOKDEMO".

2. Enter "CRM Book Demo" as the DESCRIPTION.

3. Enter the name of a valid package for your rule. For this example, use a valid package that exists in your system. Your completed entry should look similar to Figure 7.34.

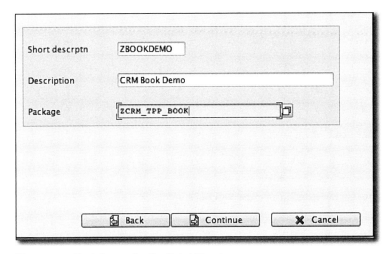

Figure 7.34 Start Screen for the Rule Wizard

Now that you've defined the name, description, and package of the rule, you can select which attributes your rule will filter on. This list of predefined attributes is automatically provided by the system. For this example, you want to determine possible organizational units by the postal code, so select POSTCODE_1 as shown in Figure 7.35. Rule attributes

Now that your rule is created, you can go to the following path in the IMG to display it: CUSTOMER RELATIONSHIP MANAGEMENT • MASTER DATA • ORGANIZATIONAL MANAGEMENT • ORGANIZATIONAL DATA DETERMINATION • CHANGE RULES AND PROFILES • MAINTAIN DETERMINATION RULES. Display rule

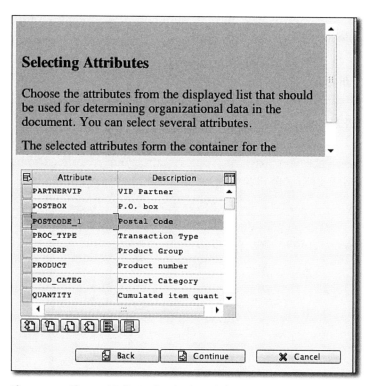

Figure 7.35 Choose Attributes for the New Rule

On the main part of this screen, press F4 in the RULE ENTRY field to search for the rule you just created by its technical name—ZBOOK-DEMO. After you select this, it will place the internal number of the rule into the RULE field, and you can click the CHANGE button to look at the contents of your rule.

Custom vs. standard rule If you examine your generated rule in Figure 7.36, you can see that it looks very similar to the standard rule that was provided by SAP. The primary differences are the function module that your rule will use and the different elements in the container. For your rule, the system will use the CRM_ORGMAN_ORGOBJECTS_FIND_1 function module. On the CONTAINER tab, you'll see that the POSTL_COD1 attribute is being used. Remember, the container specifies what data from the business transaction data is being passed into the function module for evaluation.

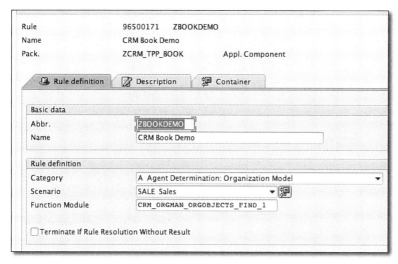

Rule	96500171 ZBOOKDEMO
Name	CRM Book Demo
Pack.	ZCRM_TPP_BOOK Appl. Component

Rule definition | Description | Container

Basic data
| Abbr. | ZBOOKDEMO |
| Name | CRM Book Demo |

Rule definition
Category	A Agent Determination: Organization Model
Scenario	SALE Sales
Function Module	CRM_ORGMAN_ORGOBJECTS_FIND_1

☐ Terminate If Rule Resolution Without Result

Figure 7.36 Generated Organization Determination Rule from the Wizard

Now that you've created a rule, you need to use it within an organizational data profile so that your business transaction can use your logic. To do this, go to the following path in the IMG: CUSTOMER RELATIONSHIP MANAGEMENT • MASTER DATA • ORGANIZATIONAL MANAGEMENT • ORGANIZATIONAL DATA DETERMINATION • CHANGE RULES AND PROFILES • MAINTAIN ORGANIZATION DATA PROFILE.

Organizational data profile

Follow these steps:

1. Click on the NEW ENTRIES button. You now need to create a new profile.

2. Use "ZCRMBOOKDEMO" as the technical ID of the profile and "Sales" as your scenario.

3. Under the DETERMINATION RULES segment, search for the rule that you created through the F4 help.

4. Mark that any organization returned via this rule must have the sales organization, distribution channel, and division to be returned in your results.

5. After your entry looks similar to Figure 7.37, you can save your work. Now that your profile has been saved, you must assign it to your business transaction.

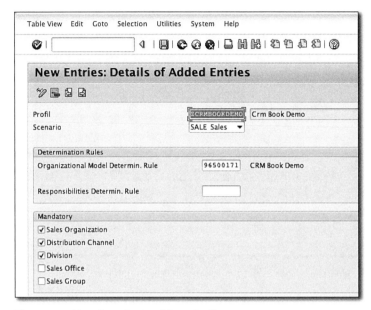

Figure 7.37 New Organizational Data Profile

Assign profile to transaction

Throughout this book, you've been working with the social media call report transaction type ZSCR. You can once again assign the profile to the transaction by going to the following path in the IMG: CUSTOMER RELATIONSHIP MANAGEMENT • MASTER DATA • ORGANIZATIONAL MANAGEMENT • ORGANIZATIONAL DATA DETERMINATION • CHANGE RULES AND PROFILES • ASSIGN ORGANIZATIONAL DATA PROFILE TO TRANSACTION TYPE.

Follow these steps:

1. In the definition of transaction types screen, select your transaction type ZSCR, and click the DETAILS button.

2. Enter "ZCRMBOOKDEMO" in the ORG. DATA PROF field, and click SAVE. Now your social call report will assign the sales organization in the transaction based on the ZIP code of the activity partner in the transaction.

Maintain attribute

Even though the system has been configured to assign the sales organizations based on the ZIP code, you also must maintain this attribute on your sales organizations to be determined when you create your social call report transaction. To do this, follow these steps:

1. Log in to the Web Client under the SALESPRO business role.

2. Choose the SALES OPERATIONS work center and the ORGANIZATIONAL MODEL link under SEARCH.

3. Search by the organizational unit to bring up the sales organization that you want to assign the new attribute. In the ATTRIBUTES block, click the EDIT LIST button.

4. Click on the EXPAND ALL button, and then scroll down to the line labeled POSTAL CODE.

5. Enter "60000" through "70000" for this example and click SAVE as shown in Figure 7.38. By maintaining this attribute, the system will now suggest this organizational unit when the activity partner on your transaction has a ZIP code within the range you just specified.

Figure 7.38 Attributes of Organization Unit in PPOMA_CRM

As you can see, the creation of custom organizational rules allows you to control the determination of the organizational unit when a more precise assignment of the organization is needed.

7.6 Summary

As a developer, this chapter provided you with the basic examples to solve Sales and Service problems and adapt them to a more complex scenario. These enhancement techniques should reduce the amount of time that you need to implement your most common business requirements. This will lead to a faster implementation that covers more of the business needs and should hopefully result in more satisfied business users.

In this chapter, we covered some of the most common enhancement requirements and solutions outside of adding new fields in a sales or service implementation of SAP CRM. Based on our past 10 years of experience in implementing and supporting SAP CRM projects, we've found that the enhancements shown here appear in almost every SAP CRM implementation in which we've participated.

Making fields required and defaulting values in new fields are two of the most common requests when implementing any process in SAP CRM sales or service. In addition, we've found that there is a need to calculate dates and propose business partners and organizational units in a business transaction beyond the capabilities of the standard SAP CRM system. These requirements can make up the bulk of the work of any SAP CRM project in sales or service.

In the next chapter, we'll look at two common BAdIs used in marketing.

In SAP CRM, there are two common marketing enhancement requests that are made in typical projects. In this chapter, you'll see the details on how to enhance the External List Management and the open channel for Campaign Management.

8   Common Enhancement Requests in Marketing

Throughout most of this book, the focus has been on the business partner, product master, and business transaction. However, an important aspect of working with SAP CRM is considering a business's marketing efforts. *Marketing* is the process of communicating the availability of goods or services that have value for customers and sales prospects. Effective marketing communication should allow you to track the receipt and sending of information in a conversation. Because these conversations are unique, SAP allows you to tailor how you track them.

In this chapter, we'll take a look at two common Business Add-Ins (BAdIs) used in the SAP CRM Marketing module. We won't cover every BAdI available; instead, we'll focus are the External List Management (ELM) BAdI and the open channel BAdI for Campaign Management. We'll review how to implement these BAdIs within your SAP CRM system. We've chosen these two BAdIs because the functionality they represent is typically part of a next phase implementation in SAP CRM after the traditional Sales Force Automation (SFA) processes have been implemented using SAP CRM.

BAdIs

Let's start with the External List Management BAdI.

8.1   External List Management BAdI

Leads from
customer lists

External List Management (ELM) is a function of the SAP CRM Marketing component that allows you to import external lists of potential customers and to generate leads or activities from that list. These external lists can be created internally or purchased/rented from a third-party source. A common requirement for ELM is to change how the business partners and/or transactions created by the tool are created. In some situations, you may want to extend the tool so that it can import custom attributes that you've created in your lead or activity transactions.

In the following sections, we'll review the BAdI that allows you to import these lists, and then we'll look at how to create an implementation of this BAdI. We'll then show you how to test the coding of your implementation.

8.1.1   BAdI Overview

CRM_MKTLIST_
BAdI

The technical name of the BAdI you'll use to import the lists and generate the leads or activities is `CRM_MKTLIST_BADI`. This BAdI is filter-dependent but has a default implementation class called `CL_DEF_IM_CRM_MKTLIST_BADI`, which means it's always invoked. The filter of the BAdI is the name of the mapping format used by ELM.

Mapping format

A *mapping format* is a set of customizing in the ELM application that defines how fields contained in a flat file will be mapped to target fields in the SAP CRM system. All mapping formats use this class for processing data. In some cases, you may only be interested in changing part of how the standard logic works but not the entire logic. We therefore recommend that you copy the default implementation class as a starting point for your work.

The BAdI has several methods that are executed. For this chapter, we'll take a look at the methods `create_business_partners` and `create_business_transactions` in the following sections.

8.1.2 Method CREATE_BUSINESS_TRANSACTIONS

This method creates leads or activities based on what was defined in the mapping customizing. This method calls `create_leads` or `create_activities`, respectively. Both the `create_leads` and `create_activities` methods call the function modules `CRM_ORDER_MAINTAIN` and `CRM_ORDER_SAVE` to create the business transactions. Most of the code involved in these methods map the data contained in the import parameters of the `create_business_transactions` method to the parameters of the `CRM_ORDER_MAINTAIN` function module.

CREATE_BUSINESS_TRANSACTIONS

In Chapter 3, we looked at the details of how to add new fields to the SAP CRM business transaction. When the fields are added by the Easy Enhancement Workbench (EEWB), Application Enhancement Tool (AET), or manually, they aren't added for use in ELM. To create new leads or activity transactions from ELM with custom attributes, you need to extend the standard delivered structures for ELM, configure a mapping format that contains your new fields, and implement the method `create_business_transactions` of the BAdI `CRM_MKT_LIST_BADI`.

Why businesses need to use this method

For ELM, there are two separate data structures provided in the system that handle leads and activity data, respectively. During the setup of the external list mapping format, you specify whether you'll be creating lead or activity transactions. Based on that specification, the system will move the data contained in the external list to the corresponding fields of the data structures that match what you're importing into the system. The structure `CRMT_MKTLIST_LEA_EXT` contains lead-specific information, and the structure `CRMT_MKTLIST_ACT_EXT` contains activity-specific information. You'll need to add any custom attributes that you want the ELM application to add to the business transactions created by the tool to these structures.

Data structures for managing leads and activity data

Structure Enhancement: Activity Transaction Data

Now that you know how this BAdI works, it's time to see it in action in this book's ongoing business example of adding social media enhancements. For this example, you want to be able to create social media call reports through ELM. As you recall, you added a new attribute to the

Call reports through ELM

call report called ZZHASHTAG in Chapter 3. You now want to have that attribute stored on the business transactions that will be created through ELM. Follow these steps:

1. Launch Transaction SE11, and bring up the structure CRMT_MKLIST_ ACT_EXT in display mode.

2. Choose the APPEND STRUCTURE button. If this structure hasn't been appended before, it prompts you to provide a name of an append as shown in Figure 8.1. Call the append "ZACRMT_MKTLIST_ACT_EXT" for this example.

Figure 8.1 Create an Append for CRMT_MKTLIST_ACT_EXT

3. Add a single COMPONENT called "ZZHASHTAG", which has the COMPONENT TYPE of "ZZHASHTAG" to your structure. Your completed append structure should look similar to Figure 8.2.

4. Activate the structure; now the field will be available for use in a mapping format definition. However, it won't process or update the business transaction with data until you implement CRM_MKTLIST_BADI.

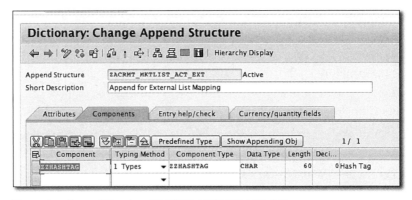

Figure 8.2 Append Structure ZACRMT_MKTLIST_ACT_EXT

Creating a Mapping Format

The next process step is to create a mapping format. The mapping format defines how the physical file containing the external list data maps into the transfer data structures used to import the data into the SAP CRM system. An external list only has one corresponding mapping format. However, several different external lists can use a mapping format.

To create the mapping format, log in to the normal Web Client under a business role that accesses mapping formats and external lists. If you don't have any custom business roles set up with this functionality, you can log in to the business role MARKETINGPRO. A quick way to access this business role (provided you have the required security) is to add the CRM_UI_PROFILE parameter with a value '*' using Transaction SU3. You'll then see a list of all business roles available in your SAP CRM system.

In the standard MARKETINGPRO business role, you can create a new mapping format by going to the MARKETING work center. Choose the link mapping format under the CREATE section to bring up the CREATE MAPPING FORMAT screen. The mapping format defines how data in an external file should be imported into the SAP CRM system. When you create the mapping file, you must provide a technical ID of the mapping and a description. You also need to choose the category of import. For this example, use the ID "ZTPP" and the description "CRM Book Example". Remember this ZTPP ID because it will serve as the filter value for your BAdI implementation.

MARKETINGPRO business role

The next part of creating the mapping format is somewhat confusing. You must provide an example data file that contains columns that you want to map the data from into the SAP CRM system. For this example, you'll open Microsoft Excel and create a new spreadsheet with the layout shown in Table 8.1. Keep in mind that you can choose whatever data you want for your testing, as long as your layout contains all of the fields listed in the table. If you don't have all of these fields, then your file can't be imported into SAP CRM where it can create activities and business partners.

Data file for mapping

Column	Field Name (Row 1)	Example Data (Row 2)
A	COMPANY NAME	My Company
B	CONTACT FIRST NAME	Stephen
C	CONTACT LAST NAME	Johannes
D	STREET	100 Example Lane
E	CITY	Saint Charles
F	STATE	MO
G	CITY	63301
H	PHONE	636-448-4595
I	HASHTAG	sapcrmtpp
J	ACTIVITY DESCRIPTION	Discussed SAP CRM Programming
H	COUNTRY	US
I	TRANSACTION TYPE	ZSCR or a valid activity transaction type in your SAP CRM system
J	MARKETING CAMPAIGN	\<Enter the ID of a valid campaign in your system\>

Table 8.1 Example of Data Mapping Information in Excel

The spreadsheet you created using the layout in Table 8.1 should then be saved as a tab-delimited file. Now that the file is created, you can switch back to your SAP CRM system. At this point, you still should be on the CREATE MAPPING FORMAT screen.

Now select a valid flat file that is comma separated or tab delimited by clicking SELECT A FILE as show in Figure 8.3.

Figure 8.3 Select File Popup for Mapping Format

For this example, select the flat file that you just created. After the layout is imported, you can map your fields form your file to the target data structures of ELM.

The category of the mapping format influences the data that will be created. You have several options, including ADDRESSES, ADDRESSES AND ACTIVITIES, ADDRESSES AND LEADS, ACTIVITIES, LEADS, and MARKETING PROSPECTS. The ADDRESSES option only creates new business partners, while the ACTIVITIES option only creates new activity business transactions. If you want to create a new business partner and assign it to an activity, you need to use the ADDRESSES AND ACTIVITIES option. A common business requirement is to load a file containing a list of new prospects along with data about the initial contact with those prospects. For this example, choose ADDRESSES AND ACTIVITIES. The social call report, as you may recall, is a business activity transaction.

Category

Now that you've selected the category, you'll also use the filter criterion to limit the display of the available fields for mapping. The custom attribute that you added previously to `CRMT_MKTLIST_ACT_EXT` will be available as a mapping target and will be shown under the ACTIVITY option (see Figure 8.4).

Filter

Field Mapping

Position	File Preview Value	Target Field	Mapping Rule
1	Partner Name	Name 1	
2	Street	Street	
3	City	City	
4	Country	ISO code	
5	Zip Code	Postal Code	
6	Telephone	Telephone	
7	Hashtag	Hash Tag	
8			

Insert Row · Delete Row · Add Mapping Rule

Available Target Fields

Map

Target Field	Target Field ID
Personalized Response Code	PERS_RESP_CODE
Coupon Code	COUPON_CODE
Campaign element	CAMPAIGN_ELEMENT
Organization ID	ORG_NUMBER
ID of the Person	PER_NUMBER
Template ID	TEMPLATE_ID
Transaction Type	PROCESS_TYPE
Transaction Descr.	DESCRIPTION
Actual Date From	ACTUAL_DATE_FROM
Actual Time From	ACTUAL_TIME_FROM
Actual Date To	ACTUAL_DATE_TO
Actual Time To	ACTUAL_TIME_TO
Status	USER_STATUS
Priority	PRIORITY
Category	CATEGORY
Hash Tag	ZZHASHTAG

Figure 8.4 New Field Available in the Mapping Format

Mapping format You can now map all of the fields of the file structure to your desired target. To do this, follow these steps:

1. Select a row on the left hand table labeled FIELD MAPPING.

2. Select a row from the list of fields that you wish to map to your file fields, which is the table on the right part of screen called AVAILABLE TARGET FIELDS.

3. Click the MAP button at the top of the AVAILABLE TARGET FIELDS table. You will repeat this procedure until all row entries in the left hand table contain a value for the Target Field.

4. Then click the BACK button, and click SAVE.

You now have a mapping format that can be used for an external list as shown in Figure 8.5. However, to get your custom field imported, you need to implement the CRM_MKTLIST_BADI.

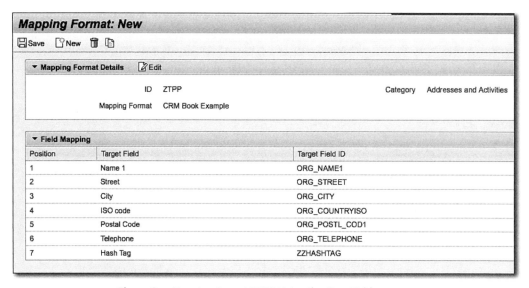

Figure 8.5 Mapping Format ZTPP Using the New Field

Implement CRM_MKTLIST_BADI

To implement the BAdI, we always recommend copying over the standard implementation class CL_DEF_IM_CRM_MKTLIST_BADI to a custom version. This class unfortunately is delivered by SAP as final, so you can't use the concept of inheritance to override just one method of the implementation and add your own logic for the methods that you're interested in.

Go into either Transaction SE80 or Transaction SE24, and copy this class to a z-version. For this example, you call it "ZCL_TPP_CRM_MKTLIST_BADI". During the copy of the class to the z-version, you'll receive some warning messages that prevent you from activating the BAdI implementation using your copied class. To fix these errors, you need to change the type of the local variable `lv_handle` in both `CREATE_ACTVITIES` and `CREATE_LEADS` from `sy-tabix` to type `CRMT_HANDLE`. This also requires you to change a parameter `IV_RFF_HANDLE` on the method `FILL_HEADER_DATA` from the type `sy-tabix` to the type `CRMT_HANDLE`. These changes allow you to generate your copied class without any syntax warnings.

Copy BAdI

However, after you test this code, you may find several calls of function modules that use the `lv_handle` local variable requiring you to create a secondary version of the variable. To solve this issue, you'll need to create a `lv_handle_tabix` local variable of type `sy-tabix` and copy the current value for `lv_handle` into the `lv_handle_tabix` before each function module is called by the system.

After your copied class is generated without warnings, you can create the BAdI implementation for `CRM_MKTLIST_BADI`. To do this, bring up the BAdI in Transaction SE18, and then choose CREATE IMPLEMENTATION. For this example, call the new implementation "ZCRM_TPP_MKTLIST", and enter the description "TPP Format List".

Create BAdI implementation

On the PROPERTIES tab of the implementation, assign the filter value ZTPP, which will match the ID of the mapping format that you created. Then move to the INTERFACE tab, and replace the name of the implementation with the copy of the class you created, which was "ZCL_TPP_CRM_MKTLIST_BADI". After you've done this, click SAVE to activate your BAdI.

At this point, the system processes the ZTPP using your BAdI implementation. However, because your implementation is a copy of the standard logic, you now need to make some changes to your code to allow your custom field to be stored in the social call report business transaction.

Make Code Changes for Custom Enhancements

The code changes will consist of modifying the `create_activities` method and adding in a new private method called `fill_customer_h_data`. For the modifications for the `CREATE_ACTIVITIES` method, you'll need to add in the data structures used by the `CRM_ORDER_MAINTAIN` function module for `CUSTOMER_H` data. You'll also need to map your custom field, which is now part of the ELM activity data transfer structure to the `CUSTOMER_H` structures required by `CRM_ORDER_MAINTAIN`.

You don't need to completely rewrite the `create_activities`; instead, you just need to make a few changes to this method. The code listing in Listing 8.1 shows the new code you've added along with a reference to where that code would be found in your copy of the standard logic.

```
METHOD create_activities.
<<unchanged code>>
* Insert new data declaration at end of method

DATA: lt_customer_h_wrk    TYPE crmt_customer_h_comt,
      ls_customer_h_wrk    TYPE crmt_customer_h_com.
*************************************************************
  FREE lt_orderadm_h.
  FREE lt_activity_h.
  FREE lt_input_fields.
  FREE lt_partner.
  FREE lt_doc_flow.
  FREE lt_outbound_details.
  FREE lt_prc.
* Add this line
  FREE lt_customer_h.
* End add this line
*************************************************************
* Create Activities
  LOOP AT it_mktlist_act INTO ls_act.
<<unchanged code>>
*    At end of loop insert the following code
  CALL METHOD me->fill_customer_h_data
    EXPORTING
      is_act        = ls_act
      iv_ref_guid   = lv_ref_guid
    IMPORTING
      et_customer_h = lt_customer_h
```

```
        CHANGING
          ct_input_fields = lt_input_fields.

  ENDLOOP.

****************************************************************
* Create Activity
  CALL FUNCTION 'CRM_ORDER_MAINTAIN'
    EXPORTING
      it_activity_h       = lt_activity_h
      it_partner          = lt_partner
      it_appointment      = lt_appointment
      it_survey           = lt_survey
      it_status           = lt_status
* Add the customer_h parameter
      it_customer_h       = lt_customer_h
    IMPORTING
      et_exception        = lt_exception
    CHANGING
      ct_orderadm_h       = lt_orderadm_h
      ct_input_fields     = lt_input_fields
      cv_log_handle       = lv_log_handle
      ct_doc_flow         = lt_doc_flow
    EXCEPTIONS
      error_occurred      = 1
      document_locked     = 2
      no_change_allowed   = 3
      no_authority        = 4
      OTHERS              = 5.

*   Remaining code in method remains the same
<<unchanged code>>
ENDMETHOD.
```

Listing 8.1 Modification to CREATE_ACTIVITIES Method

The method FILL_CUSTOMER_H_DATA maps the data from the ELM structures to those used by CRM_ORDER_MAINTAIN. You create this method as a
private method of your BAdI implementation class. The BAdI should
have a signature as shown. The IS_ACT structure contains the activity-
related fields from the mapping format. You also need to add in the
fields you're updating to CT_INPUT_FIELDS, which controls the update of

field data by Transaction CRM_ORDER_MAINTAIN. The parameters of your method should look like Figure 8.6.

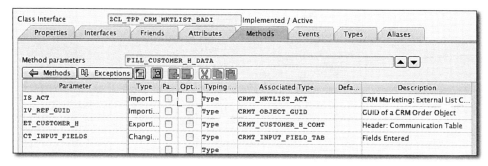

Figure 8.6 Method Parameters for FILL_CUSTOMER_H_DATA

Maintain method parameters

The parameters of the method should be maintained as detailed in Table 8.2 with none of the parameters being marked as pass value or optional. The program logic for method FILL_CUSTOMER_H_DATA is given in Listing 8.2.

Parameter	Type	Typing	Associated Type
IS_ACT	Importing	Type	CRMT_MKTLIST_ACT
IV_REF_GUID	Importing	Type	CRMT_OBJECT_GUID
ET_CUSTOMER_H	Exporting	Type	CRMT_CUSTOMER_H_COMT
CT_INPUT_FIELDS	Changing	Type	CRMT_INPUT_FIELD_TAB

Table 8.2 Parameters for Method FILL_CUSTOMER_H_DATA

```
METHOD FILL_CUSTOMER_H_DATA.

  INCLUDE crm_object_kinds_con.
  INCLUDE crm_object_names_con.
  INCLUDE crm_mode_con.

  DATA: ls_customer_h        TYPE crmt_customer_h_com.

  DATA: lt_input_field_names TYPE crmt_input_field_names_
tab.
  DATA: ls_input_field_names TYPE crmt_input_field_names.
  DATA: ls_input_fields      TYPE crmt_input_field.
```

```
  ls_customer_h-mode = gc_mode-create.
  ls_customer_h-ref_guid = iv_ref_guid.
  ls_customer_h-zzhashtag = is_act-zzhashtag.

  INSERT ls_customer_h into TABLE ET_CUSTOMER_H.

  FREE lt_input_field_names.
  IF ls_customer_h-zzhashtag IS NOT INITIAL.
    ls_input_field_names-fieldname = 'ZZHASHTAG'.
    INSERT ls_input_field_names INTO TABLE lt_input_field_
names.
  ENDIF.

  CLEAR ls_input_fields.

  ls_input_fields-ref_guid    = iv_ref_guid.
  ls_input_fields-ref_kind    = gc_object_kind-orderadm_h.
  ls_input_fields-objectname  = gc_object_name-customer_h.
  ls_input_fields-field_names = lt_input_field_names.
  INSERT ls_input_fields INTO TABLE ct_input_fields.

ENDMETHOD.
```

Listing 8.2 Method FILL_CUSTOMER_H_DATA

Testing the New Mapping Logic

To test that your BAdI implementation works correctly, create a new external list in the SAP CRM system that will use your new mapping format. You can create a new external list by logging into the Web Client using either the MARKETINGPRO business role or another role that contains the external list link within one of its work centers.

Test BAdI implementation

If you use the MARKETINGPRO role, follow these steps:

1. Go to the MARKETING work center, and then choose CREATE EXTERNAL LIST.

2. Provide a technical name for your list, and choose the origin of the list as OWN DATA along with the type of data as OWN DATA.

3. Select the mapping format that you created—CRM BOOK EXAMPLE.

4. Select the delimiter for the file as COMMA DELIMITED, and then choose SELECT CLIENT FILE. Choose the CSV file that you created on your local computer that matches the layout format you created earlier.

5. To process the data, select the checkbox next to READ FILE, choose the IMMEDIATELY time under scheduling, and click the START button at the top as shown in Figure 8.7.

6. After you click START, you will be brought to an overview screen and can see the status of reading the file. When this status is green, go back in and edit the external list to kick off the next step.

7. Select the map data, and start it again.

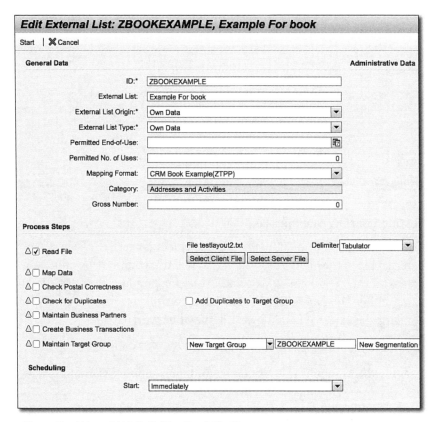

Figure 8.7 External List Definition Read File Step

We'll go through one step at a time for maintaining business partners and creating business transaction until all steps have a green status. The step CREATE BUSINESS TRANSACTIONS is the step that executes your custom logic to add the custom field to the created business transaction.

When this processing is finished, you can see the transactions created by clicking on the SHOW LIST RECORDS display on the OVERVIEW screen for your external list as shown in Figure 8.8.

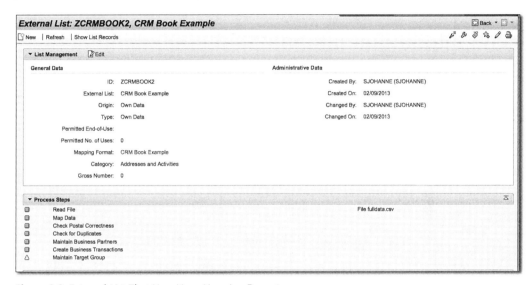

Figure 8.8 External List That Uses Your Mapping Format

This will provide you with the object IDs of the company, contact, and business transaction created (see Figure 8.9).

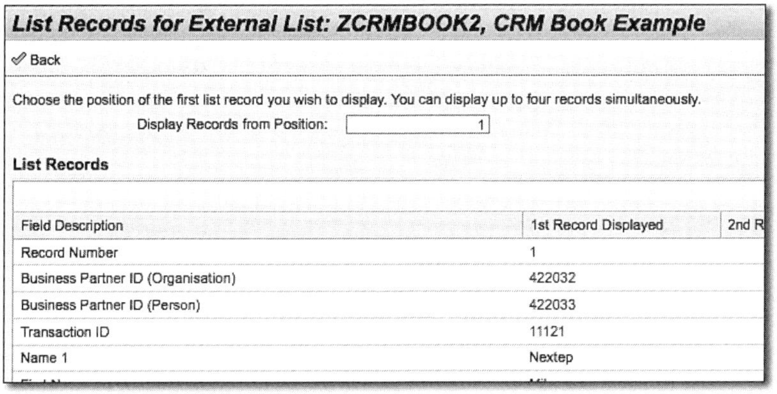

Figure 8.9 List of Imported Records Showing Created SAP CRM Object IDs

You can click on the ID of the business transaction created to see the details. You can see from the activity screen, that the value for your custom HASHTAG field was transferred successfully as shown in Figure 8.10.

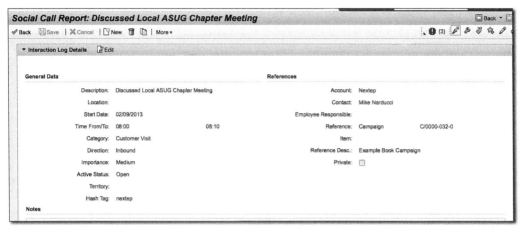

Figure 8.10 Business Activity with Custom Attribute

8.1.3 Method CREATE_BUSINESS_PARTNERS

Create/update business partners

This method creates and/or updates the business partners for both companies (organizations) and contact persons that are mapped within your file of data to be loaded. An external list can contain new business partners that can be created or existing business partners whose contact information needs to be updated.

> **Note**
>
> In processing the external list, the business partners are created in an earlier step, before the business transactions are created. The reason for this is that SAP CRM requires valid partner data to be available when creating a business transaction.

In Chapter 3, we looked at adding new fields to the SAP CRM data model. When the fields are added by the EEWB, AET, or manually, they aren't added for use in ELM. To be able to create new business partners that contain those attributes you added, you need to implement the `create_business_partners` method in the `CRM_MKT_LIST_BADI`.

In the default implementation of the BAdI, the method performs several steps to create or update the business partner data. The first check is to see if a new organization (company) partner needs to be created. If you provide an existing business partner ID to update, then it will call the private method `update_organization`; otherwise, it will call the private method `create_organization`. The `create_organization` method will call the function module `BUPA_CREATE_FROM_DATA`. If the system tells you that the organization was created successfully, then you need to create a related contact person using the `create_person` method (if the information is provided). If a contact person ID is provided in the file, then it will it will call the `update_person` method instead to update the information of an existing contact in your SAP CRM system.

Method checks

To add additional attributes to be imported on the created organizations or contact persons, you must manually enhance the respective data transfer structures for the business partner data. These structures are `CRMT_MKTLIST_PER_EXT` for the contact person and `CRMT_MKTLIST_ORG_EXT` for the organization. To enhance these structures, follow these steps:

Add attributes

1. Go to Transaction SE11, and bring up the respective structure in display mode.
2. Click on the APPEND STRUCTURE button. After you click this, the system will either display the existing append structure or prompt you to create a new append structure.
3. Add your custom fields to the structure, and they are ready for use.

> **Note**
>
> In Section 8.1.2, we reviewed the complete enhancement procedure for business transaction attributes. The same type of steps can be used for business partner data enhancement, so we won't repeat them here. Note that the one exception is that you'll need to enhance the business partner data structures and implement the `create_business_partners` method instead.

Business partner data enchancement

8.2   Open Channel BAdI for Campaign Execution

The open channel BAdI (`CRM_MKT_EXP_CAMP_DAT`) is provided to allow customers of SAP CRM to execute and export campaign information to channels beyond the standard provided communication methods in SAP

Execute and export information to custom channels

CRM. These methods include email or print campaigns. A *campaign* is an object that plans and tracks marketing activities surrounding a group of potential or existing customers around a product or service offered by a company.

In SAP CRM, the campaigns can be created and managed through the standard Web Client interface by a business user. In the campaigns, you can specify the target recipients of the campaign information along with how this information will be distributed. This distribution method is also known as a *communication media*, which is a strategy consisting of one or more communication methods in which a group of business partners targeted by a campaign are to be contacted. It doesn't specify the content of the campaign but rather the delivery of the campaign message.

Business scenario | In a normal business scenario, you may want to export the campaign information and/or communication to a third-party target that isn't currently supported by SAP CRM. This could include Twitter or Facebook marketing, or sending a transmission to a marketing agency stating who should be contacted. The open channel BAdI allows you to define a custom export of the campaign through the use of custom ABAP code.

In the following sections, we'll show you the prerequisites for using this BAdI and then explain how to implement and test it in your system.

8.2.1 Campaign Customizing for Open Channel Use

Prerequisites | Before you can use the BAdI, you must first set up a communication medium in your SAP CRM system that will use the open channel. Go to the following path in the IMG: CRM • MARKETING • CAMPAIGN EXECUTION • DEFINE COMMUNICATION MEDIUM.

Choose NEW ENTRIES. The system prompts you for a technical name of the medium and description. For this example, enter "ZTPP" as the technical name and "CRM Book Example" as the description as shown in Figure 8.11.

Communication method and medium | Click the SAVE button. You now need to assign a communication method. Select the COMMUNICATION METHOD on the left-hand tree menu. Then choose NEW ENTRIES, and add an entry for the open channel.

Because a communication medium represents the possible communication strategy for a campaign, you can have more than one communication option possible.

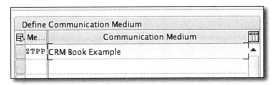

Figure 8.11 Define Communication Medium

You now need to maintain several fields on the MAINTAIN NEW ENTRY screen. The PRIORITY field orders the list of communication methods that your user will see. For this example, you'll only have one communication method, which will be the open channel. Set the PRIORITY field value to "1", choose the OPEN CHANNEL communication method, and then click the SAVE button. The resulting entry should look similar to the entry contained in Figure 8.12.

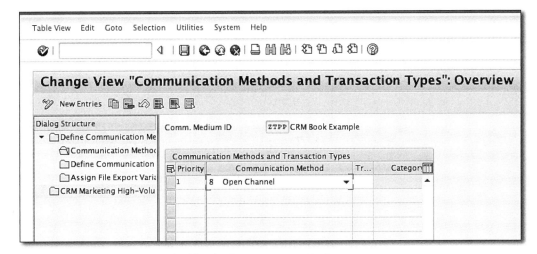

Figure 8.12 Communication Method for the Communication Medium

Now that you've created the communication medium, you need to assign it to a campaign type for use. Go to the IMG path: CRM • MARKETING • MARKETING PLANNING AND CAMPAIGN MANAGEMENT • BASIC DATA • DEFINE TYPES/OBJECTIVES/TACTICS.

On the resulting screen, several campaign types are listed. Choose the campaign that you want to assign to your communication medium and select the details. Assign ZTPP to your campaign.

Due to the complexity of configuring campaigns in SAP CRM, we won't cover the rest of the customizing options on this screen as we could write a couple chapters on Campaign Management of SAP CRM, which is beyond the scope of this book.

8.2.2 Implementing the Open Channel BAdI

The technical name of the open channel BAdI is CRM_MKT_EXP_CAMP_DAT, and it has a single method called EXPORT_CAMPAIGN_DATA. The BAdI is executed in the program CRM_MKTTGGRP_EXPORT_BATCH. SAP Note 535536 explains the general use of this BAdI.

To implement this BAdI, you create a new implementation and then also create a new communication medium that will use the open channel communication method. To do this, follow these steps:

1. Go to Transaction SE18, and select the CRM_MKT_EXP_CAMP_DAT BAdI.

2. Choose the CREATE IMPLEMENTATION option. A popup appears as shown in Figure 8.13 asking for an implementation. For this example, enter the implementation "ZCRM_TPP_OPEN_CHAN".

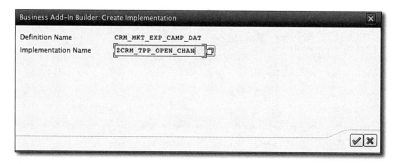

Figure 8.13 Create the New Implementation CRM_MKT_EXP_CAMP_DAT

3. Click the checkmark icon, and then enter a description for the implementation on the next screen. For this example, enter "Open Channel BAdI example" as the description.

4. Save and activate the implementation. You're now ready to code your logic in the class that was created when you created the new implementation of this BAdI.

The class interface has two methods: `export_campaign_data` and `maintain_add_camp_data`. For campaign execution, you'll implement a method called `EXPORT_CAMPAIGN_DATA`. This method has several parameters as shown in Figure 8.14, which we'll review in detail:

Coding the logic

▶ `IS_PROJECT_INFO`

This contains general information about the campaign, including the description and the start and end dates of the campaign.

Method EXPORT_CAMPAIGN_DATA parameters

▶ `IS_TASK_INFO`

If the campaign has been divided into subcampaigns, this contains the information about the subcampaign that is being executed.

▶ `IT_TARGETGRP`

This is a listing of all of the target groups being executed upon by the campaign.

Class Builder: Class ZCL_IM_CRM_TPP_OPEN_CHAN Change

Ty.	Parameter	Type spec.	Description
	IS_PROJECT_INFO	TYPE CRMT_MKT_PROJECT_INFO	CRM Marketing: Transfer Structure – Campaign Header
	IS_TASK_INFO	TYPE CRMT_MKT_TASK_INFO	CRM Marketing: Transfer Structure – Campaign Task
	IT_TARGETGRP	TYPE CRMT_MKT_PLTGGRP_T	CRM Marketing: Table for Target Group Transfer fr. Campaigns
	IT_SMARTFORM	TYPE CRM_MKTPL_TDSFNAME_T	CRM Marketing: Table for Smart Form Transfer from Campaigns
	IT_PRODCAT	TYPE CRMT_MKT_PLPRCAT_T	CRM Mkt: Table for Product Catalog Transfer from Campaign
	IS_TARGETGRP	TYPE CRMT_MKT_PLTGGRP	CRM Marketing: Row Type Target Group Transfer from Campaign
	IV_LOG_HANDLE	TYPE BALLOGHNDL	Application Log: Log Handle
	IT_SCRIPTS	TYPE CRMT_OBJECT_GUID_TAB	List of GUIDs
	IT_BP_CHANNEL	TYPE CRMT_BP_CP_CHANNEL_TAB	Table Type for Row CRMT_BP_CP_CHANNEL
	IV_PRINT_ID	TYPE CRMT_IM_PRINT_ID	Profile for Print Parameters
	IV_CHANNEL	TYPE CRM_MKTPL_CHANNEL	Communication Medium
	IV_END_OF_TG	TYPE CRMT_BOOLEAN	Logical Variable
	EV_RETURN_CODE	TYPE SYSUBRC	Return Value, Return Value After ABAP Statements
	ET_OBJ_TO_SAVE	TYPE CRMT_MKTTG_ORDER_GUIDS_TAB	CRM Marketing: Table Type for BAPIBUS20001_GUID_DIS
	ET_RETURN	TYPE BAPIRET2_TAB	Error Messages
	ET_BP_STATUS_CHANNEL	TYPE CRMT_BP_CP_CHANNEL_TAB	Business Partner Return Table for Contact Tracking

Method `IF_EX_CRM_MKT_EXP_CAMP_DAT-EXPORT_CAMPAIGN_DATA` — Inactive (revised)

```
method IF_EX_CRM_MKT_EXP_CAMP_DAT-EXPORT_CAMPAIGN_DATA.

endmethod.
```

Figure 8.14 Method Signature EXPORT_CAMPAIGN_DATA

▶ IT_SMARTFORM

This contains information about the smart form that will be used for output in the campaign. Even though this is a table, only one smart form can be assigned to the campaign.

▶ IS_TARGETGRP

This contains header information about the target group being processed.

▶ IV_LOG_HANDLE

This is the handle of the application log, so that you can add error messages as needed.

▶ IT_BP_CHANNEL

This is the key table that contains the business partners from the target group that need to be processed.

▶ IV_END_OF_TG

The system may break up the target group into smaller portions for processing. This lets you know that the target group being processed is finished.

▶ ET_OBJ_TO_SAVE

If your campaign execution creates corresponding transactions as part of the execution, this table can be used in two different ways.

▶ ET_BP_STATUS_CHANNEL

This contains the status of the export of the campaign information to each business partner that was listed in ET_BP_STATUS_CHANNEL.

Example code for BAdI implementation

Now that you understand the data provided to the BAdI and what you'll need to return, let's look at example code for this BAdI implementation. To keep this example, simple, we'll show how to export the list of target group partners to a z-table in your system. However, you can replace the export to z-table with any other type of process, such as writing the data out to a flat file or calling a web service of a third-party marketing provider.

1. Create a new z-table in your system using Transaction SE11. The z-table should be named "ZCRMTPPBOOK". For the table, you need to define the fields shown in Table 8.3.

Field ID	Key Field	Data Element
MANDT	Yes	MANDT
CAMP_GUID	Yes	CRM_MKTPL_GUID
PARTNER	Yes	BU_PARTNER
UPDATE_DAY	Yes	DATUM
UPDATE_TIME	Yes	UZEIT

Table 8.3 Z-Table Fields

2. Now that the table is defined as shown in Figure 8.15, implement the `export_campaign data` method in your BAdI implementation.

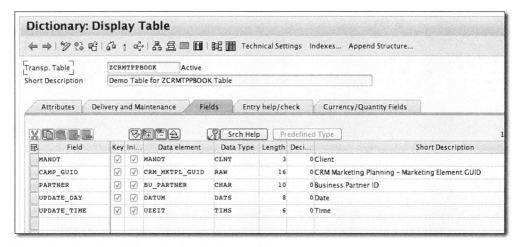

Figure 8.15 Database Table to Receive the Results of Export

3. Your coding logic should start with checking that the `iv_channel` parameter corresponds to your communication medium. Because the BAdI doesn't contain a filter, this will prevent your code from being executed for other communication mediums.

4. Loop through the `it_bp_channel` table for each business partner in the target group. Call a new method—`process_bp_ztpp`—to perform the actual action and return the status as shown in Listing 8.3.

```
method IF_EX_CRM_MKT_EXP_CAMP_DAT~EXPORT_CAMPAIGN_DATA.
   data: lv_status type crmt_bp_cp_channel.
```

```
            field-symbols: <fs_bp_channel> type crmt_bp_cp_channel.

            check iv_channel eq 'ZTPP'.
            loop at it_bp_channel assigning <fs_bp_channel>.
               lv_status = process_bp_ztpp(
                              is_project_info = is_project_info
                              is_task_info   = is_task_info
                              is_bp_channel = <fs_bp_channel> ).

               append lv_status to et_bp_status_channel.
            endloop.
         endmethod.
```

Listing 8.3 EXPORT_CAMPAIGN_DATA_METHOD

The method process_bp_ztpp contains the logic that will transfer the data to your z-table. For this example, you want to write out the campaign GUID, business partner ID, and date and time of processing. The signature of this method should contain the import and export parameters from Table 8.4 as shown in Figure 8.16.

Parameter Name	Data Type	Type of Parameter
IS_PROJECT_INFO	CRMT_MKT_PROJECT_INFO	Importing
IS_TASK_INFO	CRMT_MKT_TASK_INFO	Importing
IS_BP_CHANNEL	CRMT_BP_CP_CHANNEL	Importing
RV_STATUS	CRMT_BP_CP_CHANNEL	Returning

Table 8.4 Parameters for the Method Signature

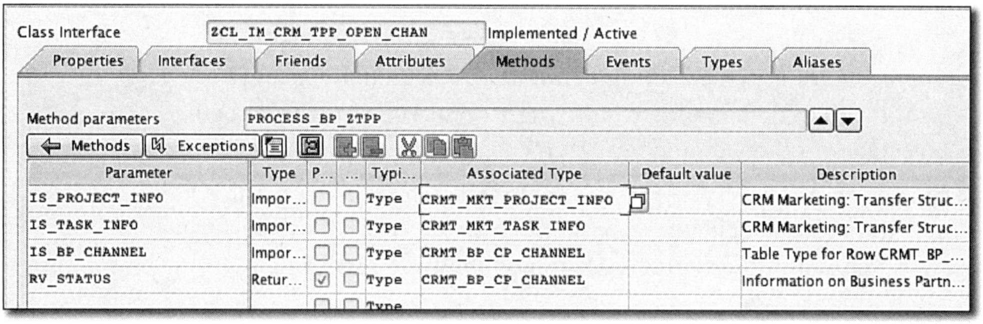

Parameter	Type	P...	...	Typi...	Associated Type	Default value	Description
IS_PROJECT_INFO	Impor...	☐	☐	Type	CRMT_MKT_PROJECT_INFO		CRM Marketing: Transfer Struc...
IS_TASK_INFO	Impor...	☐	☐	Type	CRMT_MKT_TASK_INFO		CRM Marketing: Transfer Struc...
IS_BP_CHANNEL	Impor...	☐	☐	Type	CRMT_BP_CP_CHANNEL		Table Type for Row CRMT_BP_...
RV_STATUS	Retur...	☑	☐	Type	CRMT_BP_CP_CHANNEL		Information on Business Partn...

Figure 8.16 Parameters Method BP_ZTPP

5. In this method, you insert a new record into the ZCRMTPPBOOK table. If the insert is correct, you'll set the status record back as successful. If not successful, you'll set the status record back with a technical error. The code for this method is given in Listing 8.4.

```
method PROCESS_BP_ZTPP.
* To keep things simple we will output the bp information t
o a z-table to show how this works.
data: ls_book_data type ZCRMTPPBOOK.

  move-corresponding is_bp_channel to rv_status.

  ls_book_data-camp_guid = is_project_info-guid.
  ls_book_data-partner = is_bp_channel-bp_number.
  ls_book_data-update_day = sy-datum.
  ls_book_data-update_time = sy-uzeit.
  insert zcrmtppbook from ls_book_data.

  if sy-subrc eq 0.
    rv_status-status = 0.
  else.
    rv_status-status = 5.
  endif.
endmethod.
```

Listing 8.4 Method PROCESS_BP_ZTPP

8.2.3 Testing the BAdI

To test the BAdI, you need to create a new campaign in your SAP CRM system, assign your communication medium and a target group to this campaign, and release the campaign as shown in Figure 8.17. To do this, you need to perform the following steps:

Create new campaign

1. Log in to the Web Client under the MARKETINGPRO or a similar business role that contains the create campaign link.

2. If you're using the MARKETINGPRO business role, choose the MARKETING work center and then the link campaign under the CREATE section. You will now see the campaign details screen.

3. Enter a description for your campaign.

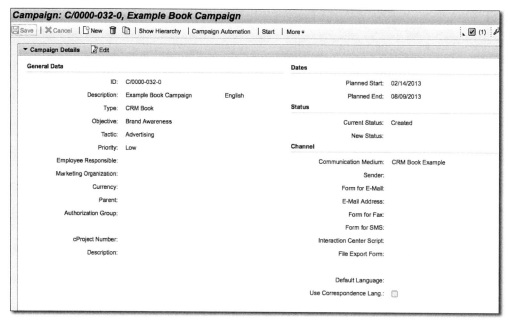

Figure 8.17 Campaign Using Your Communication Medium

4. Choose the type of campaign (this should be the one that you assigned your communication medium).

5. Enter a valid planned start and planned end date.

6. Choose the communication medium that corresponds to the one you created for the CRM book example or ZTPP and the communication medium will appear.

7. Press the SAVE button to save the campaign.

8. Click on the EDIT button to change the status of the campaign. Once you're in edit mode, choose RELEASED from the new status field and then press the SAVE button to save the campaign again.

Campaign execution

Now that you've released the campaign, you can start the campaign execution. Click on the START button in the CAMPAIGN overview screen. A popup appears asking for a job name as shown in Figure 8.18. You can choose the default value or change it to a more meaningful name. Next, choose the execution time by switching from a SCHEDULE LATER to a SCHEDULE IMMEDIATELY option. After you've entered these values, click the START button to kick off the campaign in the background.

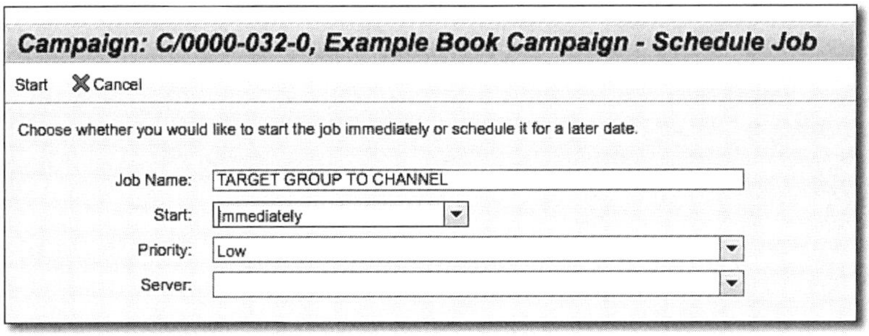

Campaign: C/0000-032-0, Example Book Campaign - Schedule Job

Start ✗ Cancel

Choose whether you would like to start the job immediately or schedule it for a later date.

Job Name: `TARGET GROUP TO CHANNEL`

Start: `Immediately` ▼

Priority: `Low` ▼

Server: ▼

Figure 8.18 Start Screen for Open Channel Communication

For campaign execution, SAP CRM schedules a batch job that executes the program CRM_MKTTGGRP_EXPORT_BATCH with a dynamic variant. You can monitor the job execution in the SAP GUI through Transaction SM37 as shown in Figure 8.19. After the job is complete, you can see the results of your coding.

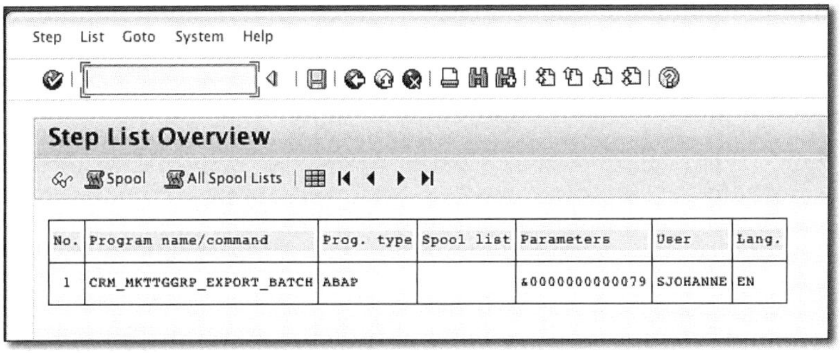

Step   List   Goto   System   Help

Step List Overview

⟨⟩ Spool   All Spool Lists | ⊞ |◀ ◀ ▶ ▶|

No.	Program name/command	Prog. type	Spool list	Parameters	User	Lang.
1	CRM_MKTTGGRP_EXPORT_BATCH	ABAP		&0000000000079	SJOHANNE	EN

Figure 8.19 Created Job for Open Channel Export

The job log shown in Figure 8.20 lists which target groups were transferred and how many partners were in each target group. If the target group was required to be split up into separate processing packets, you'll see how many packets were created as well.

Job log: results of coding

You also see the total number of partners that were sent to the open channel and how many failed. Those numbers are determined by your code sending back the correct status information for each partner transferred. It's an absolute requirement that you must send the transfer status for each partner received by your BAdI for the campaign to accurately track results.

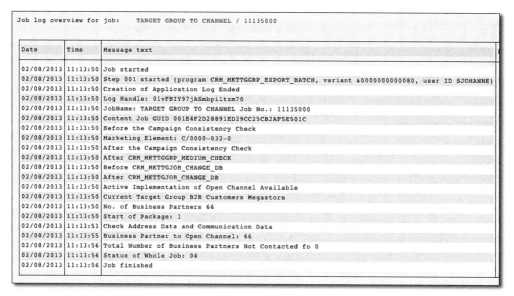

```
Job log overview for job:      TARGET GROUP TO CHANNEL / 11135000
```

Date	Time	Message text
02/08/2013	11:13:50	Job started
02/08/2013	11:13:50	Step 001 started (program CRM_MKTTGGRP_EXPORT_BATCH, variant &0000000000080, user ID SJOHANNE)
02/08/2013	11:13:50	Creation of Application Log Ended
02/08/2013	11:13:50	Log Handle: 01vFBIY97jASmbpiltzm70
02/08/2013	11:13:50	JobName: TARGET GROUP TO CHANNEL Job No.: 11135000
02/08/2013	11:13:50	Content Job GUID 001E4F2D28891ED29CC25CB2AF5E501C
02/08/2013	11:13:50	Before the Campaign Consistency Check
02/08/2013	11:13:50	Marketing Element: C/0000-032-0
02/08/2013	11:13:50	After the Campaign Consistency Check
02/08/2013	11:13:50	After CRM_MKTTGGRP_MEDIUM_CHECK
02/08/2013	11:13:50	Before CRM_MKTTGJOB_CHANGE_DB
02/08/2013	11:13:50	After CRM_MKTTGJOB_CHANGE_DB
02/08/2013	11:13:50	Active Implementation of Open Channel Available
02/08/2013	11:13:50	Current Target Group B2B Customers Megastore
02/08/2013	11:13:50	No. of Business Partners 66
02/08/2013	11:13:50	Start of Package: 1
02/08/2013	11:13:51	Check Address Data and Communication Data
02/08/2013	11:13:55	Business Partner to Open Channel: 66
02/08/2013	11:13:56	Total Number of Business Partners Not Contacted fo 0
02/08/2013	11:13:56	Status of Whole Job: 04
02/08/2013	11:13:56	Job finished

Figure 8.20 Job Log for Execution to the Open Channel

Now that you see the job has completed correctly, you can look at the contents of your z-table in Transaction SE16 (see Figure 8.21), and you can see that each member of the target group has one entry in your z-table, provided the logic in your BAdI was executed properly.

Other examples for use — Even though this was a simple example, you could expand upon this technique to send the information needed to execute a campaign to a third-party system. The only limitation is that you need to develop the logic that will call the external system and map the data from SAP CRM into the external format. This would be extremely useful for cases where you may have hired another company to send out mailings on your behalf and need to send a list of customers that should receive the literature for that campaign. The provider may require a flat file or may ask you to update this in real time.

Another option is to execute sending text messages as marketing campaign for those customers who have signed up to received text message marketing communication from your company. The standard SAP CRM system can manage the message and list of people to receive the message, and you could call or transmit to the third-party provider. These are just a few examples for which this BAdI can be used.

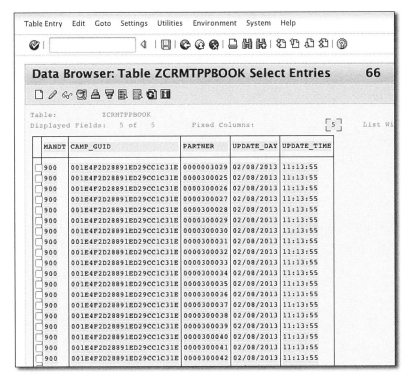

Figure 8.21 Resulting Entries in Your Z-Table

8.3 Summary

The two BAdIs explored in this chapter, ELM and Open Channel Management, allow you to meet common requirements found in projects implementing SAP CRM Marketing. The ELM BAdI allows you to add additional attributes to business partners or change how the business partners will be created. In addition to business partner data, the tool allows you to change how transaction data will be created. This flexibility can allow you to handle more complex data import requirements that go beyond the standard delivered system functionality.

The open channel for Campaign Management BAdI allows you to transfer data to a third party or external source for processing. However, you must make sure during those transfers that you provide a status back for each record transferred to ensure accurate tracking of the campaign results. The limits on where or how the data can be transferred are only limited to your knowledge of building real-time interfaces using ABAP.

These BAdIs will allow you to truly tailor the inbound and outbound information received in SAP CRM Marketing and meet the needs of your business.

In the next chapter, we'll look at common enhancements made to the analytics and reporting tools of SAP CRM.

A customer relationship management system without reports is nothing more than a fancy electronic filing system. Analytics on the data contained in SAP CRM are key to gaining valuable insight on customers. Extending those reports to reveal the new data you've added is a common step of almost every SAP CRM project.

9   Common Enhancements in Analytics and Reporting

SAP CRM provides three primary methods for performing analytics in the standard delivered system: transferring data to SAP NetWeaver BW for analysis, Interactive Reporting, and custom ABAP reports.

In this chapter, we'll look at some of the more standard SAP CRM project requirements in regards to analytics and reporting: how to enhance the standard SAP NetWeaver Business Warehouse (BW) data sources contained in SAP CRM, how to add new fields to the Interactive Reporting data sources, and how to allow users to run traditional ABAP reports in the Web Client using the Transaction Launcher. We'll limit our focus to how to set up the SAP CRM portion of these tools.

If you remember from Chapter 3, we looked at adding additional fields to the social media call report transaction. Even though you added the field to the SAP CRM system, this doesn't mean that the field will be automatically added to the reporting tools of SAP CRM. For the example business requirement, you want to make the HASH TAG field available within the reporting tools of SAP CRM.

9.1   SAP NetWeaver BW Data Source Enhancements via BAdIs

Transfer
information to BW

A common requirement in many SAP CRM implementations is to transfer information to the SAP NetWeaver BW system for analytics and reporting. For most SAP CRM customers, business transactions make up the primary information transferred for reporting. Until SAP made the interactive reports available in the newer releases of SAP CRM, there were no other methods to build reports on SAP CRM data without writing a custom ABAP program.

Manually enhance
data source

As we discussed in Chapter 3, you can enhance the SAP CRM system to add custom attributes to the business transactions. If you use the standard SAP tools such as the Application Enhancement Tool (AET) or Easy Enhancement Workbench (EEWB), the custom fields can be automatically added to the BW data source in SAP CRM. However, there are many situations in which you might want to add information to the data source that is either not a custom field or for which you did not check the option in the EEWB or AET to add the custom attribute. To get around this limitation, you can manually enhance the data source. By enhancing the data source, the new attribute will be made available to your SAP NetWeaver BW system and can be used in reports that you create on that system.

Prerequisites

To manually enhance the data source, it must be installed on your SAP CRM system for use by SAP NetWeaver BW. This process typically involves installing the data source using Transaction RSA5 in the SAP CRM system.

> **Note**
>
> We won't cover the installation of the data source in this chapter. The SAP best practices available at *http://help.sap.com/bp-crm* contain guides that detail how to install the SAP NetWeaver BW data sources on your SAP CRM system.

After the data source has been installed, you're ready to enhance the data source. This process generally requires two different steps. The first step is to enhance the data source structure. The second is to implement the BAdI `CRM_BWA_MFLOW` to enhance the extractor program for the data source. We'll discuss these steps in the next subsections.

9.1.1 Enhance the Data Source Structure

To enhance the structure of the data source, there are several steps that you'll need to follow.

Go to Transaction RSA6, and locate the data source that needs to be enhanced as shown in Figure 9.1. For this chapter, we'll examine enhancing the data source `OCRM_SALES_ACT_1`, which is used to transfer data from SAP CRM to BW for activity transactions. If you recall from Chapter 2, you created a new business transaction called a social media call report. For this social media call report, you added a new field called ZZHASHTAG via the EEWB. During that enhancement, you didn't choose to add that field to the BW source structure via the EEWB tool.

Transaction RSA6

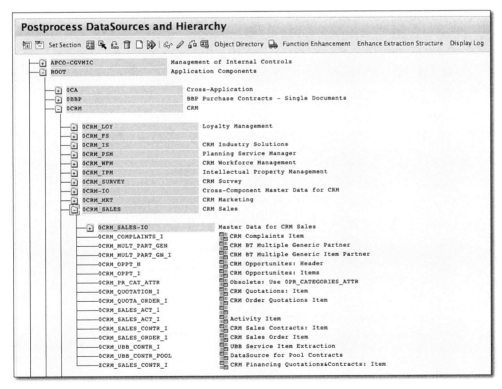

Figure 9.1 Transaction RSA6

Manually add ZZHASHTAG to the report

Now you'll need to manually add the field because you don't want to regenerate your EEWB extension. To do this, follow these steps:

1. Select the 0CRM_SALES_ACT_1 data source, and drill into the display.

2. Click on CRMT_BW_DS_ACTIVITY to pull up the data source structure in a Transaction SE11 view as shown in Figure 9.2.

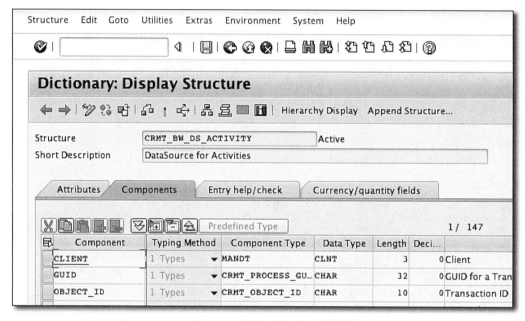

Figure 9.2 Data Structure CRMT_BW_DS_ACTIVITY

3. Click on the APPEND STRUCTURE button. Your structure doesn't contain any append structures, so you'll be prompted for the name of your new append structure as shown in Figure 9.3.

Figure 9.3 Create Append Popup Window

Add new append structure

4. Call the append "ZACRM_BW_DS_ACTIVITY".

5. Click on the checkmark icon.

6. Define fields in the append structure on the next screen. For this example, enter the description of the structure as "Activity BW Data Source Extension". In the COMPONENT section, add a new field called "ZZHASHTAG" that is of type ZZHASHTAG.

7. Save your work and assign your append structure to a transportable package.

8. You'll be prompted for a transport request. After you provide that information, the append structure will be in inactive status.

9. Activate your structure. Your new append structure will contain a single field called ZZHASHTAG and appear as active (see Figure 9.4).

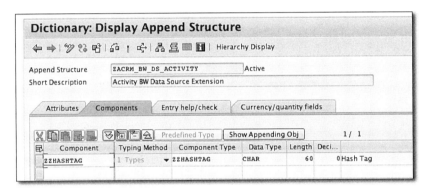

Figure 9.4 Fields of the New Append Structure

After the structure is activated, the fields show up in Transaction RSA6. By default, all custom fields added to a data source via the append structure are hidden in the data source definition as shown in Figure 9.5 (at the bottom of the screen, the new field has the HIDE FIELD checkbox selected).

To allow that data to be transferred to SAP NetWeaver BW, remove the HIDE FIELD flag, and the SAP NetWeaver BW system will be able to see that those fields are part of your data source definition (see Figure 9.6). Now that you've extended the structure of the data source, you'll need to build logic that will enhance the extractor programs to put values in your fields.

Enable data to be transferred

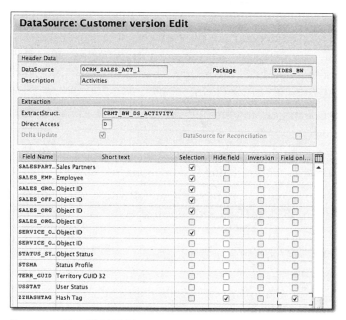

Figure 9.5 New Field Hidden

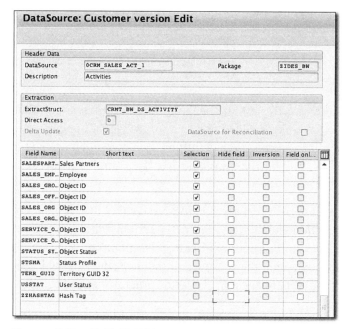

Figure 9.6 New Fields Unhidden

9.1.2 Extractor Program Logic

Now you're ready for the second step of the process. For SAP NetWeaver BW data sources, the traditional method of enhancing the extractors has been through user exits. In the SAP CRM system, those user exits are available but not used. Instead, SAP CRM has a specific BAdI for enhancements of the extractors for SAP CRM-specific data sources. This BAdI is called CRM_BWA_MFLOW. If you were using the EEWB or AET, an implementation of this BAdI would be automatically generated in your system.

CRM_BWA_MFLOW

However, in this example, because you decided not to use the tools provided by SAP and instead chose to work manually, you must implement this BAdI manually. A benefit of manually implementing this BAdI is that you can implement virtual attributes that don't correspond to physical values stored on the SAP CRM database or attributes that cross business objects. A great example is that you might want to transfer the country of the sold-to party in the data source; however, it isn't stored on your business transaction. You can then instead populate the attribute virtually by using the CRM_BWA_MFLOW BAdI.

Manual implementation

In the following subsections, we'll walk you through the steps to create the BAdI implementation and test your work. We'll also provide a quick overview of how to accomplish this with AET for your comparison.

Creating the BAdI Implementation

Follow these steps to implement the BAdI:

CRM_BWA_MFLOW implementation

1. Go to Transaction SE18, and open up the BAdI definition for CRM_BWA_MFLOW.

2. Choose IMPLEMENTATION • CREATE from the menu; you'll then see a popup window as shown in Figure 9.7.

3. Fill in the IMPLEMENTATION NAME field; for this example, enter "ZCRM_TPP_BOOK_MFLOW".

4. Click the CHECKMARK button. On the next screen, you'll need to enter a description for your BAdI implementation. For this example, enter "Activity Data Source Enhancement" as shown in Figure 9.8.

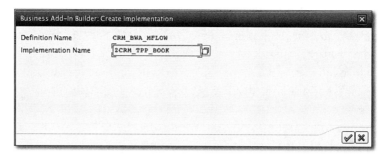

Figure 9.7 Create a New BAdI Implementation for CRM_BWA_MFLOW

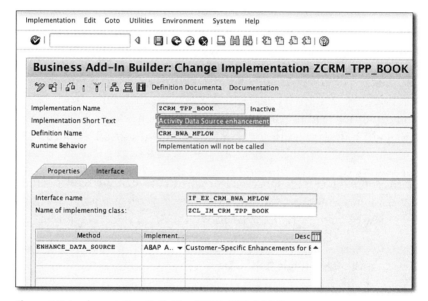

Figure 9.8 Implementation Definition ZCRM_TPP_BOOK

5. Click SAVE. You can now code the method ENHANCE_DATA_SOURCE of your BAdI implementation.

6. On the next tab, double-click on the method. The resulting screen allows you to add code to populate or change values that will be sent to the SAP NetWeaver BW system as shown in Figure 9.9.

Method code ENHANCE_DATA_ SOURCE

The code for the ENHANCE_DATA_SOURCE method follows a general pattern, which is very straightforward. You first must check to see if the data source name matches the data source you want to enhance. This is provided by the I_DATASOURCE parameter.

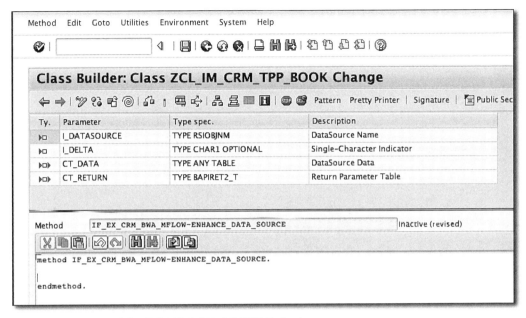

Figure 9.9 Signature of the ENHACE_DATA_SOURCE Method

Next, transfer the data to a local typed copy so you can change the fields. To do this, take the CT_DATA structure, and move the internal table to a local internal table. Finally, loop on the internal table. For each entry, use the GUID provided to find any other information on the business transaction, and then update the corresponding field.

In this example, ZZHASHTAG is stored on the CRMD_CUSTOMER_H table. You'll use the CRM_CUSTOMER_READ_OW function module to find the value of the ZZHASHTAG for each activity transaction extracted.

As the last step, you'll transfer your local copy of the data extract back to the CT_DATA parameter. Listing 9.1 shows the completed code to populate the ZZHASHTAG field through the ENHANCE_DATA_SOURCE method.

```
method IF_EX_CRM_BWA_MFLOW~ENHANCE_DATA_SOURCE.
  data:
    lt_data        type table of crmt_bw_ds_activity,
    wa_data        like line of lt_data,
    ls_customer_h_wrk type CRMT_CUSTOMER_H_WRK.
```

```
field-symbols:
    <ls_data> like line of lt_data.

  case i_datasource.
* activities data source
    when '0CRM_SALES_ACT_1'.

* copy data from extract structure to internal table.
      lt_data[] = ct_data[].
      refresh ct_data.

      loop at lt_data assigning <ls_data>.

        clear: ls_customer_h_wrk.
        CALL FUNCTION 'CRM_CUSTOMER_H_READ_OW'
          EXPORTING
            IV_GUID                 = <ls_data>-guid
          IMPORTING
            ES_CUSTOMER_H_WRK       = ls_customer_h_wrk
          EXCEPTIONS
            HEADER_NOT_FOUND    = 1
            OTHERS              = 2.

        <ls_data>-ZZHASHTAG = ls_customer_h_wrk-zzhashtag.
      endloop.
* send the changed data back
      ct_data = lt_data[].
    when others.
  endcase.
endmethod.
```

Listing 9.1 Example Code to Populate ZZHASHTAG via ENHANCE_DATA_SOURCE

Testing Your Work

Transaction RSA3: extractor checker To test your work, use Transaction RSA3. This is the extractor checker transaction that allows you to see if your BAdI is properly populating the new data source structure. As you can see from Figure 9.10, you can specify the name of your data source and pass selection parameters in to execute a test run of the extractor logic. For this example, enter "0CRM_SALES_ACT_1" as the data source name.

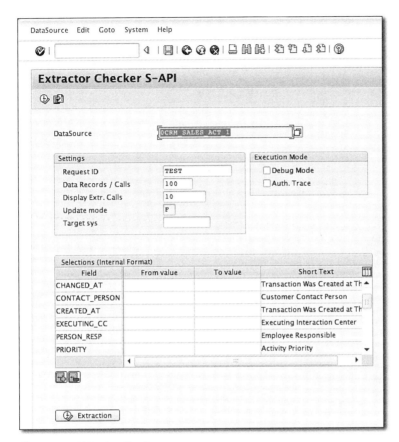

Figure 9.10 Extractor Checker

Now follow these steps:

1. Scroll down under SELECTIONS (INTERNAL FORMAT), and enter "ZSCR" as the FROM VALUE in the row with the key field of "PROCESS_TYPE".

2. Click the EXTRACTION button to run the extractor. After the extraction, another screen appears that allows you to display your results as shown in the Figure 9.11.

3. Click the ALV GRID button to get an ALV grid display of your results. This grid, as shown in Figure 9.12, allows you to verify that the extractor is now executing your BAdI logic to fill in the additional attribute to the extract structure.

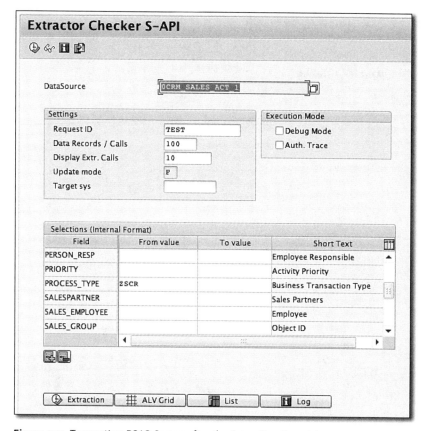

Figure 9.11 Transaction RSA3 Screen after the Extraction Completes

Figure 9.12 ALV Grid Display of Extracted Records

You can use the DETAIL display button to open a popup as shown in Figure 9.13 that will show all of the columns of the extract structure in a listing. You can see that your new HASH TAG field is indeed being populated by your extract logic.

Figure 9.13 Detail Display of the Extracted Record

Comparison against AET

For the purpose of this example, we walked through the steps of adding your custom field manually. Understanding this manual technique allows you to add fields to the extractor data source that may not be available via the AET. This could include values from related transactions instead, such as follow-up activities or tasks. However, if you had created your field using the AET, then none of the coding would be required that we just described. Instead, SAP has automatically included exits in the standard extractors to bring in the AET fields, provided that you checked the BW REPORTING checkbox when you created the field in the AET (see Figure 9.14).

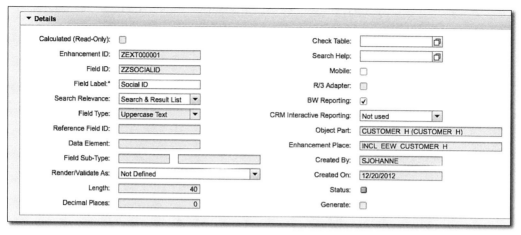

Figure 9.14 AET Field Definition for BW Relevant

Final Steps

After you've validated that the data source is properly enhanced, you'll need to work with your BW configurator/developer to enhance the SAP NetWeaver BW data structures to include your new field. This work is beyond the scope of this book; if you're interested in these steps, review the book *Data Modeling in SAP NetWeaver BW* by Frank K. Wolf and Stefan Yamada (SAP PRESS, 2011).

Standard extractor function module
    If you look at the standard extractor function module CRM_SALES_ACT_1_MAP, there is a call to the method MAP_EXT_FIELDS_FROM_BDOC of the class CL_CRM_1O_EXTENSIBILITY_TOOLS. This method takes a reference GUID, reference GUID type, objects, and bdoc structure. It then returns the changed extract structure. In the CRM_SALES_ACT_1_MAP function module, it looks for extensions in three key areas: ORDERADM_H, CUSTOMER_H, and ACTIVITY_H.

Method steps
    The method first finds the includes that are normally used to extend the object. These are predefined as part of the AET metadata model. Next, the tool determines if any of these includes have been implemented in the system. If the include has been implemented, which means that it contains an actual new field and not just the default dummy field, the tool then calls a mapper that moves the data from the passed in bdoc structure to the extract structure.

The BDoc that is used is the source data provided by the SAP CRM Middleware being sent to the SAP NetWeaver BW system. SAP CRM uses an outbound BDoc when transactions are saved to send data to the SAP NetWeaver BW system.

9.2 Interactive Reporting Enhancements

In most SAP CRM implementations, there is always a requirement to report on transaction data based on custom attributes added to your system. To avoid building new custom reports or tools, you can instead extend existing reporting tools such as Interactive Reporting. Interactive Reporting allows users to perform ad hoc analytical reporting on transactional data within SAP CRM without requiring a separate SAP NetWeaver BW system. As of SAP CRM 7.0 EHP1, it's possible to add custom fields from the business transaction to the interactive reports using the AET. There is, however, a limitation on the interactive reports because you can't manually extend these reports and must use the AET to extend the report data sources.

The method to extend the Interactive Reporting data sources is through setting the INTERACTIVE REPORTING flag attribute for the custom field you created. As you recall, you can access the details of the custom field you created using the AET by first bringing up the CREATE INTERACTION LOG screen in the Web Client. Click on the menu option SHOW CONFIGURABLE AREAS, and then click on the INTERACTION LOG DETAILS section. This brings up the screen configuration popup window. Select DISPLAY ENHANCEMENTS, and you'll be prompted to choose the object type, which is INTERACTION LOG. You'll now see a list of the fields you've added. To flag the attribute, go into the details of the field that you added, and choose one of three options as shown in Figure 9.15.

Interactive Reporting extension method

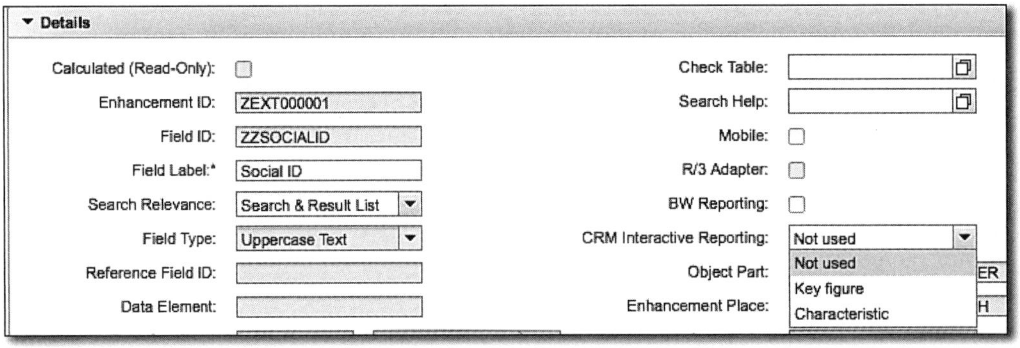

Figure 9.15 AET Field Options for Interactive Reporting

The default option is NOT USED, and the remaining options are KEY FIG-URE and CHARACTERISTIC. There are some limitations to the type of fields that can be used in Interactive Reporting, such as you can't use any field that is a free-text field in mixed case (e.g., you can't use both uppercase and lowercase letters). You can, however, use fields that are uppercase only as a characteristic in the Interactive Reporting tool. Another draw-back is that fields that were created manually through the EEWB or manual extension can't be used in the interactive report framework. This means only fields you've created via the AET can be added to Interactive Reporting.

Add the field to data extractor

After you've set your options, the field will be placed automatically in the appropriate data extractor based on the object type you've originally extended. Because you started your extension for an interaction log, the field is added to the business activity extractor for Interactive Reporting. If your system isn't correctly set up for Interactive Reporting in SAP CRM, you'll receive an error when trying to generate the AET field with the SAP CRM INTERACTIVE REPORTING flag selected for use. You must have a valid SAP CRM Interactive Reporting setup in your system before you can extend the Interactive Reporting data sources.

Verify the new field

Your next step is to verify that your new field was added and what exactly is generated in the system. When adding a new field to the business activity, the data source is /CRMBW/OLTP_ACTIVITY. You can review installed data sources in your SAP CRM system by launching Transaction RSA6.

The data sources for Interactive Reporting are located under the node Data sources
/CRMBW/ROOT • /CRMBW/OREP as shown in Figure 9.16. The data
source /CRMBW/OLTP_ACTIVITY has an extract structure called
/CRMBW/OLTP_EXT_ACT_APP.

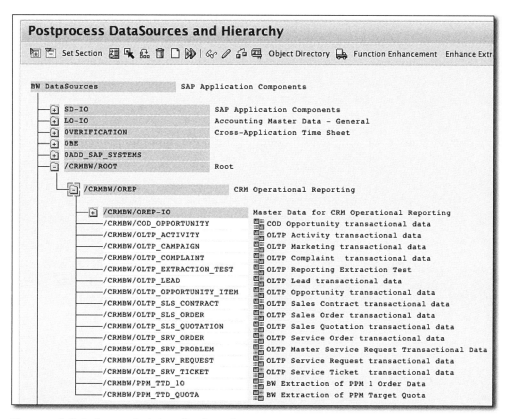

Figure 9.16 Data Sources for Interactive Reporting

When the AET generates your field and you select the field as either a
CHARACTERISTIC or KEY FIGURE for Interactive Reporting, the field is then
added to the structure. The name of your field in the structure will correspond exactly to the technical name that was defined in the AET. This
once again stresses the fact that if you don't use the technical names
provided by the AET for new fields, you should name all of your fields
starting with "ZZ", and they should be unique across all segments of the
business transaction.

Function module
/CRMBW/OLTP_
EXTRACT_ACT

The data extractor for the activity source calls the function /CRMBW/OLTP_ EXTRACT_ACT. Note that you can find the function module that gets called for any data extractor by selecting the data source extraction test button, which appears as the standard ABAP test button (which appears as a wrench) in Transaction RSA6, or by running Transaction RSA3 directly. You then can select the debug mode, which will step you into the extractor function module that will be called for the data source. The interesting part of this function module is that if you dig deeply enough into the code, you'll find that this extractor technically executes the one order search that is used by the standard searches in SAP CRM.

Function module
/CRMBW/EXTEND_
FROM_DS

On the Interactive Reporting client, the AET calls function module /CRMBW/EXTEND_FROM_DS. This is used to create the necessary Interactive Reporting objects in the Interactive Reporting client that will be used when the Interactive Reporting client is executed. Once again, the definition of all of these objects is based on the metadata for the field contained in the AET and can only be created using the AET.

As you've learned, the extension of additional fields for Interactive Reporting is limited in both what is possible and the amount of effort necessary. You must first have Interactive Reporting configured in your system before you can make any extensions to the reporting data sources.

9.3 Displaying Custom Reports Using the Transaction Launcher

One of the biggest drawbacks of reporting through SAP NetWeaver BW or Interactive Reporting is that there is quite of bit of setup required for it to work. There may be situations where you need to provide the users with the ability to report or extract data in your SAP CRM system without having to set up a full reporting system.

As you may recall, the SAP CRM system is an ABAP-based system, so you could develop ABAP custom reports. However, the problem is that most ABAP custom reports require the SAP GUI for display and execution, and the Web Client doesn't use the SAP GUI.

The way to solve this problem to create a custom report is to combine two different tools provided by SAP. The first tool is the SAP GUI for HTML, which is delivered as part of SAP NetWeaver AS ABAP. The second tool is the Transaction Launcher, which is part of the SAP Web Client. The combination of these tools will allow you to run custom ABAP reports from the Web Client for execution by your end users.

Combine tools: SAP GUI for HTML and the Transaction Launcher

The general process that you'll need to follow to achieve this is to first set up the SAP GUI for HTML on your SAP CRM system. Next you need to define a URL for the report you want to display and then configure the Transaction Launcher. All of these steps assume you've created the custom program first, as you can't add a custom report until it's built and assigned a transaction code within SAP.

Let's get started.

9.3.1 Setting Up the SAP GUI for HTML

The SAP GUI for HTML is part of the SAP NetWeaver AS ABAP. Your SAP NetWeaver system administrator will perform the task of setting up the SAP GUI for HTML for use. This process is documented by the standard SAP Help found on *http://help.sap.com* in detail.

The following are a few tips on how to verify that it has been activated:

▶ In the profile parameters for your SAP CRM ABAP AS, the parameter `itsp/enable` should be present and have a value of 1.

▶ You should validate that the system and WebGUI services have been published via Transaction SE80 and activated via Transaction SICF.

▶ You can launch the WebGUI using the URL *http(s)://<hostname>:<port>/sap/bc/gui/sap/its/webgui*, where *<hostname>* is the name of an application server where the Internet Transaction Server (ITS) has been activated, and *<port>* is the HTTP(s) port defined on the application server.

9.3.2 Defining the URL for the SAP Web Client

The Web Client Transaction Launcher allows the launching of external URLs from the Web Client. In the last step, you set up the SAP GUI for

HTML to be able to view traditional SAP GUI reports from a web browser. The Web Client allows you to create links to any valid URL using the Transaction Launcher. These links will appear as menu items in your WEB CLIENT menu. To use these URLs with the Transaction Launcher, you must first define the URL in your system. To do this, follow these steps:

Define URL 1. Go into the IMG (Transaction SPRO) to the following menu path: CUS-TOMER RELATIONSHIP MANAGEMENT • UI FRAMEWORK • TECHNICAL ROLE DEFINITION • TRANSACTION LAUNCHER • DEFINE URLS AND PARAM-ETERS.

2. In the DEFINE URLS screen, click the CREATE NEW ENTRIES button. Specify the following details for the entry to be created.

   ▶ Provide a technical ID for the URL.

   ▶ Choose the type of URL as a NON-BSP URL. Because the SAP GUI for HTML is part of the SAP NetWeaver AS ABAP, select the DETERMINE HOST/PORT checkbox.

   ▶ For the logical system, choose OWNLOGSYS because you're working in the same client as the Web Client.

   ▶ Define the URL for the Transaction Launcher as "sap/bc/gui/sap/its/webgui/!?~transaction=SE38".

> **Note**
>
> For your own custom report transaction, you would replace *SE38* with the appropriate transaction code.

The completed URL definition should look similar to Figure 9.17. Now that this is done, you're ready to configure the Transaction Launcher.

9.3.3 Configuring the Transaction Launcher

The Transaction Launcher is used by the Web Client to launch external applications and pass data to those applications. You'll need to use the Transaction Launcher wizard to create a new entry. This Transaction Launcher entry will form the basis of a logical link in the menu of the Web Client.

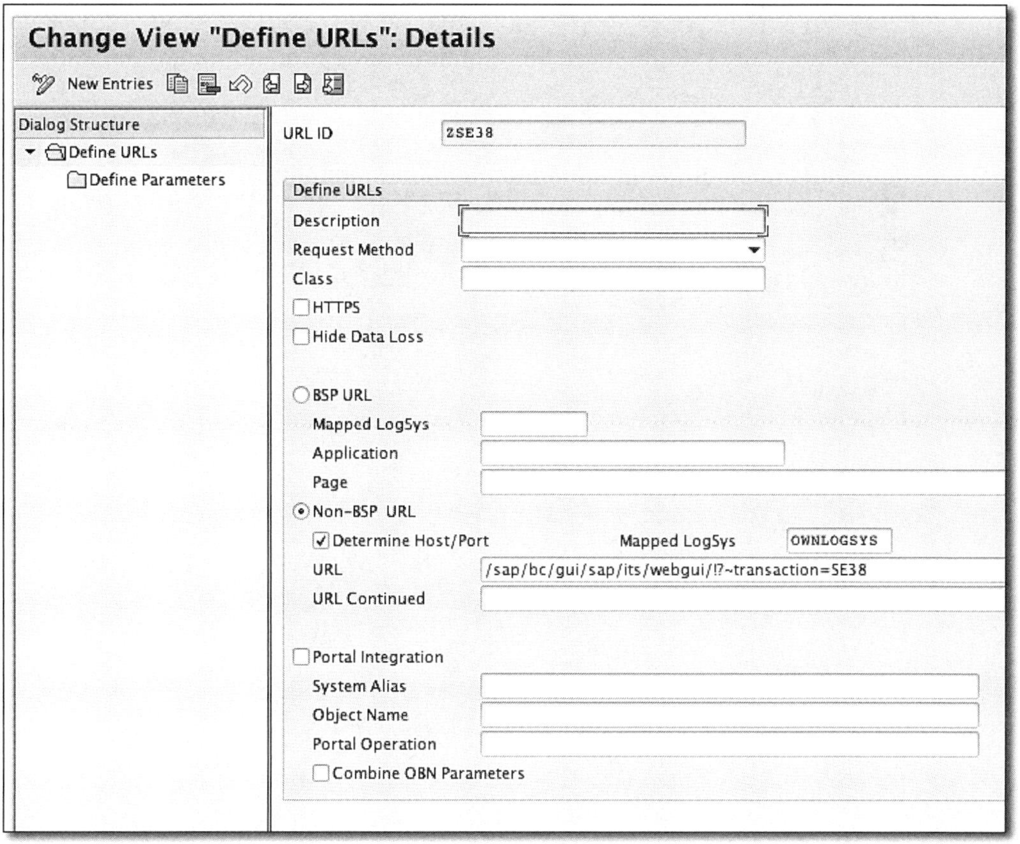

Change View "Define URLs": Details

New Entries 🗋 🖺 🏱 🖺 🖺 🗗

Dialog Structure
- ▾ 🗁 Define URLs
  - 🗀 Define Parameters

URL ID `ZSE38`

Define URLs

Description	
Request Method	▾
Class	
☐ HTTPS	
☐ Hide Data Loss	

○ BSP URL
  - Mapped LogSys
  - Application
  - Page

◉ Non-BSP URL
  - ☑ Determine Host/Port   Mapped LogSys   `OWNLOGSYS`
  - URL   `/sap/bc/gui/sap/its/webgui/!?~transaction=SE38`
  - URL Continued

☐ Portal Integration
  - System Alias
  - Object Name
  - Portal Operation
  - ☐ Combine OBN Parameters

Figure 9.17 Define the URL for SAP GUI for HTML Transaction

Transaction Launcher Wizard

Launch the wizard from the following path within the SAP CRM IMG: CUSTOMER RELATIONSHIP MANAGEMENT • UI FRAMEWORK • TECHNICAL ROLE DEFINITION • TRANSACTION LAUNCHER • CONFIGURE TRANSACTION LAUNCHER. The initial screen asks you to define the technical name of the transaction launch ID. For this example, name this "ZCRM_BOOK_SE38" as shown in Figure 9.18.

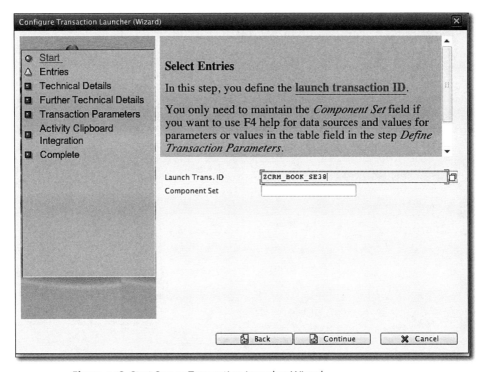

Figure 9.18 Start Screen Transaction Launcher Wizard

Now, follow these steps:

1. Click CONTINUE to move to the next screen.

2. Provide a description of your launch transaction. In this case, enter "SE38".

3. Provide the name of an ABAP class that will be generated by the wizard. This name can be any valid class name within your customer namespace. For this example, enter "ZCL_TPP_BOOK_SE38".

> **Note**
>
> It's important to note that the class generated is a local object assigned to the $TMP package. You must remember to change the package of the class if you plan on moving it within your landscape from the development system to your test and production systems.

4. Select the RAISE VETO flag. Your completed entry for this step is shown in Figure 9.19. This will require users to confirm that they want to continue when clicking on the link if they are coming from a screen where they are editing data.

5. Click CONTINUE to move to the next screen.

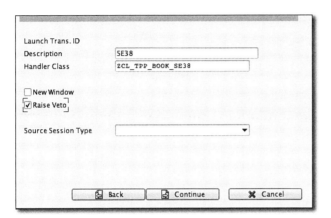

Figure 9.19 Define Details of the Launch Transaction

6. On the next screen, define the launch transaction to be of type URL. Provide the technical ID of the URL that you defined in the previous step, which is "ZSE38", as shown in Figure 9.20.

Define the launch transaction

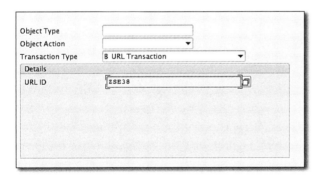

Figure 9.20 Define the URL Launch Transaction Type

7. Click CONTINUE, and a screen appears to confirm your entries. When you're finished, a screen summarizing your choices appears. Click FINISH.

The system will generate a Transaction Launcher class and entry in Customizing for your Transaction Launcher that will look similar to Figure 9.21.

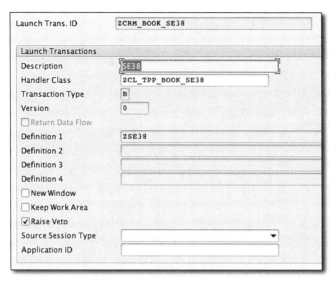

Figure 9.21 Fully Configured Launch Transaction

Defining the Logical Link

Logical link *Logical links* are the building blocks of all menu items within the Web Client. For your newly defined launch transaction to appear within the menu that your business user would use, you need to create a logical link for the launch transaction.

To do this, go into the IMG, and then go to the path CRM • UI FRAMEWORK • TECHNICAL ROLE DEFINITION • DEFINE NAVIGATION BAR PROFILE. An overview screen appears with several options that define a navigation bar profile (see Figure 9.22). A navigation bar profile is essentially the definition of a menu in the Web Client. The navigation bar profile consists of several layers; the lowest layer is the logical link, which is the menu item. These links are then grouped together in work center link groups. The link groups are then assigned to work centers, which are the main grouping parts of the Web Client menu.

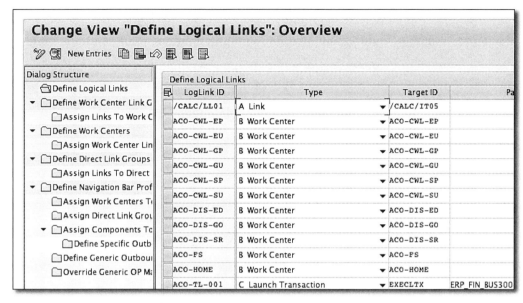

Figure 9.22 Navigation Bar Profile—Define Logical Links

From the overview screen, follow these steps:

1. Choose the submenu on the left-hand side logical links.

2. Choose CREATE NEW ENTRY.

3. A new entry screen appears. Provide a technical ID for your logical link. Use "C Launch Transaction" as the logical link TYPE. The technical TARGET ID is "EXCELTX". This corresponds to a "plug name" within the framework of the Web Client components. The PARAMETER should be the name of your launch transaction, which was "ZCRM_BOOK_SE38". The PARAMETER CLASS should be "CL_CRM_UI_LTX_NAVBAR_PARAM".

4. Provide the TITLE of how the link should be placed in the Web Client menu and the DESCRIPTION so that when you add this to a link group, it's visible. The resulting entry should look similar to Figure 9.23.

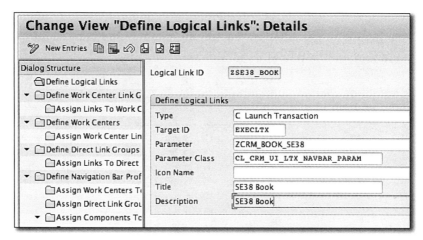

Figure 9.23 Logical Link Definition in the Navigation Bar Configuration

Add link to navigation bar profile

At this point, the link can be added to a navigation bar profile through a series of steps:

1. Add the link to an appropriate work center link group, or create a new work center link group.

2. Add the work center link group to a work center if you created a new link group.

3. After the link has been added, go into the CUSTOMIZING business role, and mark the item as visible to the user.

> **Note**
>
> Because the scope of this book isn't a full dive on Web Client customizing, we recommend that you review *SAP CRM Web Client: Customizing and Development* by Michael Füchsle and Matthias E. Zierke (SAP PRESS, 2010) for further explanation on how these tasks work.

Final step: report link to menu

When you're finished, your new report will be linked in your menu; in this case, it was the SE38 ABAP Editor transaction. When you launch Transaction SE38 from the Web Client, you'll see a screen as shown in Figure 9.24 (the one shown here is cropped for space), which is an HTML rendering of an SAP GUI screen. All of the limitations of the SAP

GUI for HTML apply, so we strongly recommend that this technique is used for quick and simple reports or as a way to allow users to run update programs without the need for an SAP GUI. In terms of security, standard SAP security practices for custom reports apply, so you'll need to provide your users with the appropriate S_TCODE access and make sure your reports check authorizations appropriately.

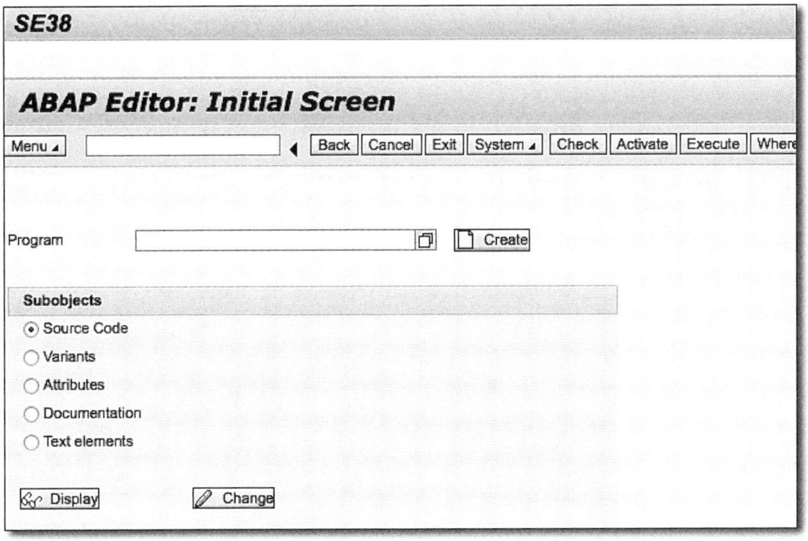

Figure 9.24 Transaction SE38 via SAP GUI for HTML

Although we don't recommend that the Transaction Launcher reports should replace a full-fledged analytics solution, they provide a nice alternative of providing reporting access to data in a quick fashion when there isn't enough time to develop a full report or proper UI using the Web Client. Keep in mind that this technique shouldn't be used to launch the no longer supported SAP data maintenance transactions such as CRMD_ORDER or BP, which were replaced by their respective Web Client counterparts. In addition, be aware that the SAP GUI for HTML will require additional resources of your SAP CRM servers, so validate your system sizing in terms of memory and processor before running this productively.

9.4   Summary

Accurate and useful analytics are necessary to measure the effectiveness of any business process supported by SAP CRM. As SAP has provided methods to extend the data model and processes of SAP CRM, additional methods have been provided so that the analytics will be extended also. If you use the AET provided by SAP, then you don't need to manually enhance the analytics data sources in SAP CRM. When you can't use the analytics tools provided by SAP, you can use the Transaction Launcher to run your own custom reports to provide quick and dirty access to the data contained within your SAP CRM system.

In the next chapter, we'll examine your last set of options to meet your business requirements when all other options fail.

SAP CRM projects shouldn't fail because the technical team is unable to meet a business requirement. In those situations where everything has been exhausted, there are methods of last resort that can conquer the most complex challenges.

10　When All Else Fails

In the last several chapters, you've learned about the data model, enhancement techniques, and methods to retrieve and extract data from the SAP CRM system. For most situations, the techniques you examined will allow you to meet the needs of your business users. However, there are certain situations when you'll need to pull out the methods of last resort to meet the requirements.

In this chapter, we'll look at three methods when all else fails to solve your SAP CRM problems. The three primary techniques are implicit enhancements, core modifications, and community resources. As you'll learn, implicit exits and core modifications should be considered methods of last resort. Community resources will show you how to effectively use the power of social networking to support your SAP CRM implementation and solve your problems.

10.1　Implicit Enhancements

Implicit enhancements were introduced by SAP in the SAP NetWeaver Application Server as a way to bridge the gap from the provided user BAdIs and user exits and core modifications. In most applications delivered by SAP, there is gap between the BAdIs provided and the enhancement options desired by an SAP customer. The primary purpose was to provide a way to enhance the standard delivered SAP applications in a way that could be upgradeable and would not directly change SAP code. The drawback of implicit enhancements is that there are only certain

Bridge between BAdIs and enhancement options

points where they can be inserted. Thus, you may not always be able to insert an implicit exit at the correct point in application processing.

Your options for implicit enhancements are available typically at the beginning and end of a subroutine, function module, or a method call. The primary benefit is that they are always available, and SAP doesn't have to deliver a predefined enhancement spot for every single piece of code in your system.

10.1.1 Create an Implicit Enhancement

To create an implicit enhancement, follow these steps:

1. Open up the source code editor of the function module, subroutine, or method call to be enhanced.

2. Click on the ENHANCE SOURCE CODE button in the source code editor to put the source code editor into enhancement mode.

3. Find the available implicit enhancement points on your system. Choose EDIT • ENHANCEMENTS • SHOW IMPLICIT ENHANCEMENT OPTIONS. It's important that you turn on the enhancement mode first because even if you can show the enhancement options without being in enhancement mode, the system will reset the display of those enhancements when switching into enhancement mode.

   In the source code editor, you'll now see a highlighted line that will appear at the beginning and the end of any code contained within a function module, subroutine, or method call, as shown in Figure 10.1.

Figure 10.1 Implicit Enhancement Spot

4. Move your mouse pointer onto the line, and then choose EDIT • ENHANCEMENT OPERATIONS • CREATE ENHANCEMENTS. The system will ask if you want to create the enhancement via declaration or code.

5. Choose CODE, and a popup appears asking for a technical name and description. For this example, enter "ZST3_BOOK_EXAMPLE" as the

technical name, and enter the description as "Book Example" (see Figure 10.2).

6. Click the CHECKMARK button to continue.

Figure 10.2 Create Enhancement Implementation Popup

7. You'll now see the inline code editor for your enhancement as show in Figure 10.3. At this point, you can add your logic and then save the code and activate as any normal ABAP program.

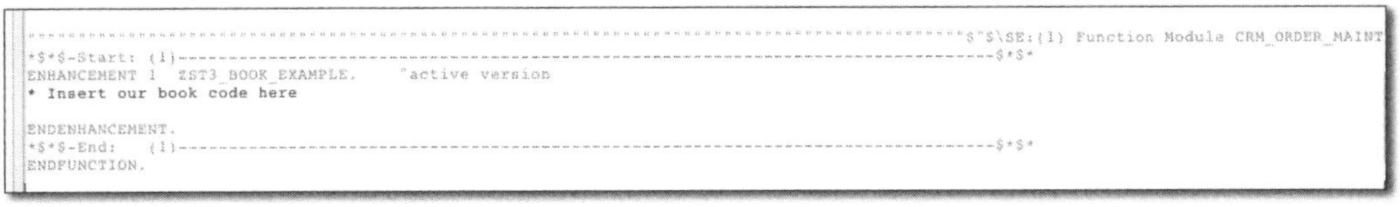

Figure 10.3 Inline Enhancement Editor

Now that you understand the basic mechanics of creating an implicit enhancement, you may wonder what you can do with them that can't be done with BAdIs. Let's move on to that topic in the next section.

10.1.2 Common Uses of Implicit Enhancements

One common technique is using implicit enhancements to retrieve intermediate values for use in later program calls. You may have a requirement that can be met by a BAdI, but the BAdI doesn't receive all of the information needed for the requirement. The BAdI is called by another program, which does have the required information.

In this situation, you can use implicit enhancements to export the information in the program that calls your BAdI to either a static method of a class that updates a static variable of a class or a function module call that updates the global variable of its function group. This scenario is the

Export information

best use of implicit enhancements because you didn't change the SAP logic completely, but rather used the implicit enhancements as a way to make the BAdIs provided in your system more effective.

Function group method

The *function group method* works because global variables of a function group retain their values from the point of the first call of a function module that is part of that function group. To use this method, you'll need to build a new function group that contains global variables to store the data being transferred, a function module to store the data being collected, and a function module to retrieve the data being collected.

Follow these steps:

1. Go into Transaction SE80, and choose FUNCTION GROUP as the OBJECT TYPE in the repository browser.

2. Enter a name for your function group, and click DISPLAY.

3. A popup appears as shown in Figure 10.4. Choose YES, provide a description for the function group, and click the SAVE button.

Figure 10.4 Create Function Group

4. For this example, call the function group "ZST3_BADI_TRANSER" and enter the description as "Implicit Exit Data Transfer Example" (see Figure 10.5).

5. You are then prompted to choose a package, and if you don't make it a local object, a transport request.

6. Save the function group. You can now see the left-hand tree structure in Transaction SE80. Expand the structure, and drill into the top include of the function group as shown in Figure 10.6.

7. Open the top include for editing, and then declare the variables that you want to store in the global memory of the function group.

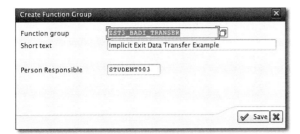

Figure 10.5 Create Function Group Details

Figure 10.6 Function Group Structure

For this example, declare a global variable called "GV_SOCIALTAG of type CRMT_DESCRIPTION".

8. Save your changes, and then activate the code.

9. Now you need to create a function module to retrieve the value you just created. For this example, call it "ZST3_BADI_TRANSFER_GET" as shown in Figure 10.7.

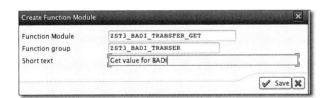

Figure 10.7 Create Function Module

10. The function module must contain one exporting parameter that has the same type as the global variable you created for the function group. In this example, name the export parameter "EV_SOCIALTAG" and enter the type as "CRMT_DESCRIPTION" as shown in Figure 10.8.

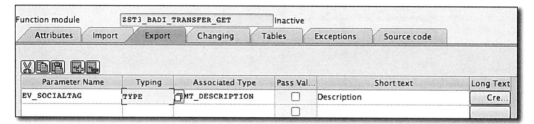

Figure 10.8 Export Parameter for the Get Function Module

Function module
code

For this function module, the code is very simple, as shown in Listing 10.1.

```
FUNCTION ZST3_BADI_TRANSFER_GET.
*"----------------------------------------------------------
*"*"Local Interface:
*"  EXPORTING
*"    REFERENCE(EV_SOCIALTAG) TYPE  CRMT_DESCRIPTION
*"----------------------------------------------------------
  EV_SOCIALTAG = GV_SOCIALTAG.
ENDFUNCTION.
```

Listing 10.1 Function Module ZST3_BADI_TRANSFER_GET

11. You now need to create another function module that allows your implicit enhancement to set the value that you want to pass to your BAdI. Call this "ZST3_BADI_TRANSFER_SET" as shown in Figure 10.9.

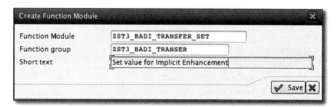

Figure 10.9 Create Setter Function Module

12. The function module must contain one importing parameter that has the same type as the global variable you created for the function group. In this example, name the import parameter "IV_SOCIAL-TAG" and enter the type as "CRMT_DESCRIPTION" as shown in Figure 10.10.

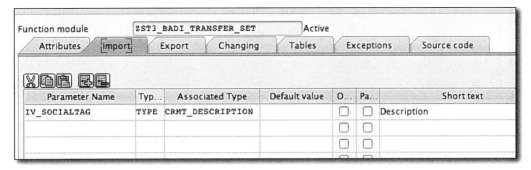

Figure 10.10 Import Parameter for the SET Function Module

The code for the function module to set the values is also very simple. A single import parameter sets the value of the global variable (see Listing 10.2).

```
FUNCTION ZST3_BADI_TRANSFER_SET.
*"----------------------------------------------------------------
*"*"Local Interface:
*"  IMPORTING
*"     REFERENCE(IV_SOCIALTAG) TYPE  CRMT_DESCRIPTION
*"----------------------------------------------------------------
   GV_SOCIALTAG = IV_SOCIALTAG.
ENDFUNCTION.
```

Listing 10.2 Setter Function Module ZST3_BADI_TRANSFER_SET

Now that you've created the function group and the corresponding set and understand function modules, you can use this to extend the values known to a BAdI. You can call the SET function module in the implicit enhancement and the GET function module within the BAdI. As you can imagine, the example here is quite simple, but the technique can be applied to more complicated logic.

Extend values to a BAdI

10.1.3 Upgrades

Another point to keep in mind when using implicit enhancements is that during upgrades, the system will recognize whether the enhancement technically conflicts in the new version. This, however, doesn't change the fact that the logic of the upgraded system may cause your assumptions of standard behavior to become invalid. However, you'll have standard tools to go through all of the created implicit enhancements during upgrade adjustment work to make sure they are still technically correct.

Even though implicit enhancements should always be treated as a method of last resort in your list of ways to solve a business requirement, they provide a powerful way to enhance the system when there are no other options. The tools provided by SAP NetWeaver AS ABAP to manage implicit enhancements will minimize the amount of effort during an upgrade to adjust the code to a new version. Implicit enhancements allow you to further extend the capabilities of BAdIs and should normally prevent you from using core modifications, which we'll discuss next.

10.2 Core Modifications

We're going to start off this section with the recommendation that you shouldn't perform core modifications. However, any proper discussion of techniques to enhance SAP CRM to solve common business requirements should have a discussion on when core modifications are appropriate and the reasons not to use them. Due to the very nature of core modifications, we aren't going to provide an example of how to create one. For that information, there are other resources that are available, including the standard SAP help.

Data integrity errors

There are many reasons not to perform core modifications. The most practical reason is that you don't always understand the full design of the code delivered by SAP, and a change could introduce side effects that cause data integrity errors or unexpected program behavior. The counter-argument has always been that the SAP-delivered system isn't flexible enough or didn't deliver the enhancement spots that would eliminate the need for a core modification. In the oldest versions of SAP CRM and SAP ERP, this counter-argument was valid; however, as of the current version of SAP CRM, there are enough ways to enhance the system to meet almost every business requirement without a core modification.

The next issue is that when you make a core modification within a standard program, it may prevent SAP from fully supporting your system when a problem arises, without that core modification being removed first. Even though your core modification may not be responsible for a system issue, as part of a standard troubleshooting routine, there is a tendency to remove all customer adjustments before saying that a standard delivered code does contain an error. Although the amount of enforcement on this can vary between customers, it's still a valid point to take into consideration.

The last issue on core modifications is that when someone else is performing the work for you, this may be a sign that they don't understand the options delivered. A skilled consultant or resource should always present the core modification as the last choice and not your first choice to meet a business requirement.

However, if you must modify standard SAP-delivered code within SAP, we recommend using the modification to modify the code in the following fashion. In the source code editor of any standard delivered SAP program, there will be additional buttons to INSERT, REPLACE, or DELETE SAP-delivered code. To make a modification, click on the section in question, and then select the appropriate action. You then insert your code to make the adjustment.

Modify source code

However, you'll be prompted by SAP to enter a modification key for the program. One option to bypass this is to manually adjust the delivered code. You can do this by going to EDIT • MODIFICATION OPERATIONS • SWITCH OFF ASSISTANT. We don't recommend doing this, however, because the system will no longer track your changes and instead just notes that the object you modified is changed. By using the modification assistant, you minimize the amount of effort it takes to reconcile your changes back to the SAP-delivered code during an upgrade project.

Modification assistant

When researching this book, it was very difficult to find a valid example for a core modification, given all of the other enhancement techniques provided by SAP. Therefore, our final recommendation isn't to make a core modification to the system unless directed by SAP. Before you create a core modification, it's always wise to ask other SAP CRM customers about the problem, which we'll examine in the next section.

10.3 Community Resources

As in sports, "there is no I in team" when it comes to successfully using SAP CRM. Although you may have the benefit of working in a large implementation, there are many people who must work on small teams. The challenge for the small teams is that there may be only one SAP CRM technical and functional expert available within a company. In many cases, there is no room in the budget to maintain a large team to support SAP CRM.

In addition, members of the team that support SAP ERP typically don't have the knowledge about the SAP CRM solution. This can be the case even when the SAP ERP support team consists of a hundred people, and the SAP CRM team still only has two people assigned.

To overcome the limitations of the knowledge of your immediate team members, there are community resources available around the world that can be used to gather knowledge about SAP CRM. These resources include the SAP Community Network, SAP user groups, and social media.

10.3.1 SAP Community Network

When SAP CRM was first launched as a product, the concept of social networks to exchange information about supporting SAP was very limited. In fact, the SAP Developer Network (SDN) didn't exist. Most knowledge exchanges about SAP CRM were limited to either personal exchanges or the occasional ASUG chapter meeting. Although both methods were and still are a great way to share knowledge about SAP CRM, there are limitations to these methods.

ASUG The first issue with the ASUG method is that the in-person meetings are normally on a limited basis with the primary focus being the annual conference. Although the annual conference is an excellent place to get SAP CRM content, the drawback is that most of the content tends to be geared toward business case presentations instead of technical development. In addition, other events such as SAP TechEd tended to focus on pure development, rather than application-specific development. This left developers who focus on SAP CRM enhancements stuck without a particular resource to attend.

As SAP CRM installations grew, there became a knowledge gap on how to perform various enhancements on SAP CRM. The problem was that SAP didn't offer on a regular basis any classes to explain how to enhance the system. In addition, the publicly available documentation was not sufficient to meet the needs of most SAP CRM customers. The only way to learn the SAP CRM solution from a technical point of view was to work on an implementation project. If you were lucky enough to get on a project you would get hands-on training. Because the number of knowledgeable resources was few and far between, it was easy to get work as an SAP CRM technical consultant.

In 2003/2004, SAP Introduced the SAP Developer Network (SDN). At the time, SDN was not focused on any traditional SAP solution and even included forums for topics such as ABAP. SAP then introduced an ABAP forum and as a result, the community grew to become a case study in business-to-business online community networks.

SAP Developer Network (SDN)

In late 2004/early 2005, SAP introduced the first technical forum dedicated to SAP CRM on SDN. This forum was known as SAP CRM General and Framework. In this forum, many people connected and gathered to share and answer SAP CRM questions. Some of the early members of this community eventually became moderators of the community. In this forum, unknown concepts such as the XIF adapter were introduced, along with discussions on how to use the various BAdI frameworks in SAP CRM and the BTE framework. As SDN grew and became the SAP Community Network (SCN), the SAP CRM forum grew into several spaces dedicated to both technical and functional SAP CRM topics.

In the early part of 2012, SAP relaunched the SAP Community Network on a new technology platform called Jive. This platform combined several distinct areas on the old platform into one unified interface. The SAP Community Network (SCN) SAP CRM (*http://scn.sap.com/community/crm*) space as shown in Figure 10.11, along with the "subspaces," is a key knowledge source for information on the technical aspects of enhancing SAP CRM.

SAP Community Network on Jive

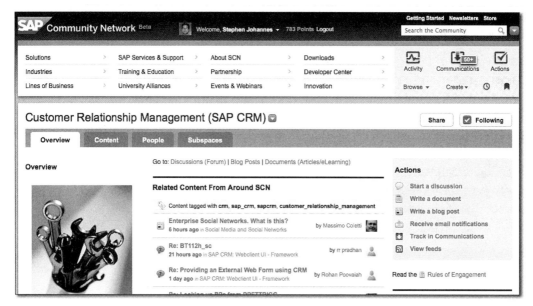

Figure 10.11 SAP CRM Community on SCN

We've used SCN extensively since 2005 to answer and research questions on the enhancement of SAP CRM. There are no longer "forums" on SCN but rather spaces that focus on different SAP solutions. On SCN, there is a general space dedicated to any SAP CRM topic that doesn't fall into one of the following categories: Web Channel, Interaction Center, PCUI, Sales, Marketing, Service, Mobile, Upgrades and Enhancement Packs, and Web Client UI Framework. In the spaces, you'll find discussions, blog posts, and articles on various SAP CRM technical topics.

The most interesting aspect is that most of the content historically has been generated by people who aren't employees of SAP. You'll find, however, that product managers and developers form SAP will contribute content in terms of blogs or even answering an discussion question. However, the scope of knowledge also extends to an SAP CRM wiki that contains the answers to many frequently asked questions on SAP CRM.

Search for answers One of the biggest questions when it comes to SCN is how to find the answer to your problem effectively. To get the best response for your problems, you'll need to put some effort in on your end to first look for that answer and also provide the information that someone would need to solve your problem. Before you ask a question, you should consult reference resources such as *http://help.sap.com*, *http://service.sap.com*, and even this book. When you are convinced the answer isn't in those places, then perform a search on SCN for your topic.

Now keep in mind that the search isn't perfect, so the more you know about the problem area, the better luck you'll have with search results. If your issue is with loading product data with the XIF adapter, your results will be worse if you only search for "XIF". Instead, you should search for "XIF product load." This will provide better search results than a general search. Keep in mind that it will take some practice when searching to learn how to get the results you want. You can see an example of this search in Figure 10.12.

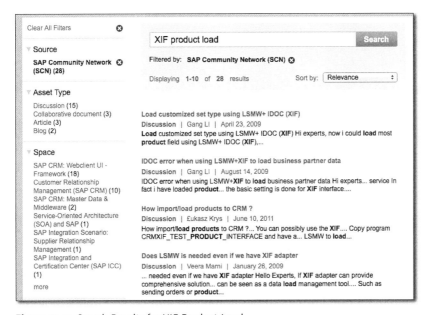

Figure 10.12 Search Results for XIF Product Load

Now that you've searched and you can't find what is needed anywhere, it's time to ask a question. The first part in asking your question is to make the subject of the question briefly describe your problem. In the full description of the problem, you should mention your release of SAP CRM and talk in specifics about what you were doing. A bad example of a description is: "I'm trying to load product data into SAP CRM via XIF

Ask a question

and it gives me an error, please help." Instead, your description should be: "I'm working with SAP CRM 7.0, and I'm trying to load product data via the XIF. I am using the LSMW IDoc interface and have tried mapping the description into the system, but when I run the data conversion, I receive an error about no valid description was provided for the material. Could someone please assist." The more information you provide will help in getting a better response.

Now when waiting for a response, please keep in mind that SCN is a community so there is no Service Level Agreement for people to respond. Instead, try to be patient and if after a week, someone hasn't answered your question, ask a moderator to "bump" your question up or bump up your question by replying to it. Sometimes, no one will be able to answer your question, just because it's too specific to your business requirements and difficult to recreate. Don't be discouraged if that happens. We've encountered that many times when using SCN and eventually we solved our problems.

If you do solve your problem before someone answers, then post your resolution back to your question. The benefit of doing this is that someone else can learn from what you did, and then you have another source of documentation on how you resolved a particular issue.

SCN is a very effective tool in helping to solve technical problems with SAP CRM in terms of enhancements and other requirements. The developer community on SCN for SAP CRM consists of many individuals across the globe who understand the SAP CRM solution on a deep technical level. These community members understand the value of sharing their knowledge to help other people solve their problems.

Pay it forward A great example of this is called the pay it forward concept. You can read the article here: *http://scn.sap.com/docs/DOC-5222*, but we'll summarize the article here as well.

Many years ago, a moderator of the SAP CRM community answered a question for another member. The member who answered the question was then asked to take the final resolution to their problem that used the answer to the question and document it for the whole community. This member then documented the answer in a wiki making it easily available for future use. This use of the wiki lead to more and more people building wiki pages for general FAQs for SAP CRM technical topics.

About SAP Mentors and SCN

It would be hard to mention the SCN without mentioning the SAP Mentor Program. According to *http://sapmentors.sap.com*, SAP Mentors "engage in collaborative activities in their area of expertise that proactively improve or influence products and services of SAP along with the relationships of SAP with its customers, partners and prospects."

They are at the heart of SCN and are the top community influencers in the SAP ecosystem. They can be found at many SAP events, including SAPPHIRE and TechEd wearing a special SAP Mentor shirt. Known as the friendly SAP Mentor Wolf Pack, they offer advice, but aren't afraid to challenge SAP constructively on its approach and direction.

There are several current and former SAP Mentors who focus on SAP CRM. They are a great resource to contact when you have a "big picture" issue about SAP CRM and have run out of people for ideas. The SAP Mentor may not solve your problem, but more than likely can connect you with other people who might be able to help. For more information on how to contact them, visit *http://sapmentors.sap.com*.

This concept doesn't require community members to contribute on a frequent basis but rather contribute when they have something of value to share. The impact of one quality contribution when combined with many other individual contributions has a multiplying effect on the knowledge available to everyone. The SCN SAP CRM space is a must-visit community for all developers working with SAP CRM.

10.3.2 SAP User Groups

Around the world, there are various SAP user groups that allow users of SAP to exchange knowledge and influence SAP on the direction of its products. One of the most prominent user groups is ASUG. There are many other user groups in the world that cooperate all together under the SUGEN umbrella, but for the purposes of this chapter we'll focus on ASUG as an example. Keep in mind that activities performed by all user groups worldwide are very important in helping users of the SAP solution.

ASUG ASUG is one of the largest SAP user groups in the world. It has more than 100,000 members at various customers and partners running SAP solutions. ASUG has several special interest groups that focus on the various aspects of the SAP-delivered solution. One of the interest groups available has a focus on SAP CRM. This interest group conducts year-round meetings and also works on content selection for the ASUG Annual Conference. The ASUG Annual Conference features presentations on many different topics from customers running SAP solutions. There is normally an entire track dedicated to SAP CRM-related topics at the conference. As mentioned earlier, this track doesn't tend to focus on SAP CRM development but rather the business use of SAP CRM. You may find on occasion some more technical-related content during this annual conference.

Feedback sessions Another important aspect of ASUG and SAP user groups is the concept of influence. ASUG and other SAP user groups participate in customer feedback sessions with SAP to better improve the products that SAP provides. There have been feedback sessions for SAP CRM that have resulted in new features in SAP CRM. The role of SAP user groups is very important regardless of whether the focus is on developer-related issues. In many cases, these features have reduced the need for custom development, which allows you to focus on the many other requirements still left on your list of requirements from your business users.

Even though traditional user groups such as ASUG haven't provided a defined place where developers who focus on SAP CRM can communicate, the network from these user groups still allows communication to take place. By talking to other customers of the SAP CRM product through a user group, you might be able to connect with others who have seen a similar issue or will be facing the same problem.

10.3.3 Social Media

Beyond the SAP community, there is another channel to solve SAP CRM problems through social media. The best example is Twitter. As you likely are aware, Twitter is an online social networking tool that allows for the concept of "micro-blogging." Micro-blogging refers to recording short messages that express a thought or idea on a publicly available website. To use Twitter, you can sign up for an account on *https://twitter.com* through a computer or mobile device.

To use Twitter to solve SAP CRM-related issues, you need to follow people that focus on SAP CRM on Twitter and then send them a brief message about your issue. On Twitter, hashtags represent conversations about a topic. The hashtag for SAP CRM-related topics is #sapcrm. You'll find a lot of information on #sapcrm in a mix of functional and technical conversations. By viewing these conversations, you can see who is talking about SAP CRM, which will give you a better idea on who to follow. In addition to using this method to find people, we've created a list of interesting SAP CRM technical- and functional-related individuals at *http://twitter.com/sjohannes/sap-crm-folks*.

A normal SAP CRM technical conversation on Twitter will usually mention an SCN forum thread or basic problem concept and some SAP note number describing the issue. With only 140 characters to use, there are some limits on how much can be described. In many cases, it may take a series of messages to explain the issue or start as a way to send a private email to the other person with the issue. It's possible, however, to solve issues through this method, as there have been several past Twitter conversations between developers who focus on SAP CRM enhancements on problems that they have faced.

Other social media channels such as Facebook or Google+ tend to not be used as much for technical conversations on SAP. Although you'll find SAP-related content on those channels, the best resource for connecting with other developers who focus on SAP CRM enhancements is through Twitter or SCN.

10.4   Summary

Regardless of how many enhancement options are provided by SAP for SAP CRM, there always is one business requirement that will challenge the most experienced developer. In those situations, you must pull out your most powerful set of techniques for the issues that require a more creative use of the SAP CRM system. As you've discovered, you can use implicit enhancements and core modifications to enhance the system when there are no other options. Implicit enhancements can be used to get around the limitations of BAdIs. Core modifications are something that every SAP CRM implementation should challenge the need to make. However, if you do have to make a core modification, there must be a 100% business and technical case on why any other enhancement concept, including creating custom code, won't meet the requirements.

In the modern era of social networks, the SAP Community Network and SAP user groups provide a way to discuss and solve problems with other people facing the same issues. SCN provides an online repository of already solved SAP CRM technical problems, along with the chance to ask and answer new questions. Using a global community to solve your problem will allow you to spend less time on the problem and meet the requirements of your business without needing a huge team to perform the work. Remember, your SAP CRM implementation doesn't have to be limited to those who actually work on your system and/or project.

Throughout this book, we've given you examples and information to tackle common business requirements found on SAP CRM projects. We hope that by using the knowledge gained here, you can implement the necessary enhancements to your SAP CRM system to meet your business requirements. This book isn't a complete reference on every possible scenario, but we have provided some additional resources in this chapter so that when all else fails, you have some options.

A   Common Mistakes When Setting Up an SAP CRM Development System

During our more than 10 years of experience supporting and implementing SAP CRM, we've found some common mistakes that lead to project failure or make the support of SAP CRM much more difficult. These mistakes include setting up multiple clients in the development system, not having a sandbox system available, and trying to implement SAP CRM when the design of SAP ERP isn't complete. In this appendix, we'll review these mistakes and why you should avoid them for your SAP CRM implementation.

Multiple CRM Clients in the Development System

In a traditional SAP ERP landscape, the development system normally contains one or more clients: one client for development, a gold client for customizing, and a unit test client in the SAP ERP development system. SAP CRM wasn't originally designed to use more than one client due to the limitations of its middleware. Unless you're running a multiple exchange project, you should pay attention to this recommendation.

Traditional landscape

In your SAP CRM development system, you should have one client that will contain all of your work. When connected to a corresponding SAP ERP system, an SAP CRM system must receive all of the baseline configuration from the SAP ERP system. In addition, you can only have one middleware connection between an SAP ERP and SAP CRM system, which means if you want to test the download of master data into your SAP CRM system, you must use the unit test client of your SAP ERP system as the source system for your SAP CRM system.

Today's SAP CRM system

A gold client in SAP CRM doesn't make sense because the Customizing for SAP CRM when connected to SAP ERP must be downloaded. Therefore, a single client in SAP CRM is recommended that contains Customizing, master data, and transactional data. By using multiple clients and trying to set up multiple middleware connections, you'll cause unnecessary work and effort on your project unless you're attempting a multiple exchange project.

Single client

In the past 10 years, we've never needed multiple SAP CRM clients in any of the SAP CRM implementations we've worked on or supported when involving a single SAP CRM system connected to a single SAP ERP backend. Keep in mind that the interactive reporting requires a separate reporting client, which isn't considered a primary client as part of this discussion.

As a developer or consultant, if you find that you have someone on your project team considering this idea, please show them this book. If that still doesn't convince them, please have them contact me directly at *sjohanne@gmail.com* so I can tell them personally that it's a bad idea.

Lack of a Sandbox System

In other SAP solutions, not having a sandbox system sometimes can be overcome by creating multiple clients in the development system. For SAP CRM, we don't recommend having multiple clients in any system (except for an additional interactive reporting client); instead, you need another place to prototype your work.

Prototype work | In this situation, we recommend that you make the investment in a sandbox system to prototype the work you're doing. A great reason for doing this is that the tools such as the Application Enhancement Tool (AET) will generate code and extensions to tables. If for some reason these tools fail or you can't reverse something that changed, your development system will end up in an inconsistent state.

We admit that we've spent around six combined years without a sandbox system. The biggest drawback is that we have to be extra careful when designing a new requirement for the business. Most of the time, our mistakes don't cause any issues and we can clean up the mess within an hour or so. However, there have been cases where the mistakes have broken the development system to the point where it has taken a few days to fix the problem. In addition, the ability to validate advanced corrections from SAP to see if they work correctly before applying them in your development system is also a benefit.

Visualization | Even though a sandbox system is an additional cost without a direct business benefit, the ability to design without interrupting production support will pay off in the long run. If you aren't already using virtualization in your landscape, this would be a great use case for a virtualized system.

Implementing When SAP ERP is Not Ready

If you're running your SAP CRM as a standalone system without an SAP ERP backend, then you can ignore this section. However, if your company is performing a brand-new implementation of the SAP Business Suite, we strongly recommend that you don't try to configure SAP CRM until you've finished up the design of your SAP ERP system.

SAP CRM is very much dependent on the design of the customer master, material master, organizational model, general Customizing, and much more in the SAP ERP system. It's hard to design a system to support customer-facing processes when you don't know how the customer will be modeled in the enterprise. In past experience, we've found that changes in the SAP ERP customer master or other design will normally just cause the SAP CRM to have to redo the middleware initial downloads and start configuration all over again.

SAP ERP dependent

B The Author

 **Stephen Johannes** is a system analyst who currently supports a productive SAP CRM implementation for a large specialty chemical company in the United States. He graduated from the University of Missouri-Columbia. He has worked with the SAP CRM solution as a developer since 2001, providing enhancements to the standard platform for SAP customers in both consulting and application support roles. During this time frame, he has gradually become a functional/technical resource on SAP CRM and will claim that he only codes when necessary or is just in the mood.

Stephen has also been a moderator on the SAP Community Network (SCN) for the Customer Relationship Management Space since 2009 and has been actively answering questions off and on since 2005 on SCN. He was recognized in 2009 as an SAP Mentor for his contributions to the SAP ecosystem through SCN and remained active as an SAP Mentor until early 2012. He's currently looking at rejoining the SAP Mentor program in 2013.

To make sure that his life is busy 24/7, he's married to his wife Karon and is the proud father of two children: Emily and Zachary. He's an avid St. Louis Cardinals and Mizzou Tigers Fan. In addition to watching sports, he's a slow but steady recreational runner who enjoys running outdoors when the weather permits.

You can reach Stephen via Twitter *@sjohannes*.

Index

D

Interested in reading more?

Please visit our website for all new
book and e-book releases from SAP PRESS.

www.sap-press.com